FRAMING AUTHORITY

FRAMING AUTHORITY

SAYINGS, SELF, AND SOCIETY IN
SIXTEENTH-CENTURY ENGLAND

MARY THOMAS CRANE

PRINCETON UNIVERSITY PRESS

PRINCETON, NEW JERSEY

Library of Congress Cataloging-in-Publication Data

Crane, Mary Thomas, 1956–
Framing authority : sayings, self, and society in sixteenth-
century England / Mary Thomas Crane.
p. cm.
Includes bibliographical references and index.
ISBN 0-691-06947-6
1. English literature—Early modern, 1500–1700—History and
criticism—Theory, etc. 2. Literature and society—England—
History—16th century. 3. English literature—Classical
influences. 4. Frame-stories—History and criticism.
5. Commonplace-books—History. 6. Authority in literature.
7. Rhetoric—1500–1800. 8. Self in literature. 9. Humanists—
England. I. Title.

PR418.S64C7 1992   92-19878
820.9′003—dc20   CIP

This book has been composed in Adobe Sabon

Princeton University Press books are printed
on acid-free paper and meet the guidelines for
permanence and durability of the Committee on
Production Guidelines for Book Longevity
of the Council on Library Resources

Printed in the United States of America

10 9 8 7 6 5 4 3 2 1

For Gregory, Thomas, and Parker

CONTENTS

ACKNOWLEDGMENTS

IN THE COURSE of writing this book I have been helped by many institutions and individuals. Parts of chapter 6 originally appeared in *Studies in English Literature* and are reprinted here with permission. Similarly, part of chapter 7 first came out in a *Harvard English Studies* volume entitled *Renaissance Genres*. Librarians at the Houghton, Folger, and British Libraries helped me track down elusive commonplace book manuscripts, and most of this book was written in Harvard's Child Memorial Library. Boston College funded the final stages of research with a Distinguished Junior Faculty Research Award, and the Radcliffe Childcare Center helped me find the time to do both research and writing.

At Harvard, Steven Berkowitz, John Klause, and the late Herschel Baker all encouraged my interest in this topic in its earliest stages. Colleagues in Child Library, including Kimberly Van Esveld Adams, Joseph Bartolomeo, Harbour Hodder, Carol Ann Johnston, Maryclaire Moroney, and Frederick Wegener helped out with information and advice. Richard Tarrant, Claudio Guillen, and G. Blakemore Evans all read and provided useful commentary on parts of an earlier version of the manuscript.

At Boston College, I have enjoyed the support of many people, but especially of Anne Ferry, Dayton Haskin, and Alan Richardson. Mary Jo Kietzman cheerfully photocopied, checked references, and visited libraries, and Roy Galang of the Computer Help Center provided patient counsel.

Elsewhere, conversation and correspondence with a number of scholars, including Judith Anderson, Janel Mueller, Anne Lake Prescott, Jane Tylus, and especially Ann Baynes Coiro and Victoria Kahn, have shaped my ideas as I worked on this project. Heather Dubrow has aided me in ways too numerous to list here and continues to be a model of generous support for younger scholars.

Barbara Lewalski took this project (and me) in hand when we were both stuck in the Middle Ages. Without her prodding, advice, and example, it and I would still be languishing in the twelfth century. I could not have written this book or survived the dual demands of assistant professorship and motherhood without close friends who also endure one or both of these states. My telephone bill attests the extent to which I have relied on Emily C. Bartels, Laura Lunger Knoppers, and Naomi J. Miller.

My late parents supported and encouraged my education for many years, and I regret that they have not lived to see this tangible product of it. I have dedicated this book to my husband and sons; the former provides a copious source of valuable information for gathering, and the latter offer a daily (and wonderful) demonstration of resistance to framing.

FRAMING AUTHORITY

INTRODUCTION

My tables—meet it is I set it down
That one may smile, and smile, and be a villain!

(1.5.107–8)

HAMLET here, as most readers probably realize, refers to the practice of jotting down memorable sayings in a commonplace book. Ralph Bolgar has most thoroughly traced the history of this activity in the Renaissance, from Manuel Chrysoloras's fifteenth-century revival of Quintilian's recommendation that students keep a notebook, preserving notable fragments encountered in the course of their reading, through its most influential restatement in Erasmus's *De copia*.[1] Although many scholars acknowledge that the notebook method was widely practiced in England and elsewhere during this period, most of them marginalize, dismiss, or even excoriate its impact on discourse.[2] Thomas Greene, for instance, argues that "the work of cataloguing and of rote memory required by this method could not in itself produce sensitive understanding and creative imitation."[3] H. A. Mason describes the fondness for commonplaces as "pathetic," a "weakness . . . at the heart of Humanism," while Paul Oskar Kristeller suggests that "the frequency of quotations and of commonplaces" gives to Renaissance moral philosophy "an air of triviality that is often very boring to the modern critical reader."[4] Even Bolgar, who emphasizes the importance of the notebook in assimilating ideas from the vast space of Greek and Latin literature, nevertheless confines it to the status of a "mnemotechnical aid."[5]

It will be my purpose here to resituate the commonplace book in its intellectual, social, and ideological milieus, and to argue that in sixteenth-century England the notebook method was far more than just a mnemotechnical aid involving the cataloging and rote memorization of aphorisms. During this period, the twin discursive practices of "gathering" these textual fragments and "framing" or forming, arranging, and assimilating them created for English humanists a central mode of transaction with classical antiquity and provided an influential model for authorial practice and for authoritative self-fashioning.[6] Gathering and framing were not just rhetorical strategies; they were basic discursive practices, formulated in response to the pressures and opportunities of the historical moment (the shift from feudalism to capitalism, the rise of the powerful Tudor monarchy, the bureaucratization of government and temporary

decline of the aristocracy) and constitutive of social, economic, political, and literary discourse.[7] I hope to show that gathering and framing were, in sixteenth-century England, the basis for a theory and practice of reading, writing, education, and social mobility that developed alongside and in partial resistance to the individualistic, imitative, imaginative, and aristocratic paradigms for selfhood and authorship that we tend to associate with the English Renaissance.[8]

Reliance on these discursive practices meant that English humanists often seemed to think of ancient literature as a space containing textual fragments, and that they imagined their interaction with that literature as the collection and redeployment of those fragments and not, in many cases, as the assimilation and imitation of whole works.[9] It also meant that a central part of humanist education in sixteenth-century England involved the use of aphoristic fragments to constitute and control a middle-class subject able to move upward within the changing hierarchies of the early modern state.[10] This educational program in turn gave rise to a version of authorship that was collective instead of individualist, published instead of private, inscriptive instead of voice-centered, and aphoristic or epigrammatic instead of lyric or narrative, but which shaped and informed the lyric tradition even as it countered it. I hope to show that the attitudes toward text and subject fostered by the notebook method left their mark on most forms of literary and political discourse in sixteenth-century England.

My account of the nature and development of the commonplace tradition is divided into two parts, which might be loosely described as "theory" and "practice" (although, as we will see, the very notion of "commonplace" resists such a division).[11] The theory of gathering and framing is articulated most basically in the logic and rhetoric texts that were influential in sixteenth-century England and in the pedagogical theory with which they are inextricably linked in the humanist project. The first section of this book (chapters 1 through 3) examines a number of logic, rhetoric, and pedagogic treatises (in both Latin and English), tracing the formulation of these discursive practices in sixteenth-century England. Gathering and framing were central to this program in several ways; gathering offered a way to excerpt the most authoritative fragments of ancient literature and collect them as an easily displayed sign of status as an educated person. Because the fragments to be chosen were already "framed" by their participation (as commonplaces) in the dominant cultural code, would-be educators and advisers could offer to construct authentic and stable discourse, and authoritative but controlled subjects.

In the second section (chapters 4 through 8) I have chosen to investigate the practice of gathering and framing through a series of texts that both exemplify the notebook method of composition and try to work through some of its problems and changing implications: these texts include school curricula, political and economic treatises, letters seeking preferment, letters of advice, contemporary biography, collections of epigrams, descriptions of courtly festivals, and poetic miscellanies. In these texts, commonplaces that were important nodes of stress in humanist theory recur and reveal the English humanists' continued reliance on gathering and framing in response to anxiety about social status and the accumulation of wealth. In these chapters I trace the development of rival courtly and humanist versions of subjectivity and authorship. This section of the book turns on two pivotal dates: 1520, when a controversy over methods of pedagogy and authorship delineated the differences between courtly and humanist modes of writing and behavior, and 1571, when William Cecil became Baron Burghley and began to force a younger generation of writers to attempt to frame themselves in accordance with mutually exclusive social and literary paradigms. I have chosen to focus on epigram and lyric as the literary exempla of gathering and framing because these forms were themselves often gathered and framed as sayings and because they were closely involved in the development of the rival aristocratic and humanist versions of subjectivity and authorship in the period.[12]

It may be helpful to say a few words about some especially problematic issues of terminology and methodology, and, in particular, to justify the use of two terms ("humanist" and "saying") that were not used in the period in quite the sense that they appear here. It is probably necessary, first of all, to clarify what I mean by "humanist," a term that is both historically and ideologically vexed. Historically, of course, there is an ongoing controversy about the definition, nature, and, in England especially, influence of humanism.[13] Ideologically, anyone who attempts to discuss humanism must be aware of, on the left, Althusser's critique of its implication in bourgeois individualism, and, on the right, religious opposition to "secular humanism" and, at the same time, conservative attempts to preserve a traditional humanist canon and curriculum.[14] It is not surprising, given these pitfalls, that many New Historicist readings of sixteenth-century England have tended to ignore or marginalize those texts (for example, Elyot's *Governor*, Ascham's *Scholemaster*, the Neo-Latin tradition in general) conventionally associated with the humanist movement. As Stephen Greenblatt has explained, to the modern critic, "the great syncretic structures of the Renaissance humanists no longer seem as intellectually compelling or as adequate to the period's major works of art as they once did."[15]

It is precisely to recuperate such texts and structures into our readings of sixteenth-century English culture that, despite these problems, I want to retain the term "humanist" to describe what seems to me to be an identifiable position in early modern England. As several scholars have asserted, humanism was essentially a program of educational reform that sought to replace the existing scholastic and professional training with a curriculum based on the rhetorical study of classical authors and designed to teach its students to speak fluent, classical Latin.[16] In England, I intend to argue that this project was largely based on the collection, assimilation, and redeployment of textual fragments, and I consider as "humanist" any person who advocates or uses this method of composition and teaching.[17] I have been influenced by revisionist and Marxist historians (such as Lawrence Stone, Perry Anderson, Mervyn James, Alistair Fox, and John Guy) in stressing the social and political as well as intellectual contexts of English humanism.[18] Thus, my humanists are distinguished by their common background and common aims, as well as their education in the use of common discursive practices. They are virtually all members of the merchant or lower gentry classes who conceived and promulgated a theory of language and education, based on the gathering and framing of fragments of authoritative texts, which they managed to institute (in opposition to existing aristocratic credentials) as a necessary form of cultural capital for upward mobility in the newly bureaucratized state, and upon which they relied, in various ways, to provide at least a provisional guarantee of authenticity and stability in the face of rapid social, economic, and intellectual change.[19]

I intend to argue, however, that this movement was not "humanist" in the Althusserian sense; that is, although it was bourgeois, it was not, at least in England, necessarily "individualistic."[20] Especially in its earlier stages (before 1550), English humanism fostered, alongside existing aristocratic individualism, concepts of a socially constituted subject, common ownership of texts and ideas, and a collective model of authorship.[21] Although this project participated in the process of forming the "modern subject" as a "self-regulating bourgeois individual," it emphasized the cultural determinants of self-regulation at the expense, under certain circumstances, of individuality.[22] In theory at least, all texts formed a common storehouse of matter, validated by existing cultural codes, from which all educated people could gather and through which all educated subjects were framed. This common textual matter provided a form of symbolic capital that could be accumulated without threat to the existing hierarchy, and the social mobility that it enabled could be imagined as a collective project which did not involve dangerous singularity or personal aggregation of power. This capital could be manifested through the strategic use of commonplaces and aphorisms in letters, treatises, translations, and poems which, when published, made that capital the common property of an even wider audience. The aristocratic "stigma of print" was not operative in the humanist system, which embraced print technology and was shaped by it in important ways.

These humanists first achieved a measure of success under Wolsey (around 1520), when, appropriating certain aspects of the theories of Agricola, Erasmus, and Vives, men like William Lily and Thomas More established a link between government preferment and a particular educational curriculum. Their ideology and practice was carried on throughout the Henrician years by Thomas Elyot, Richard Pace, Richard Morison, John Cheke, and John Palsgrave; it was carried into the Elizabethan period by Thomas Wilson, Ralph Lever, Roger Ascham, William Cecil, Richard Tottel, George Gascoigne, and, with qualifications, Sir Philip Sidney. Although there were changes in allegiance as well as disagreements among these men throughout the century, I hope to show that their version of "humanism" does represent a nexus of ideas and practices that can be usefully differentiated from, for example, the aristocratic and courtly tradition. Some of the most interesting and complex texts of the period (for example, the poems of Wyatt, Sidney, and Shakespeare) were situated in the margins *between* these positions and are, in many ways, products of and responses to that gap. This study is, in a way, a "defense" of English humanism, arguing that it possessed greater theoretical sophistication, manifested a more complex and problematized ideological stance, and exerted a more pronounced (but different kind of) influence than has generally been recognized.

The second issue of terminology involves the lack of an adequately comprehensive collective term for the matter to be gathered in a commonplace book. I often use the word "saying," although it is unsatisfactory in several ways: it stresses the oral/aural aspects of this material at the expense of its equally important textual and inscriptive qualities, and it tends to exclude certain less sententious forms (exemplum, analogy) that were often included under the rubric of "commonplace." It is, however, more inclusive than "aphorism," "maxim," "proverb," or "adage," and will work in contexts where the names of specific forms are too limiting.

There are several reasons for the lack of an adequate collective term for such material. In the first place, such gathered matter bore an enormous and internally contradictory burden in the humanist attempt, through theory and education, to ensure the authenticity of discourse. "Sayings" were a useful tool because they were supposed to combine matter and words (*verba* and *res*), to transmit the authority of antiquity without transgressing modern cultural codes, to provide the matter for copious speech while making sure that speech was grounded and controlled, and to provide a socially and politically empowering facility with language while making sure that its wielder remained within the existing social hierarchy. Too strict or prescriptive a definition or term—confining the collected matter to proverbs, for example, or to sententious maxims— would forestall the flexibility informing the belief that gathering and framing could carry out such conflicting mandates.

The typical sixteenth-century definition of what ought to be gathered focuses on two seemingly contradictory attributes of sayings: they are at the same time both "common"—based on the commonly accepted beliefs and standards of the prevailing cultural codes—and "uncommon"— stylistically unusual in such a way as to make their common content seem striking, memorable, persuasive, and true.[23] The paradoxical juxtaposition of common and uncommon is, as we shall see, what enables this material to be conceived of as simultaneously verbal and material, empowering and controlling, enabling and limiting. Advocates of gathering sometimes provide helpful lists of some of the kinds of matter that a student might look for without, however, providing a collective term. Such lists often include proverbs, aphorisms, maxims, similitudes, exempla, fables (collapsed into their moral), and apothegms.

Ultimately, however, the exact criteria for and means of selection were, perhaps consciously, mystified. The experience of humanist education was designed precisely to teach you to know what to gather, but that knowledge could not be conveyed in a definition or single prescriptive statement.[24] It was, instead, the product of initiation into humanist practice, acquired over years of example, indoctrination, and exercise.[25] The student learned to gather what was already framed as a saying, it framed his character, and he, in turn, reframed it in his own writing as a sign that he had received the prescribed education.[26] Most of the treatises that describe the notebook method thus focus on the practices of gathering and framing rather than on the nature of the matter to be gathered, and my account will reflect that emphasis.

Nevertheless, my understanding of the nature of gathered matter has been informed by several critics' work. Although sententiousness—brevity, prescriptiveness, and strong closure—was not the only criterion for inclusion in a sixteenth-century notebook, it was a significant factor. Geoffrey Bennington's poststructuralist analysis of sententiousness in eighteenth–century French writing has been particularly helpful, especially in its discussion of the difficulty of defining even this small subset of gathered matter according to conventional generic or rhetorical criteria.[27] For Bennington, the supplementarity of the sententious fragment is a crucial feature. He describes sententiousness as "the text's difference from itself,"noting that "maxims in texts are thus substantial and excessive, the best of the text and the rest of the text, a surplus." Such fragments stand out from their context (and can be identified for gathering) because they both sum up its most central meanings and provide extraneous ornamentation.[28] Bennington's discussion of the problematic relationship between sententiousness and narrative is also useful in its emphasis on the ways in which one both counters and gives rise to the other.

Despite Bennington's critique of rhetorical definitions, the status of sayings as rhetorical devices remains important in my study. I have tried, however, to build upon the summarizing and restatement of definitions from rhetorical treatises that has tended to characterize this approach to aphoristic material.[29] Two recent studies in particular have influenced my treatment of the theoretical implications of rhetoric. Both Patricia Parker and Derek Attridge stress, like Bennington, the problematic status of rhetoric as a supplement to "natural" speech, and both also consider the social implications of the humanist rhetorical project.[30] Father Walter Ong's work on the changes in discourse theory as culture shifted, in the sixteenth century, from primarily oral in its orientation to primarily visual and spatial, has also been important.[31] Various sociolinguistic accounts of how proverbs function in ordinary speech have been less directly helpful, largely because English humanists were frequently concerned to obscure sociological distinctions between, say, folk proverbs and learned maxims. Still, such studies emphasize the complex role of apparently simple sayings, establish their basis in cultural codes, and suggest that they can be read more carefully than they usually are.[32]

Readers will notice in this book what may seem to be a methodological peculiarity. Throughout, I have used, as well as traced the history of, the practices of gathering and framing. That is, I have read texts from the period as I argue that sixteenth-century humanists did, by gathering commonplaces and reframing them in their contemporary system of signification. To some extent, this method resembles the Derridean technique of deconstructive reading, in which a text's metaphors are scrutinized for signs of rupture and contradiction in its logical argument.[33] I have, however, focused not only on metaphors but on a series of commonplaces, aphorisms, and proverbs that recur throughout the texts I discuss. I believe, as well, that the decision to concentrate on selected fragments is not just a modern interpretive tool, but that it represents (in many cases) a more accurate reflection of sixteenth–century English practices of thought and composition than would an attempt to discern a coherent line of argument, or to trace the influence of whole texts or philosophical systems.

Indeed, the frequency with which key commonplaces recur vindicates this method of reading: metaphors of hunting and gathering, planting and harvesting, poison and cure, engraving, beating, as well as commonplaces about the nature of common and uncommon property, trifle and commodity, are used almost relentlessly throughout the period and create a flexible and useful system of significances. When read in the context of this system and in light of its social and political valences, the most trivial commonplaces assume precise, and even sophisticated, connotations. Sixteenth-century theory was expressed almost entirely through commonplaces; we need to learn how to read it according to its own rules, tracing its reiterated terms and figures as they accumulate and shift meanings.[34]

I have also gathered and reframed concepts from a number of partially incompatible modern theories. Throughout this study I have used elements from the work of several influential theorists without, however, necessarily accepting all of their assumptions or implications. Readers will recognize in these pages the Derridean supplement, Foucauldian "discipline," Lacanian subject-formation, Pierre Bourdieu's theories of cultural capital and symbolic violence, and Althusser's "anti-humanism," to name only a few of the most obvious. Such a mix of theoretical fragments, divorced from their respective systems, runs the risk of appearing to represent merely a superficial appropriation of terminology.

My justification is again based on the demands of historicism. Most contemporary theory—Freudian, post-Marxist, structuralist and post-structuralist—is itself historically placeable as an ongoing attempt to respond to (and dismantle) the social, philosophical, ideological, and literary formulations of the nineteenth century. This is obvious in the cases of Freud and Marx, but we may not always be aware of the extent to which more recent theoretical systems are constituted by the lingering influence of nineteenth-century ideas about voice, presence, individualism, and transcendence against which they react. We are also not always sufficiently aware of the extent to which "our" Renaissance is the product of the nineteenth century: its texts, its authors, its concepts of self and authorship were necessarily shaped by the ideology and assumptions of the scholars who did the monumental work of rediscovering and reformulating them. Recent applications of theory to Renaissance texts thus represent the first steps in a necessary process of deconstructing that nineteenth-century "Renaissance."

But, as Greenblatt and others have suggested, those nineteenth-century concepts of self and work had not yet been fully formulated in the Renaissance.[35] Theory-based critiques thus have moments of almost uncanny success, and also moments of blindness, because they are based on opposition to concepts that were, in the Renaissance, only in the process of being constituted. Some of the best recent studies have begun to trace, with considerable historical specificity, the halting and uncertain movement in this period toward "modern" concepts of self and work.[36]

I am concerned here to excavate traces of sixteenth-century *difference* from these modern concepts. In the long process of creating the individual, the transcendent work, and the lyric voice, early modern writers tried a variety of possibilities, some of which look forward to those concepts as we recognize them, and some of which lead in other directions.[37] The commonplace book method and its practice of gathering and framing might be described as a false start, which, in many respects, points away from these ends. Nevertheless, overly teleological accounts of the period that do not give such false starts their full weight may misrepresent early works and may fail to understand an important constituent—if only through opposition—of later ones. I thus have gathered and used only those elements of theory which have helped me to push aside anachronistic assumptions about the nature of the self, the text, and the world, in order more clearly to perceive the crucial ways in which sixteenth-century concepts differed from nineteenth-century constructions. Although I realize that this version of the sixteenth century is necessarily shaped by my own beliefs and concerns, it has nevertheless seemed possible, particularly at this historical moment, to achieve some measure of internal distantiation, to stand as it were *between* the theoretical systems of our age and the previous one in order to see, however partially, our common past.

Chapter I

FINDING A PLACE:
THE HUMANIST LOGIC OF GATHERING
AND FRAMING

LOGIC TEXTS are the logical place to begin this study because they furnish the most basic articulation of the grounds for gathering and framing. Of course, humanist logic treatises are not really logics at all.[1] Instead, they constitute a kind of rhetoricized dialectic, a quasi-logical basis for the rhetorical program offered by humanists as a replacement for the Scholastic arts curriculum.[2] In northern Europe and England, such logicians as Rodolphus Agricola, Thomas Wilson, Ralph Lever, Abraham Fraunce, and Dudley Fenner wrote texts designed to serve as pragmatically oriented guides to thinking, reading, teaching, speaking, and writing, and to establish the discursive practices of gathering and framing as the primary constituents of those activities.[3] Although their treatment of the "places" is derived from the Aristotelian and Ciceronian systems of topoi or strategies of argumentation, they shift the concept of commonplace to mean, among other things, a fragment of text suitable for gathering. In addition, their texts themselves serve as commonplace books offering a collection of fragments from whatever sources each writer wishes to valorize. Indeed, the nature and goals of the humanist project are articulated in these commonplaces and analogies as well as in the more conventionally discursive passages of their texts; through them we can trace both the epistemological implications of gathering and framing as means of authenticating and controlling discourse, and also the ideological implications of gathering as a flexible posture for upward mobility in an intensely hierarchical society.

Terence Cave and Thomas Greene have described Continental humanists' anxious search for "authentic discourse" and their newly troubling perception of "the ungrounded contingency of language."[4] The logical and rhetorical treatises of English humanists are manifestations of this more general desire to realize a stable and authoritative language, and the operations of gathering and framing are offered as the primary means of accomplishing this impossible goal. These writers instruct their readers to cull only those fragments of text that articulate elements of the prevailing cultural code, the usually implicit rules which govern a culture's "language, its schemas of perception, its exchanges, its techniques, its values, the hierarchy of its practices."[5] By identifying and excerpting bits of texts where the writers of classical antiquity seem to accord with modern consensus, they made imaginable a stability transcending the contingency of language. And by reifying the code in the form of these fragments of text, individual readers and writers were able to appropriate its authenticity for their personal use.

In English logical and rhetorical treatises, anxiety about the authenticity of language can be traced to two separate but related problems: the problem of having nothing to say, and the inability to control one's language, or (and this is closely related) to control others with that language.[6] The operation of gathering, represented in these texts under the rubric of "invention" and deeply involved in the concept of *copia*, is essentially a response to the first, while framing, associated primarily with arrangement or "disposition" but also with the "matter" of copia, responds to the second. Sayings provide a central means of resolving what might initially seem to be a conflict between a need for copia and a need for control by offering a source of matter that has already been framed, both by its accordance with the prevailing cultural code, and by its place in an organized system of thought.

Although Derrida has established the universality in Western culture of both a fear of lacking voice or presence and an awareness of the difficulty of controlling language, these anxieties were, for a number of reasons, particularly intense in northern Europe in the late fifteenth and early sixteenth centuries. The decline of feudalism and the Roman Catholic consensus of belief meant that accepted values and practices, and the linguistic structures that constituted them, were either disappearing or changing. In England particularly, as Henry VII and Henry VIII began to erode the feudal nobility's power and establish a powerful, centralized monarchy, these anxieties were accompanied by opportunities for new men from less than aristocratic backgrounds to move into positions of authority. But while the feudal magnates and Catholic clergy had possessed a well-developed system for establishing, manifesting, and protecting their powerful presence, would-be bureaucrats had no such technology. Humanist education—its logic, rhetoric, and pedagogy—was designed to supply that lack: to establish an authentic language and powerful presence for secular teachers and bureaucrats.

This sense of lack was also intensified by a basic tenet of the humanist program that originated in Italy. Northern European humanists established a need for their educational program in part by accepting and promulgating the idea that modern men ought to learn to speak and write classical Latin. Many humanist rhetorical and educational reforms were, in fact, aimed at achieving this ambitious goal. Few modern scholars have registered the fundamental strangeness of this project of reviving a difficult, dead, and thus essentially written language in contemporary speech.[7] The Latin logic of Rodolphus Agricola and the Latin rhetorics of Erasmus all reflect and disseminate a quite understandable fear of having nothing to say in Latin, and an equally understandable fear of lacking voice or presence in discourse based on a written language. The proliferation of printed editions of classical texts in this period made the written ancient languages seem inimitably copious and impossible for the modern student to assimilate. The commonplace book was an aid to managing these multiplicitous texts, and the collection of idiomatic expressions in commonplace book collections such as Nicholas Udall's *Floures For Latine Spekynge* (1553) provided a means of gathering fragments of speech from written texts.[8]

In England, poverty of expression becomes an issue in several different ways. Latin speaking never caught on there outside the schoolroom.[9] Even at school, records show that much effort went into cajoling and even forcing students to speak in Latin alone, and to acquire the necessary store of matter and language for fluent Latin speech.[10] As the sixteenth century got under way, humanist scholars in England increasingly wrote in the vernacular and addressed the use of the English language.[11] Because the humanist project was heavily invested in the restoration of pure, authentic Latinity, the vernacular necessarily carried a taint of inferiority (even to its defenders) as a supplementary mode of speech for those who could not use the ancient language.[12] English, specifically, was thought to be an impoverished and ineloquent language, lacking an adequate number of words to express the concepts found in ancient texts, and unamenable to rhetorical ornamentation.[13] English logics and rhetorics play on the fears of those confined to the vernacular that they lacked the copious and authoritative voice of Latin speech, and here again the notebook provided an important way to enrich the vernacular by borrowing fragments from ancient literature.

The other central anxiety—that of lacking control—is raised and exploited by both Latin and English texts. In Latin, as Terence Cave has argued, there was persistent nervousness that too copious speech in this powerful language would get out of control.[14] This is partly based on a fear that words (*verba*), ungrounded in matter (*res*) or in the authority of a speaking presence, would become empty verbiage. Anxiety about control was intensified in the case of the vernacular by the belief, current in sixteenth-century England, that English had no grammar and was thus by nature an "unruly" language.[15] Also, as Thomas Greene has shown, humanists realized that the meanings of words were unstable, changeable over time, and thus difficult (if not impossible) to translate from Latin or

Greek to the vernacular without loss of control over meaning.[16] Because classical authors were pagan, they were operating under a cultural code that was in many ways radically different from that of Renaissance readers. As a result, classical texts were, at least in places, potentially dangerous to Christian readers, and some form of control had to be exerted over reading as well as writing. The notebook method offered a way to choose out only those fragments in which the cultural codes of pagan antiquity and Christian Europe intersected. And finally, although rhetorical texts promised to teach their readers how to achieve control over an audience through language, the fact that this control could be taught offered the possibility of subversion of the social hierarchy, and had itself to be hedged and controlled in various ways.[17]

Social and economic conditions in early modern England may have contributed to the intensification of the two lacks upon which humanist discourse theory was based. As feudalism began to give way to early forms of capitalism, a number of changes took place.[18] Estates were bought up and enclosed for wool farming, and peasants were physically dislocated and separated from their means of production. This "deterritorialization" of the peasantry was accompanied by the dislocation and deregulation of trade, as specific and carefully controlled market*places* gave way to an abstract "market," which, as Jean-Christophe Agnew describes it, "now referred to acts of both buying and selling, regardless of locale, and to the price or exchange value of goods and services."[19] This transition was accompanied by a phase of "primitive accumulation" of capital, when "the factors and products of production" were "monetized," and the market was increasingly based on exchange of that most "liquid" medium—money.[20]

This process, like most contemporary changes, carried both opportunity and danger: on the one hand, the possibility of accumulating new power and resources, and on the other, nervousness about the dislocation and motility of what had previously seemed to be established and controlled. English humanists frequently used economic or monetary language to talk about their discursive practices, and they apply similar commonplaces to discussions of the economy as to discussion of language and education.[21] It seems clear that "gathering" was meant to be a version of primitive accumulation that was based on the liquidity of printed texts but which "rematerialized" itself through the concept of content as "matter," and which "reterritorialized" itself through the system of logical and rhetorical "places." By inventing a less threatening form of capital to accumulate, humanists attempted to create for themselves a stable place in society between the landed nobility and the deterritorialized merchant class.[22] Thus Pierre Bourdieu's concept of "cultural capital" is not quite accurate to describe the humanists' conscious and literal attempt to find an intellectual counterpart, or replacement for, contemporary economic processes.

However sincerely humanist logicians and educators felt these anxieties about language and society, they also learned to exploit them for their own benefit. Unless kings could be convinced of their need for educated advisers, and unless subjects could be convinced of their need for humanist teachers, there could be no place in society for such people. The humanists who wrote the most important logics and rhetorics in this period were engaged in constructing a place for themselves in society by establishing their ability to teach others how to have something authoritative to say, how to control it, and how to use it to control others.

Their project was, however, complicated by a number of constraints. As several critics have recently shown, rhetoric and other *artes* could not be considered authentic unless they were in some sense natural, perfect, and God-given, while at the same time they could not be taught as skills unless they were also artificial, and unless the natural, God-given state was in need of completion by artificial means. These critics point out the logic of supplementation in the Derridean sense at work in sixteenth-century rhetoric; according to this scheme, rhetoric is depicted as a natural faculty of divine provenance, both complete in itself and at the same time in need of supplementation by the artificial techniques taught by the rhetorician.[23]

These critics, however, have not explored in sufficient detail the usefulness of supplementation to the rhetoricians' own attempts at self-empowerment.[24] Teaching and writing treatises on logic and rhetoric are, after all, valid activities only if such supplementation is necessary. Indeed, the social roles that humanists fashion for themselves all involve supplementation: as advisers they supplement the powerful authority of the monarch; as teachers, they supplement the existing perfection of the material they teach as well as the natural gifts of (often) socially superior students; and as writers, they supplement the existing body of literature inherited from classical antiquity.[25] The humanist writer could not present himself as the *source* of the authority he promised to convey without subverting the hierarchy into which he wished to insert himself. Supplementation allowed these men to present a double face to power, claiming that they were simultaneously both essential and inessential to its assertion.

"Gathering" and "framing," as described in the logic and rhetoric texts written by sixteenth-century English humanists, reflect these writers' reliance on supplementation even on a textual level. As a gatherer, the writer does not produce his own matter; instead, he supplements his natural ability with fragments borrowed from existing literature. These fragments are in turn supplemented by acts of selection, rearrangement, and assimilation (all part of the process of framing).[26] The fragments he borrows are themselves delineated by their supplementarity; that is, they stand out both as the essential matter of the text and as excerptible excrescences—as Geoffrey Bennington has put it, "the best of the text and the rest of the text."[27] Through the collection of such fragments, the authority of the source is maintained while the production of new texts is made possible. These new texts, as we shall later see, are strongly marked by their author's position as supplemental gatherer; they are best described not in terms of an author-centered imitative model, but as the products of a true intertextuality of fragments.

. . . . .

Rodolphus Agricola's *De inventione dialectica* (ca. 1479) has long been recognized as the preeminent humanist "logic." Walter Ong describes in detail how Agricola replaced more rigorous medieval logic with what is essentially a method of rhetorical invention based on the topoi, loci, or "places," a list of categories of relationship that could be used to analyze a topic and come up with ideas or arguments suitable to it. He suggests that the *De inventione* might more accurately be entitled "Thoughts on Discourse and How to Teach It."[28] Agricola's treatise was extremely influential in England, where traces of its attitudes and methods show up in virtually all logic texts (and some rhetorics) written in both Latin and English in the first two-thirds of the sixteenth century.[29]

Agricola is especially important to a history of the commonplace book because he reestablishes for the later Renaissance the logical basis for the practice of keeping one, and because his text enacts the shifting definition of "commonplace" as a space or category and as a textual fragment subject to gathering.[30] In the course of that shift, Agricola seems to perform a process of intellectual reterritorialization; he teaches his readers both to accumulate matter for copious speech from texts, and to map or classify those collected fragments according to the schema of the places. His treatise powerfully, and rather poignantly, conveys a deep anxiety about lack of fluency in Latin, and establishes the need to supplement natural abilities with a systematic technology of discourse. Agricola also establishes the commonplace book method as a means of appropriating the cultural code as a basis for authentic discourse, and in so doing he forges a link between gathering as a means of rhetorical invention and as a means of social self-definition.

The Aristotelian place or topos is a technique or strategy for "inventing" (that is, discovering) arguments on those controversial subjects which cannot be proven with scientific certainty.[31] The list of places (*topoi* in Greek, *loci* in Latin) passed on from Aristotle—through Themistius, Cicero, Boethius, and Peter of Spain—to Agricola varies but usually includes "definition," "genus," "species," "wholes," "parts," "adjacents," "relatives," "comparisons," "opposites," and "witnesses or pronouncements."[32] The places, then, are essentially a way of systematically classifying accepted ideas about how things relate to each other. They become useful in inventing arguments because they provide a reminder of what kinds of things might be said about anything. When discussing or thinking about "justice," for instance, one goes to the place "definition" in order to find ideas or arguments related to or stemming from accepted definitions of that concept.

In the Aristotelian tradition, the space which the places map is that of the *doxa*, or common beliefs of a culture.[33] According to dialectical tradition, such beliefs, when textualized as sayings, are found under the specific place "witnesses or pronouncements."[34] Daniel Kinney, for example, identifies Erasmian adages as "basic, enduring components in a structure of social *consensus*. The adages are building blocks of common knowledge and thus basic elements of social cohesion."[35] Although Agricola begins with something like the Aristotelian notion of place as strategy or technique based in the doxa, he persistently textualizes the concept until, in books 2 and 3, the space becomes ancient literature and the places in it the textual fragments that articulate common belief. For Agricola, places are finally signposts that give access to and control over the space of authentic discourse: at first, this is imagined as a space where the mind can participate in matter in order to comprehend its nature according to the sanctioned concepts of a culture. Later, when he shifts to a focus on texts rather than nature, it comprises the fragmentary textual spaces where the cultural codes of antiquity and fifteenth-century Europe intersect.[36]

Agricola's most basic concepts of language are deeply involved with the humanist social agenda and its strategies of supplementation. From the first sentences of the *De inventione*, he closely identifies dialectic, and, indeed, language itself, with the power relationships attendant upon the activities of teaching and advising. He begins the treatise with his definition of "speech" (*oratio, sermo*): "Every act of speech through which we reveal the thoughts of our minds has as its first and proper purpose the teaching of something to whoever hears it."[37] He goes on to emphasize the usefulness of his dialectical program to those "who govern a republic through their advice."[38] Speech itself is closely identified with power relationships; it enables the speaker to teach and to govern. Although Agricola initially defines speech as the natural expression of human presence ("through which we reveal the thoughts of our mind"), he immediately shifts to describing it as an instrument for imposing authority on someone else. But in both cases, the speaker's power is qualified by the presence of a more powerful listener: the one who hears the teacher and must be convinced to learn what he teaches, and the one who actually governs, having heard the adviser's counsel. Agricola's treatise establishes the traditional humanist occupations of adviser and teacher as "natural" properties of speech, which, however, need to be supplemented with instruction in dialectic in order to be carried out effectively.[39]

Agricola ties the need for instruction in dialectical invention to a vividly conveyed anxiety about lack of things to say in Latin. Although speech is a natural "gift" that God has given to man ("deus loquendi atque orationis indulserit munus"), it can only be wielded effectively by those with a greater measure of this gift:

> Some men are ingenious and think up an ample and ready argument (which, as Cicero says, is something convincing discovered to produce belief); others on the contrary, are less resourceful and, becoming confused when they examine things, either discover nothing to say about a given subject or find it too late.[40]

Although Agricola acknowledges the existence of a fortunate few with a natural gift for speech, he spends more time on a moving description of how it feels to lack that gift, and to grope blindly for words and ideas that come too late.

Agricola offers a system of gathering from the places as the solution to the pressing needs of those who find Latin speech difficult, and the fundamental strangeness of speech in classical Latin is perhaps most tellingly conveyed by the implication that thinking must become an out-of-body experience, carried on at least in part outside the speaker's living presence: "They seem to have done something extremely useful, who have discovered certain 'seats' of arguments (which are called places). By the warning of these places, as by certain signs that they give, we can take our mind through the very things themselves, and we can see whatever is probable about anything and whatever is suited to our speech."[41] The most notable feature of this supplement to natural speech is the idea, vividly conveyed here, that thinking takes place outside the speaker's body: we are instructed to take (*circumferremus*) our minds through "the things themselves" in order to find the ideas that we need.[42]

Agricola persistently describes thought as the supplementation of natural presence by going to the places, gathering ideas, and bringing them back: "We can go, and draw back from thence an argument suited to the things proposed."[43] Agricola's language for describing the act of gathering from the places is always metaphorical, and he frequently uses the apologetic qualifiers ("sedes *quasdam*," "signis *quibusdam*") that conventionally accompanied metaphorical language in Latin prose. The places are simultaneously signs to remind you of ideas, places where ideas are located, and signs pointing the way to a place where the mind can gain contact with "the things themselves."[44] In this ambiguity, Agricola wa-

vers between imagining the places textually, as signs, and spatially, as giving access to some place outside the mind. The bizarre scenario of thought taking place outside the body persists because Agricola has such a deep need to ground thought (and speech) in a presence more stable and authoritative than the speaker's mind, and to give to ideas the material existence they need to be authentic.[45]

Agricola explicitly relates the link between mind and matter (*animum* and *res*) forged by gathering from the places with the mastery of the cultural code necessary to a political adviser. He argues that mind must be in contact with matter outside itself in order to attain the prudence needed to give advice, and in so doing he conflates "matter" with social consensus about the nature of matter: "Nor does this faculty seem to aid only the mouth, and supply simply copia for speech; rather, it seems to provide the mind with foresight [*providentia*] and to open the path for giving good advice. For prudence does not appear to consist of anything but seeing what is placed in any thing whatsoever, and in collecting what agrees and disagrees with it, where it leads, and what can result from it."[46] "What is placed in any thing," as well as what agrees and disagrees with it: these are the ideas about natural relationships delineated by the doxa. The places provide something that transcends mere verbiage because they "open the path" that gives access to a culture's implicit beliefs. By describing the social consensus about "things" as located in those things and subject to collection as material fragments, Agricola allows the speaker to collect bits of the cultural code and assimilate them as the symbolic capital commonly termed prudence.[47] The authority needed for advice giving can only be gained through Agricola's method and the access to "things themselves" that it offers.

The method of dialectical invention is itself described as the result of a similar gathering operation. According to this scenario, the places themselves exist in nature, but they are useless unless gathered and systematized:

> There is in all things a certain common condition [*habitudo*] (although each is differentiated by its own signs), and all things tend toward a resemblance in their nature; for example, the fact that everything has substance (each has its own), or that all things arise from some sort of cause, and that all things end in certain effects. The most brilliant of men have gathered from the vast variety of things these common headings, such as substance, cause, effect, and the rest which I will soon name, so that when we turn our minds to considering anything whatsoever, following those headings, we can at once go through the whole nature and parts of the thing, and through everything that agrees or disagrees with it, and bring back an argument suited to whatever is mentioned.[48]

According to this passage, the commonplaces give access to natural properties that inhere in things themselves, acting as verbal headings or "signs" that lead a speaker to these natural resemblances. Once again, Agricola represents commonly accepted ideas about things (everything has a substance, a cause, effects) as partaking of the nature of things themselves. Ordinary people, confused by the "vast variety of things," will be unable to perceive these helpful resemblances unless they are aided by "the most brilliant men" (dialecticians) who have attached textual signs to these concepts and gathered them into a systematic method. Agricola offers his own treatise as a guidebook for visiting and exploiting the properties of things that lurk just out of sight of the uninitiated.[49]

The shift from describing the places as verbal signs of common properties in nature to describing them as fragments to be culled from literary texts occurs gradually through the course of the *De inventione dialectica*. As Agricola lists and discusses each individual place in the first book, he explicitly confines "pronouncements" taken from letters, books, speeches, sayings of learned men, and the common talk of the people, as was conventional, to the place "witnesses" or *pronuntiata*.[50] The other places, however, tend to be treated as categories under which commonplaces are grouped, and as a result what one gathers from each place is often a saying. Under "definition," for example, Agricola finds this sententious definition of law: "Law is the decree of a greater power, for preserving the state, instituted from equality and good." Under the place "proprium," we find that "the property of man is that he was born to laugh."[51] In practice, the "natural properties of things" to which the places are supposed to give access are represented by articulations of common beliefs about the natural properties of things, Aristotle's doxa, in the form of sententious fragments.

In book 2, Agricola's emphasis shifts to practical methods for parlaying knowledge of the places into fluent, copious Latin speech. In practical terms, literature rather than nature offers the readier source for copia, although this source is not without its dangers. He initially relates the places to ancient literature when he advocates their use as a kind of defense against its powerful force:

> The next step in knowledge of the places, which is more difficult, involves returning the arguments handed down by authors to their places. This practice is useful both in helping you to understand the strengths of these authors, and in discerning the varied methods of argumentation among them, as when sometimes they strike their adversaries with many arguments quickly joined together, as with frequent and continuous blows; and when their argument has been copiously and broadly joined so that they equal the force of many with one blow; so that now they stab with their pointed wit, now they overthrow

their opponent with their strength, now they make a judgment; now wherever there is too little trust in the case, having turned their speech to the opposite point of view, they win with an artful shift.[52]

The combat metaphor (derived from ancient discussions of the "pointed" force of sententiae) emphasizes the Renaissance reader's helplessness in the face of the overwhelming copiousness, variety, power, and duplicity marshaled by the native speakers of Latin who produced the literature they must attempt to understand, assimilate, and equal.[53] Although the violence is described as directed against an ancient opponent, it is so vividly portrayed here that a reader cannot help feeling threatened by the proliferation of punches, stabs, and wrestling holds that emanate from the ancient text. Agricola offers knowledge of the places as a kind of inside information that will provide some defense against these powerful texts. If a modern reader can gather fragmentary arguments from these texts and return them to the controlled space (that is, the systematized cultural code) delineated by the places, they will be disarmed. Here the technique of gathering textual fragments allows the reader to divide and conquer his powerful predecessors.[54]

A study of the places found in ancient works also has positive, as well as defensive, value. Agricola argues that by identifying the places in ancient authors (especially Demosthenes and Cicero), the modern student will gain a store of arguments or things to say that go along with his knowledge of the nature of "things themselves." This amounts to an articulation of his own practice in book 1, where the sample arguments found in each place tend to take the form of quotable fragments. Through this approach to studying ancient literature, "a certain copia and storehouse is prepared, which will always be had in readiness, so that as often as we look for similar places among things, similar arguments will run to meet us."[55] The spatiality of this program is revealing: a person who is about to speak searches (*quaeremus*) for places among things, and appropriate fragments of text run to meet him (*occurrant*) from the storehouse he has prepared by locating corresponding places in literature. The places delineate a space where nature, text, and mind can meet, and where the common beliefs of antiquity correspond to those of the modern reader.[56]

Not surprisingly, Agricola explicitly links knowledge of the places in literature with the preparation needed to hold public office. Here the places provide a carefully delineated common ground to which those already in power and those seeking power have access in different ways:

It is from Plato, Aristotle, Cicero, Quintilian, and the rest whose names are among the famous, that knowledge of all arts and humanity shines forth. Practice and the custom of listening and experiencing supplies this knowledge to those who are employed among the people and the greater crowd of civil businesses. But I do not know where those who prefer the indoors and hide themselves away among the secrets of studies can get such knowledge, unless they can gather it from those who have put these things in writing.[57]

Those who are already in power can experience the places in nature, while those who are still students need the help of the supplementary places found in famous literary works. Agricola's spatial metaphor, however, lets him imagine the knowledge as the same.

Agricola also offers his "commonplace book" method of gathering the places from ancient literature as the key to successful imitation of the ancients. He stresses that this gathering of fragments from a wide range of authors is the best way for modern writers to "follow in their footsteps, which to be able to follow from however far off is, I think, in this slothful age of ours, a particular virtue."[58] Agricola here acknowledges the painful distance between modern imitators and their sources that Thomas Greene has stressed as a central component of Renaissance imitation theory.[59] But Agricola avoids the apian, filial, and digestive metaphors that, according to Greene, express the Renaissance writer's goal, when imitating whole texts, of "making one's own the external text in all its otherness."[60] Agricola's spatial metaphor (following in the footsteps of the ancients) seems to indicate a concept of intertextuality that differs from Greene's voice-centered model. The modern imitator does not devour a text and reconstitute it as his own. Instead, he perceives certain fragments of the ancient text as *vestigia* or traces of the author's participation in a consensus about the "nature of things" that the modern reader shares. He is to follow those footprints to the space where words and things, ancient and modern, meet to form a reservoir of common matter for the construction of authentic discourse.

Once in that space (and he can only get there with the help of Agricola's dialectical method), the would-be writer is free to use this matter as is, or to reconstitute it in various ways. Agricola recommends that once arguments have been collected from classical authors, they may be made briefer or more copious, reordered, or contradicted.[61] The verbal form of these arguments is of little interest to the dialectician and only becomes an issue in rhetorical treatises. If these fragments are gathered and framed, however, Agricola concludes triumphantly that the speaker "will be able to speak expeditiously, copiously, and spontaneously on any thing that is proposed."[62]

Agricola sometimes acknowledges that his scheme for enabling authentic discourse is neither simple nor foolproof. Although he believes in the copia that it provides, he also worries about problems of control that can arise at various points in the process. One nagging worry is that the matter contained both in the world and in ancient literature is just too enormous to fit into the Agricolan mental, or extramental, space. When explaining the nature of the places early in book 1, Agricola reiterates his belief in the common nature of things but acknowledges that "there are, however, an immense number of things and their properties and diversities are equally immense. As a result of this, no speech, no force of the human mind, can possibly embrace one by one all things that join with or differ from single things."[63] The dialectical method offers a way to control this inflationary proliferation of concepts, since it relocates (or reterritorializes) them under "common headings gathered from the wide variety of things." The Agricolan method deals with fragments rather than wholes because they are less overwhelming, and easier to categorize.

Literature shares with nature this overwhelming copia, suggesting that Agricola's nervousness about the immensity of things may be related to the proliferation of new editions of classical texts that followed the invention of printing. In book 2, Agricola admits that arguments in ancient writers can be difficult to "place" because they are hidden by the very copia that they enable: "For often they hide, and conceal themselves in the copia of language itself, or they are concealed by various figures of speech."[64] Knowledge of the places can help the reader to locate the real matter of a work hidden beneath its deceptive verbal surface, providing a means of controlling the duplicity of copious language, even in Latin.

Agricola's *De inventione dialectica* provides an early and influential description of a version of the commonplace book method. But even more important, it establishes the act of gathering (*colligere, excerpsere*) as the central means of reading, thinking, and writing or speaking. In searching for a way to help modern students speak Latin with a fluency and authority approximating that of the Romans, Agricola constructs a system for dismantling the bewildering variety of ancient literature and choosing from it the most useful and authoritative bits. The basis of this system is an imaginary space, outside author, text, and reader, where words, things, and minds from different cultures can interact and ensure the authenticity of discourse. This space is that of the doxa, in this case the intersection of the cultural codes of antiquity and fifteenth-century Europe. Although its ubiquity and intangibility suggest the newly abstracted and deterritorialized market, Agricola's doxic space offers a form of symbolic capital that is both liquid and tied to a system of places. The modern student who has been trained in Agricola's systematic method of classifying common beliefs is able to locate the fragments of ancient text which articulate those beliefs and to recycle them in discourse that he produces.

This system thus claims to give its students access to the very source of authority of the ancient text: its basis in generally accepted truth about external nature, and its author's skillful manipulation of that truth.

Knowledge of the places offers to students a way to control both the immensity of nature and the powerful influence of ancient literature. It furnishes a safer way than imitation of whole texts to transfer that power to the modern writer, because it teaches him how to recognize the traces of authenticity in the ancient text and appropriate them for himself. It offers not a voice-centered, organic model of imitation, but a spatial, external, and fragmentary intertextuality that is simultaneously liberating and constraining. And although Agricola does not articulate clearly how the appropriate places in literature are to be recognized, he does introduce the complex psychology, sociology, and epistemology of gathering as a central linguistic maneuver.

English vernacular logics of the sixteenth century all show signs of the *De inventione*'s influence. But the problems they attempt to resolve are slightly different, and gathering and framing are put to different uses in these texts. Their central goal is not to enable Latin speech, but to transfer the authority, matter, and control of Latin into English speech. English was, at least in the early sixteenth century, widely considered to be a poor language, lacking in vocabulary and eloquence, and also an unruly one, lacking a grammar and standard orthography to control it.[65] The remedy for the lack of matter and eloquence is the gathering of matter from ancient languages, as expressed in the following passage from Ascham's *Scholemaster*:

> the prouidence of God hath left vnto vs in no other tong, save onelie in the *Greke* and *Latin* tong, the trew preceptes, and perfite examples of eloquence, therefore must we seeke in the Authors onelie of those two tonges, the trew Paterne of Eloquence, if in any other mother tong we looke to attaine, either to perfit utterance of it our selves, or skilfull iudgement of it in others.[66]

Many scholars assume that Ascham is talking about imitation here as a way to improve the vernacular. However, he describes Greek and Latin literature as the source of "preceptes" and "examples," both of which represent the kind of fragmentary matter included in most lists of what ought to be gathered in a commonplace book.[67] We see here also the language, familiar from Agricola, of "seeking" matter and finding it in other texts. And the gathering of this matter from ancient literature is seen as contributing to the two parts of dialectic: invention or "perfit utterance of it our selves," and "skilfull iudgement of it in others," according to a scheme like Agricola's.

In practical terms, the issue becomes how one properly manifests one's intellectual capital, the possession of a humanist education in classical literature, while speaking or writing in the vernacular. In these English texts, the social goals of achieving the authority necessary to teach and provide political counsel are even more prominent, and these activities were increasingly carried out in English.[68] English logic texts are generally directed at the special problems of authenticating English discourse in acceptable ways, and it becomes especially important that what is gathered from ancient literature contain matter and not just words. Although some authors suggest translation and the borrowing of foreign ("inkhorn") terms as means of enriching the vernacular, each of these methods had problems that prevented it from being widely embraced. Inkhorn terms were widely criticized as empty verbal affectations, and translation in itself did not directly enrich speech; both methods are tainted by the belief that they involved borrowing foreign matter and shifting words from their natural location.[69] Using language similar to that used by sixteenth-century theorists of the mercantilist balance of trade, English logicians generally deplore the importation of foreign words as in some way weakening the English intellectual economy. The gathering of commonplaces provides a solution because they were thought to contain matter in a way that single terms could not, and because, as statements of ideas that the two cultures held in common, they were uniquely translatable.

The role of gathering and framing in English logics must also be examined in light of the particular purpose for which each text was written. For although these treatises all contribute to the general ongoing search for a means of producing authentic discourse, each author has his own ax to grind, and his own reason for wanting to make that discourse possible. Logic in school was still taught largely in Latin, and as a result these vernacular texts are aimed at different audiences, each with a different purpose. Both religious and economic goals determine the special interests of these authors.

Thomas Wilson's *Rule of Reason* (1551), for example, is usually discussed as if it were simply a nationalistic attempt to provide England with a vernacular logic to rival Agricola in Latin.[70] But Wilson's choice of subject matter (he focuses on judgment, whereas Agricola restricts himself to invention) and examples (they are virtually all concerned with matters of religious belief) suggest that he had a different purpose: that of convincing a middle-class audience, literate in English but not in Latin, that Protestant beliefs were logical, and that they could be effectively marshaled and controlled through the practices of gathering and framing.

Wilson's *Rule of Reason* intends to prove that Protestant doctrine, expressed in the vernacular, is itself an authentic form of discourse and that it occupies the space of doxa. He also takes pains to associate his dialectical method with the construction of a Protestant bureaucracy under Edward VI, to whom the treatise is hopefully dedicated. Metaphors of dismantling or "unknitting" erroneous beliefs and replacing them with a carefully constructed single edifice (or "frame") of Protestant truth replace Agricola's images of searching and collecting. In this sense, Wilson typifies the English tendency to stress framing or control over gathering and copia, but he goes further than other English writers in constricting the common mental space he tries to delineate. At its most extreme, Wilson's "common place" is confined to a single line of Protestant belief, based on the use of fragments of Scripture according to a strict "rule of reason." Ultimately, Wilson discounts gathering because he believes that those who are saved have the necessary matter imprinted through grace on their hearts.[71]

He begins, interestingly, by defining "the rule of reason" as primarily useful for advising rather than teaching: "In euery cause that man dooeth handle, this one Lesson should first bee learned. Never to entre upon any matier nor yet ones to talke, without good aduisement. Artes therefore were inuented, wisemen are yet for the same cause estemed, and sage counsaillours had in moche honour."[72] Unlike Agricola, Wilson does not at this point mention the natural gift of speech, and his greater emphasis on control becomes evident when he stresses that speech should be preceded by advice, which he identifies with the "arte" of dialectic. The supplemental technology here, oddly, precedes and supersedes the natural act. He reveals the motivating force behind his social goals when he directly links the invention of supplemental arts with the "esteem" and "honour" given to advisers. His treatise will simultaneously establish the need to frame thought, speech, and society according to Protestant rule, and the need to elevate those who do the framing to positions of authority.

Wilson more clearly presents his version of the relationship between the natural and the supplemental when he links the need for the art of logic to the Fall:

> Manne, by nature hath a sparke of knowelge [*sic*], and by the secrete woorking of God, iudgeth after a sorte, and discerneth good from euil. Before the fal of Adam, this knowelege was perfeicte, but through offence, darkenesse folowed, and the bright light was taken awaie. Wisemen therefore, consideryng the weaknesse of mannes witte, and the blindnesse also, wherin we are all drouned: inuented this Arte, to helpe us the rather, by a natural order, to find out the trueth.(8)

Here again Wilson's concern is not with finding something to say, but with finding a "natural order" through which man can control and confine his speech to "the trueth." His attempt to define his art as a "natural order" recapitulates with wonderful economy Agricola's idea that the places are simply found, already framed, in nature, and gathered by the dialectician.

In justifying his decision to treat judgment before invention, Wilson reveals the roots of his emphasis on framing rather than gathering:

it is more meete that the ordryng of an Argumente should be first handled: forasmoche as it shall no more profit a manne, to find out his argumente, excepte he first know, how to order the same, and to shape it accordyngly, (which he dooth not yet perfeictly knowe) then stones or timber shal profit the Mason or Carpenter, whiche knoweth not how to woorke upon the same. A reason is easlier founde, then fashioned, for every man can geue a reason naturally, and without Arte, but how to fashion and frame the same, accordyng to Arte, none can dooe at all, excepte thei be learned.(9)

Wilson's idea that "every man can geue a reason naturally" is, of course, completely at odds with the basic assumptions and purpose of Agricola's text. Writing in the vernacular, with religious controversy in the back of his mind, it seems to Wilson that there is a dangerous proliferation of arguments or matter. The problem is that they lack the "order" and "shape" of Protestant truth. While Agricola's concern was to locate and make available a space of shared consensus between the ancient and modern worlds, Wilson wants to redefine the consensus of his own day in terms of that delineated by a Protestant reading of Scripture. His treatise will demonstrate the proper way to frame, fashion, or construct arguments in English that are congruent in shape with Protestant doctrine. And he will try to show that this shape occupies the space of doxa, of common sense and logical validity.

Despite his emphasis on framing, Wilson nevertheless assumes that some form of material must be gathered. His definition of place is often quoted because of its lively metaphor:

A Place is, the restying corner of an argumente, or els a marke whiche geueth warning to our memorie what wee maie speake probably, either in the one parte, or the other, vpon al causes that fal in question. Those that bee good harefinders will soone finde the hare by her fourme. For when thei see the ground beaten flatte rounde about, and faire to the sighte: thei have a narrowe gesse by al likelihode that the hare was there a litle before. Likewise the Huntesman in huntyng the foxe, wil soone espie when he seeth a hole, whether it be a foxe borough, or not. So he that will take profeicte in this parte of Logique, must bee like a hunter, and learne by labour to knowe the boroughes.(90)

Agricola's double sense of place as sign and as space has obviously influenced Wilson here. But he departs radically from Agricola in his whimsical images of the "harefinder" and "Huntesman." He may use this metaphor at least in part as a way to make his subject understandable and appealing to a (relatively) uneducated audience, attempting to convince them that the space of logic intersects with the fields of rural England.[73] But his metaphors also convey distrust of the arguments to which knowledge of the places gives access. Although they do not stab and hit like those found in Agricola's description of ancient literature, they are swift, slippery, and cunning. No longer seen as inert bricks and timber, these arguments occur naturally and numerously, but are extremely difficult to find and control.

Wilson's treatment of the place "witnesses" where sayings were usually located reveals the specific nature and source of the constrictions through which he hopes to control his version of gathering and framing. Although the main outline of his treatment of this place follows convention, he diverges from the tradition in his concern to delineate strictly the difference between divine and human sayings and how they may be used:

> Al soche testimonies maie be called, sentences of the sage, whiche are brought to confirme any thing, either taken out of old aucthours, or els soche as have bee vsed in this common life. As the sentences of noble men, the lawes in any realme, quicke saiynges, prouerbes, that haue been vsed heretofore, or bee now vsed. Histories of wise Philosophers, the iudgementes of learned men, the common opinion of the multitude, olde custome, auncient fashions, or any suche like. Testimonies are twoo waies considered. For either thei are soche as partein to God, or els to man. (121)

His list of types of "testimonies" is conventional and also resembles a list of the kinds of matter that are to be copied into a commonplace book. He reproduces Agricola's language of gathering when he speaks of such sayings being "brought" for confirmation and "taken out of old aucthours."

He begins to differ from Agricola and other dialecticians when he distinguishes sharply between divine sayings, which "are vndoubtedly true, neither can thei bee false" (121) and human authority, which "hath no soche great force" (122). This stricture clearly stems from the Protestant doctrine of *sola scriptura*, the idea that Scripture (and not ecclesiastical tradition) is the sole source of Christian belief. According to Wilson's "rule," one may reason affirmatively from human testimony, arguing, for example, that "the best thinges are first to bee learned, for so dooeth Quintilian teache" (122). But one can reason negatively only from Scripture: "We read not in all the scripture, from Genesis to the Reuelacion of saincte Ihon, that euer there was Frier, Monke, Nonne, or Chanon, ergo let theim goe from whens thei came" (123). His logic here is, of course, ridiculous, as it is at many such points. Wilson departs from valid logic in his attempt to restrict the shape of argumentation from gathered sayings in conformity with Protestant belief. And there is no room in Wilson's system for places not found in the specially authoritative space of Scripture: "let theim goe from whens thei came."

Wilson also departs from dialectical tradition in his definition of a third category of testimony, neither completely divine nor fully human.[74] In this concept of "natural law," he relocates the space of authority:

"Herunto might be added al soche sentences as by the lawe of nature are graffed in man. As these folowyng. Dooe as thou wouldest be dooen vnto. Be thankfull to him that dooeth thee a pleasure. Honour thy father and thy mother. Knowe there is a God. He that hath not these opinions naturally fastened in his harte, he maie iustly be thought rather a beast, then endued with reason" (123). Here, God's gift of reason takes the form of a "graft," a supplement that is both natural and artificial.[75] The supplement in this case consists of various divine and human "sentences" that a human being is supposed to have "naturally fastened in his harte." Without this textual supplement, one cannot be naturally human. According to this version of dialectical invention, knowledge of the places gives access to one's own heart, which has always already internalized the necessary fragments of text (most of which also appear in Scripture). We can now better understand Wilson's sense that gathering is unnecessary: the elect already possess the matter that they need, which has been gathered for them by God: the rest are beasts incapable of reason. Such reasoning would, in fact, invalidate his project of constructing a Protestant logic if it were rigorously followed. The importance of gathered sayings becomes clear, however, when they are imagined as a primary sign of God's grace.

Wilson concludes with instructions on how to dismantle false reason: "to confute, is nothing els but to iudge false packyng and to vnloose by reason, thinges knit together by crafte" (157). His goal is to destroy false buildings and replace them with those constructed on "some staie or sure foundacion of Goddes truthe," so that "all we maie drawe after one line, and seke one uniforme and sound doctrine" (217).[76] His emphasis on proper framing is clear in this conclusion where the space of doxa shrinks to "one line." Although other English logicians will not constrict this space so severely, Wilson's desire for a "staie or sure foundacion," and his sense that sentences (even when preengraved on the heart) contribute to that foundation, remain influential.

Ralph Lever's *The Art of Reason* (1573) continues Wilson's emphasis on building and framing but uses these metaphors to convert the space of logic into an English marketplace.[77] Lever's text is designed to present logic as a valuable commodity for the upwardly mobile, and under his system gathering and framing are ways to collect and market ideas as goods. Lever's own mercantile metaphors strikingly anticipate and make literal Bourdieu's concept of the "primitive accumulation of cultural capital" that takes place in societies as literacy and education become more widespread.[78] Thus, when Lever shares the Agricolan and Wilsonian emphasis on the places as a way to ground speech in matter, and explicitly associates this kind of grounding with verbal sententiae, his epistemology can be directly related to his desire to re-create ideas as a liquid but material commodity that can be accumulated and sold.

Lever dedicates *The Art of Reason* to "the right honorable Lorde, Walter, Earle of Essex, Viscount Hereford," who was in 1573 attempting to colonize Ulster and bring it under English control.[79] Lever was evidently tutor to the earl in his youth and offers this vernacular logic to him as a self-help guide to the art the nobleman failed to master when he studied it, presumably in Latin, with his tutor.[80] Lever attempts to persuade his former student that mastery of this art is a necessary supplement to power, since "he that is cunnyng in this facultye, shall seme ignoraunt in no learning: and who that is altogether unseene in this, can be depely seene in none. Doubtlesse a wise man must needes take great pleasure, and wonder, to see a fewe rules lead men to an infinite knowledge."[81] Lever builds on the anxiety of a reader who did not master an important subject, and offers that subject as a kind of academic snake oil to cure all intellectual ills—or, at least, the appearance of ills, since Lever's emphasis here is on the appearance ("seme," "seene") of learning and not the actuality. Contrary to Wilson, who wants to constrict intellectual space, Lever promises his reader access to "infinite knowledge."[82]

Lever's book is designed to appeal to the unlearned reader in several important ways and, at the same time, to create a flexible and controlled intellectual economy. First, not only is it written in English, but it makes a point of eschewing inkhorn terms and replacing them with English neologisms. Thus, instead of the Latinate "preface," Lever writes a "forespeache," and such logical terms as "predicate" and "definition" become "backsett" and "saywhat." In addition, Lever's "rules" are presented not in paragraph form but as numbered steps that systematically map the space of logic and can be more easily learned. Finally, Lever chooses his illustrative examples not from classical literature (as Agricola did), nor from Scripture and religious controversy (as did Wilson), but from the homely activities of everyday life: he compares his step-by-step presentation, for example, to "billets in a pile of wood" (viii). By gathering the matter of his logic from mundane manifestations of the cultural code, Lever reassures his readers that they in fact already have some access to logic. The emphasis throughout, then, is on the great gains that can be made, using his method, with little pain or effort.

Lever recapitulates the language of gathering and framing as he begins to describe his method. Logic is primarily a

> searching facultie, by reason whereof she teacheth a man the sooner to espy, what is right [and] what is wrong. . . . Shee sorteth all wordes, and placeth every kind by it selfe, [t]eaching what they signifie, as they are considered, and taken alone. shee declareth what sense words do make, when they are coupled and knit together: shee painteth forth the perfect forme of a reason by rule. And to conclude, shee doth minister matter to confirme, and laye forth a troth: and teacheth a way, howe to disprove, and discover an errour. (viii)

For Lever as for Agricola and Wilson, the primary operations of logic are to "search" out and "minister matter" and to "sort" and "rule" that matter once it has been found.

Although Lever, like Wilson, places judgment before invention and spends more time on it (books 1–3 on judgment, book 4 on invention), his treatment of judgment actually deals with gathering matter. He begins with the Aristotelian "predicaments," which he renames "storehouses" and treats essentially as places: "There are tenne generall woordes whiche may well be called storehouses, not onely for the store of woordes, whiche they conteyne (comprising all playn meaning words). . . . But also for the good order they keepe in placing of wordes in their particular roumes, with breefe rules, (as notes sette on packets), declaring theyr nature and properties" (7).[83] Although he does here discuss the abundance of matter furnished by the "storehouses," his emphasis is on their help in keeping words in "good order," confined to their "particular roumes," handily labeled "as notes sette on packets." Control seems important in this case as a kind of inventory-taking procedure ensuring that you know what ideas you have in stock and can produce them on demand.

In book 4, when invention is directly treated, the mercantile implications of Lever's logic become even more explicit. Invention is for Lever the means to "get store of proving termes," and his own method promises an orderly way to do this:

> For as the good and ready marchaunt provideth store of sundry wares, and sorteth every kinde by it selfe, adding special markes for his better direction, that hæ may with convenient speede fit and serve his customer when he calleth: So the quick and sharpe reasoner, must gather general rules together, and place them in order, that he may have in a redinesse when need shall be, store of reasons, for proofe or disproofe of matters in doubt. (137)

This method of sorting and labeling involves the places, which Lever also decides to call "storehouses" (141). His emphasis here is again on sorting and marking reasons so that they can be readily called into use whenever there is a market for them. Lever's concept of the space to which the places give access is in some ways quite different from Agricola's. Although it still constitutes the doxa, the places themselves seem to be imagined as shelves or pigeonholes in which to store and classify ideas that accord with common belief. By classifying these ideas according to Lever's scheme, the student is presumably able to accumulate as private property concepts that belong to the communal space of the doxa.

The reasons found and stored in the storehouses, as noted above, tend to take the form of the commonplaces of daily life. Under the place "number" (*quantitas*), for example, we find this list of examples:

5 If you will builde with speede, hire many laborers; for many handes make radde woorke.

6 And againe, strive not against many: for force lieth in a multitude.

7 Item, pardon mee this fault: it is the firste

8 Item, forgeve this second trespasse: for twice is not often.

9 The force of these and suche like reasons consist in number. (164)

These "reasons" (they are evenly divided between advice and excuses) are ostentatiously based on commonsense observations of daily life. It seems hard to believe that one would need to study logic to come up with these ideas, and, indeed, this is the point of Lever's book.[84] The reader will find that, in fact, he already practices the "art of reason" without understanding the terms. Because dialectic is based on the doxa or common beliefs of a society, its matter will always be commonplace. Lever recognizes that the difficulty lies in the special terminology of the discipline, and by simplifying that, he demystifies what must have seemed to the uninitiated a powerful and exclusionary discourse. But lest his own treatise seem an unnecessary supplement, he also emphasizes the need to sort and classify the morass of common belief. He thus implies that by collecting and classifying these concepts according to a "logical" scheme, the student will be able to own them himself and sell them to others.[85]

This is not to say that Lever is indifferent about the authenticity of the discourse produced by his method. Like Agricola and Wilson, he is concerned that speech be grounded in matter, although for Lever the materiality seems inextricably associated with the production of a commodity. Like other dialecticians, Lever must begin by defining speech in its natural state. Unlike the others, however, Lever's emphasis is on production: "words are voyces framed with hart and toung, uttering the thoughtes of the mynde"; "wee have also framed unto our selves a language, wherby we do express by voyce or writing, all devises that wee conceyve in our mynde: and do by this means let men looke into our heartes, and see what we thinke" (iiii). For Lever, the spoken or written word has already been framed: that is, an immaterial "device" invented in the heart of the speaker has been given material form. These devices cannot be offered to the public until they have been framed into material existence. And the framing process can be aided by knowledge of logic, which is, after all, "a cunning to frame and to answer a reason" (1).

The importance of sayings or sententiae as guarantors of authenticity is made clearer by Lever than by either Agricola or Wilson. Although words are framed into materiality by the organs of speech, they lack the sure grounding in matter of sayings: "Both words and sayings are meanes to express the thoughtes of the minde: but sayings express the thoughts of the mind, as matter is coupled to matter: and words express the

thoughtes of the minde without any ioyning of thyngs together at all"
(65). Like Agricola, Lever is concerned that discourse be grounded in
matter or things (*res*), but, as he makes clear, single words "expresse the
thoughtes of the minde without any ioyning of thyngs together at all."
"Saying" is used here as Lever's vernacular term for *propositio*, and he
goes on to define it as "a voyce whose several partes do by consent signifie
some matter" (66). He also mentions sayings under the place "witnesses"
in the usual sense as maxims or *sententiae* "which doe arise of the matter
itselfe," and it seems clear that he means something like the same thing in
both places. Sayings for Lever are more than collocations of words. Like
Agricola's places, they provide a link between mind and matter by articu-
lating common beliefs about things. Thus, discourse is authentic only
when it contains sayings to ground it in matter; it is useful only when that
matter renders it sufficiently material to be offered as a commodity.

The materiality of sayings gives them a crucial role in the transfer of
matter from ancient literature to modern discourse. A major concern of
Lever's "forespeache" (or preface) is, as noted earlier, a defense of his
decision to use English neologisms instead of Latinate inkhorn words for
the technical terms of logic. He poses the problem in economic terms:
"nowe the question lyeth, whether it were better to borrowe termes of
some other toung, in whiche this sayde Arte hath bene written: and by a
litle chaunge of pronouncing, to seeke to make them Englishe, whiche are
none in deede: or else, of simple usual wordes, to make compound" (v–
vi). Lever recognizes that translating or "borrowing" words from other
languages will lead to intellectual bankruptcy, and chooses instead to
"compound" words that are already in the vernacular wordbank. But
even these newly coined English words are open to problems of misinter-
pretation. Thus, although neologisms present a compromise solution to
the problem of terminology, they do not solve the problem of how best to
enrich English with ancient matter. Here again, sayings provide an answer because their matter remains the same even when they are translated: "Thoughtes of the minde, and matters whereof men use to speake
and to write, be in all countryes one and the same in kind: but letters and
the voyce whereby suche things are uttered, are not. . . . A saying is a
voyce whose several partes do by consent signifie some matter" (65). In
order to recycle ancient texts into authentic grounded discourse, one must
gather sayings instead of borrowing single words.

Lever, then, makes clear the importance of the commonplace book in
the commodification of knowledge. Thought and discourse must be reduced to material fragments that can be inventoried, labeled, framed into
new devices, and sold to whoever will buy them. "Framing" is Lever's
all-purpose word for the transformation of immaterial idea into salable
commodity. The inner thoughts of the human subject are worthless in

their natural state; supplementation is necessary before they can be sold: "Thus ye may see the originall groundworke and beginning of artes. Man firste doth conceyve trim devises in his heade, and then (as the Poetes do feigne of Jupiter) is pained as a woman in travaile, till he have uttered and published them, to be sene, and commended of others" (v). However "trim" such devices may be, they are of no use until "framed" into a form that others may commend and buy.[86] Lever's own art of dialectic teaches a ready and easy way to convert the raw material of commonplace ideas into the goods (in the form of gathered sayings) of symbolic capital, labeled for sale as "infinite knowledge."

I want to close this section with a brief look at Dudley Fenner's *The Artes of Logike and Rhetorike* (1584) and at Abraham Fraunce's *The Lawiers Logike* (1588). As these texts reveal, to the extent that it conceives the essential operations of discourse to be gathering and framing, Ramism represents, in some ways, not a new direction but a culmination of the tendencies we have seen so far.[87] Fenner's treatise is essentially an unacknowledged translation of Ramus's *Dialecticae libri duo* and Talaeus's *Rhetorica*.[88] Fenner resembles Wilson in gathering his examples from Scripture and Protestant doctrine; he resembles Lever in his explicit attempts to present his treatise as a commodity. Fraunce's text is itself a commonplace book which attempts to prove that English law is "logical" by gathering from it textual fragments which correspond to fragments from ancient and modern literature: he concludes by wishing "the whole body of our law to be rather logically ordered then by alphabeticall breviaries torne and dismembered," and demonstrates such ordering with the "analysis" of Virgil's second "Eclogue" and two law cases.[89] Such seemingly bizarre juxtapositions make perfect sense under a system that seeks fragmentary traces of the same cultural code in all texts. Fraunce, like Fenner, articulates a kind of compromise between Wilson's Protestant narrowing and Lever's mercantile expansion of the space of authentic discourse.

Fenner's preface, addressed "To the Christian Reader," uses a version of the gathering metaphor in defending his decision to translate two Latin treatises into English: "seeing the common use and practise of all men in generall, both in reasoning to the purpose, and in speaking with some grace and elegancie, hath sowen the seede of these artes, why should not all reape where all haue sowen?"[90] Because logic is based on the common cultural code, Fenner feels justified in translating it out of Latin, a language that he calls "the storehouse of the worlde for these commodities" (145). Here, as translator, Fenner presents himself as the gatherer of logic out of classical languages; indeed, his debt to Ramus may remain unacknowledged as a means of insinuating that he is gathering his matter from classical texts. His purpose in gathering this matter is explicitly tied to its status as a commodity: he has prepared this treatise "that everie one who had neede, might buie of the same" (146). He does not explicitly acknowledge his other goal, which is, like Wilson's, to demonstrate that the Bible and Protestant doctrine share with classical literature the space of doxa, and that religious as well as secular fragments may be repackaged as a useful commodity.[91]

Fraunce, like Fenner, goes further than previous logicians in confining the operations of both logician and student to gathering and framing. His distinction between natural and artificial logic represents supplementation entirely in terms of these operations:

> Artificiall Logike is gathered out of divers examples of naturall reason, which is not any Art of Logike, but that ingraven gift and facultie of wit and reason shining in the perticular discourses of severall men, whereby they both invent, and orderly dispose, thereby to iudge of that they have invented. This as it is to no man given in full perfection, so divers have it in sundrie measure. And because the true note and token resembling nature, must be esteemed by the most excellent nature, therefore the preceptes of artificiall Logike both first were collected out of, and alwayes must be conformable unto those sparkes of naturall reason, not lurking in the obscure head-peeces of one or two loytering Fryers, but manifestly appearing in the monumentes and disputations of excellent autors.[92]

Fraunce offers the expected description of natural reason as "that ingraven gift and facultie of wit and reason," borrowing Wilson's metaphor of engraving on the heart as a way of describing the natural supplement of grace. But for Fraunce, this natural "spark" (another word of Wilson's) exists only as it manifests itself in discourse: "shining in the perticular discourses of severall men, whereby they both invent, and orderly dispose." Fraunce skips over the inner state and moves directly to the product to which the gift leads. He acknowledges, as did Agricola, that different people possess this gift "in sundrie measure," and as a result, a method of artificial logic is needed to supplement the gift. And for Fraunce, as for Agricola and Fenner, this art is itself gathered: the difference is that Fraunce gathers not from nature, but from the traces of nature in texts, "manifestly appearing in the monumentes and disputations of excellent autors." As in Wilson's text, there is some limitation of texts where these traces are to be found, but Fraunce would delete only those fragments "lurking in the obscure head-peeces of one or two loytering Fryers." Like Agricola and Wilson, Fraunce sees the art of gathering as a solution to the confusing variety of things in the world, but he departs from Agricolan theory in his surprising claim that the greater order of the supplemental art makes it superior to nature: "And then is this Logike of Art more certain than that of nature, because of many particulers in nature, a generall and unfallible constitution of Logike is put down in art" (2r).

Fraunce thus carries the textualization of logic to its logical extreme. Like Agricola, Fraunce acknowledges the need to supplement thought with matter gathered from outside: unlike Agricola, Fraunce suggests that this matter is to be found solely in a textual space. Like Wilson, Fraunce is concerned to locate the origin of thought in God's grace, and to confine the space of knowledge to texts that accord with it: he differs in widening the space of allowable texts. Like Lever, Fraunce offers logic as a practical commodity for lawyers: he differs in locating the source of matter in texts alone. This extreme textualization manifests itself in Fraunce's definition of "place": he begins by calling places "generall heades of arguments," which, he says, other authors have termed "categories," "locos, sedes, fontes, places, seates, springes or fountaines . . . principles, Elementes, Reasons, Proofes, Argumentes, Termini, and Media" (10v). He will use the terms "Argument, and sometimes Reason, and proofe, as most usuall and significant, the rest being rather straunge and metaphoricall" (10v). Fraunce condenses Agricola's progressive textualization into a single paragraph that begins with the Aristotelian category, proceeds through the spatial concepts of topos as seat or fountain, and ends by choosing to consider the textual manifestations of places—reason, argument, proof—as the places themselves.

Fraunce concludes by suggesting exercises in reading and writing that correspond closely to those recommended by Agricola.[93] First, he offers what he calls "genesis," a gathering and framing exercise designed to "breede a great plentie and varietie of new argumentes" useful both "in making and enditing our selves, or els in resolving, and as it were dismembring that which others have doone" (81v). The student is directed to "draw any one woord through these generall places of invention"; this is done, according to Fraunce's example, by finding sayings in various authors that correspond to the various types of argument delineated by the places. In effect, Fraunce takes the word "nobilitas" and uses it as a commonplace book heading, collecting statements about it from various sources. Then, for the exercise of "analysis," Fraunce finds all of the arguments, corresponding to the places and pertaining to the word "amicitia," that he can find in a single text, Cicero's De amicitia. Here, he demonstrates how to mine a single text for matter. Note that Fraunce no longer imagines the ancient text as something against which a defense must be mounted. Instead, the student dismembers that text for his own use.

Thus, when Fraunce concludes his book with tables analyzing the arguments found in Virgil's second "Eclogue" and two law cases, we can see the method in his madness. He can only prove that English common law is "logical" if he can demonstrate that it contains fragments which accord with ideas found in ancient literature. As Fenner does with Scripture, Fraunce is concerned to show that English law shares the space of doxa and thus admits commodification. These English Ramists also want to demonstrate that humanist education and its commonplace book method can be sold to Protestants and lawyers as well as to teachers and advisers. In these goals, Fenner's and Fraunce's Ramism simply continues and intensifies trends present in English logic from the beginning of the century.

Agricola, Wilson, Lever, Fenner, and Fraunce all present different versions of the same basic system for the manufacture of authentic discourse. For all of them, authentic discourse depends not on inspiration, imagination, or creative imitation, but on the ability to recognize fragmentary traces of a shared cultural code in other texts, and to frame those fragments into a reordered whole. The space of that shared code is variously imagined, depending on the author's image of what constitutes authentic discourse. Agricola, for example, sees fluent Latinity as authenticating and is concerned to teach modern minds, as far as possible, to inhabit the entire space of Latin and Greek literature. Wilson and Fenner are concerned to show that Protestant doctrine expressed in the vernacular at least partly shares the space of doxa as defined by ancient texts. Wilson imagines God's grace as the engraving of textual fragments on the heart and constricts the space of authenticity to a building constructed on those texts' foundation, or, ultimately, to a single doctrinal line. Lever wants to enable authentic discourse for those lacking an adequate classical education. He first plays on their anxiety that they lack access to the privileged space, and then allays it by showing how common sense and general knowledge can be repackaged as logic. He assures his readers that they already inhabit that space and only need to relabel it in order to possess sufficient intellectual capital. Fenner similarly tries to market a logic based on Scripture and Protestant doctrine under the rubric of Ramus's simplified method. Fraunce culminates this tradition by redefining thought as the manipulation of texts.

All of these writers are concerned with giving their readers or students access to a common space, that of the doxa or cultural code. They pay little attention to how this code articulates itself in texts, beyond listing forms such as proverb, aphorism, exemplum, and the like. And they seem uninterested in formal properties that might define or differentiate sententious forms. These distinctions are left to rhetoricians, who continue the language of gathering and framing but who are less certain about the relationship between authentic discourse and the "common" beliefs of society.

Chapter II

COMMON PEOPLE, UNCOMMON WORDS:
THE POWER OF RHETORIC

THE LOGICIANS, then, established gathering fragments of other texts as a central means of producing authentic discourse. These fragments were described as the portions of a text that reflected common ideas about extratextual things, places in the text where the cultural codes of antiquity, Scripture, and sixteenth-century England intersected. Logic texts define the verbal form of such fragments only implicitly when they list kinds of "argument" that are especially efficacious, usually "example," "sentencia," and "proverb."[1] Logicians prefer not to consider the purely stylistic qualities that identify these forms for gathering. Their main concern is that the gathered fragments be grounded or framed in things rather than words, and that they represent common ideas about those things. In fact, despite the implicitly rhetorical nature of the copia that their program enables, these writers tend to regard the verbal stylistics of texts with distrust, as constituting a copia that obscures the matter of the text, or as aggressive weapons directed against the unwary reader.[2] For the logicians, the fragments upon which authentic discourse should be constructed are imagined as the raw materials of construction—bricks and timber, or basic commodities arranged for sale.

Rhetoric, of course, concerns itself with verbal ornamentation as a means of persuasion and has often been seen as logic's harlot sister, the mother of lies.[3] Where logic is natural, plain, and grounded in things, rhetoric is artificial, bedizened, and concerned largely with the manipulation of words. Rhetoricians tend to represent gathered fragments as ornamental flowers, or jewels, unlike the plain bricks and timber of logic. Sixteenth-century English rhetoricians, as several critics have pointed out, were in the position of defending their art as a safe, truthful, and necessary supplement to logic, and to natural powers of speech.[4] I want to argue that these rhetoricians took over from logic the concepts of gathering and framing as the central means of making their form of discourse seem grounded, authentic, under control, and able safely to assert control.

The social role of the humanist writer, and of the discourse he enables, becomes even more problematic when rhetoric, with its dangerous manipulations of truth and emotion, is at issue.[5] Rhetoric, based in part on the gathering of ornamental fragments framed only by devices of style, and designed to exceed the limits of common speech and to manipulate the emotions of the common people, posed a threat both to the grounding of discourse in significant matter and to its framing in accordance with the hierarchical social code. Rhetoric, that is, promised to teach a way to control others without necessarily being able to control itself. Also, when rhetoricians advocate the borrowing of ornamental "jewels" and "flowers" from foreign texts into English, they seem in opposition to the logicians' mercantilist concerns about the intellectual balance of trade.[6]

Of course, English rhetoricians try in various ways to forestall these problems; to ground their borrowed tropes in substantial matter, to frame the power of rhetoric within accepted cultural codes, and to limit its social agenda. The words "common" and "uncommon" become key terms in the discussion of appropriate discourse and map the intersection of the social and the stylistic. Rhetoricians embrace the authenticating force of social consensus and at the same time acknowledge the need to construct a discourse that is superior to and able to manipulate common belief. Sententious forms are now explicitly defined in terms of style as well as content; they become a crucial factor in negotiating the distance between logic and rhetoric because they can be defined as both uncommon and common, verbal and material, ornamental and substantial, imported and native, empowering and controlled.

Most rhetorical treatises begin with an assertion, familiar to us from logic texts, of the need for this art as a supplement to natural ability—and now, to logic itself. As in the logic texts, English humanist rhetoricians emphasize the importance of this art in their supplemental activities of teaching and advising. The rhetoricians place more emphasis on the control over the audience that their faculty makes possible, and they also show more nervousness about that control and its social implications. Leonard Cox offers modest claims at the beginning of his school text, *The Arte or Crafte of Rhethoryke* (1530), offering that "crafte" as "very necessary to all suche as wyll eyther be aduocates and proctoures in the lawe, or els apte to be sente in theyr pryneces Ambassades, or to be techars of goddes worde in suche maner as maye be moste sensible and accepte to their audience."[7] The power of the successful rhetorician is here described as directly dependent on the audience's acceptance and not as powerful in itself. Thomas Wilson's *Arte of Rhetorique* (1560) reveals more clearly a typical nervousness about the social implications of teaching rhetoric. He seems first to make a strong assertion of his own power as teacher, describing rhetoric as "so necessarye: that no man oughte to be withoute it, whiche either shall beare rule over manye, or must have to doe wyth matters of a Realme."[8] But he quickly recalls the superior position of his dedicatee, Lord John Dudley, and reroutes the path of supplementation: "you wil so farre be better than this my boke, that I shall . . . be driven to sette this simple Traictise to your Lordshyppe to Schole" (8).[9] Whether he chooses to define himself as grantor or recipient of this powerful skill, Wilson remains the conduit for the interchange of supplemental instruction.[10] Henry Peacham, in the second edition of his *Garden of Eloquence* rather neatly asserts a claim to power and then undercuts it by acknowledging the supplementarity of the humanist position: the man who adds instruction in eloquence to natural wisdom "hath bene iudged able, and esteemed fit to rule the world with counsell, prouinces with lawes, cities with pollicy, and multitudes with persuasion."[11] Peacham's students, like Cox's, will be able to rule, but only indirectly, through counsel, laws, policy, and persuasion. Like Wilson, he makes a claim for the importance of rhetoric and then retreats from it.

As in logic, a key part of the humanist writer's flexible posture is his reliance on gathering and framing both as his own method for writing the treatise and as that which the treatise teaches. Scholars traditionally identify three kinds of rhetorical treatise in sixteenth-century England: the Ciceronian, or full five-part treatment; the stylistic, or list of schemes and tropes; and the formulary, or collection of patterns and exercises.[12] Leonard Cox's *The Arte or Crafte of Rhethoryke* (London, 1530) treats the first two parts (invention and disposition) of the Ciceronian type, while Thomas Wilson followed his logic with *An Arte of Rhetorique* (London, 1553), a five-part Ciceronian rhetoric.[13] Richard Sherry's *A Treatise of Schemes and Tropes* (London, 1550) and Henry Peacham's *The Garden of Eloquence* (London, 1577, 1593) are stylistic rhetorics comprising lists of schemes and tropes, and Richard Rainolde's *A Book Called the Foundacion of Rhetorike* (London, 1563) is a formulary rhetoric and consists of a translation into English of Aphthonius's *Progymnasmata*.[14]

The language of gathering and framing enters into these different types of text in varying ways. Because Cox and Wilson include treatment of invention and disposition, the two parts that rhetoric shares with logic, they import the concepts of gathering and framing directly from the logical tradition. Cox gives a definition of invention that would be at home in any sixteenth-century logic: "Invencyon is comprehended in certayn placys, as the Rhetoriciens call them, out of whom he that knoweth the facultye may fetche easyly suche thynges as be mete for the mater that he shal speke of."[15] As in logic, the student is directed to gather "thynges" out of "placys." Cox stresses that those who know the faculty may easily "fetche" suitable things, in contrast, perhaps, to "farfet" metaphors, which are usually condemned as rhetorical excess.[16] Wilson similarly begins his discussion of invention with the instruction that the student "must . . . to his boke, and learne to be well stored with knowledge, that he maie be able to minister matter, for all causes necessarie" (28), and he goes on to define invention as "a searchyng out of thynges true, or thynges likely, the which maie reasonablye sette furth a matter, and make it appere probable. The places of Logique, geve good occasion to finde out plentifull matter" (31–32). Again we can recognize from the logics Wilson's typical emphasis on "searching, matter," and the conflation of going "to his boke" and to the places.

Gathering and framing are not, however, confined to the sections of these texts that overlap with logic. Wilson, when he takes up style or "elocution," and also Peacham and Sherry, whose treatises are confined to that part of rhetoric, transfer these operations to the collection and use of figures of speech.[17] Wilson, for example, calls his third book "Of apte chusyng and framyng of wordes and sentences together, called Elocucion" (323). Sherry and Peacham both entitle their books in ways that identify their own roles as gatherers of figures. Sherry's full title is "A treatise / of Schemes and Tropes / very profytable / for the better understanding of good / authors, gathered out of the best / Grammarians and Oratours / by Rychard Sherry Lon/doner.[18] The title of Peacham's second edition includes the information that it is "*Manifested, and furnished with varietie of fit exam/ples, gathered out of the most eloquent Ora/tors, and best approued authors, and / chieflie out of the holie / Scriptures. /Profitable and necessarie, as wel for private speech, / as for publicke Orations.*" Peacham, in fact, represents the acts of gathering and framing (or ordering) as providing assurance that his rhetoric is grounded in matter: "now, lest this part should seeme an emptie art of wordes, without wisedome or substance of matter, I haue gathered out of the most excellent Orators, and best approued authors, varietie of fit examples for everie figure by it selfe: which figures or formes of speech, I have disposed into orders" (ABivr).

Both Sherry and Peacham also recommend gathering and framing as activities to be undertaken by those who want to learn how to use the figures effectively in both reading and writing. Sherry instructs that "oute of thys great stream of eloquucion, not only must we chose apte, and mete wordes, but also take hede of placinge, and settinge them in order" (18). Peacham similarly notes that "the wisdome of man hath invented and found out an Art, not onely teaching where apt translations [i.e., tropes] may be found, but also giving excellent rules and certain directions, how they should be most aptly and properly applyed" (2). Here, of course, "chose" and "found" are synonyms for gathering, "placinge" "settinge them in order," "aptly and properly applyed," for framing.

The imitative exercises of formulary rhetoric are sometimes cited as evidence that rhetorical instruction in the sixteenth century was based on imitation rather than on the commonplace book method. W. S. Howell, for example, stresses their aim of providing "models for imitation."[19] But Richard Rainolde's translation of Aphthonius, *The Foundacion of Rhetorike*, is as deeply marked by the operations of gathering and framing as any other logic or rhetoric written in sixteenth-century England. A formulary rhetoric traditionally consists of a set of "orations" along with directions to the student for imitating each kind of speech. The "orations" themselves, however, are categorized not by subject but by the form of matter upon which they are based. Rainolde includes orations based on fable, narration, *chria* (a proverb), sentence, confutation, confirmation, commonplace, praise, dispraise, comparison, *ethopeia*, description, *thesis*, and *legislatio*.[20] In effect, the student is directed to write essays based on various kinds of gathered matter.

Rainolde, as we might expect, presents his own role in the project as that of gatherer rather than translator. He has "chosen out in these Oracions soche questions, as are right necessarie to be knowen and redde of all those, whose cogitacion pondereth vertue and Godlines" ("To the Reader"). Both his instructions to the student and the examples themselves are full of references to gathering and framing. He defines the moral of a fable, for example, as something "out of the whiche some godlie precepte, or admonicion to vertue is given, to frame and instruct our maners" (2v), since "fables dooe conteine goodlie admonicion, vertuous preceptes of life" (3r). When writing an oration on a fable, the student is to begin with praise of the author, "whiche praise maie sone bee gotte of any studious scholer if he reade the auchthours life and actes therin, or the Godlie preceptes in his fables" (4v). Rainolde's example of an oration on a fable by Aesop includes this praise of his fables: "herein ample matter riseth to Princes, and governours, to rule their subiectes in all godlie lawes" (5v). Under chria, we learn that a sentence or saying "dooeth containe so great matter, and minister soche plentie of argumente" (16v). These exercises involve not imitation of whole texts but a method of extracting moral "preceptes" that can be rearranged according to set instructions for framing, and which themselves provide a source of matter and a source of rules for ordering subjects.

Stylistic and formulary rhetorics are thus equally concerned to provide instructions for gathering and arranging figures of speech effectively and appropriately. And although sententious sayings such as "proverb," "sententia," "gnome," and "precept" might seem at first to be treated as specific figures of speech, it soon becomes clear that the figures themselves, especially closural figures such as isocolon and antithesis, function as verbal signposts for delineating the matter to be gathered.[21] For most of the century, rhetoricians resist the idea that the verbal wit and closure provided by the figures is as important as congruence with doxa in making sayings seem true and material. They do not want to admit that sayings simply seem true because of rhetorical tricks rather than actually embodying authentic and stable truth, that they are delineated by form rather than content. But by 1589 and the publication of Puttenham's *Arte of English Poesie*, this disturbing idea can be explicitly acknowledged.[22]

All of these writers do, in accordance with classical tradition, define sententious forms explicitly under a single figure or group of figures. Sherry, for example, includes them under his discussion of the place "Indicacio, or authoritie," and includes seven "kyndes," which seem related to the kinds of formulary rhetoric: common moral sentence, common rules, proverbs, chria ("short exposicion of any dede or worde wyth the name of the author recited"), enthymeme (which he defines as "a sentence of contraries"), aenos ("a saying or a sentence, taken out of a tale"), or a commandment of God (92–93). Wilson identifies the "thirde kinde of Amplifiynge" as "when wee gather suche sentences as are communelye spoken, or ellse use to speake of suche thynges as are notable in thys lyfe," for example "Likeryshe of tongue, lighte of taile" (246–47). Peacham separately treats "Paroemia, called of us a Proverbe, . . . a sentence or forme of speech much used, and commonly knowen" (29), and "gnome, otherwise called sententia, [which] is a saying pertaining to the maners and common practises of men, which declareth by an apt brevitie, what in this our life ought to be done, or left undone" (189). In these instances, various kinds of saying are identified primarily on the basis of their common matter—that is, in the same way that they are designated in logic. Only Peacham specifies a stylistic criterion when he notes that the gnome must also have "apt brevitie."

In practice, however, sayings of various kinds are closely associated with the rhetorical figures in general. Many figures in these treatises are exemplified, as their title pages warn us, by sayings taken from famous authors. This practice of gathering serves a double purpose: it authenticates the figures by deriving them from the doxic fragments of authoritative texts, and it also authenticates the treatise by presenting it as a commonplace book offering useful fragments of text framed in an orderly fashion. Under "similitude," for example, Wilson tells us that "the proverbes of Heiwode helpe wonderfull well" (375) for providing examples of this figure.[23] Peacham tends to illustrate his figures with sayings taken from classical literature, folk wisdom, or the Bible. Diaphora, for example, is exemplified by "Phisition heale thy selfe if thou beest a Phisition" (45), while homeoptoton yields "a friend in neede is a friend indeede," or "foolish pitie undoeth many a citie" (54).[24]

Wilson directly articulates the close connection between the figures of speech and sententious sayings. Having commented on the use of "delightfull sayings, and quicke sentences," he tells us that "pleasantnesse in a saiyng, is stirred by the quicke altryng of some one worde, or of some one sentence" (281); for Wilson, a "figure" is "a certaine kinde, either of sentence, oration, or worde, used after some newe or straunge wise" (340). Figures of speech were usually divided into "schemes" and "tropes," both terms indicating etymologically that they represent a turning or altering of words from their usual order or meaning.[25] According to Wilson, then, sayings are stylistically delineated by the figures of speech that give them their witty sententiousness.[26]

In the introduction to his *Adagia*, Erasmus lists some of the kinds of figures that define his adages. He emphasizes primarily such tropes as metaphor, allegory, riddle, allusion, and pun that involve the alteration of meaning.[27] These forms help to authenticate the adage in various ways. Metaphoric references to homely activities call attention to the origins of sayings in the cultural code, while the shifts of meaning involved in riddle or pun stress the ways in which the uncanny resemblances of language can support and comment upon the code. Erasmus also mentions the use of schemes involving "repetition of the same or a similar word, or by the putting together of opposite words."[28] Here, devices of sound provide stylistic support for the ethical closure of the doxa.[29]

Peacham also acknowledges a close link between sayings and figures of speech. He defines eleven different types of sententia, the last of which opens out to include all the figures of speech: "the eleventh is a figured sentence, wherof there be as many kindes, as there be figures: If it be figured, it beareth the name of the figure wherewith it is ioyned" (190–91). George Puttenham, whose *Arte of English Poesie* is a rhetorical treatise specifically addressing the composition of poems, defines an entire category of figures as "sententious, otherwise called Rhetoricall": "your figures rhethoricall, besides their remembred ordinarie vertues, that is, sententiousness, and copious amplification, or enlargement of language, doe also conteine a certaine sweet and melodious manner of speech." He alone articulates the close connection between sententious style and weighty content in making such sayings seem true: "therefore the well tuning of your words and clauses to the delight of the eare, maketh your information no lesse plausible to the minde than to the eare: no though you filled them with never so much sence and sententiousnes."[30]

Rhetoric thus offers the possibility that the gathered material of discourse is defined not only by its "sence" or congruence with the cultural code, but by its skillful manipulation of style. The dangerous secret, which most of these texts repress, is that "the well tuning of your words and clauses to the delight of the eare, maketh your information no lesse plausible to the minde." Although Puttenham, writing probably in the late 1580s for a courtly audience, can openly acknowledge this as a fact, earlier writers could not.[31] To do so would be to admit that they were teaching the production of discourse that was ungrounded in truth, only as stable as words which were twisted out of their normal meanings, and designed to manipulate audience reactions purely through style. Of course, we would now recognize this as precisely a description of the aims of rhetoric. But sixteenth-century English humanists, at least before the 1590s, for both social and intellectual reasons, go to great lengths to avoid depicting rhetoric in this light. We can trace their uncertainty about the implications of stylistic power in their nervous accounts of the relationship between "common" and "uncommon" discourse. Sayings, by definition both "common" and "uncommon," provide a means of negotiating this dilemma.[32]

Logic—even the rhetoricized logic of the humanists—was traditionally associated with the expression of matter in plain or "common" language, while rhetoric involved some sort of elaboration in unusual or "uncommon" language. Cox explains the distinction clearly:

> The Logycyan in disputynge obseruythe certayne rules for the settynge of his words [,] beynge solycytous that ther be spokyn no more nor no les then the thynge requireth / and that it be even as playnly spoken as it is thought. But the Rhetoricyan seketh abought and boroweth when he can asmuche as he may for to make the symple and playne Logycall argumentes gay and delectable to the aere. so then the sure Judgement of argumentes or reasons muste be learnyd of the Logycyan but the crafte to set them out with pleasaunte fygures and to delate the matter longith to the Rhetorycian.[33]

Even here, in the introduction to a rhetorical treatise, logic is associated with "certayne rules," "Judgement," and "playn" speaking, while rhetoric implies borrowing language that does not quite fit (as opposed to gathering what is plain and suitable).[34] Cox associates rhetoric with "crafte," a synonym for "art" that could also imply crafty deception. Cox cannot help reflecting his sense that rhetoric is a dangerous supplement to plain-speaking logic.[35]

Other rhetoricians reflect a similar sense that rhetoric is a supplement to logic but make greater efforts to assert its utility in a fallen world. Wilson acknowledges that a speaker's first duty is "utter his mind in plain wordes, suche as are usually received, and tell it orderly, without goyng aboute the busshe" (25). But he goes on to say that "quicknesse of witte must be shewed, and suche pleasaunt sawes so well applied, that the eares maie finde muche delite . . . and assuredly nothyng is more nedeful, then to quicken these heavie loden wittes of ours, and muche to cherishe these our lompishe and unweldie natures." A marginal note here explains the context of Wilson's sense that his hearer's "wittes" were "heavie" and suggests his ambivalence about commonness in discourse: "Preachers not so diligently heard as common plaiers" (27). Although plain, common speech ought to be sufficient, most people prefer the elaborated speech of common players. We should note that a central part of Wilson's solution is the inclusion of "pleasant sawes" or sayings. In order to speak pleasantly, Wilson advises that "every Orator should earnestly laboure to file his tongue, that his woordes maie slide with ease" (26), and his use of the words "file" and "slide" convey his doubts about the ethical status of rhetoric, even when the failings of the audience are taken into account.[36]

Wilson and Sherry both use the concept of a gift of eloquence to assert the naturalness of the rhetorical supplement. Wilson argues that "many are wise, but fewe have the gift to set furthe their wisedome. . . . Now an eloquent man beyng smally learned, can do muche more good in per-swading, by shift of wordes, and mete placyng of matter: then a greate learned clerke shalbe able with great store of learnyng, wantyng wordes to set furth his meanyng" (323–24). Here, "wisedome" and "store of learnyng" gained by gathering are described as common attributes, and eloquence becomes a "gift," rare, but still natural. Thus, artificial rhetoric simply supplements a natural gift of eloquence that is separate from the artificial yet common wisdom supplied by logic. The word "shift," how-ever, implies doubts about the grounding of rhetoric in truth; it refers explicitly to the arrangement or framing of words but could also suggest "a fraudulent or evasive device."[37] Further emphasis on "mete placyng of matter" only partially offsets the suggestion of shiftiness. Sherry uses the same strategy when he asserts that "howe to finde out matter, and set it in order, may be comen to all men, whyche eyther make abridgementes of the excellent workes of aunciente wryters, and put histories in remem-braunce, or that speake of anye matter themselves: but to utter the mynde aptely, distinctly, and ornately, is a gyft geven to very fewe" (18–19). Here again, store of matter is associated with an artificial practice, while rhetorical ornamentation becomes, again, a natural "gyft."

The figures of speech, involving as they do the concept of altering the natural order of speech, or borrowing foreign meanings, form the most questionable part of rhetoric. Peacham defines "schemates rhetorical" as "those figures or forms of speaking, which do take away the wearisom-nesse of our common speech, and do fashion a pleasaunt, sharpe, and evident kind of expressing our meaning: which by the artificial forme doth give unto matters great strength, perspicuitie, and grace" (40). He repeats Wilson's idea that common speech is "wearisome" and also in-cludes the admission that "artificial forme" serves to make matter more convincing. Sherry provides a similar definition of figure and makes ex-plicit the social implications of this kind of supplementation: a figure is "the fashion of a word, sayynge, or sentence, otherwyse wrytten or spo-ken then after the vulgar and comen usage" (25). Here, unfigured speech is associated with "vulgar and comen usage"; this connects lack of figures with the vernacular and implies that figured speech provides a mark of social distinction.[38]

If common people *use* unfigured language, however, they are especially susceptible to the persuasive power of the figures. Sherry expresses this idea most directly when he advocates the use of *amplificacio* to make a matter "lesser or greater then it seemeth to manye. For the rude people have commonly a preposterous iudgement, and take the worst thynges for the beste, and the beste for the worst" (70).[39] Wilson, in a famous passage, stresses the role of rhetoric to "wynne folke at their will, and frame theim by reason to all good order. . . . For what manne I praye you being better able to maintayne him selfe by valeant courage, then by living in base subjection: would not rather loke to rule like a lord, then to lyve lyke an underlynge" (18–19).[40] He later recommends a number of figures, including "delitefull saiynges, and quicke sentences," which enable the speaker to have "mennes hartes at his commaundement, beyng able to make theim merie when he list" (279).

These treatises thus make a double promise: they will teach their readers how to surpass common speech themselves, and also how to rule over common people with that speech. Adepts will be able to frame their own sentences with the figures; they will use those sentences to frame less educated people to the hierarchical social order. Such power, however, cannot be offered without attendant misgivings and anxieties. Although rhetoric may well offer this power over language and over others, it can also be seen as power based on the cynical and amoral manipulation of emotion, and involving discourse ungrounded in matter. Logic was grounded because it was based on the collection and recombination of fragments which expressed common truth—common in the sense that the places deal with relationships common to all things in nature, and also in the sense that they coincide with the doxa, or common beliefs of the culture. When rhetoric offers the power to supersede common language, it threatens to lose touch with the basis of its authenticity and with the social constraints that keep the potentially dangerous power of language under control.

In the first place, if rhetoric promises to teach its students how to control the emotions of the mob, it offers a means of fomenting sedition. In order to defuse this possibility, humanist writers often pull back from asserting absolutely the emotive force of the figures. Rainolde, for example, associates copious expression with the ability to "incense" and "inflame" its listeners: rhetoric "setteth out small thynges or woordes, in soche sorte, with soche aboundaunce and plentuousnes, bothe of woordes and wittie invencions, with soche goodlie disposicion, in soche a infinite sorte, with soche pleasauntnes of Oracion, that the moste stonie and hard hartes, can not but bee incensed, inflamed, and moved thereto" (A1v). However, when he begins to consider the uses of rhetoric in a political context, he attributes to it the opposite force: those who can "copiouslie dilate any matter or sentence" are able "to drawe unto theim the hartes of a multitude, to plucke doune and extirpate affeccions and perturbacions of people" (A1v) Wilson's assurance that rhetoric serves to "frame" its hearers (through "reason," not emotion) "to good order," and that if emotion is involved, it "make[s] theim merie" rather than inflaming them, serves a similar purpose.

Another safeguard against the excessive power of rhetoric is the claim that it is being taught not to enable powerful speech, but as a defense against powerful texts.[41] In this sense the concept of gathering ensures that rhetoric does not become too powerful. Both Sherry and Peacham seem at times unsure whether their texts are intended to help the reader in reading or in writing. Sherry, for example, seems to blur these two different aims into one purpose in arguing that knowledge of "schemes and figures" is necessary when "to set out the matter more plai[n]ly we be compelled to speake otherwyse then after common facion, onles we wil be ignorante in the sence or meaninge of the mater that excellente authors do wryghte of" (13). Here syntactical confusion serves to gloss over a conceptual ambiguity; the sentence begins by associating knowledge of the figures with speech, ends by associating them with reading, and separates the two with an "onles" which suggests that the second provides a reason for the first. His title implies that the treatise is intended to aid reading alone: it is "very profytable / for the better understanding of good / authors." The title of Peacham's 1577 edition offers the treatise for a double purpose as "very pro/fitable for all those that be studious of Elo/quence, and that reade moste Eloquent / Poets and Oratours, and also / helpeth much for the bet/ter understanding of / the holy Scrip/tures."[42]

Sayings, despite their close association with the figures, form another central means of ensuring that rhetoric was grounded and safe. They are uniquely able to do so because they are simultaneously common and uncommon, composed of solid matter and figured words. By presenting the gathering and framing of sayings as a central component of rhetoric, humanist rhetoricians ensured that their art was continuous with logic, solidly and safely grounded in doxa, efficacious for the defensive reading of dangerous texts, and that its persuasive force was directed toward acceptable moral goals. In the context of sententious sayings, the rhetorical closure of the figures could be seen as confirming the moral closure of the doxa. At the same time, however, they could offer their art as a necessary supplement to logic, promising a way to transcend common speech and to frame common listeners.

Rhetoricians almost universally define sayings of all kinds as simultaneously both common and uncommon. Although we can make some sense of this paradox by assuming that it refers to common ideas expressed in an uncommon manner ("what oft was *Thought*, but ne'er so well *Exprest*"), this distinction is not always maintained.[43] Instead, humanists find a variety of ways to express the sense that sayings bridge the gaps between nature and supplement, commoners and courtiers, common belief and uncommon style, logic and rhetoric.

Erasmus's famous definition of an adage, for example, reflects the tendency to define a saying as simultaneously common and uncommon. For Erasmus, an adage is "a saying in popular use, remarkable for some shrewd and novel turn." He goes on to say that an adage is characterized by "common usage and novelty," and that its "shrewd turn" serves to "distinguish it from ordinary talk."[44] An adage thus has its base in the strength of the doxa ("in common use") but also gains force from the fact that it is at the same time unusual or striking. Erasmus associates the novelty of the adage especially with the figure of metaphor but in his initial definition does not tie it so specifically to style. He does construct a definition that ensures sayings a base in the doxa, and also a connection to some form of uncommon expression. Similarly, Wilson describes the third kind of amplification as "when wee gather suche sentences as are communlye spoken, or elles use to speake of suche thyngs as are notable in thys lyfe" (247). His sententiae are both common and notable, and in this case both qualities are associated with matter rather than style.

Peacham's definitions of both paroemia (proverb) and gnome (sententia) reiterate the paradoxical conflation of common and uncommon even more explicitly than either Erasmus or Wilson:

> *Paroemia*, called of us a proverbe, is a sentence or forme of speech much used, and commonly knowen, and also excellent for the similitude, and signification: to which two things are necessarily required, the one, that it be renowned, and much spoken off, as a sentence in everie mans mouth. The other, that it be witty, and well proportioned, whereby it may be discerned by some speciall marke and note from common speech, and be commended by antiquitie and learning. (29–30)

Peacham's proverb must be both "commonly knowen," and "discerned by some speciall marke and note from common speech." It must be "in everie mans mouth," and also "commended by antiquitie and learning." The paradox reflects the strange logic of supplementation. Peacham wants to assert that his rhetoric, through this important figure, is based both in the natural, common, doxic discourse associated with logic, and also that it enables a powerful discourse which establishes the speaker's social and intellectual superiority. In this context, fragments that bridge the cultural codes of "antiquitie" and contemporary culture are prized not, as in logic, for their commonness, but for their difference, as cultural capital. Proverbs thus enable a discourse of great social flexibility, because they can be at the same time vulgar and learned, in accordance with the doxa and set apart from it.

Peacham's discussion of sententia embraces both the common and the uncommon in a slightly different way:

> Gnome, otherwise called *Sententia*, is a saying pertaining to the maners and common practices of men, which declareth by an apt brevitie, what in this our life ought to be done, or left undone. First it is to be observed, that everie sentence is not a figure, but that only which is notable, worthie of memorie, and approved by the iudgement and consent of all men, which being such a one, maketh by the excellency thereof the Oration not onely beautifull and comely, but also grave, puissant, and full of maiestie. (189)

The interplay of common and uncommon is even more complex here. First, a sententia is common because it pertains to the "common practices of men," human actions as they are constrained by the cultural code of their society. Sententiae, however, are able to "lay down the law" about such practices because of their stylistic difference from other discourse, their "apt brevitie."[45] Peacham expresses the prescriptive nature of sayings in a phrase ("ought to be done, or left undone") that echoes the prayer book, thus seeking to associate the moral efficacy of sententiousness with religious orthodoxy.[46]

Peacham more specifically addresses the relationship between moral sentences and figurative language when he admits that "everie sentence is not a figure." First it seems as if only the uncommon or stylistically notable fragments are to be included, but he then seeks again to associate such figured sentences with social consensus, identifying them as "approved by the iudgement and consent of all men." Here the very definition of a figure includes both the standard idea that it differs from common speech, and a new idea, tied to the stylistic effects of moral sententiae, that it must also accord with the cultural code. Unlike Puttenham, Peacham does not attempt to address the relationship between style and content in acquiring the "consent of all men." He concludes with an account of the effects of sententiae on discourse in general, and his list of the qualities they confer remains paradoxical. Sayings make a speech both "beautifull," or rhetorically ornamented, and "comely," in accordance with common standards of decorum.[47] They impart power or "puissance," social distinction or "maiestie," and moral seriousness or "gravity." In this case the potentially dangerous power and majesty conferred by the uncommon aspects of sayings are balanced by the gravity and decorum stemming from their accordance with doxa. Once again, the saying negotiates a series of tensely balanced antitheses in order to define itself as a natural supplement.

Sayings were as important to humanist rhetoricians as they were to logicians in their ongoing project of making authentic discourse possible, and of fashioning a flexible social posture for themselves. By basing rhetoric as well as logic on the gathering and framing of textual fragments, rhetoricians could assert that rhetoric shared the material ground or authenticity of logic. But the basis of sayings in the doxa and their tendency to address ethical issues that were of central importance in the cultural code gave them the power to offset the potentially dangerous malleability of the rhetorical figures. A rhetoric based on sayings retained its grounding in matter, as well as the decorum that comes from according with the doxa. However, because sayings are also distinguished from common discourse by the figures, they allowed the rhetorician to offer to initiate his students into a socially marked discourse, superior to the speech of common people and effective in manipulating the emotions of those commoners.[48] In the case of some sayings, the social marking could retain an extremely complex and flexible ambiguity, sharing in the property of homely occupations, and also in the cultural capital of classical education. Finally, should this power seem threatening, both teacher and student could take refuge in their supplemental status as mere "gatherers" and could call on the defensive importance of gathering when reading dangerous texts.

The practice of keeping a commonplace book may indeed have involved simple "cataloguing" and "rote memory," but we have seen that it was reformulated and disseminated in response to complex and deep-seated insecurities about language. In sixteenth-century England, the very fabric of discourse theory was permeated by the concepts of gathering and framing upon which the commonplace book was based, and these concepts gave rise to attitudes toward reading and writing that were very different from those conventionally attributed to writers of the period. English rhetoricians did not always emphasize the imitation of whole works or distinctive styles; indeed, they did not seem to conceive of texts as "works," organic wholes identified by their style or voice. Instead, literary texts were imagined as fields or containers from which fragments of matter could be gathered. Early in the century, intertextuality often seemed to involve not the deep incorporation and imaginative re-creation of classical works, but the recycling of significant fragments of text. The identification of aphoristic sayings as those significant fragments was itself based on sophisticated ideas about the authenticity of discourse, and it provided a flexible medium for expressing one's stance in relation to the past and within the present social system. The commonplace book and its attendant practices of gathering and framing thus shaped the theory of discourse in this period; as we shall see, through its role in education, it shaped human subjects as well.

Chapter III

SEED OR GOAD:

EDUCATING THE HUMANIST SUBJECT

THE LOGICAL and rhetorical treatises examined in the preceding chapters were, of course, intimately related to the humanist educational project as it was carried out in sixteenth-century England. These works articulated the theoretical bases of the project, and some of them served as school texts through which it was carried out. But another group of texts written in the early years of the sixteenth century might more accurately be called educational treatises; unlike the logics and rhetorics, which emphasize the reshaping or framing of texts, these stress the ways in which texts can be used to frame the student. Works dealing directly with education in this way can be divided into two types: theoretical works, such as Erasmus's *Institutio principis Christiani* and *De ratione studii*, Juan Luis Vives's *De tradendis disciplinis*, Roger Ascham's *Scholemaster*, Sir Thomas Elyot's *Boke Named the Governor*, and William Kempe's *The Education of Children in Learning*, which attempt to lay out and justify a particular pedagogical theory or method, and practical documents such as school curricula and elementary textbooks, which reveal what actually went on in the classroom.[1] I will look at the theory of education in this chapter and turn to its practice in the next.

The gathering and framing of sayings, and the use of those sayings to frame students as well as texts, are central aspects of both humanist pedagogical theory and classroom practice.[2] The basis of the humanist curriculum in England (at the grammar school level) was the inculcation of sententious precepts and examples in order, as Kempe put it, to "teach [the student] all things, framing him to eloquence in talke, and vertue in deedes."[3] Anthony Grafton and Lisa Jardine have recently explored the gap between humanist educational ideals and their teaching practice, concluding that in northern Europe especially, the connection between learning Latin and becoming a better, wiser person was assumed but never explained or interrogated.[4] In their generally excellent account of what went on in sixteenth-century classrooms, they underemphasize the role of sayings and the notebook method.[5] As we shall see, for Erasmus, Vives, and English theorists, the gathering and framing of sayings provided a central means of linking *eloquentia* and *sapientia* within the student, "framing him to eloquence in talke, and vertue in deedes."

Like their logic and rhetoric, humanist education concerns itself with the supplementation of the speaking self by carefully chosen fragments of text. This supplementation is perceived as simultaneously necessary, since English boys are not born speaking fluent Latin, and potentially dangerous, since the plenitude and empowerment conveyed by these potent texts could elude rational control to yield an endless chain of anarchic signification or a more dangerously anarchic subversion of the social hierarchy. We have seen how logicians and rhetoricians relied on the twin operations of gathering and reframing sayings in order to stabilize the tension between copia and closure, fertility and control, style and content in discourse. In educational theory, the dialectic between plenitude and control causes even more anxiety since teachers must worry about their students' ethical, as well as rhetorical, development, and about what they will do, as well as what they will write.

Humanist educators cope with this anxiety by positing two mutually exclusive, but inextricably linked, versions of the action of the text on the subject in the educational process. These imagined scenes of education are themselves described through commonplaces, some familiar from logic and rhetoric, and some either newly coined or derived from classical sources. One version imagines the individual student as a plant or fountain that organically assimilates fragments of text which shape and control its growth and plenitude. In this scenario, the psyche is an integrated whole that can be cultivated into a productive, powerful, rational being. But the other version, almost always present alongside the first, envisions the rational self as a wall containing and controlling an unruly unconscious. In this scenario sententious texts frame and shore up the wall but remain alien to an invisible and ultimately uncontrollable inner self.

These two supplemental accounts of instruction imply quite different conceptions of the relationship between text and self, work and author. The first "organic" model approximates the individualism usually attributed to humanist education, although it diverges somewhat from that model in acknowledging the constitutive power on the subject of language and the cultural code.[6] The other "inorganic" model posits a fragmented subject (rather than individual) consisting of a textual superego and a powerful but repressed (and wordless) unconscious. These two versions of the relationship between text and self have important implications for the act of authorship in the period. If an author believes that education involves the deep assimilation of important texts into his very being, he will imagine authorship as involving the rearticulation of those transformed texts in distinctive individual writing. But if he imagines the inner self as impermeable to texts which surround and wall it in, the act of authorship will involve an intertextuality that is not necessarily mediated by voice. Most educational theorists seem torn between these two possibilities, imagining education as involving both kinds of textual interaction at once.

Humanist educators' concern with, on the one hand, growth and accumulation, and, on the other, limitation and control, and the metaphors they use to convey these ideas, at times correspond with almost uncanny prescience to Pierre Bourdieu's theories about education as a form of "cultural capital" and "symbolic violence."[7] But the humanists' "storehouse" of sayings, and their disciplinary "goads" belong to a historical moment quite different from the present, a time when the very concept of an educational system was first being formulated, and when the element of misrecognition so central to Bourdieu's theories was much less important. These educators were engaged in constituting a uniform educational system designed to counter an existing aristocratic training in the display of natural superiority in aristocratic pastimes such as hunting, dancing, and erotic exchange.[8] In the early sixteenth century, it was the aristocratic program that was based on what Bourdieu calls "the subjective experience of the cultural arbitrary as necessary in the sense of 'natural,' " and the new humanist curriculum that presented itself as an openly artificial supplement, in opposition to that dominant cultural arbitrary.

Educational theory takes over from logic and rhetoric the commonplace analogies between accumulated sayings and a storehouse of accumulated treasure or goods, thus openly and literally representing itself as a form of cultural capital. In so doing, it sought a middle way between the old feudal system of power based on the display of inherited natural gifts, and the new and frightening possibilities offered by the accumulation of monetary capital. Educational capital in the form of sayings, was, as noted earlier, both liquid and tied to a system of places. In educational theory, metaphors of accumulation often shift between treasure and seeds, offering a possibility that the capital to be accumulated is natural and, unlike money, capable of natural growth and reproduction.[9]

The concept of symbolic violence is, in these treatises, openly acknowledged when they describe the "beating in" of precepts, and when the action of the collected matter on the mind is described as a sharp goad or weapon. This acknowledgment of the role of violence in education also serves to mediate between old and new cultural codes. Mervyn James has shown how, in sixteenth-century England, Tudor monarchs sought to gain legislative and judicial control over the aristocracy's old feudal code of honor and violence, and thus to arrogate to itself a "monopoly" of violence. Humanist educators participated in this project: first, by replacing the aristocratic training in martial skills with a conspicuously nonviolent education in discursive skills; and second, by including within their curriculum the actual violence of corporal punishment and the metaphoric violence of a coercive cultural code as substitutes for the old displays of violence as power. When sayings are described as "goads," they represent an internalization of symbolic violence designed to replace the openly violent codes of feudalism.[10] But again, misrecognition is not a goal. Humanist educators are eager to acknowledge an element of violence in their program so that it will seem equivalent to the aristocratic codes it seeks to replace.

In England, humanist educational theorists were especially concerned to argue that their new curriculum provided access to the authority needed by those who would wield power in the state. Like their logics and rhetorics, educational works openly stress the importance of humanist supplementation of power in the form of education for future leaders and advice for present ones. Treatises addressed to princes emphasize the importance of education, as well as good counsel (and thus humanist advisers and teachers), as a means of ensuring effective leadership. But princes were a limited audience, and early humanists also recognized that their power had to be supplemented by lesser administrators and bureaucrats: "it is expedient and also nedefull, that under the capitall governour be sondry meane authorities, as it were aydying hym in the distribution of justice."[11] In England, humanists in the early sixteenth century were remarkably successful at establishing their brand of teaching as a necessary credential for upward mobility in service to the state.[12] Their treatises are full of optimistic promises that they offer a brand of "learning, which doth not only support, but exalte: not availe, but advance unto a wonderfull height of magnificent and pompous honour."[13]

The wide acceptance of their educational program gave humanist educators and their students a share of power.[14] Richard Pace, John Colet, Sir Thomas More, Thomas Wolsey, Roger Ascham, Sir Nicholas Bacon, and William Cecil are only a few of the men to achieve an influential place in society at least partly because of their possession and transmission of the credentials provided by the new education. Comparing the education of Henry VIII's two sons offers one index of the increased status of teachers.[15] His illegitimate son, Henry Fitzroy, duke of Richmond, was raised according to the old, aristocratic curriculum, which stressed martial skills. His tutors, John Palsgrave and Richard Croke, were given to constant complaints that they had little authority over their reluctant student, who spent most of his time hunting and hawking. Edward, on the other hand, was educated by Richard Coxe and John Cheke according to the humanist method. His teachers evidently had great power over him as a child and retained influence after his accession.

Despite their increased status and power, humanist teachers remained ever aware of the supplemental nature of their project. The power of the monarch was great, and human nature was depraved. Any attempt to encroach on the one or ameliorate the other was fraught with danger and uncertainty. In their educational treatises as in their logics and rhetorics, humanist teachers stress their own supplemental and mediatory role, as gatherers of bits from ancient literature, and as framers of students in accordance with the hierarchical order of the prevailing cultural code.[16] They are always aware of the dangers of the power that they offer to inculcate in students, and as in logic and rhetoric, every claim to power is hedged with safeguards to keep it in control. These preoccupations come out most clearly in the metaphors that these writers use to describe the educational process: gathering, treasure, bees, (in)digestion, planting, fountains, weeding and pruning, antidotes, fortification, and engraving.[17] Metaphors of gathering and treasure, of course, continue from logic and rhetoric to represent the empowering potential of education. Likening education to digestion, gardening, and fountains tends to stress the organic assimilation of material, while metaphors of fortification and engraving represent the more cautious and restrictive model of teaching. However, the more liberal models are almost always carefully hedged: digestion and fountains with the need for antidotes, and planting with accompanying emphasis on weeding and pruning.

The ideas that books contain matter, that reading consists of gathering that matter, and that writing consists of reusing it are as prominent in educational treatises as they were in logic and rhetoric. Here, however, emphasis falls on the importance of choosing properly, and of the teacher's role in facilitating that choice. Juan Luis Vives, for example, describes how a teacher ought to "pick out for the use of his pupil" the best sayings from pagan and sacred authors.[18] Thomas Elyot similarly stresses his own efforts as a gatherer, identifying authors suitable for the school curriculum on the basis of the extent to which "good and wise mater may be picked out" of them (51v).[19] Even Roger Ascham, who is more critical of the notebook method than most English humanists, nevertheless praises those who "gather examples to give light and understanding to good precepts."[20]

The source of this collected matter is not necessarily confined to classical literature. Many writers identify the space or container from which sayings are to be gathered as including pagan literature, Scripture, patristic texts, modern writings, and personal experience. Thus, Sir Thomas Elyot promises that his *Boke Named the Governor* is full of "mater I have gathered as well of the sayenges of moste noble autours (grekes and latynes) as by myne owne experience" (A2r–v). Similarly, John Foxe urges students of theology to gather in their commonplace books the exempla that "offer themselves not only among sacred writings but even in daily life."[21] Vives observes that "experience" itself is most easily gained from "adages and sentences, in a word, all those precepts of wisdom which have been collected from the observations of the wise, which have remained amongst the people, as if they were public wealth in a common storehouse" (38).[22]

These educational theorists frequently use an analogy with picking flowers to convey the importance of choosing proper matter. All of literature, pagan and Christian, along with daily experience, is described as a field or meadow from which the teacher plucks appropriate sayings or flowers for the use of his students. To read on in Vives is to learn that "it will be easy for the teacher to pick out for the use of his pupil little flowers from the philosophers and sacred authors, as it were, from the most verdant meadows" (84).[23] This metaphor lies behind the common idea, often reflected in titles during this period, that a commonplace book or collection of poems is a bouquet of flowers.[24] Nicholas Udall's *Floures For Latine Spekynge*, for example, describes its Terentian idioms and sententiae as "all selected and plucked, as it were, from the most fragrant garden."[25]

The metaphor of flower picking was used to convey a number of important considerations that both students and teachers should bear in mind when gathering sayings. Sometimes it was used to counter the proponents of Ciceronian imitation with the argument that flowers should be chosen from the whole garden of literature and not from one author alone. It also worked to suggest the benefits that the student could derive from doing his own gathering instead of relying on florilegia prepared by others: "for we might freely make use of little flowers plucked by another hand, but when we are ourselves strolling among the greenery of the meadows and with free choice pick what we desire, still breathing scent, from the root, a double pleasure is felt."[26]

Most frequently, however, this metaphor is used to stress the importance of proper choice. When one reads pagan works, especially, it is vital to choose out only the good passages and to leave the bad behind. The notebook method thus becomes a central means through which pagan works are made to accord with the contemporary cultural code. Vives cautions that students should "begin the reading of the heathen, as though entering upon poisonous fields. . . . Let the scholar remember that he is amongst the heathen, that is, amongst thorns, poisons, aconite, and most threatening pestilences, that he is to take from them only what is useful, and to throw aside the rest" (125).[27] Elyot similarly urges that

> sens good and wise mater may be picked out of these [pagan] poetes, it were no reason for some lite mater that is in their verses, to abandone therfore al their warkes, no more than it were to forbeare or prohibite a man to come into a faire gardein, leste the redolent savours of swete herbes and floures shall meve him to wanton courage, or leste in gadring good and holsome herbes he may happen to be stunge with a nettile. No wyse man entreth in to a gardein but he

sone espiethe good herbes from nettles, and treadeth the nettles under his feete whiles he gadreth good herbes. (51v–52r)

Only by selectively gathering "wholesome" matter can pagan poets be read safely by the Christian student. According to Vives, it would be the teacher's duty to pluck the good bits, and, in case of exposure to something bad, to choose from Scripture "some passage to be as it were remedies of diseases" (89).[28] Criteria for choice are not specified by Elyot, who assumes that a "wyse man" will already possess this knowledge.

Several theorists use a common variant of the flower gathering metaphor in which the choice is made not by men but by bees. Erasmus, for example, sums up his description of the notebook method in *De copia* by describing how "our student will flit like a busy bee through the entire garden of literature, will light on every blossom, collect a little nectar from each, and carry it to his hive."[29] Thomas Greene and G. W. Pigman III have identified this "apian" metaphor as one of the most common humanist analogies for the imitation of ancient authors.[30] Both Greene and Pigman stress the ways in which this metaphor implies "a capacity for absorption and assimilation on the part of the poet, a capacity for making one's own the external text in all its otherness," although they also note that a version of it, derived from Lucretius and Horace, emphasizes gathering rather than transformation.[31] They neglect another classical source for this metaphor, however, that was probably more influential in sixteenth-century England. Plutarch's essay "How the Young Man Should Study Poetry" emphasizes the importance of choice in gathering, if poetry is to be morally helpful: "Now the bee, in accordance with nature's laws, discovers amid the most pungent flowers and the roughest thorns the smoothest and most palatable honey; so children, if they be rightly nurtured amid poetry, will in some way learn to draw some wholesome and profitable doctrine even from passages that are suspect of what is base and improper."[32] In general, English theorists tend either to avoid digestive metaphors in describing their relationship to classical texts or else to progress quickly from digestion to concerns about poisons and antidotes.

Daniel Kinney has shown how Erasmus, in contrast to Boccaccio's attempt to reconstitute ancient myth whole, "insisted in theory and practice throughout the *Adagia* that the fragments [of antiquity] were better left fragments and could best be assimilated as such. Reconstituting the totality of pagan wisdom meant for Erasmus incorporating successfully the totality of available fragments as such into his own Christian, modern-day context."[33] For Erasmus, Vives, and English theorists of education, sayings of all kinds, because of their fragmentary and extractable nature, provided a way to isolate and extract the bits of text where the cultural codes of antiquity and modern Europe coincided. Collection of these fragments would ensure that students had a store of morally efficacious and rhetorically powerful matter for composition. Metaphors of educational gathering stress the importance of this piecemeal approach to imitation and mystify the schoolmaster's knowledge of which fragments to gather. Because these fragments restate the cultural code, the wisdom collected as in a common storehouse for humanity, anyone ought to be able to recognize them. Yet schoolmasters must also stress the necessity of education to make this common storehouse accessible.

English educational theorists are also notable in their avoidance of specificity when describing the criteria according to which proper choice is to be made. Several of these educators provide lists, familiar from logical and rhetorical treatises, of the forms of "matter" that ought to be gathered. Foxe, for example, variously lists similitudes, allusions, metaphors, proverbs, descriptions, emblems, rhetorical figures, witty phrases, sententiae, epithets, "flowers" of poetry, definitions, arguments, objections, physical causes, and the nature and properties of things, as matter to be included by the student in his commonplace book.[34] The first part of his list bases recognition of suitable matter primarily on form, and the last part (definition, argument, and so forth) on content. Erasmus (in his *De copia*) similarly considers both form and content when he includes fables, exempla, sententiae, clever sayings, proverbs, metaphors, and analogies in his list of material suitable for the notebook.[35]

When they do offer criteria, these writers usually repeat the paradoxical formulation used by rhetoricians: extractable material must be both common and uncommon, morally serious and rhetorically pleasing. Udall's preface to Erasmus's *Apophthegmata* describes its "saiynges" as having "appropriated vnto them, a certain reason and marke of their own whereby to iudge, so that thei doe plainly expresse and sette out, the verie naturall inclinacion and disposicion of eche speaker that thei procede from, briefly, finely, quippyngly, and merily, within the boundes of good maner."[36] They are plain, natural, and in accordance with good "maner," as well as fine and quipping. Foxe urges that sayings be chosen on the basis of "weight of subject matter, gravity, wisdom, brilliance, learning, methodicalness, and felicity of treatment."[37] Vives notes that ancient books contain "the knowledge of antiquity and of all human memory, of so many words and deeds, keenly, seriously, gaily, and piously expressed, by which [prudence] is cultivated, and helped" (49).[38] Ultimately, however, the ability to recognize proper fragments on the basis of their adherence to the cultural code and rhetorical efficacy is the mysterious and mystified wisdom transmitted by humanist education. These authors repeatedly note that the "good teacher" and the "wise man" are able to cull suitable sayings. Education presumably conveys this knack to students, although theorists cannot specify how it does so. By gathering sayings students become wise, and by becoming wise they learn how to gather sayings.

These writers also mystify the process through which the collected fragments were to affect, form, or help the student. Their texts are riddled with contradictions and inconsistencies when they consider whether the student simply copies these sayings, memorizes them, or assimilates them more deeply.[39] Even a single writer tends to give multiple accounts of the extent to which these sayings transform the student, and how they might do so. They use quite different metaphors to describe the actual process of education through gathering and framing, and they place this process in different parts of the mind. Thus, the mechanics of the link between wisdom and eloquence remains hidden, but not because these writers avoid treating it. They try repeatedly to imagine an interaction between text and student that would achieve a delicate balance between empowerment and control, but their attempts to do so almost always end in self-contradiction and rupture.

Most scholars who have discussed the collection of commonplaces believe that the fragments were assimilated through memorization, and relate the use of commonplace books to the systems of "artificial memory" whereby images standing for ideas were memorized in imaginary "places" (arranged around the walls of a house, for example). Sayings cannot be exactly related to artificial memory, however, since as Frances Yates points out, memory systems almost always rely on images or pictures instead of words.[40] Greene dismisses the notebook method as "a work of cataloguing and rote memory" that "could not in itself produce sensitive understanding and creative imitation."[41] But English theorists in the sixteenth century wanted to believe that the commonplace book led to assimilation and understanding just as deep as those offered by other versions of *imitatio*, although they were unable to describe how this actually worked.

Some educational theorists do describe the notebook as a supplement to natural powers of memory and, as does Ralph Lever in his dialectic, see the collection of sayings as a way to "possess" classical literature as a commodity, to accumulate it as visible intellectual capital. Foxe, for example, offers his blank commonplace book to students as a means of helping memory to accommodate the increasing store of available texts: "Since faced with such a great crowd of writers no one's memory would be sufficient to retain everything, it will surely be not a little useful to have supported the fragility of memory through the security of writing and noting down, making use of a commonplace book, in which as in a memorial library, it will be possible to heap up all the wealth of your learning." In another place Foxe urges that the commonplace book be used to supplement (*supplere*) memory with the commodity (*commoditas*) of art.[42] In these passages we see signs of an anxiety, similar to that revealed in Agricola's dialectic, about the difficulty of assimilating the totality of ancient literature (the "great crowd of writers") made available by print technology. Foxe seems to view these texts as a potential source of intellectual capital ("wealth" or "commodity"), if only the student can find a way to possess and store it.[43]

Other educational theorists share Foxe's sense that the commonplace book aids students in acquiring their education as a kind of valuable property, to be stored up in memory and in the book. We can recall Vives's idea, cited above, that sayings represent "public wealth in a common storehouse" of literature from which the student can gather what he needs. Ascham, however, replaces this notion of intellectual communism with a more elitist version of textual wealth: "in the Greek and Latin tongue, the two only learned tongues which be kept not in common talk but in private books, we find always wisdom and eloquence, good matter and good utterance, never or seldom asunder."[44] Humanist education, of course, gives students access to the storehouse of these learned tongues, and the notebook method provides them with "private books" of their own in which to store the "good matter and good utterance" that they gather. All of these writers use such terms as *apotheca, thesaurus, aeraria*, and *supellex* to describe the commonplace books in which students accumulate their hoard of learning.[45]

Sayings themselves are also often described as precious jewels, a metaphor that implies, in addition to value as a commodity, qualities of timelessness and ornamentality. As Geoffrey Bennington has noted, the jewel metaphor expresses the basic "ambivalence of the maxim" as constituted by both content and style, common and uncommon language, since it "has at once an attractive surface brilliance but is also made of a substance of the highest value."[46] Erasmus, for example, relates adages to jewels because they are valuable despite their small size: "If the adage seems a tiny thing, we must remember that it has to be estimated not by its size but by its value. What man of sane mind would not prefer gems, however small, to immense rocks."[47] He goes on to say that "so to weave adages deftly and appropriately is to make the language glitter with sparkles from antiquity, please us with the colors of rhetoric, gleam with jewel-like words of wisdom."[48] Vives, describing the teacher's role in the notebook method, advises, "Let each boy have an empty paper book divided into several parts to receive all that falls from the teacher's lips, since this is not less valuable to him than precious stones" (108).[49]

But despite their sense that the sayings gathered in a commonplace book provide a way for students to possess and retain the most valuable fragments of an immense body of texts, educational theorists also want to believe that their curriculum leads to deeper assimilation of values and, ultimately, to moral transformation. Northern European humanists frequently associate medieval (Scholastic) education with rote memorization and strongly contrast their own pedagogy, which, they claim, leads to more profound absorption or digestion of material. Erasmus, for example, recommends the notebook method as an alternative to the practice of those who "have much material stored up so to speak in their vaults, but when it comes to speaking or writing they are remarkably ill-supplied and impoverished."[50] In the *Antibarbari*, he castigates Scholastic writers whose habit is to "put down nothing of their own, but to collect the sayings of others picked out here and there. . . . It is enough for them to have piled up heaps of stuff."[51] Greene quotes a passage from Erasmus's *Ciceronianus*, contrasting digestion with memorization:

> That must be digested which you devour in your varied daily reading, must be made your own by meditation rather than memorized or put into a book, so that your mind crammed with every kind of food may give birth to a style which smells not of any flower, shrub, or grass but of your own native talent and feeling.[52]

The process described here involves not imitation of a single work but the absorption of selections from "varied" (*varia*) reading. The contrast is not between use of commonplaces and imitation, but between true and false uses of both imitation and commonplaces.[53]

The passage from Erasmus's *Ciceronianus* contains a complex mixed metaphor, moving from digestion to birth to gardening, all of which were common analogies for the educative and imitative processes. Exploration of the digestive metaphor sheds further light on the contrast (as the humanists represented it) between medieval and humanist uses of authoritative sayings. Medieval authors themselves tend to stress the importance of having collected sayings readily available for use, often in "chests," a common medieval metaphor for memory. Hugh of St. Victor says in his *Didascalion* that "we ought, therefore, in all that we learn, to gather brief and dependable abstracts to be stored in the little chest of memory, so that later on, when need arises, we can derive everything from them." He continues with a curious "indigestive" metaphor: "These one must often turn over in the mind and regurgitate from the stomach of one's memory to taste them, lest by long inattention to them, they disappear."[54] Ascham echoes this analogy or something like it in a more pejorative sense when he remembers the program of rote learning in the schools of his youth: "their whole knowledge, by learning without the book, was tied to their tongue and lips, and never ascended up to the brain and head, and therefore was soon spit out of the mouth again."[55] The contrast in the humanist passages (unwittingly corroborated by Hugh of St. Victor) sets

up a superficial knowledge, related to the faculty of memory and expressed by conventional metaphors of storage in chests or spitting out,
against some mysterious process of digestion by which the material in
question is truly assimilated. This process of digestion, at least in sixteenth-century England, was closely related to the collection and assimilation of sayings.

Sayings are often depicted as particularly palatable, wholesome, and
easy to digest. By definition, they stand out from the surrounding discourse as morally "wholesome" and as lively and interesting in ways that
were deemed especially attractive to students. As Vives explains:

> the teacher will spice all these with jokes [lit. "salty jokes"], witty and pleasant
> stories, lively historical narratives, with proverbs, parables, apophthegms, and
> with acute short precepts, sometimes lively, sometimes grave. Thus the pupil
> will drink in willingly [and with great fruitfulness], not only the language, but
> also wisdom and experience for life as well. (133)[56]

Here Vives describes the familiar components of the commonplace book
as condiments that the students will readily imbibe, simultaneously di-
gesting wisdom and eloquence. Richard Coxe, in a letter of 10 December
1544 describing the education of Edward VI, notes that he is ready to
begin reading Cato's *Distichs* and Aesop's fables, sententious works
which offer "holsom and godly lessons."[57]

Sayings are also frequently described by analogy to taste, although authors represent them as both condiment and substantial food, that is, as
simultaneously the main matter of a text and as supplemental ornamentation. Thomas Elyot, in the preface to his *Bankette of Sapience*, plays
extensively on a complex of associations between wisdom and food,
punning on the Latin etymology of *sapiens* and *sapor*, on the idea of a
symposium, and on Wisdom's banquet depicted in the Book of Proverbs,
in order to stress the ingestibility of the sayings that he has collected in the
volume.[58] Erasmus, in a passage quoted above, associates sayings with
the "sweetest nectar," which, presumably, a student would willingly
drink in; and in *Adagia* he expands on the notion that sayings are spicy
condiments which lure us to eat: "We should treat them not as food but
as condiments."[59] Nicholas Udall's translation of the preface to Erasmus's *Apophthegmata*, however, sees sayings as both food and spice:
"soche saiynges of mirthe, are but here and there in fewe places, enter-
medleed emong saiynges of grauitee and sadnesse, as sauces of the feaste"
(xxvi).

Despite this well-established tradition that sayings are a particularly
wholesome and palatable food, humanist educators retain lingering
doubts about the ability of students to digest this material, or to be un-
harmed by it as they absorb it. Although Ascham associated indigestion
with the rote memorization used in older schools, he also fears that stu-

dents will be unable to retain wholesome humanist teaching: "if we suffer the eye of a young gentleman once to be entangled with vain sights, and the ear to be corrupted with fond or filthy talk, the mind shall quickly fall sick and soon vomit and cast up all the wholesome doctrine that he received in childhood, though he were never so well brought up before."[60] Here, a single exposure to "vain sights" is enough to empty the student of the wholesome doctrine so carefully inculcated at school.[61] Vives also cautions teachers to respect the small capacity of the boys' minds, "like a vessel with a narrow neck, which spits out again the too large supply of liquid which the teacher attempts to pour in. Let instruction therefore be poured in gradually, drop by drop" (106).[62] English humanists (as perhaps all experienced teachers must be) seem generally more preoccupied with the possibility of indigestion than confident in their ability to cause lasting assimilation in their students.

More troubling are hints that the wholesome food is actually poisonous, and that as a result the transformation wrought by education will not be to the good. Vives cautions that careful choice is important when the student reads pagan authors because "yet amongst these so healthy characteristics, they mix dangerous gifts, not a few, like as sometimes honey or the sweetest wine is mixed with poison" (49).[63] Although this passage is similar to the one (cited above) in which Vives warns the student to leave aside thorns and poison and choose only healthful herbs, its implications are more disturbing. Although herbs may be easily discerned and separated from surrounding thorns, healthful honey and wine cannot be separated from poison that has been intermixed with them. According to this scenario, the student cannot read pagan authors safely simply by gathering good sayings and leaving aside the bad; if what he reads transforms him deeply, there will be a chance that what is bad, even ungathered, will effect an unfortunate transformation. There seems to be a lingering fear, even among the most idealistic humanists, that exposure to the pagan cultural codes of antiquity might be damaging.

The solution to this problem is to regard morally efficacious sayings as "antidotes" to the poison offered by the parts of pagan texts that manifest frighteningly alien mandates of the cultural code. Both Erasmus and Vives use the phrase "fortified with an antidote" (*antidoto praemunitus*) to describe the preparation needed before one undertakes to read classical works.[64] Erasmus specifies that the sententious portions of the Bible (Proverbs, Ecclesiasticus, and Wisdom) can serve as this antidote, and Vives similarly urges the teacher to "choose some passages [of Scripture] to be as it were remedies of diseases."[65] Erasmus also occasionally refers to a secular saying as a "philtron" or a law as a "pharmacon," both able to serve as antidotes or remedies for moral poisons or ills.[66]

Of course, as Derrida has noted, a *pharmakon* is always at the same time both a remedy and a poison, because it cures by causing pain, and, more important, because it serves as an artificial supplement to what should be a natural state of health.[67] The very need for an antidote suggests the dangers inherent in the humanist program. Having posited a lack in human nature in need of supplemental education, English humanists set off a potentially unending chain of supplementation. The concept of saying as antidote implies, first of all, that even carefully educated students require help, a textual supplement, in order to read the pagan texts upon which their curriculum is based. And once the power of digested fragments over a student's moral development has been posited, fears are bound to surface that poison and antidote, disease and remedy are two faces of the same unnatural supplement.

The importance of reading classical texts and the political significance of classical education are linked by humanists in a complex of metaphors, closely related to those of poison and antidote, involving fountains and springs of water. Water in this context represents powerful eloquence or the authority of antiquity as source, and figures a relationship among sayings, antiquity, and political power. Erasmus begins his *De copia* with a metaphor that expresses the power of copious speech: "The speech of man is a magnificent and impressive thing when it surges along like a golden river, with [*sententiae*] and words pouring out in rich abundance."[68] This river represents speech as a natural outpouring of authoritative presence: it "surges along," seemingly without effort; its "rich abundance" is the natural expression of its speaker. The *De copia*, however, is a treatise designed precisely to teach students how to supplement their natural faculty of speech in order to achieve this fluency by artificial means. Vives similarly expresses this mixed sense that authentic speech is both natural and learned when he says that "the first thing man has to learn is speech. It flows at once from the rational soul as water from a fountain" (90).[69]

These passages express the familiar dilemma of education as supplement. Speech *ought* to be a natural power that expresses the inner nature of the speaker, yet the educator offers necessary instruction in how to speak powerfully and well. Humanists seek to naturalize their particular version of the educational supplement by describing ancient literature as a similar watery source. Both John Guillory and David Quint have traced the figure of the river or fountain as a representation of authoritative origin, and references to antiquity, especially Greece or Scripture, as a source or fountain are common in Renaissance theorists.[70] Erasmus describes Greek in these terms as a source, arguing that "almost all knowledge of things is to be sought in the Greek authors. For in short, whence can one draw a draught so pure, so easy, and so delightful as from the very fountain-head."[71] Vives represents both Latin and Greek as authoritative supplements to speech in this way:

From the knowledge of Latin, too, they would render the native language of their fathers more pure and rich, even as a copious stream is derived more purely from its source. How many matters are handed down to memory in Greek literature, in history, in nature-knowledge, private and public morals, medicine, piety, which we drink in more easily and more purely from those very sources themselves. (94)

According to Vives, natural speech (the native language of their fathers) becomes, paradoxically, purer when it has been adulterated through supplementation. There is no sense of rupture between ancient text and modern speaker since the modern speaker can "drink in" and assimilate the text. Ancient and modern can flow as one "pure" stream, however, only insofar as the values and codes that they represent are the same.[72]

As a result, it is to be expected that sayings are often identified as components of the fountain or spring of eloquence. Erasmus urges students to gather and emulate "a passage from some author where the spring of eloquence seems to bubble up particularly richly."[73] Vives recommends that the teacher "have an ample and copious equipment of Latin words so that his boys may be truly able to draw from him as from a fountain" (103).[74] That fountain, as demonstrated by a passage cited above, is to be made up of "jokes, witty and pleasant stories, lively historical narratives, . . . proverbs, parables, apophthegms, and . . . acute short precepts" through which the students are said to "drink in willingly, not only the language, but also wisdom and experience for life" (133).

There are, of course, particular dangers attendant upon transferring the power of the source to students, particularly to students who will themselves become sources of power. Erasmus frequently likens the prince to a fountain and bewails the misfortunes that occur "if from him the greatest part of the evils of a republic arise, where there ought to be a fountain of good things."[75] Richard Mulcaster extends this property to magistrates, who are "the principall springs of most good or euil in anie state."[76] In this context sayings are once again described as antidotes against poison in the public fountain. Erasmus, for example, describes those who corrupt a prince in his youth as poisoners of a public fountain; he recommends this remedy: "As early as infancy, [the teacher] should introduce pleasant fables, festive tales, charming similes, which afterwards will be taught with graver seriousness." To a prince, flattery is a poison (*venenum*) which must be countered by sayings as an *antidotus*, *philtron*, and *pharmacon*.[77] Yet, as Derrida notes, "water, pure liquidity, is most easily and dangerously penetrated then corrupted by the *pharmakon*, with which it mixes and immediately unites."[78] The price of imagining the process of education as merging the streams of ancient text and modern speech is precisely the threat of contamination and corruption. The teacher's informed choice of matter is once again a crucial safe-guard, but the water metaphor reveals its precariousness. And when the stream of classical eloquence is to be diverted in the service of political power, the stakes are especially high, and the dangers especially great.

Yet another series of metaphors retains the promise of organic assimilation and transformation through education, but attempts to attribute greater control over the process to the teacher. The teacher as gardener chooses seeds from ancient texts and plants them in the student, ensuring that the student's mind reproduces the ancient plant. Elyot, for example, describes the teacher as "a wyse and counnynge gardener," who "will first serche throughout his gardeyne, where he can find the most melowe and fertile erth; and therin wil he put the sede of the herbe to growe, and be norrished: and in most diligent wise attende that no [w]eede be suffred to growe or aproche nyghe unto it" (16r).

English theorists are particularly obsessed by the idea that liberal education must bear "fruit" that is of practical value to the state. Elyot argues for the continuation of study after age thirteen because "if the elegant speking of latin be nat added to other doctrine, litle frute may come of the tonge: sense latin is but a naturall speche, and the frute of speche is wyse sentence, whiche is gathered and made of sondry lernynges" (47v).[79] The student is to gather seeds in the course of his reading so that he can bear fruit himself, in the form of the expression of his own "wise sentence." Richard Pace entitles his defense of the humanist program *De fructu qui ex doctrina percipitur*, "the fruits that proceed from learning."

At first it might seem as if careful gathering of appropriate sayings as seeds insures that the plant will grow as it ought to. Vives explains that ancient poets have "sowed the seeds of all kinds of knowledge which were scattered about in their works," and that the student who studies ancient literature will "receive many seeds of the material of knowledge remaining to us" (129, 94).[80] Richard Morison similarly promises that his translation of Vives's own collection of moral sayings "introduceth wysedom unto you, rootyng the love and desire of vertue in your hert, extirping from it all maner of vice and uncleannesse."[81] Morison's use of the metaphor introduces a hint of anxiety into this georgic paradise, however, when he admits that weeds are a problem even if the seeds are chosen carefully.

In fact, most examples of this metaphor stress pruning and weeding as heavily as they do the sowing of proper seeds and nurturing of the plant. Erasmus explains that "as much as the nature of the soil is better, by so much the more is it corrupted, and seized by useless herbs and fruits, unless the farmer is vigilant. Similarly, the *ingenium* of man, by as much as it is more blessed, more generous, and more upright, by so much it is overspread by many foul vices, unless it is carefully cultivated with helpful precepts."[82] Erasmus here clearly associates education with repres-

sion, rather than cultivation, of the individual. Kempe views schoolmas-
terly planting in a similarly coercive light when he notes that it is the
teacher's duty "to prescribe good order both for manners and learning,"
and that he does so by "sowing in their tender mindes the seedes of Christian holinesse."[83] Ascham cautions against both stylistic and ethical
weeds, noting that faulty Latin syntax "taking once root in youth, be
never or hardly plucked away in age," and also urging parents to be "as
well ware in weeding from their children ill things, and ill company as
they were before in grafting in them learning."[84]

   The restrictive side of humanist horticulture responds to two threats.
The first is that rhetorical training will plant in the student an eloquence
that will grow out of control. The moral dangers of wild growth are vividly expressed in Plutarch's influential essay on poetry, where he suggests
that there is no need to "root up or destroy the Muse's vine of poetry, but
where the mythical and dramatic part grows all riotous and luxuriant,
through pleasure unalloyed, which gives it boldness and obstinacy in
seeking acclaim, let us take it in hand and prune it and pinch it back."[85]
Elyot, however, conflates this fear with an anxiety that is less easily
allayed:

> I verily do suppose that in the braynes and hertes of children, whiche be mem-
> bres spirituall, whiles they be tender, and the little slippes of reason begynne in
> them to burgine, ther may happe by ivel custome some pestiferous dewe of vice
> to perse the sayde membres, and infecte and corrupte the softe and tender bud-
> des, wherby the frute may growe wylde, and some tyme conteine in it fervent
> and mortal poyson, to the utter destruction of a realme. (17r)

Elyot's solution is that nurses and teachers of young children should pro-
tect them from "wanton and unclene" acts and words, and yet we know
that the problem runs deeper than that. If education makes use of powerful texts to transform and empower students, there is always a chance
that this power will "growe wylde," or, even worse, that it will affect that
child as a "poyson," with dire political results. And while wild growth
can be controlled by careful choice of matter, the specter of poison raises
the more difficult problem of the supplement.

   This is why horticultural analogies for textual education, which begin
as idealistic visions of nurturant cultivation, tend almost inevitably to
bring in pruning, weeding, and other versions of control. Francis Clement, in his *Petie Schole* vividly displays the contradictions with which
the Tudor view of liberal education is riddled. He promises that his book
will offer

> wholsome and savyng counsell, whereby I wish to persuade thee to the delite
> and love of learning, even now in these greene and tender yeares of thine infan-
> cie and childhoode: wherin as all children are by nature inwardly fraught (as

saith the wise Solomon) with folly and ignoraunce: so may they be readily
reformed by diligent nourture and erudition, which that wise king termeth the
rod of correction.[86]

On the one hand, children are "greene and tender" plants, able to be
persuaded to a love of learning and "readily reformed by diligent nourture and erudition." On the other hand, however, they are "by nature
inwardly fraught . . . with folly and ignoraunce," and thus only to be
reformed by the "rod of correction." The Solomonic precepts here function, as Erasmus suggests this part of the Bible can, as a pharmakon or
antidote to humanist (pagan) optimism. They tell us that "nourture"
must be the same thing as discipline, and that sayings which provide the
matter of forceful and fruitful copia must at the same time control it.
Although humanists hoped that careful choice of the "matter" of education might enable them to imagine it as the cultivation of the natural self,
the poison of pagan heresy and original sin threaten to corrupt their project at every turn. Ultimately, an organic model for the educational transaction between text and student is just too threatening. As much as they
would like to promise that their curriculum effects a deep ethical transformation and equally deep linguistic assimilation, the risks attendant upon
such a claim were great. In England, as Clement's passage shows, "nourture" all too quickly becomes a violent and coercive "rod of correction."

One problem with the horticultural metaphor and its concomitant organic view of education lies in the psychology available to these theorists.
Renaissance educational theorists rely, with some minor variations, on
the account of the mind found in Aristotle's *De anima* and passed down
through the Middle Ages by Scholastic philosophy. Briefly, this theory of
"faculty psychology" involved a tripartite division of the mind; the five
"outer" senses take in information and convey it to the three "inner"
senses (imagination, common sense, and memory), which then pass it on
to the highest rational part of the brain (wit, reason, or *ingenium*, and
will), which judges and analyzes the information and passes it back to the
memory for storage.[87] According to this schema, memory and imagination are similar in that they are both located in the central part of the
brain, both serve as "messengers" between the senses and the rational
faculty, both deal in images rather than words, and together they represent the only parts of the mind that are capable of retaining material.[88]
They differ sharply, however, in that memory always reproduces exactly
what it takes in, whereas the imagination distorts, recombines, and multi-
plies the images that it carries.[89] Because of its unreliability and its tendency to transmit a flood of random, confusing, and bizarre images, the
imagination was greatly distrusted in the early sixteenth century.[90]

Walter Ong makes an interesting slip when he refers to the notebook
method as a way of "stocking the imagination with 'matter' by means of

wide and selective reading."[91] Sayings stock the mind with matter that it digests and recombines to produce original work; this process would seem, as Ong suggests, to have more to do with the workings of the imagination than with the memory. J. L. Halio demonstrates that metaphors of conception and birth were used to represent the workings of the creative imagination in the Renaissance, and Erasmus, in a passage quoted at length above, said that a mind "crammed" with matter collected in the course of varied reading "may give birth to an original style."[92] But most English educational theorists scrupulously avoid the birth metaphor, and they virtually never associate copia with imagination. Educational seeds are planted in the mind (*animus*) or the rational faculty (*ingenium*), although strictly speaking this was not possible, since only memory and imagination could retain matter. When the operation of gathering is related, even obliquely, to the fancy or imagination, that operation is viewed with considerable distrust. Richard Morison, for example, describes how metaphorical or allegorical sayings are absorbed: "morall preceptes pleasantly set out in feate colours of witty phantasies both crepe faster into our bosomes, and also tary there with muche more delectation and profite, than they would beyng playnly spoken."[93] Here sayings "clothed" in images are related to the fancy, and they are seen to "crepe" rather sneakily into the student's "bosom."

Humanist representations of the educational assimilation of classical texts tend to rupture, at least partly because, in the early years of the century, their psychology did not offer a vision of a stable and unified mind, or a creative imagination. Our view of humanist individualism, then, must be tempered by the fact that their psychology offered them a mind oddly similar to a Freudian or Lacanian "partitioned subject, incapable of exhaustive self-knowledge," with parts that "speak different languages and operate on the basis of conflicting imperatives."[94] The imagination, able to deal only in images and both unpredictable and uncontrollable in its random associations, seems closely akin to the unconscious, while reason, able to deal in words and highly predictable and controllable, resembles the superego.[95] Obviously, Renaissance psychology differs from Freudian or Lacanian versions in its hope that the rational faculty could control human actions. But theories of literary education foundered on their inability to imagine a safe way for texts to be assimilated into the mind and to transform it. If texts are only memorized, then their pedagogy remains superficial. If, however, they are more deeply absorbed and transformed, the imagination must come into play. Sayings form the ideal basis for a nonimaginative theory of invention, partly because they do not necessarily involve images, and partly because they are so often moral. Nevertheless, any version of education based on deep assimilation and transformation necessarily admits the dangerous possibility that the imagination will become involved.

Thus, these educational treatises often turn from nurturant, organic models of pedagogy to more openly violent and coercive strategies designed to control the dangerous parts of the mind. The use of sayings and the notebook are still central here, but more emphasis is placed on framing than on gathering. In this sense, students are framed along with their texts, and the word comes to mean not only "build up," but also "contain" and "control." In some cases, it approximates what Foucault means by "discipline," although it also carries a suggestion of duplicity and deceit. The concept of framing is closely related to a number of inorganic metaphors for the process of education, including fortification and engraving.

Framing, of course, was, in rhetorical treatises, a common term for putting ideas into words in an orderly fashion. Educational treatises retain this sense of the word, as when Ascham complains about "ill framing of the sentence" learned in poor schools, or about the nobleman's child who could "in no wise frame his tongue to say a little short grace, and yet could roundly rap out so many ugly oaths."[96] In the second instance, however, "frame" begins to take on connotations of control and discipline, since it is lack of discipline in the home that has caused the child's tongue to be so unruly. Thus, as we noted at the beginning of this chapter, Kempe could speak of a schoolmaster as "framing [the child] to eloquence in talke, and vertue in deedes." And uneducated children could be described by Richard Rainolde as "without all civilitie, unframed to vertue, ignoraunte of all arte and science."

Descriptions of the process of framing do not always clearly separate grammatical from ethical framing; it is as if learning to frame a proper sentence is the same as learning to frame a life. Richard Coxe's description of Prince Edward's educational progress expresses this conflation of framings and also hints at the political implications of the process:

> These parts [the accidence] thus beten downe and conquered, he begynneth to buylde them up agayn and frame them after his purpose with dew ordre of construction, lyke as the Kyng's maiesti fframed up Bullayn whan he had beaten it downe. He understondeth and can frame well his iii concordes of grammar and hath made all redy xl or l prety latyns. . . . Euery day in the masse tyme he redeth a portion of Salomon's proverbs for the exercise of hys reding, wherin he deliteth much and lerneth ther how good it is to geve eare vnto dyscipline.[97]

The process of framing the prince entails a mixture of destruction and construction, submission and assertion. The basic rules of grammar that Lily suggests need to be "beaten in" have been "beten downe and conquered" by the prince so that he can use them to "frame" up new sentences "after his purpose," but also "with dew ordre of construction."

This is analogous to his father's destruction of Boulogne so that he could build it up again according to his own rule and purpose. The prince has been so framed by the rules of grammar that his own framings are informed by them. Similarly, his reading of Proverbs "deliteth" him but also frames him to "dyscipline." Education is empowering but carries within itself subtle controls on the exercise of that power. By reading the quintessential framing text (Proverbs), the prince learns that he must "geve eare" to humanist advice.[98]

Sayings, as we saw in the logic texts, were considered to be framed in several senses. As illustrative examples of grammatical or rhetorical rules, they were obviously framed by them. And as moral precepts, they were equally obviously framed by the cultural code. Thus, sententious readings (like the Proverbs of Solomon) could both frame a child and serve as an antidote to harmful ideas. As frame, however, they exercise a control that is subtler (because the child is insensibly shaped by it), more coercive (because it involves shaping the self instead of simply providing a counterforce against bad influence), and more empowering (because it builds up a self according to the hierarchical mandates of the cultural code, and prepares it to insert itself into the upper reaches of that hierarchy). As Rainolde defines the sententia, it is "an oracion [i.e., speech act] in fewe woordes, shewyng a godlie precept of life, exhorting or diswaydyng: the Grekes doe call godly preceptes, by the name of *Gnome* or *Gnomon*, whiche is asmoche to saie, a rule or square, to direct any thyng by, for by them, the life of manne is framed to all singularitie."[99] The achievement of "singularity" in Tudor society is based on deep inculcation of its rule.

Framing, then, implies the construction of a self in accordance with a preexisting rule, both grammatical and ethical. Related to this is the idea that education uses precepts to provide a kind of fortification for the mind. Again we can recall from both Erasmus and Vives the phrase "antidoto praemunitus," fortified with an antidote. Fortification, however, implies that evil is kept out of the self completely, not just counteracted after it has been let in, and also that bad impulses are contained. The Italian educator Aeneas Sylvius Piccolomini similarly identifies the duty of the schoolmaster to be "to fence in the growing mind with wise and noble precepts and example," thus simultaneously curbing the growth of the plant and keeping weeds away from it.[100] Erasmus urges that just as "we are accustomed to fortify most diligently those shores, which receive the most violent force of the wave. . . . By so much the more diligently he [the prince] ought to be fortified against them [evil impulses] with the best sayings and deeds of praiseworthy princes."[101]

It would seem that these accounts of fortification with moral precepts confine the effects of education to a kind of superficial defense. They make no claim to transform the individual or self but simply imagine the sayings as forming a kind of wall or fence around the mind, keeping out bad influences, and keeping in bad impulses. Erasmus, however, in another passage, seems to imply that fortification with sayings can have a transformative effect: he suggests that the prince's teacher "where he feels him inclining toward vice, here first he should fortify his mind with helpful rules and suitable precepts; and let him try to turn his still pliant ingenium onto a different path."[102] Erasmus's depiction of precepts bending the *habitus* of the mind in a different direction seems to press beyond a theory of superficial fortification and to reflect, once more, a desire to believe that sayings act to transform the very self. Medieval writers such as Aquinas and Bonaventure believed that a man's habitus was *difficile mobilis* and, once inclined to vice, moved only by the grace of God.[103] Erasmus, however, depicts educative sayings working directly on the ingenium in order to transform the very habit of the self; he does not, however, attempt to describe how fortification can do this.

Another metaphor seems similarly torn between imagining the action of sayings on the mind as superficial and imagining it as deeply transformative. Engraving or carving sayings on the mind is an extremely common analogy and is often related to the literal carving of sayings on surfaces. Erasmus, for example notes that

> it is not enough simply to relate moral sayings which deter the student from vice or incite him to honest actions; they must be drilled in, they must be plowed in, they must be hammered in, and other memorable forms, such as a sententia, a fable, metaphors, examples, apophthegms, or proverbs, must be carved on rings, fastened to tablets, inscribed on charts, and if there is anything else which a person of the student's age particularly likes, it should be done there too, so that he will be surrounded by moral sayings.[104]

Similarly, Elyot gathers certain precepts "out of holy Scripture as out of warkes of other excellent writars of famouse memorie" and advises that they be "wel and substancially graven in a noble mannes memorie, it shall also be necessary to cause them to be delectably writen and sette in a table within his bedde chamber" (102r, 104v).

H. A. Mason expresses contempt for this practice, calling it "pathetic to see the Humanists in all walks of life supposing that the mere writing up on the wall of a wise saying will make a difference to those who read the writing on the wall."[105] Mason, however, does not acknowledge the close connection between the engraving of sayings on walls and the idea, according to faculty psychology, that ideas retained in the memory were engraved on its walls. This metaphor also calls on the concept of artificial memory, where natural memory could be improved by visualizing whatever one wanted to remember placed on the walls of a house.[106] This advice was taken quite literally by Sir Nicholas Bacon, who had the walls of the great chamber in his house at Gorhambury decorated with moral sayings.[107] Here the inculcation of sayings is kept from involvement with imagination through their confinement to memory; it is stressed, however, that such methods lead not to the superficial retention of medieval rote learning but to a deep and permanent engraving of moral precepts on the mind. Of course Bacon's great chamber also served as a public manifestation of his possession of a liberal education, an external representation of the walls of his own memory.[108]

Sayings are, for several reasons, particularly suited for mental engraving that simultaneously preserves the controlling compartmentalization of the mind and also deeply influences it. Sayings were, in several ways, associated with writing rather than speech, and thus with stable truth transcending fallible human authority. First of all, there was a tradition, going back to antiquity, that moral sayings engraved in stone represented the only surviving fragments of ancient philosophy. Sometimes this engraving was even given religious significance, as if the gods themselves did the engraving.[109] Erasmus notes in the *Adagia* that adages "were written on the doors of temples, as worthy of the gods; they were everywhere to be seen carved on columns and marble tablets as worthy of immortal memory."[110] Francis Clement remarks on the saying "gorgeously graven" at Delphi, and the "learned sentence . . . engraven at the entry unto *Isocrates* his Schoole in letters of gold," emphasizing the artistry and value of these engravings, but attributing the act to no identifiable human agent.[111] Sayings were also associated with the writing on the soul that Plato associates with the source of speech. Through these associations, the engraving of sayings on the mind and on the wall takes on an almost occult significance.

More disturbingly, sayings are often described as acting violently as they penetrate or cut into the mind. Again, humanist educators openly acknowledge the symbolic (and literal) violence that is a part of their curriculum. The rhetorical devices that give them their novelty or closure are often associated, in both Latin and English, with metaphors involving sharpness: "point," "acuteness," *argutia*. Vives, for example, notes that "Seneca has elegant, sharp and brief sentences, which he hurls like thonged darts" (193).[112] Clement explains that he has included sayings in Greek and Latin in his treatise for young children "that even the same may be as a spurre and goade to incite and provoke thy forwardnes to the speedier obtaining the excellent treasure of learning."[113] And John Stanbridge interestingly conflates corporal punishment with the memorization of Latin sentences: "the rodde must not spare / You for to lerne with his sharpe morall sense." The "sharpe morall sense" of corporal punishment is closely related to the force of the sentences themselves "These latyn wordes in your herte to impresse."[114] With these violent metaphors, humanists again reach toward transformation of the self but can only depict it as a painful violation, closely related to corporal punishment.

Educational theorists thus place the gathering and framing of sayings at the very heart of their method's efficacy to empower, to control, and to instill wisdom and eloquence. Sayings were useful not least because they lent themselves to a variety of scenarios. They could be precious jewels encapsulating much wisdom in a small chest, a treasury of liquid capital that anyone could accumulate, flowers of morality amid heretical thorns, drops of water in the fountain of eloquence, tasty morsels of wisdom, seeds of learning, building blocks to frame up and fortify the self, laws engraved in stone, sharp weapons with which to engrave those laws. Because they combine, in small and portable fragments, eloquence and wisdom, pleasure and seriousness, fertility and closure, they helped humanists to believe that their curriculum could carry out their complex and contradictory project. Using sayings, they could give students access to powerful and copious speech with built-in controls, they could reconcile pagan and Christian codes, they could provide an education that could be possessed and displayed as a sign of fitness for power, and they could preserve their own delicate position as supplements to power.

Problems surface when humanist teachers try to envision an educational process that uses ancient texts to transform the student. Although on one level they must believe that their innovative program surpasses medieval education precisely by effecting this kind of ethical transformation, they also realize that such a transformation, especially if based on pagan works, is dangerous. Thus, although they often formulate elaborate organic analogies to depict education as a transformative process, they inevitably back away from the disturbing implications of this model and move toward a view of education as controlling, rather than transforming, the self. These educators cannot quite believe in the whole, rational individual that they long for; they exhibit a strong countertendency to depict their students as fragmented subjects, both alienated from and controlled by language.

Chapter IV

EDUCATIONAL PRACTICE IN
EARLY SIXTEENTH-CENTURY ENGLAND

A T THIS POINT, I want to turn from theory to practice, or from discussions of how gathering and framing ought to work to some of the existing textual traces of humanist attempts to use these practices in school, at court, and in print. The line between theory and practice is, however, as Victoria Kahn has argued, impossible to draw with certainty.[1] Theoretical discussions were themselves largely carried out through gathered commonplaces, and those same concepts and analogies—hunting, planting, poison and cure, fortification and goad, common and uncommon—resurface in practical texts and remain vehicles even in those contexts for theorizing about discourse, subject-formation, and the economics of power.

By practical texts, I mean documents such as school curricula, textbooks, letters, political and economic treatises, and even poems, which constituted the humanists' attempts to establish gathering and framing as the basis of a new curriculum, to secure that curriculum as an accepted credential for political office, to transform existing cultural values in accordance with their aims, and to display their own grounding in this program as a sign of fitness for preferment. As in the three previous chapters, I have read these texts by focusing on their commonplaces. I believe that such a reading establishes the centrality of humanist practice across a wide discursive field, and that the continuing presence of those practices shaped basic attitudes toward language, selfhood, and power in ways that have not been adequately acknowledged. Thus, alongside the imitation of whole texts, we find an intertextuality of fragments. And alongside aristocratic individualism, absolutism, imperialism, and a strong assertion of the authorial voice, we find an emphasis on collectivism, shared resources, concern with a balance of power and balance of trade, and a communal voice.

In the tracing of humanist practice, historical specificity becomes more important, as attitudes and alliances changed from decade to decade. Two dates stand out, at each end of the century, around which a nexus of ideas and positions can be discerned. In 1520, Richard Horman's *Vulgaria* was published and adopted for use at St. Paul's School, and Richard Croke, with Wolsey's support, was named reader in Greek at Cambridge.

These events signal early signs of humanist success at achieving the support of the monarch (through Wolsey) for the institutionalization of their curriculum, but there were also concurrent signs of aristocratic resistance to this program. The Grammarians' War and the conflict of Greeks versus Trojans at Oxford pit humanists from the merchant or lower gentry classes (More, Wolsey, Lily, Constable) against the conservative writers Robert Whittinton and John Skelton who uphold the traditional educational methods (combining rudimentary instruction in Latin grammar with the teaching of manners, dancing, music and table service, and practice in hunting) and traditional attitudes toward hierarchy and authority shared by the aristocratic Howard family.[2] The humanists won, in the sense that their curriculum remained dominant and, through the 1530s and 1540s, its products achieved positions at court as advisers, tutors, and propagandists.

But success had its price, and contact with power strengthened already-existing doubts about the moral efficacy of humanist practices in a repressive monarchy and in an increasingly capitalist society. During these years humanist writings of all kinds respond to a contemporary crisis of value by establishing a code, based in important ways on the practices of gathering and framing, to rival aristocratic traditions. Instead of the display of innate superiority at such courtly pastimes as hunting, singing, dancing, and romantic interchange, English humanists sought to establish a serious demeanor, aphoristic style, and constructive use of time as the signs of a powerful subject. During these years, too, poetry becomes a battleground on which aristocratic and humanist versions of that subject vied for dominance.

The other date is more specific, and its specificity attests the concentration of power in the hands of one man. In 1571, when William Cecil was made Baron Burghley, the aristocratic and humanist systems were forcibly joined. Cecil, along with Roger Ascham, Nicholas Bacon, and others, had carried into the Elizabethan Age both the discursive practices and the upwardly mobile, antiaristocratic values of humanism. But Cecil, always deeply conservative in his attitudes toward hierarchy and degree, harbored a lingering sympathy with aristocratic codes. This became more pronounced when he was made Lord Burghley and he effectively established a combination of aristocratic and humanist credentials as preconditions for elevation to power. In practice, Burghley's mixed signals combined with a decreased need for public servants to create a bottleneck for upwardly mobile young men. Burghley exercised considerable bureaucratic control over traditional aristocratic prerogatives, as well as over humanist education; but in fact, he seemed to eschew both sets of criteria for preferment. The 1570s and 1580s, then, were a period of particularly fertile confusion as ambitious men were forced to work out some sort of compromise between two mutually exclusive sets of practices and values. The Sidney and Devereux families were important focal points for this activity, and their vehicles include the impresa, the epigram, and the sonnet. The result was perhaps the first manifestation of the modern self—the bourgeois individual as it was constructed out of both aristocratic and humanist codes.

Rather than proceeding according to this chronology, however, I have chosen to examine the impact of humanist practices in three different fields: in the schoolroom, at court, and in poetic miscellanies. In the areas of courtly and literary endeavor, however, it has been necessary to look separately at the Henrician and Elizabethan periods. Since educational practice remained virtually the same throughout the period, an examination of the humanist curriculum can remain confined to the years between 1520 and 1540 when it was established.

.   .   .   .   .

Many scholars seem to hold an overly idealized view of humanist education in sixteenth-century England, and, as a result, it is important to try to establish what was actually done in the classroom. Too often, critics assume that a work listed on a school curriculum was read in its entirety and interpreted as we would read it today. There has also been a tendency to overlook differences in canon, stressing those works which we value and ignoring other, perhaps more central works, which seem less obviously interesting to us. Above all, the centrality of gathering and framing as the primary pedagogical practices during this period has been underestimated. Although I do not mean to imply that whole texts were *never* read, I do want to suggest that texts were not always read as wholes.[3]

A commonly accepted view of humanist education stresses the creative imitation of classical texts and their exemplary authors through a process that gradually leads to originality and empowerment. Italian humanists do seem to view imitation in this way, stressing a relationship to prior texts in which, as Thomas Greene describes it, "the modern voice distinguishes itself from the older voice, finds its own public accent, but it does so, can only do so, after sensitively apprehending the other accent in something like its particular timbre and personal force."[4] In this kind of imitation, "the object of knowledge is perceived to be composed not by a kernel of moral, religious, or philosophic wisdom, but by what might be called a *moral style*."[5] But in England, humanist pedagogy fostered an approach to reading and writing which stressed precisely those kernels of knowledge, often at the expense of "voice" or "moral style."

A close examination of English school curricula and textbooks reveals the extent to which basic instruction in Latin grammar, the reading of classical authors, and the composition of "original" themes and verse were based on the recognition, assimilation, and redeployment of fragmentary sententiae. In these texts as in logical and rhetorical treatises, sententiae include a variety of forms, variously called arguments, precepts, examples, similitudes, axioms, aphorisms, and figures, but all defined by their expression of a commonplace idea in a rhetorically distinguished form. Moreover, those commonplace ideas generally contribute to a kind of moral framing, repeatedly indoctrinating students with values—the importance of education and hard work, a more assertive attitude toward authority—that would support the humanist project.[6]

What, then, were the curriculum and methods of a typical early sixteenth-century English school? Although there were minor differences from school to school, Grafton and Jardine have convincingly established that humanist efforts to make the grammar school curriculum methodical and uniform throughout England were largely successful.[7] Thus, the curricula of Eton (1530), Winchester (1530), St. Paul's at Canterbury (1541), and Ipswich (1529), as well as the textbooks widely used in that period, display similar methods and goals.[8]

Students (always boys) came to grammar school knowing how to read and write in English. The first three forms at school were devoted to teaching them the basics of Latin grammar and the application of those basics in the composition of simple sentences in Latin. In the next three forms, students focused on the reading of prescribed classical authors, and in the final two added instruction in dialectic and rhetoric as well as more complex exercises in composition.

In the first form, students were required to memorize the "accidence" (declensions and conjugations) and "concordences" (rules of syntax) in English and Latin.[9] Usually, the schoolmaster read out the rule itself and an example, which the students memorized and later recited: "The Under Master shall come into school at 6 a.m., and immediately after saying the prayers to God which we have prescribed, shall make his scholars daily say by heart one of the eight parts of speech until they are ready in each."[10] Both precept and example were often couched sententiously as an aid to memorization.[11]

In the early years of the sixteenth century, there were two rival methods for teaching basic Latin grammar. A traditional method, centered on texts written by John Stanbridge and Robert Whittinton, emphasized the memorization of rules or precepts and the exemplification of those rules in practical sentences (called "vulgars") coined by the author of the text. The humanist method, which was centered on the so-called Lily's Grammar, consisted of a group of texts by several men that de-emphasized the memorization of rules (although this task was still required) and stressed instead the assimilation of sentences taken from classical authors, sentences that exemplified the rules which framed them. Lily's Grammar itself consisted of an accidence and syntax in English and Latin, and was often used in conjunction with a new *Vulgaria* by Robert Horman.

Around the year 1520, the so-called Grammarians' War, waged through polemical prefaces and epigrams in an attempt to secure the court's support for one of these methods, reveals what was really at stake.[12] In actuality, this "war" represented a displacement of the ongoing and more central struggle between the old feudal custom of training young aristocrats in noble households and the new humanist system based in schools.[13] As often happens in curricular reform, a relatively minor methodological disagreement took precedence over (and stood for) the larger conflict. Thus, although the argument explicitly centered on the memorization of rules as opposed to early exposure to rule-exemplifying sentences from classical authors, the real issue was a conflict between the "traditional" educational program, which sought to preserve the existing aristocratic power structure, and the humanist model with its promise of empowerment and upward mobility. John Skelton's involvement in this "war" may even signal the indirect involvement of Wolsey's powerful aristocratic enemies, the Howard family.[14]

Whittinton's method followed the essentially medieval program of grammatical instruction based on Donatus.[15] This curriculum emphasized memorization of grammar rules and of colloquial phrases, "vulgars," which provided students with a practical (but unclassical) basis for daily conversation. Such a curriculum was ideally suited to the education of minor clerics or secretaries, whose spoken Latin would be confined to conversational interchange and memorized ritual, or to aristocrats, who might need some practical knowledge of Latin for diplomatic exchange. The Lily method de-emphasized the memorization of rules (which were, however, despite Whittinton's accusations, still studied) and stressed instead the assimilation of classical examples, fragments of text that were "framed" by the rules in question. Horman's *Vulgaria* was based on fragments gathered from classical authors and consisted, in addition to useful phrases for daily speech, of sententiae, precepts, observations, definitions, and practical advice designed, in the words of a prefatory epistle by Robert Aldrich, to provide "many things suited to almost every human situation and profession."[16] The goal of this program was the production of subjects who could speak elegantly and, as we saw in the previous chapter, who had internalized a classicized cultural code. These boys were intended to be not minor clerics but bureaucratic functionaries who would usurp aristocratic prerogatives in government.

The texts by Stanbridge and Whittinton tend to present grammatical rules in some form that could be easily memorized, while their examples are diffuse and expressed in unclassical Latin.[17] Stanbridge's *Accidence* teaches the parts of speech in English prose, using a question-and-answer format derived from Donatus: "How many partis of reason ben there (eyght)."[18] Exceptions to the rules are given in Latin hexameter verses, a mnemonic device that must have been of limited help to students who knew virtually no Latin.[19] Stanbridge's *Vulgaria* consists of useful vocabulary, again in Latin hexameters, moving from head to foot and outward to areas of human endeavor: "sinciput et vertex caput occiput et coma crinis" is followed by definitions of the words in English: "hoc sinciput /is the fore parte of the heed."[20] The latter part of this volume, the *Vulgaria* proper, consists of useful phrases given in English and Latin: "Good morowe: Bonum tibi huius diei sit primordium" (13). Most of these sentences are expressed in nonclassical Latin and many of them are, literally, vulgar: "I am almost beshytten. sum in articulo purgandi viscera"; "profred seruyce stynketh. ministerium oblatum sordescit"(17, 15).

Whittinton's *Vulgaria* actually consists of the "concordes" or rules of syntax. Whittinton gives the rules first in English prose, then in Latin hexameter, then provides examples in Latin and English, and finally, sometimes, cites "Authorities" for the rule taken from classical works: "The verbe shall accorde with his nominatyfe or vocatyue case in persone and nombre / as appereth here folowynge by rule and example. Verbum cum recto casu quinto ve coheret / Persona et numero. docet ut Maro /marce doceto. Example: My chylde gyf dylygent hede to thes instruccyons. Mi puer diligenter inuigilato his preceptiunculis."[21] The rule, given in Latin hexameter and including within it the classical "authority," is more memorable than the example, which is neither sententious nor observant of classical word order or idiom.

Lily's versions of the same rule of syntax provide an instructive comparison. His emphasis on classical examples of each rule implies that the rules themselves are simply gathered from correct Latin speech and avoid the "vulgar" Latinity of Stanbridge and Whittinton which, according to Ascham, led to "ill framing of the sentences."[22] His section of "concordes" first gives the rule in English prose: "A Verbe Personall agreeth with his nominative case, in numbre and person: as Praeceptor legit, vos vero negligitis, The Maister readeth, and ye regard not."[23] The second part provides rules and examples in Latin prose: "Verbum personale, cohaeret cum nominatiuo in numero et persona: ut *Nunquam sera est ad bonos mores via. Fortuna nunquam perpetuo est bona. . . .* Ovidius *Tu dominus, tu vir, tu mihi frater eris.*"[24] Here, the rule is in unmemorable Latin prose, while the examples are memorable sententiae, either imitating classical construction or actually derived from classical authors.[25]

The difference between the rival methods is perhaps most obviously revealed by the ideological content of the "examples" that they furnish. Whittinton coins his own examples, and they are both deeply suspicious of upward mobility and extremely subservient to established authority. One series of examples explicitly comments on the fortunes of merchants and lawyers whose upward mobility furnished students for humanist schools: "we se how lyghtely ryches chaunseth to marchauntes men of lawe / and suche other as blynde fortune enhaunseth. . . . and sodenly in an houre they be lost / or scauntly remayn to the thyrd heare / but to his trouble or vndoynge. . . . This shold be to euery wyse man a spectacle / or presydens [t]o remembre suche hasty auaunsement" (82). His advice to a would-be courtier is similarly cautious and deferential to authority: "he that hath a rowmeth in ye kynges court" must "applye hymselfe to agre with all maner of persones to cory fauell craftely / to daunse / attendaunce at all houres to be seruyable." He must be "redy whan his superyour commaundeth hym" and should "compare not with suche as be his betters: though he excell them in ony vertue. but lowly gyf them premynens" (83, 85).

Stanbridge's phrasebook provides evidence of the literal violence of prehumanist education. He offers a veritable conjugation of beatings: "I was beten this mornynge"; "The mayster hath bete me"; "I shall be bete" (15, 22). Whittinton similarly offers: "He [the master] hath made me to renne a rase (or a course) that my bottokes doeth swette a blody sweat" (89). More tellingly, Whittinton assumes that the school curriculum should include traditional aristocratic training in manners and table service: "it belongeth vnto a mayster to teyche his scholars both maners and lernynge" (109), since manners are the "chefe thynge requysyte in a chylde" (115). His lengthy instructions for table service reflect once again careful attention to social hierarchy: "let hym [the student] also take dylygent hede to set his cuppe surely before his superiour discouer it and couer it agayn with curtesy made" (119). Here again, emphasis is on observing proper forms of respect for authority that were central to the feudal system but almost antithetical to the humanist project.[26]

Horman's *Vulgaria* makes direct use of gathering and framing in both the stylistic and the moral sense. It is literally a commonplace book filled with information and advice designed to provide the student with authoritative information and advice pertaining to virtually every area of life, and to inculcate him with proper attitudes toward all of those things. Its contents are, as a prefatory epistle tells us "pure, chaste and true Latin, chosen and brought from the best and most famous Latin writers, through long and certain judgement."[27] Its design is admittedly to further the revival of classical Latin against certain bad teachers (it does not name, but clearly implies, Whittinton and his supporters) who "are trivial and trifling imposters to our credulous youth."[28]

The book itself is arranged under commonplace headings that are clearly designed to shape students' beliefs and values as well as their Latin style. They include both practical and ethical topics, such as "De pietate," "De inpietate," "Medicinalia," "Coquinaria," "De civile administratione," and "Nuptialia."[29] The sayings themselves, which appear in English and Latin, cover the range of gathered matter. Under "De pietate," for example, we find aphoristic statements ("Man is naturallye dysposyd to have a mynd and reverence towarde God. Homini ingenita est religionis cura") as well as topical observations ("Kyng Henry dothe many dyvers myracles"), precepts for behavior ("say thy service without stopps or interruptyon"), theological sentences ("The lawe of Moses was holy"), and useful phrases for everyday life ("the sexton hath embesled offerynge money and iewelles") (A1r–B1r).[30]

All of the headings include material designed to initiate students, to inculcate them with the beliefs and values of the humanist cultural code, teaching everything from basic physiology ("there be foure humours bloode / color / fleme / and melancolye") to attitudes toward learning: "There is no nere wey to come to connynge: than to rede good authours / and drawe to lerned men"; "I rejoyce in the increase of cunnynge: that is now adayes. Laten speche: that was almoste loste: is nowe after longe absens recovered and come ageyne"; "Gentyll mennys children shulde be most courtese and redy to do well"; "the moste parte of techers of grammer make most of the worst authors" (B1r, P1r, P2r). "Learning" for Horman, in contrast to Whittinton, is based on the study of "good authours" and does not seem to include training in table service.

The section "De civilibus" outlines humanist attitudes toward hierarchy, authority, and duty that are also quite different from Whittinton's ideas on those subjects. The assumption here is that the student will some day occupy a position of authority: "Haute delynge and solemnes / maketh a man to be disdayned: and lesse set by in his office" (M5v). Instead of Whittinton's constant emphasis on respect and service to "superiours," Horman suggests that "I owe obedience to the: but no bondage" (M5v). And instead of Whittinton's dark predictions about upwardly mobile merchants and lawyers, Horman's quotations encourage hard work and high goals: "with unthrifty ydylnesse / all grace and goodnesse wasteth aweye"; "He is nat very besy: but slacke and shamfast in preferrynge hym selfe" (M5v).

In accordance with humanist practice, Horman's gathered sayings touch on many areas of life and include both the idealistic and the practical, the high and the low. Even vulgar language is de-emphasized rather than excluded: "that reason is nat worth a pyggis turde. Ea ratio non aequat succerdam" (293v).[31]

The Lily method also differs from Stanbridge and Whittinton in the greater role it gives to teachers as the gatherers of examples:

> When these Concords [rules of syntax] be wel knowen unto them, an easy and
> a pleasaunt payne, if the foregrounds be wel and throughly beaten in, let them
> not contynue in learnyng of theyr rules orderly al as they lye in theyr Syntaxe,

but rather learne some preaty book, wherein is conteyned not onely the eloquence of the tongue, but also a good playne lesson of honesty and godlynes,
and therof take some little sentence as it lyeth, and learne to make the same
firste out of Englishe into Latine, not seying the booke.[32]

We should note first that Lily does not dispense with memorization of
rules: the "foregrounds" (accidence) are to be "wel and throughly beaten
in," an injunction that was all too literally carried out by many schoolmasters in the period. Lily, however, probably means to replace actual
with symbolic violence, as did the theorists discussed in the previous
chapters. Rules then give way to exercises based on sayings gathered from
"some preaty book" (at St. Paul's School "preaty" books included the
Psalter and the biblical books of Proverbs and Ecclesiasticus).[33] These
sayings or "little sentences" are defined in a way that closely resembles
the definitions found in rhetorical treatises. They are "playne" and make
didactic reference to the cultural code ("lesson of honesty and godlynes"),
but are also distinguished from plain speech by their rhetorical elaboration, "the eloquence of the tongue." Note, too, the assumption that the
"preaty book" *contains* its style and content in the form of extractable
sayings, as well as the fact that the schoolmaster, rather than the gram-
marian, is given responsibility for gathering the sayings. Part of the lesson
would be exposure to the act of gathering and assimilation of the criteria
(both moral and rhetorical) upon which proper choice would be based.

Once gathered, the sayings, already framed in English, are to be reframed in classical Latin by the schoolmaster, and the students are then to
copy the correct version into their notebooks. Wolsey's instructions for
the schoolmaster at Ipswich (based on the curriculum at St. Paul's) reflect
the emphasis on proper framing of these sayings in several senses. The
schoolmaster of the second form is

there to be accustomed to speak *Latin*, and to translate into that Language,
from their Mother-Tongue, somewhat that is pretty and pertinent, and upon
such a Subject as to convey a sensible, elegant Meaning, accommodated to the
Capacities of Boys. As soon as this is translated they are to transcribe it in
Roman characters; and you are every Day to take Care, that all the Boys of this
Form keep their Books very correct, and very fairly transcrib'd in their own
Hand-writing.[34]

Similarly, Lily stresses in his *Carmen de moribus* that the boys keep notebooks instead of loose sheets of paper, and that they write in (literally
insero, "ingraft") the sayings neatly.[35] Several of the practical instructions
for notebook keeping expressed here by Lily and Wolsey reiterate the
concern with order and discipline found in educational theory. Wolsey
stresses that the saying should be in the boys' "own Hand-writing," but
specifies that they use "*Roman characters*," creating a tension between

originality and uniformity.[36] Both writers emphasize the care with which the sayings are to be framed: they should be neat, correct, fair, and neither blotted nor erased. Finally, they are to be kept together in a notebook as the cultural capital that signifies the possession of a humanist education.[37]

Whittinton seems in a way to have won the grammar wars, since he was made schoolmaster to the king's "henxmen" (pages) in the late 1520s.[38] He was thus in a position to carry on traditional methods of aristocratic education at the very center of the court. However, in the long run, Lily won out over Stanbridge and Whittinton when, in 1549, King Edward VI made Lily's Grammar the only grammar that could legally be used for the teaching of Latin. This meant that his humanist method became the standard of education in the schools and influenced many students for many years. Under this method, the earliest instruction in Latin grammar would have conveyed several important attitudes to the students. First, they would learn from the very beginning that the basic unit of discourse was a sentence, whether precept or example, that was framed in such a way as to be easily memorized. They would be taught to view texts as containers of fragments that could be possessed by memorization and by transcription in a notebook. Emphasis on the physical act of transcribing the sayings in neat roman characters gave them the status of material possessions, the signs of successful education. Students would also learn, by the teacher's example, to discern valuable sayings through a combination of moral and rhetorical criteria, assimilating both proper classical Latin style and humanist ideology.

In the second through the sixth forms, the boys would continue to review the rules of grammar and transcribe Latin sentences. But they would also begin reading a prescribed canon of classical works. The first point worth emphasizing here is the difference of this canon from our own sense of which classical works are central to the education of students.[39] In the first through third forms, students read *The Distichs of Cato*, a collection of sententious epigrams from late antiquity; Lily's *Carmen de moribus*, an imitation of the *Distichs* that outlines proper behavior in school; Aesop's fables in Latin; and selections from Terence and Lucian.[40] These works were the privileged texts for beginning students not because they were distinguished by their style or imaginative originality, but because they contain an abundance of "preaty sentences." Cato and Lily are entirely composed of aphoristic sentences, and Aesop's fables were thought to have been "invented for the moralles sake."[41] Terence was considered to be a "storehouse" of idiomatic sentences in pure, colloquial Latin, and selections were probably read along with a book like Nicholas Udall's *Floures For Latine Spekynge* (1533), which goes through the *Andria* scene by scene, gathering idioms and sayings of various kinds. Udall notes in a prefatory letter to students that his collection of "flowers" is designed to help them move from the precepts of grammar to eloquent and copious Latin speech, and his very title emphasizes that the book consists of gathered fragments.[42] Lucian's dialogues were used as a similar source, both in Greek and in Latin translation, of fragments of conversational idiom.[43] None of these works, with the possible exception of Terence and Lucian, would be included in the classical canon for modern students, and for this reason their influence on Renaissance texts is largely unacknowledged.[44]

In the fourth through sixth forms, the canon expanded to include works that are central to a modern program of classical education: Virgil's *Eclogues*, Ovid's *Metamorphoses*, Cicero's letters, selections from Sallust and Caesar, as well as Erasmus's *Colloquies* and *Parabola*. It is wrong, however, to imagine that Renaissance students necessarily approached the works as organic wholes with identifiable and imitable "voices" or styles. Instead, they seem to have treated these works more or less as they treated the aphoristic works listed above: as containers of extractable fragments of wisdom and eloquence.

Because most curricula simply list the recommended authors, it is a bit difficult to ascertain exactly how the canonical texts were studied. However, it is fairly clear that students proceeded through each work at a painfully slow pace. One curriculum specifies that the schoolmaster should cover twelve lines of the *Metamorphoses* per week, and at that speed it would take almost twenty years to get through the whole thing (it would take sixty-five weeks just to complete book 1).[45] It would be very difficult for students taught in this way to grasp the shape of the work as a whole.

The title page to John Palsgrave's *Acolastus* (1540) provides a useful clue to what English schoolmasters actually *did* to the texts on their list. Palsgrave published a text, translation, and commentary on this Neo-Latin play by Fullonius to be used as a school text in the Lily/St. Paul's curriculum. It was designed to provide a single model for the reading of authors, just as Lily's Grammar was to provide a single model for the teaching of grammar. The title page explains the steps involved in reading a text "after suche maner as chylderne are taught in the grammer schole":

> first worde for worde, as the latyne lyeth, and afterwarde accordynge to the sence and meanyng of the latin sentences: by shewing what they do value and counteruayle in our tongue, with admonitions set forth in the margyn, so often as any suche phrase, that is to say, kynd of spekying vsed of the latyns, whiche we vse not in our tonge, but by other wordes, expresse the sayde latyn maners of speakinge, and also Adages, metaphores, sentences, or other fygures poeticall or rhetorical do require, for the more perfyte instructynge of the lerners.[46]

Palsgrave differentiates between translation "worde for worde," which is a preliminary stage, and sentence by sentence, which is performed subsequently. Only units of the sentence can convey the "sence and meanyng"

from one language to the other, and only sentences contain "value" that can be materially transferred. The key to an equivalent transaction between Latin and English is once again the recognition of idioms ("latyn maners of speakinge"), adages, metaphors, sentences, and figures. Palsgrave's English text is, as this statement of his method implies, virtually unreadable. He proceeds through the text phrase by phrase, offering first a literal translation, then one or more idiomatic renderings of the same phrase, with adages and sententiae duly noted in the margins. Although a modern editor has described this text as "displaying and even exaggerating the errors and follies inherent in the system which produced it," it must fairly accurately render the experience of "reading" a classical author in a sixteenth-century school.[47]

William Kempe's directions for reading canonical works similarly urge students to view the texts as compendia of examples that illustrate the rules of grammar, logic, and rhetoric. Students are not to be concerned with interpretation of the whole, but with identification of its parts. When the student turns to such works as Cicero's *Offices* and orations, Caesar, Virgil's *Aeneid*, Ovid's *Metamorphoses*, and selected works by Horace, "he shall observe the examples of the hardest poynts in Grammar, of the arguments in Logike, of the tropes and figures in Rhetorike, referring every example to his proper rule."[48] In carrying out a "reading" of this kind, the student is made constantly aware of the rules that frame and order proper speech.

Finally, in their seventh and eighth forms, the students turned to more sustained exercises in composition. Sixteenth-century writers often use the term "imitation" to describe their approach to composition, but, in England at least, they do not go about it as we would. According to school curricula, composition began with some formal study of dialectic and rhetoric, a process that, as we saw in the first two chapters, would stress the gathering of matter (commonplaces) and the eloquent framing of that matter (through gathered tropes and figures). William Kempe, for example, suggests that students begin the study of composition by learning "the precepts concerning the divers sorts of arguments in the first part of Logike . . . [and] then shall followe the tropes and figures in the first part of Rhetoryke." Then, he should practice finding "examples of the hardest poynts in Grammar, of the Arguments of Logike, of the tropes and figures in Rhetorike" in the authors that he reads, and finally, "let him have a like theame to prosecute with the same artificiall instruments, that he findeth in his author" (232–33). Imitation, then, is a question of gathering and reusing the "artificiall instruments" provided by grammar, logic, and rhetoric.

After this material had been learned, students began to write their own Latin compositions, usually based on the graduated program found in

Aphthonius's *Progymnasmata*. Students in England usually used Agricola's Latin translation of this work, and it was also available in Rainolde's English version, *The Foundacion of Rhetorike*.[49] Although the *Progymnasmata* does provide composition models and instructions for imitating them, it is nevertheless, as we have seen, deeply informed by the mental habits of gathering and framing.[50] First of all, the different "oracions" that it offers for imitation are based on forms of commonplace material: fable, narration, chria (saying of a famous person), sentence, commonplace, praise, dispraise, confirmation, destruction. It would be the schoolmaster's responsibility to provide the fable or saying to serve as the basis of the students' compositions, yet another version of the teacher's role as gatherer.

The "oracions" themselves tend to rely on sententious fragments as the basic units of composition. The first exercise, for example, provides instructions for writing on a fable. First, the student should "recite the fable, as the aucthour telleth it" (A4r). The next section, praise of the author, is to be gathered from two sources: "whiche praise maie sone *bee gotte* of any studious scholer, if he reade the aucthours life and actes therin, or the Godlie *preceptes* in his fables" (A4r; my emphasis). The third section is "the *morall*, whiche is the interpretacion annexed to the Fable, for the fable was invented for the moralles sake." The student is then to "declare the nature of the thynges, conteined in the Fable," and is to gather this material by "naturall witte, or by reading, or sences." Next he should "sette forth the thynges, reasonyng one with an other, as the Ant with the Greshopper." Here each side will no doubt employ arguments gathered from the places and couched with sententious force. The student is told to "make a *similitude* of the like matter," and then to "induce an *example* for the same matter to be proved by" (A4r). Similitude and example were, of course, forms frequently listed by rhetoricians as material to be gathered. Finally, the student writes an "epilogus," which, in the sample oration provided by Rainolde, is itself highly sententious: "Therefore fained offers of friendship, are to bee taken heede of, and the acte of every man to bee examined, proved, and tried, for true friendship is a rare thyng, when as Tullie doth saie: in many ages there are fewe couples of friendes to be found, Aristotle also concludeth the same" (C1v). Imitation according to the Renaissance "Aphthonius" did not involve the deep assimilation and reconstitution of a "classical idiom" or "moral style."[51] Instead, students learned to deploy recycled fragments of various kinds upon a set of organizational frames loosely based on the parts of a classical oration.[52]

Even when students progress beyond Aphthonius to the imitation of classical authors, they are still instructed to rely on the familiar operations of collecting sententious matter and placing it on an appropriate frame. Ascham's methods of imitation and double translation, for example, are approached by the kind of identification and collection of fragments that we have been noting. Although Ascham does propose to supplement the notebook method with his own program of "double translation"—from Latin to English, and back to Latin—this process is itself informed by gathering: "and to conclude in a short room the commodities of double translation, surely the mind by daily marking, first, the cause and matter; then, the words and phrases; next, the order and composition; after, the reason and arguments; then, the forms and figures of both the tongues; lastly, the measure and compass of every sentence must needs by little and little draw unto it the like shape of eloquence as the author doth use which is read" (87). Ascham does envision something akin to what we usually mean by "imitation": the mind is to "draw unto itself the like shape of eloquence" by close study of classical works. But he retains the usual practice of breaking down the work into fragments. The student would rely on knowledge of the "places" in "marking . . . the cause and matter" and the "reason and arguments." He would use his knowledge of grammar to identify the "words and phrases," and would rely on rhetoric to note the "order and composition" and the "forms and figures." By "marking" these bits as he translates, the student will in effect be gathering a store of the kinds of matter that he is used to collecting in his notebook.

Ascham, in fact, goes on to relate his concept of "imitation" even more closely to the Erasmian notebook. He urges that someone compile a book entitled "De imitatione," which would contain "a certain few fit precepts unto the which should be gathered and applied plenty of examples out of the choicest authors of both the tongues [i.e., Latin and Greek]" (127). Although Ascham says that such a work has not yet been written, he does admit that "Erasmus . . . seemeth to have prescribed to himself this order of reading; that is, to note out by the way three special points: all adages, all similitudes, and all witty sayings of most notable personages" (127). Ascham's projected "De imitatione" differs from the Erasmian project chiefly in drawing on a much more limited canon of writers deemed suitable for imitation. Whereas Erasmus urged the student to read all Greek and Latin authors in this way, Ascham would stick to Plato, Xenophon, Isocrates, Demosthenes, Aristotle, and, especially, Cicero—all authors noted for their exemplary prose style and moral judgments. Ascham further objects to most contemporary commentaries on Aristotle because "they be rather spent in declaring schoolpoint rules than in gathering fit examples for use and utterance" (131). He suggests that someone ought to illustrate precepts from Aristotle by examples taken from Plato, since "such a labor were one special piece of that work of imitation which I do wish were gathered together in one volume" (131).

William Kempe, another proponent of composition through "imitation," provides a particularly detailed account of how the student should base his transaction with the ancient model on sententious fragments. He provides his own example of an imitation of Cicero's "In ambitionem" (against ambition) in the form of a theme "In avaritiam" (against avarice), in which "for the most part wee have expressed phrase for phrase, trope for trope, figure for figure, arguments for argument, and so the rest" (234). Kempe advises students to observe four general precepts when carrying out this kind of imitation:

> First, that if the author whom he imitateth, have generall *sentences*, he may reteyne the very same. . . . Secondly, that he may leave out thimitation of some sentences or arguments. As Tullie setteth forth the *similitude* by the authoritee of African, and the relation of Panetius: whereas only the protasis of the first part of our similitude is attributed but to Cato, for want of a like similitude garnished with like authority. Thirdly, he may adde more than his author hath: as here the *example* of Cleope is added to recompence that which wanteth in the similitude. Fourthly, he may in some part alter the method, forme of syllogismes, axiomes, arguments, figures, tropes, phrases and words. (236; my emphasis)

Here we see Kempe imitating Cicero by gathering "sentences" of various kinds and reframing them to suit his slightly different topic.

Finally, students were often given published gatherings of sentences and phrases to aid them in composition. There were collections of Ciceronian sententiae and idioms for help with prose, and dictionaries of poetical phrases for students required to write imitative verse.[53] And although Ascham criticizes such *epitomes* and dictionaries as "a silly, poor kind of study," he objects not to the gathering of pertinent fragments but to the fact that the gathering is not done by the student himself: "*Epitome* is good privately for himself that doth work it, but ill commonly for all other that use other men's labor therein" (106). Like Erasmus, Ascham simply wants to stress that the student himself must learn how to gather matter from what he reads.

Of course, it is quite true that the sixteenth-century writers whose works we value today were not bound by this rather pedestrian method of imitation. And it is equally true that we can discern examples of what Greene would describe as "heuristic imitation," the deep assimilation and transformation of classical texts, in sixteenth-century England. But it also seems inevitable that the daily activities of the classroom would leave their mark on even the most gifted students.

First of all, their sense of the literary canon and the criteria for choosing it would be quite different from our own. They would have been taught to value texts that contained the greatest store of matter in the form of moral aphorisms, proverbs, similitudes, and striking idioms; this led to the valorization of "unimaginative" forms—such as the aphoristic epigram, the moral epistle, the epideictic oration—that we esteem far less. More important, the concepts of creativity, imagination, and self-expression did not figure in the scenario of authorship constructed in these schools. Instead, students were encouraged to view all literature as a system of interchangeable fragments, and to view the process of composition as centered on intertextuality rather than imitation in the usual sense. Texts were seen as containers and not, primarily, utterances, a fact that implies a conception of authorship radically different from that usually associated with the Renaissance. Our canonical sixteenth-century English literature was deeply marked by the humanist schoolroom, even if only by a desperate struggle to reject it.

That literary struggle can only be understood, however, in the context of the power struggles at court that shaped its directions and contributed many of its terms. Crucial both at court and in the literary text were questions of value and, even more important, of the nature of authority and of the individual. The struggle between what I call the humanist and aristocratic educational systems spills over into political and economic theory, and into the daily exchanges of aspirants for power at court. The next two chapters will trace the ways in which humanist values and practices—still based on gathering and framing—were of central importance in shaping the forms and discourses of power right on through to the end of the century.

Chapter V

PASTIME OR PROFIT:

ARISTOCRATIC AND HUMANIST IDEOLOGY,

1520–1550

I F HUMANISTS were largely successful in instituting their curriculum in schools all over England, they met mixed results in achieving the second part of their goal, the acceptance of a humanist education as a recognized credential for preferment at court. As we have seen, humanist logicians, rhetoricians, and educators continually emphasized that their aim was the construction of a form of discourse and a kind of subject that would be uniquely suited to teach future leaders and to provide prudent political advice. As soon as humanist values and practices move out of the classroom, however, they encounter problems and resistance that theorists only sometimes envisaged. It is in the courtly arena that we see the most intense signs of aristocratic opposition to the humanist project. There we also see a growing awareness among humanist writers themselves of the problems and dangers attendant upon translating theory into practice amid the Tudor court's complex power struggles.

Nevertheless, a variety of court-centered texts from the 1520s through the 1540s (including letters, pamphlets, and such works of political theory as More's *Utopia*, Starkey's *Dialogue*, and Elyot's *Image of Governance*) reveal traces of humanist theory at work in the political arena. Gathering and framing remain effective strategies for the articulation of authoritative but nonthreatening supplements to the monarch's power. As a rhetorical strategy, the collection and redeployment of commonplaces provided a relatively safe way to discuss the balance of power at court. Rival aristocratic and humanist factions used some of the same commonplaces about advice giving to lay claim to a share of power; however, because of their training in the use of such material, humanists were able to establish a special claim to the status of adviser. The humanist education outlined in the previous chapter was also useful to the men who were hired by Henry VIII to compile collections of gathered evidence adducing the support of various authorities for his marital and religious reforms. The skillful citation of maxims and commonplaces became a way of displaying the fruits of humanist education when seeking preferment and, in the right hands, proved to be an extremely flexible and effective political tool.

As we have seen in previous chapters, however, gathering and framing imply an ideology as well as a rhetoric, formed in opposition to both aristocratic and mercantile values. The commonplaces that humanists gather tend to reinforce a value system already suggested by the nature of the practices themselves. In opposition to aristocratic codes of honor, violence, and frivolous display, humanist teachers and writers sought to instill respect for learning, hard work, and serious devotion to duty. The very process of reading through approved texts, selecting their most pithy and useful bits, and laboriously transcribing them in a notebook reinforced these values.[1] And in opposition to the merchants' accumulation of capital and precipitous mobility based on wealth, humanists sought to foster a controlled and controlling accumulation of cultural capital. Thus, midcentury theories of the political and economic commonwealth were, I intend to argue, directly shaped by the humanist commonplace.

I want to show, then, that the humanist model of counselor, and the discursive practices of gathering and framing which shaped it, contributed a strong and viable set of gestures of courtly authority, and that these gestures were influential at court throughout Henry's reign, and, as I will show in the following chapter, well into Elizabeth's. The strategic deployment of sayings in discourse and the authorship of aphoristic works was the central credential of this advice-giving persona. Discussions of how sayings helped to form the political self which emerge from a courtly context differ from educational treatises in their growing sense that the "wise counselor" was itself just another pose. This change is reflected in the shifting connotations of the word "frame," which for logicians and educators implied stability and solidity, but which can also mean "counterfeit."[2] Fears that the empowering force of sayings might disrupt the social hierarchy resurface with new anxiety, leading, on the one hand, to the rearticulation of alternative aristocratic credentials for success and, on the other, to the formulation of "commonwealth" theory as a way of justifying humanist ambition. Metaphors of gathering, framing, gardening, and the cure continue to serve as vehicles for the examination of language and its role in the formation and manifestation of the powerful subject.

The political role of humanists and humanism at the court of Henry VIII and in the govermental reforms of that period has been much discussed and is highly controversial. One view, perhaps most clearly represented by James McConica's *English Humanists and Reformation Politics* or Arthur Ferguson's *The Articulate Citizen and the English Renaissance*, attributes to humanism responsibility for the moderation, "realism," and "fresh" ideas that resulted in striking religious and political reforms during Henry's reign.[3] On the other hand, Alistair Fox has argued that although humanism during the reign of Henry VIII "furnished a new ideal of what constituted a gentleman," it is "seriously to be doubted" that "impractical" Erasmian humanism had any "direct . . . influence on political decisions."[4]

Despite their difference of opinion about the actual role of humanism at Henry's court, Ferguson and Fox (and other historians as well) are in agreement about the uselessness of the aphoristic generalizations that humanists in the period so frequently employ. Fox blames the political failure of "Erasmian" humanists on their aphoristic idealism. He argues that Sir Thomas Elyot's "humanistic study had furnished him with a wealth of moral precepts . . . but the very nature of the wisdom Elyot had gathered ensured that he would not be listened to in a world dominated by corrupt 'affects.' "[5] Ferguson identifies the aphoristic language of counsel with "medieval" attitudes and laments its lasting influence on Renaissance texts that otherwise display a "modern . . . preference for the data of experience over the precepts of traditionally accepted authority."[6] Thus, despite its acknowledged importance in the period, historians, like literary critics, have relentlessly marginalized the giving of aphoristic advice.[7]

The giving of such advice was, I want to argue, itself a sophisticated maneuver in the game of courtly power, of use both to those in power and to those seeking it. To the monarch, the act (or appearance) of seeking advice was a necessary means of avoiding the accusation of tyranny and was also the basis of a useful and effective form of propaganda. For constitutional theorists, reformers, and even rebels, discussions of counsel and advice, conducted largely in commonplaces, provided a (relatively) safe vehicle for speculating about the ways in which the monarch's power could be supplemented. For those seeking preferment, aphoristic citations of classical and sacred texts demonstrated intellectual and doctrinal credentials. The gathering of abstract, moralistic "advice" couched in aphorisms was much safer than giving concrete, possibly unpalatable advice about contemporary issues, and concrete advice couched in aphoristic form retained a protective generality. Since the sayings cited by humanists almost always reinforce the hierarchical cultural code, they provide a way to keep ambition and social mobility within acceptable bounds. Also, in an era of shifting power and loyalty, aphoristic language could be reframed and recycled to signal allegiance to figures as different as Wolsey, Cranmer, Somerset, Gardiner, and Cecil.[8] Finally, for some, the use of moral sententiae provided a way to grapple with their growing concerns about the duplicity needed to survive and thrive at court, while for others, it provided a way to hide that duplicity from themselves and from others.

The idea that good counsel is a necessary supplement to the monarch's power was commonplace in England as early as the thirteenth century. According to Ferguson, such medieval works as the *Song of Lewes* and *Mum and Sothsegger* offer "good counsel" as "the master remedy prescribed for the political ills" of the time. For Ferguson, this emphasis grows out of an overly "personal" view of government, "the implication being that the king alone is the source of policy."[9] Ferguson does, however, praise Fortescue's fifteenth-century *Government of England* for the way in which it "embodied" commonplaces about good counsel "in a specific recommendation for reform of the actual group of councilors surrounding the King."[10]

Fortescue was perhaps to first to articulate and explore the idea that the English monarchy was not absolute, but limited.[11] He defined the English monarchy as a "dominum politicum et regale," a constitutional monarchy, in which, as G. R. Elton puts it, "monarchy exists under the law and is fully active in co-operation with Parliament."[12] According to Elton, the Tudor monarchs (along with most of their subjects) accepted this general notion, although exactly how the power of the monarch was to be supplemented by Parliament and council was not clearly established.[13] The monarch did have prerogative that "accorded privilege to the personal concerns and possessions of the sovereign," but this prerogative was granted by law. Not until James I did an English monarch attempt, with disastrous results, to assert that his power was without human limit.[14]

Thus, although Henry may at times have seemed to be, as Greenblatt calls him, an "autocrat," and although the Elizabethan court may have appeared to its courtiers to embody what Whigham calls a "repressive absolutist climate," under law and according to contemporary constitutional theory such claims to absolute power would have seemed to constitute illegal tyranny.[15] In the early sixteenth century, tyranny was at least in part identified as a refusal to accept good counsel and a reliance, instead, on corrupt and flattering "favorites." In order to demonstrate the disastrous effects of bad counsel, political theorists and commentators gather exempla of such notorious tyrants as Nero, Domitian, Rehoboam, Edward II, and Richard II. Fortescue, for example, argues that while the Roman emperors "were reuled bi the counsele of the Senate," the country prospered. But

> whan themperour lafte the counseill of the Senate, and somme of theime, as Nero, Dommacion, and other, had slayne grette partey of the Senatours, and were reuled by their privat counsellours, thastate of themperour fill in dekeye. . . . We also Englishemen, whos kinges som tyme were counseled by sadde and wele chosen counseilloures, bete the mightieste kinges of the worlde. But sithen our kinges have been reuled by private Counselloures. . . . we have not be able to kepe our owne lyvelode.[16]

Fortescue notes, vaguely but ominously, that "thastate" of rulers who listened to favorites "fill in dekeye," but under more pressing circumstances the same commonplaces could carry an explicit threat. In his "book of advice" addressed to the rebels during the Pilgrimage of Grace (1536–1537), Sir Thomas Tempest urges that "who reydes the crownakylls of Edwarde the ij. [will see] what juperdy he was in for Peres de G[ave]stun, Spenseres, and susche lyke cunsellars and . . . Rycharde the ij. was deposyd for folowing the cunsell of susche lyke."[17] On the other hand, Thomas Starkey, who prefers an elected monarch and believes that subjects have a duty to depose a tyrant, nevertheless upholds Henry's right to rule because he "ys euer content to submyt hymselfe to the ordur of hys conseyl, no thyng abusyng hys authoryte."[18]

Clearly, a monarch who did not appear to be accepting wise and impartial advice was in bad company and was also in danger of rebellion that might even be legally and morally sanctioned.[19] Who ought to be giving this advice—and what institutional procedures might assure it— were, however, hotly debated, each rival group asserting the familiar commonplaces in support of its own claim to a share of power. In the fifteenth century, Fortescue was concerned to insure that the ongoing consolidation of power in a central, bureaucratic monarchy would not lead to tyranny. He favored institutionalizing a representative council so that the king would be advised not by "menn of his chambre" but by "a counseill of Spirituall men xij, and of temporel men xij, of the mooste wise and indifferente that can be chosen in alle the londe."[20] Thomas Tempest seems to echo Fortescue's concerns when he urges Henry to have a council of "susche vertus men as woylde regarde the communwelthe abuffe their princys lo[ve]," but he and the other "Pilgrims" of 1536 were really demanding that the king accept the advice of aristocrats like themselves and not "upstart" humanists favored by Cromwell.[21] In this context, bland assertions that the king needs wise and virtuous advisers represent a claim to power and a sanction for sedition should such power not be extended to the claimants.

While political theorists and aristocratic rebels used these commonplaces to explore the roles of king, council, and Parliament in Tudor England, humanists recognized their special usefulness in their own cause. As we saw in earlier chapters, English humanists focused their educational program on preparing themselves and their students for the supplemental roles of teacher and adviser. According to political theory (and royal ordinance), the king needed advisers who were "honourable, virtuous, sad, wise, expert, and discreet"—exactly the qualities, coupled with eloquence, that a man framed by gathered sententiae would possess.[22] As we recall from educational theory, good advisers need "prudence" consisting of a store of sayings, exempla, and precedents that could frame the judgment to provide proper advice.

Humanist political theory takes pains to gather from classical sources injunctions that establish wisdom (rather than birth or wealth) as the criterion for advancement to positions of authority at court. In these passages we can quite clearly see the link between discursive practices and ideology. William Baldwin's influential *Treatise of Morall Philosophie* devotes its longest section to aphorisms "Of Kings, Rulers, and Governours, and how they should rule their subiects," where we learn that according to Protagoras "most miserable is the state of that country and common-wealth, where rich men that be fooles are more commonly chosen, then rich wise men, or poore men enriched by wisedome, to governe in the common-wealth."[23] Here, a complex series of puns suggests that the Commonwealth itself ought to be based on a common wealth of wisdom rather than on actual monetary wealth. We also learn that, according to Alexander Severus, those who rule should be "sufficiently furnished with wisdome and gravitie," and that according to Marcus Aurelius, "princes live more surely with the gathering to them men of good living and conversation, then with treasures of money stuffed in their chests."[24] Good government is based on proper gathering, not of money, but of men who have themselves gathered a store of wisdom. A humanist who wanted a job at court—whether as adviser, tutor, propagandist, ambassador, or secretary—would display an aphoristic style as a sign that he was "sufficiently furnished with wisdome and gravitie," and capable of "good conversation."[25]

Examples of aphoristic self-advertisement can be found in letters written by office seekers to those in power.[26] Roger Ascham, writing to Thomas Cranmer, as McConica notes, under the "slender pretext" of seeking a dispensation from fasting but with the actual purpose of demonstrating his humanist and Protestant credentials for preferment, provides an excellent example of this style.[27] In support of his requested dispensation he cites St. Paul (in Greek) and recounts an exemplum from Herodotus that he cleverly turns to a critique of papist superstition. He also quotes sententiae attributed to Cicero and Plato, mentions Augustine, Aristotle, Thucydides, Xenophon, Homer, Sophocles, Euripides, Terence, and Virgil, and explicitly cites the humanist theory behind his use of such aphorisms and references when he remarks that "I apply Plato and Aristotle to this matter, from which fountains speaking among the Greeks the quality of prudence is best able to be drunk in."[28] Here, the reference to the apostle demonstrates a Protestant predilection for the Pauline books, knowledge of Greek, and the ability to cite Scripture to support Protestant doctrine. The use of Herodotus reveals the ability to use classical sources, wittily, for a similar purpose, and the references to Cicero, Plato, and Aristotle claim access to privileged sources of political and moral wisdom. And in case Cranmer missed the point, Ascham reminds him that such sayings provide evidence that the writer has drunk deeply from the fountain of prudence.

Although they could be used to register allegiance to specific political and religious causes, the fact that sayings were by nature detached and "gathered" from their context gave them strategic flexibility. We find Ascham, for example, citing the same aphorism from Sophocles (still showing off his Greek) in letters asking preferment from Stephen Gardiner under Mary and again from Cecil under Elizabeth. Ironically, the line, in Ascham's translation, claims a unique relationship to a single patron: "I have that I have only by you and by no mo."[29] By expressing this idea in the form of a gathered quotation, Ascham distances himself from it and masks his political opportunism with a demonstration of learning.

In a similar letter to Cromwell (of 24 July 1536), Thomas Starkey defends his political and religious orthodoxy with reference to commonplaces that he has "geddryd [gathered] of scripture . . . wych though they may peraventure appere vulgare and commyn and to be but of smal moment and weyght, yet by them I doo examyn al the wrytyngys, sayinges, and doyngys of thys tyme."[30] Here, echoing humanist rhetorical theory, Starkey defends against a charge of heresy by stressing that his judgments are framed by common belief. In Starkey's *Dialogue*, Reginald Pole's fitness to serve as adviser is attributed to the fact that he has been "so wel nuryschyd and brought vp, so wel set forward to geddur [gather] prudence and wysdom" (3), qualities that he demonstrates in the *Dialogue* with his store of sayings.[31]

In practice, however, even humanists who were selected by the king, Wolsey, Cromwell, or Cranmer for preferment did not necessarily end up giving prudent advice to a grateful monarch. Cromwell, as McConica has shown, took on Starkey and other humanists to serve as propagandists in support of the divorce and the Act of Supremacy.[32] Their training in gathering authoritative sayings provided an ideal background for their work, which consisted largely of searching libraries and questioning eminent scholars in order to compile weighty support for the king's position. Ferguson disparagingly asserts that in their pamphlets they "drew mainly on the stock of ideas common to late medieval Christendom and spent most of their ingenuity in a desperate and pragmatic search for the most impressive precedents and the most useful authorities."[33] These precedents were necessary, however, and works such as the *Collectanea satis copiosa* enlist the powerful notion of gathered copia in support of the idea that Henry was acting in accordance with the legal and moral cultural codes, as a recipient of good advice, and not as a tyrant led solely by his passions or "affects."

It was thus of vital importance that influential advisers acknowledge the force of collected commonplaces on Henry's side. Starkey, who was assigned to "collect" the opinion of Reginald Pole, offers Pole, in a letter of 1535, a rather desperate lesson in gathering: if he will "way the placys of the gospel and scripture" he will "fynd non manyfestly prouyng" papal supremacy, but, on the contrary, "the commyn placys you know how yt they are understood contrary therby diverse and many, as when the dyscypelys of chryste contendyd for superiorite you know what chryst sayd; you know how poule confessyth [he] knowyth only christ for heed, cyuyle and polytyke hedys he confessyd many, *sed iure divino, nullum.*"[34] Pole, of course, did not agree, and in his *Pro ecclesiasticae unitatis defensione* he formulates an early version of resistance theory based in part on equating tyranny with bad counsel.[35] Indeed, Henry's repeated efforts to secure the approval of influential and learned men like Pole and More suggest how important he felt it was to appear to be receiving, if not advice, then at least humanist sanction after the fact, and also how important gathering was in providing that sanction.

The success of humanists in exploiting the monarch's need for their gathering skills and gathered wisdom should not, however, obscure the doubts and problems that necessarily accompanied the translation of their theories into practice. We have seen how, in theory, humanists felt constrained to accompany their claim to power with the reassurance that their power was limited by its basis in common belief: thus, their own social mobility did not (in theory) present a threat to hierarchy because it was grounded in the cultural code of a hierarchical society. The sayings that politically ambitious humanists "gather" and display are, almost invariably, deeply conservative, thus representing a uniquely nonthreatening form of primitive accumulation. The motto of the powerful Nicholas Bacon, gathered from Seneca, was *medocria firma* (roughly "the middle way is secure"). William Cecil adopted mottoes expressing stability (*cor unum, via una*; "one heart, one way"), cautious prudence (*prudens qui patiens*; "he is prudent who is patient"), and awareness of his place in the hierarchy (*nolo minor me timeat, dispiceatve major*; "I do not want any lesser person to fear me, or any greater to despise me").[36] M. E. James has shown how the "Tudor magnate" Henry, fifth earl of Northumberland, expressed his acquiescence in the humanist and bureaucratic centralized administration of the Tudors with a series of "proverbs" painted "in the roofe of the hyest chambre" of his house. These sayings transform the old Percy motto *esperaunce* into moral *sententiae* that disclaim ambition: "Esperaunce en dyeu / Trust hym he is moste trewe," "Esperaunce in exaltation of honoure, / Nay it widderethe away lyke a floure."[37]

In practice, however, it was a deeply threatening idea that a particular kind of education (or, indeed, a prose style indicative of that education) could replace birth and wealth as criteria for access to power. It posed the greatest threat, as Lawrence Stone points out, to the aristocrats whom it disenfranchised, and until they were able, in the seventeenth century, to recast educational credentials on the basis of attendance at certain elite (and expensive) schools, they were forced to reassert an alternative training for aristocratic youth.[38] It also threatened the humanists themselves, who saw in their own upward mobility not only potentially dangerous eminence but also a disquieting acquiescence in capitalist and republican tendencies and a palpable threat to the concepts of order and hierarchy that they promulgated. These issues surface (in the 1520s through the 1540s) in the form of preoccupation with "value," and in discussions of what society ought to value and how "wealth" (both monetary and cultural) should be displayed and shared.

Stone has shown how the "educational revolution" effected by English humanists contributed to the "crisis of the aristocracy" in the seventeenth century. He argues that in the sixteenth century, the new ideal of "gentleman" based on education "increased the opportunities of the gentry to compete for office on more equal terms with the nobility."[39] There are signs, however, of aristocratic resistance to the humanist system of counsel, and in this resistance lie the seeds of the alternative model of courtly advancement, the Italianate courtier. According to this model, "worth" is manifested through the conspicuous consumption of "worthless" trifles (clothes, jewelry) and participation in frivolous pastimes (hunting, dicing, dancing, composing love lyrics).[40]

As noted in previous chapters, the traditional youthful training for aristocrats in prehumanist times took place in aristocratic households and centered on instruction in music, service at table, and hunting.[41] Of these activities, hunting is most often used to represent this curriculum in contrast to the humanist program. A famous remark related by Richard Pace in his *De fructu qui ex doctrina percipitur* (The benefit of a liberal education) sets up the paradigmatic conflict between study and hunting. Pace tells how a drunken nobleman claims that it is more suitable for "sons of the nobility . . . to blow the horn properly, hunt like experts, and train and carry a hawk gracefully" than to go to school.[42] Hunting represents training in martial skills necessary to noblemen under the older feudal system and also, increasingly, participates in what Frank Whigham calls the "fetish of recreation": noblemen indulged their preoccupation with sport in order to demonstrate a "mode of life characterized by leisure, spontaneity, the private, the casual."[43] Only aristocrats possessed the status and wealth that enabled development of skill in "trifling" pastimes. Aristocratic training also valued natural grace and ability more than the diligent labor necessary in the humanist classroom. Thus, educated aristocrats are often described as *cultus* ("cultivated," implying the cultivation of natural talents) and educated humanists as *doctus* ("learned," implying exposure to a given curriculum). In addition, hunting reinforced the chivalric code of honor, which, in a feudal society, served to "legitimize and provide moral reinforcement for a politics of violence" antithetical to humanist ideology.[44]

Humanists who acted as tutors to a royal or noble family in the early years of the sixteenth century felt the aristocratic resistance to their program most directly. John Palsgrave and Richard Croke, humanist tutors to Henry Fitzroy, duke of Richmond and illegitimate son of Henry VIII, complained repeatedly that their charge was surrounded by men who encouraged him to hunt and hawk and neglect his studies.[45] Resistance to humanism in this case was probably exacerbated by the location of Richmond's household far from London in the conservative, aristocratic north of England.[46] Writing to Sir Thomas More around 1529, Palsgrave complained that the duke "hathe all redye and euery day schall haue more and more sondry callers vpon hym to bryng hys mynde from lernyng, som to here a crye at a hare, somm to kyll a bucke with hys bow, somtyme with grayhowndes and somtyme with buckhowndes."[47] Furious at the constant subversion of his humanist program, Croke writes to Wolsey demanding that Fitzroy

> shuld wryte noo thyng of his owen hande but in Latten . . . to thentent he myght more fermely imprynte in his mynde both wordes and phrases of the Latten tonge, and the soner frame hym to some good stile in wrytinge whereunto he is now very ripe. . . . and that no man may force hym to wryte oonles I be there presente, to dyrecte and forme his said hande and stile.[48]

To the freedom of hunting is opposed the discipline of humanistic study, intended to "fermely imprynte" the mind, and "frame," "dyrecte and forme" handwriting, style, and, by extension, belief and behavior. Both tutors are concerned to defend the authority of the humanist teacher and his curriculum, and to maintain the teacher's right to impose discipline on a person of superior rank. Hunting, on the other hand, is entirely the prerogative of the duke and his aristocratic companions.

Interestingly, Thomas Cromwell, identified by McConica as the primary humanist patron during Henry's reign, seems to have consulted both paradigms when planning the education of his own son Gregory. Gregory's tutor Henry Dowes, in a letter to Cromwell, reports on an educational program that combines both humanist and aristocratic values in a curious mix. Dowes interprets his assignment as being "to instructe hime with good lettres, honeste maners, pastymes of instrumentes, and suche other qualities as sholde be for hime mete and conveniente."[49] Instruction in humanist "good lettres" consists of reading one of Erasmus's colloquies, comparing the Latin with an English translation, and giving special emphasis to "the preceptes of the same." Gregory Cromwell also practices his handwriting and reads Fabian's chronicle, but "the residue of the day he doth spende upon the lute and virginalls." Far from discouraging hunting, Dowes notes approvingly that "for his recreation he useth to hawke and hunte, and shote in his long bowe, which frameth and succedeth so well with hime that he semeth to be thereunto given by nature."[50] Dowes is concerned not to frame Gregory in prudence and wisdom but to reassure his (upwardly mobile) father that his son's skill in chivalric pastime frames itself in him as in a true aristocrat.

In contrast to the Cromwell curriculum, the royal school organized by Catherine Parr for the education of Edward, Elizabeth, and various noble children seems to have chosen a humanist (and Protestant) rather than aristocratic curriculum. This change may reflect Catherine's own beliefs as well as the increasing influence of the humanist model. As we saw in the previous chapter, Grindal, Cheke, and Ascham sought to inculcate their charges with the practices of gathering and framing. Part of this program involved conveying to Edward especially that his power required supplementation by humanist advice.

Edward's own early letters are in strict accordance with the humanist aphoristic epistolary style. Writing to Cranmer in 1546, Edward notes that he has "received much fruit from your letters, because in them you urge me, and apply a kind of goad to me to learn 'good letters,' which will be of use to me when I am grown up."[51] Edward has picked up the language of his teachers and a properly submissive attitude toward educational authority: he has gathered "fruit" from Cranmer's letter that also acts as a disciplinary "goad." In the remainder of this short letter Edward cites sententiae by Aristippus and Cicero. Edward was clearly being brought up to resemble Elyot's description of the ideal ruler, Alexander Severus, who "loved all men that were learned, and feared them also," and "ordeyned greatte salaryes to be gyven to rhetorycians, teachers of grammar," and other learned men.[52] Unfortunately (for his tutors at least), Edward did not live long enough to establish this humanist paradise.

Henry, of course, did not have such a submissive attitude toward humanist advice. Although he recognized its uses and the necessity of appearing to receive it, the dangers attendant upon failing to give him the advice he wanted are well documented. Indeed, the dangers of giving unpalatable advice to a ruler were a major theme informing discussions of advice giving or the "problem of counsel." Discussions of this "problem" become particularly pointed under the pressures generated by humanist expectations and courtly reality, and texts by Thomas More, Thomas Elyot, and Thomas Starkey manifest a range of approaches to it. All of these writers attempt to represent a version of the ideal state in which commonplaces of advice are accepted and humanist credentials are valued above all other signs of worth. Particularly interesting is their changing sense of the relationship between texts and the educated subject, the growing sense that courtly service requires some sort of dissimulation, and their uneasiness about the radical social implications of the humanist project.

Thomas More's career as Henry's "pet humanist," his advancement to the Privy Council and chancellorship, his refusal to countenance the divorce and break with Rome, and his subsequent execution are well known.[53] Equally well known is his discussion of what J. H. Hexter calls "the humanist dilemma" in book 1 of *Utopia*, the fact that although "wise, and learned councilors" are needed to advise the king, courts are "nests of evil, ruled by flattering sycophants," which wise and learned men will try to avoid.[54] In his "dialogue of counsel," Morus and Hythlodaeus debate the relative merits and disadvantages of humanist service at court, a debate given point by Erasmus's recent appointment as "counselor" to Charles, archduke of Burgundy, and Henry's offer of employment to More.[55]

Utopia, published in 1516 when Wolsey's ascendancy and patronage of humanists like More and Lily sparked hopes that the humanist program was on the verge of success, nevertheless seems designed to reveal fissures and inconsistencies within that program which many humanist treatises attempt to mask. Instead of offering commonplaces in the subjunctive mood couched as advice (as do Starkey and Elyot), More literally gives those commonplaces a "place," called "no place," where everything is common. The commonplaces upon which Utopian society is founded are helpfully noted in the margins, and they span the range of gathered matter from cited sententia to aphorism, to fable, to proverb.[56] We learn, for example, that Utopian communism has been gathered from Plato ("These features smack of Plato's Community"), their agrarian program from Virgil ("The Usefulness of Gardens Proclaimed also by Virgil"), and aspects of their governmental system from the aphoristic formulations of the cultural code ("Tyranny Hateful to the Well-Ordered Commonwealth").[57]

The "dialogue of counsel" provides a helpful introduction to Hythlodaeus's ideal humanist state. In the dialogue, Hythlodaeus appears as a rigidly moralistic reformer who rejects humanist compromise for a more radical "cure." Morus, on the other hand, takes the pragmatic strain of humanist thought to an extreme, arguing that it does not really matter if the prudent adviser is just another pose. For Hythlodaeus, only communism can provide the radical realignment of value necessary to, in effect, cause every person to internalize humanist advice.

Stephen Greenblatt has emphasized Morus's description of the theatricality of courtly performance.[58] He contrasts Morus's advocacy of "accommodation to the play at hand" with Hythlodaeus's defense of "authenticity," of behavior as a direct reflection of a stable inner self. The theatrical metaphor and its implication that the adviser's self-conscious display of prudential advice is simply a pose, rather than an expression of an authentic and carefully framed self, departs radically from the accounts of framing that we saw in educational treatises. More's treatment of the problem of counsel echoes a number of humanist metaphors, however, and examination of those metaphors reveals the extent to which his conception of the issue of counsel has been shaped by the humanist project. Finally, however, both Hythlodaeus and Morus, in different ways, reject the logic of gathering and supplementation.

Hythlodaeus is introduced as a strongly humanist figure who has, as one critic has noted, "a certain unnerving resemblance" to Erasmus.[59] His "sunburnt countenance" represents, to be sure, the effects of travel, but it also alludes to the common description of the humanist scholar as burned by prolonged exposure to the "sun" of ancient literature.[60] It is Morus, however, who begins the "dialogue" by repeating several humanist commonplaces: "From the monarch, as from a never-failing spring, flows a stream of all that is good or evil over the whole nation" (57). He joins Peter Giles in urging on Hythlodaeus the humanist assumption that a wise and learned man has a duty to ensure the purity of this fountain.

Hythlodaeus counters this suggestion with a conflation of humanist metaphors of planting and disease. Kings, he says, are commonly "infected" from childhood with "wrong ideas," so that "if I proposed beneficial measures [lit. *decreta sana*, healthy precepts] to some king and tried to uproot from his soul the seeds of evil and corruption, do you not suppose that I should be forthwith banished or treated with ridicule" (86–87).[61] Despite his humanist training, Hythlodaeus denies the efficacy of "decreta sana" as a cure for monarchal infection. Although he imagines the "seeds of evil and corruption" as susceptible to weeding, Hythlodaeus predicts that the king will deny his need for the supplemental cure and will banish the physician and gardener.

Morus responds first by denying Hythlodaeus's organic metaphors for the self. He suggests that a counselor should not expect to act at court in accordance with the ethical precepts with which he has been framed, nor should he expect to cure or cultivate the king. Instead, he should employ an approach that "knows its stage, adapts itself to the play in hand, and performs its role neatly and appropriately [*concinne et cum decoro*]" (98–99). The humanist adviser's Senecan sententiae and pointed references to Nero are themselves, to Morus, simply a role in a play, and an inappropriate one in the courtly farce. Morus's perception of the counselor's authorizing gestures as simply an assumed role, rather than the expression of his wisdom and prudence, marks a radical departure from humanist theory and serves as a threatening demystification of it.

Indeed, even Morus pulls back from this view and appropriates Hythlodaeus's organic metaphors: "If you cannot pluck up wrongheaded opinions by the root, if you cannot cure [*mederi*] according to your heart's desire [*ex animi tui sententia*] vices of long standing, yet you must not desert the commonwealth. You must not abandon the ship in a storm because you cannot control the winds" (98–99). Morus cedes Hythlodaeus's perception that the kingly self cannot be supplemented against his will, and then shifts to an inorganic metaphor which reflects a less personal view of government. The king becomes a wind that blows against the ship of state, and the humanist adviser becomes the captain of that ship. Hope inheres in a theory of government that does not attribute absolute power to a capricious monarch.

Hythlodaeus will not accept this, or any, compromise. He stubbornly maintains his organic metaphor and concludes that he would "share the madness of others as I tried to cure their lunacy" (101). Again, Hythlodaeus perceives the logic of supplementation whereby the cure becomes a poison, the doctor himself the patient. His answer is to reject supplementation altogether in favor of various forms of absolutism. He rejects, for instance, humanist accommodation of Christian and pagan truth, criticizing those who treat Christ's absolute law "as if it were a rule of soft lead" (101). Finally, he seeks a complete cure for the ills of society in a radical reorganization of property, which would do away with the need for humanist wisdom altogether.

Morus realizes the threat of Hythlodaeus's solution to the humanist project: "How can there be a sufficient supply [*copia*] of goods when each withdraws himself from the labor of production?" (107). Although his comment directly addresses the production of actual goods, it also extends to the humanist intellectual program. If ideas and texts cannot be gathered and owned, there will be no incentive for education or scholarly work, and thus no copia of words or ideas. Morus, however, has not imagined the full disciplinary technology of Hythlodaeus's communist society, where learning is valued as an empowering possession, but also, more importantly, as a system of control.

Utopian society resembles subsequent humanist utopias in its rejection of the conspicuous consumption of trifles as an aristocratic credential of value. This is probably the most memorable feature of Utopian culture, not surprisingly, since it becomes a virtual obsession. Much of the state apparatus of Utopia seems aimed at avoiding the situation common in other cultures where, since "money [is] the standard of everything, it is necessary to practice many crafts which are quite vain and superfluous [*inanes prorsus ac superfluas*], ministering only to luxury and licentiousness" (130–31). In order to avoid distinctions based on consumption, Utopians live in identical houses that are exchanged by lot every ten years (120–21). They share the humanist aversion to such trifling pastimes as dicing and hunting, which are described as "senseless delights" (*ineptias laetitias*; 170–71). Necessary hunting for food is assigned to slaves in order to prevent its use as a sign of social status (as well as its brutalizing

PASTIME OR PROFIT 107

influence). The Utopians have also constructed elaborate practices to de-value gold and precious jewels, practices which would presumably be unnecessary in a society that had never valued such things. The marginal notes in this section reveal the affinities between Utopian hatred of jewelry and humanist desire to discredit aristocratic credentials: "Foolish Honors," "Meaningless Nobility," "Pleasure from Gems most Foolish" (168–69). All of these precautions are intended to remedy a state of affairs that Hythlodaeus perceives in the rest of the world, whereby "a blockhead who has no more intelligence than a log and who is as dishonest as he is foolish keeps in bondage many wise men and good men merely for the reason that a great heap of gold coins happens to be his" (157).

In the absence of monetary or material credentials of success, Morus's prediction that there will be no "place" for authority or respect for magistrates might seem accurate. However, an alternative system of valuation gradually becomes apparent. At first, Hythlodaeus seems to imply that all Utopian citizens share the same education and the same social status and responsibilities. Initially, Hythlodaeus's account implies that all education is vocational, and there is no mention of "good letters": "besides agriculture (which is, as I said, common to all), each is taught one particular craft as his own" (125–27). Here one's only private property is his craft. The marginal comments emphasize the universality and uniformity of this training: "Trades to be Learned with an Eye to Necessity, not Luxury"; "No Citizen Lacking a Craft."

It might seem, then, that Louis Montrose's comment about the Utopian work ethic is true: "Idleness—an aristocratic prerogative in Renaissance Europe—must be rigorously excluded from the lives of *all* Utopians. Labor, both manual and intellectual, is at once an acknowledgment of the defective human condition and the means of its repair."[62] A few pages later, however, we begin to learn that intellectual labor is considered as exemption from work, and even as a form of "vacation" or idleness carrying a concomitant social cachet. Here, marginal notes again reinforce the idea that everyone has the same status, but More's use of litotes suggests that this concept is being eroded. We learn first that "Not Even the Officials Stop Working" (131), which introduces the possibility that social status *might* result in exemption from work, and this expectation is realized, although qualified, when we later learn that "there are not many in each city who are relieved from all other tasks and assigned to scholarship" (159).[63] The means for determining this exemption is confusingly described: "The same exemption is enjoyed [*gaudent*] by those whom the people, persuaded by the recommendation of the priests, have given perpetual freedom from labor [*vacationem*] through secret vote of the Syphogrants so they may learn thoroughly the various branches of knowledge [*disciplinas*]" (130–31). We are left unsure as to whether this decision is in the hands of the people, the priests, or the Syphogrants, but it is clear that such an exemption is prized: those who have it are said to "enjoy" their freedom from work, and a bit later it is described as an attribute of social class.[64] Workmen who show special aptitude in scholarly pursuits are "advanced into the class of the men of learning," from which class "ambassadors, priests, tranibors, and finally the governor himself" are chosen (133). What begins as a society of workers with no "place" or status becomes a meritocratic hierarchy ruled by a class of nonworking scholars.[65]

We might ask at this point how the Utopian workers are persuaded to accept the valuation of scholarly credentials and the devaluation of money. Hythlodaeus tells us that the success of Utopian society is based on the "good opinions" held by its people, opinions which are a result of their "upbringing, instruction, and reading good books" (*educatio, doctrina et literis*). Although less than five hundred people devote all of their time to scholarly pursuits, all citizens are "introduced to good letters" (*imbuunter literis*, lit. "imbued with letters"). Priests are in charge of this education, which is described in terms combining nurturance and coercion in ways that are familiar from humanist educational treatises. The priests are said to "take the greatest pains from the very first to instill into children's minds, while still tender and pliable, good opinions which are also useful for the preservation of their commonwealth. When once they are firmly implanted in children, they accompany them all through their adult lives and are of great help in watching over the condition of the commonwealth" (229).[66]

The implantation of good matter in a child's tender mind is a common humanist trope, but the idea that such "opinions," once implanted, become a kind of perpetual and personal "big brother" who accompanies and watches over each citizen goes beyond anything imagined by educational theorists.[67] There is no need for supplemental advice in this society because such advice is internalized by each person. More strikingly anticipates Foucault's ideas about the internalization of discipline, and the most frightening thing about Utopia is not the cancellation of the self, but the extent to which education is used to create a kind of surveillant double.

As a result, the total cure that Hythlodaeus believes communism alone can effect is itself revealed as problematic. Although communism is supposed to cure social problems, the Utopians tend instead to exclude potential agents of disease (such as slaughterhouses and hospitals) from their cities.[68] The effect of this is not to cure disease, but to spread it more widely abroad. The Utopian work ethic is also described as a cure for the infertility of the earth: "Thus the earth is cured by industry" (178).[69] However, as we saw, public acceptance of the curative powers of communism and universal labor can only be enforced by exempting some citizens from them. That labor is a cure and idleness a disease can only be accepted if certain people are exempted from work in order to indoctrinate the rest. Education is thus, even in Utopia, both cure and disease, and More's use of the cure metaphor serves finally to make drastic institutional change seem both necessary and problematic.[70]

Utopia thus reveals itself to be in part a humanist wish-fulfillment fantasy where everyone is equal but humanist scholars are more equal than others. Although Hythlodaeus avoids simply substituting intellectual capital for money, his picture of good opinions as disciplinary technology is more chilling. Like Morus's theatrical metaphor, Hythlodaeus's ideal state glimpses realities not widely recognized in this period; in fact, most humanist discussions of counsel use commonplaces and commonplace analogies to efface or conceal these realities. Thus, the humanist states envisioned by Starkey and Elyot are based upon many of the same commonplaces as Utopia, but they are not concerned to address, as More seems to be, the problems that would accompany their successful adoption. Instead, Starkey and Elyot are increasingly concerned to defend the place of the humanist adviser and his commonplaces in the political arena from charges of both personal and systemic failure. In their works, aphorism and commonplace become defensive strategies that cover up, rather than reveal, the problems inherent in the system.

Thomas Starkey was initially fairly successful at achieving and maintaining his place at court. Hired to solicit Pole's opinion on the divorce and supremacy, he at least survived the king's disappointment in the results. His letters reveal some of the reasons for his staying power. In the wake of the Pole disaster, Starkey makes brilliant use of humanist commonplaces to defend himself in this letter of 1536 (probably to Cranmer or Cromwell):

> I forge no mean but that wych I fynd wryten in goddys worde, and approuyd by the iugement of our clergy. Trothe hyt ys that I can not frame my iugement to plese al men, beyng in such varyety of sentence and controuersye, for some perauenture yet thynke truthe to be treyson, and some perauenture that hyt ys heresye, betwyx whome I stond, and wyl so long as I schal stond in thys lyfe. from thys truthe you schal fynd me my lord to be no sterter, wauerar, nor hengar in the wynd, for thys ys goddys truthe, lying betwyx this sedycyouse extremytes.[71]

Starkey claims here that he has not invented ("forged") his moderate position but has gathered it from Scripture. He presents himself as solidly grounded in this gathered truth, unable to "frame" (in the pejorative sense) his opinion to please those in power. He contrasts the stability of his gathered truth with the windblown wavering of Machiavellian time-servers. Of course, Starkey might also be accused of similar framing and forging: he advertised his close friendship with Pole in order to get his assignment and then claimed after the fact that he had always known Pole's judgment to be corrupt.

A letter to Henry reveals Starkey's adept use of familiar humanist commonplace to palliate specific advice. Concerned to insure that land and money received from the suppressed monasteries be used for relief of the poor and to support learning, Starkey carefully couches this unwelcome advice in sententious form: "When I consydur your graces hygh wysedome and prudence wherby your hyghnes most clerly seeth how the welthe of al pryncys hengyth chefely of the welth of theyr subyectys, and how penury ever bredyth sedytyon, and how the hepyng of tresure wythout lyberalyte, hathe always brought in ruyne and destructyon of euery commynalty, I am then certayn and sure that" the king will "most lyberally dyspense thys tresure and dyspose thys ryches, to the ayd succur and comfort of your most louyng and obedyent pore subjectys." He is equally sure that the king will support men who are "necessary to the mayntenance of commyn pollycy, that ys to say, men of letturys and lernyng, and men exercysyd in featys of armys and chyualrye."[72] Like More, Starkey sees "hepyng of tresure" as a threat to the humanist project, but instead of arguing for the eradication of monetary value, he is concerned merely to guarantee that scholars get a piece of the action. He cleverly attributes an adviser's prudence and knowledge of commonplaces about the distribution of wealth to the king himself. By so doing, he distances himself from what may be unpalatable advice and attempts to ground that advice in the cultural code. He also subtly reminds the king that acting against prudent advice (and failing to reward learned advisers) can lead to "sedytyon."

Starkey appears to have been undisturbed by the possibility that his clever use of humanist rhetoric was simply an expedient pose. His *Dialogue*, however, reveals that he *was* bothered by the social implications of advancement based on educational credentials rather than birth, and by the capitalist implications of the aggregation of knowledge as a commodity. Starkey belonged to the "Commonwealth" school of political theory, a group of thinkers in the middle years of the century who formulated the concept of the commonwealth as a transitional form of government between monarchy and representative democracy, feudalism and capitalism.[73] Under this system, every man, including the monarch, had a duty to consider first the common good of the country. In Starkey's radical version of this theory, the monarch would ideally be elected. Failing that, he must be advised by a council selected by Parliament who would ensure his concern for the commonwealth. Fiscally, individuals are encouraged to consider not personal profit but the common good, and policy is designed to prohibit financial dealings that are not beneficial to all, especially the exportation of staples in exchange for luxury goods that benefit only the rich.[74]

According to this theory, humanist "gathering" of knowledge for ambitious ends might well resemble the "hepyng of tresure" that, as he reminded Henry, "hathe always brought in ruyne and destructyon of euery commynalty." His *Dialogue* thus sees as a central "problem of counsel" the justification of the would-be counselor's ambition for advancement. The dialogue form allows him to displace this ambition onto the ambiguous figure of Pole, and onto Pole's friend Thomas Lupset, who seeks to convince Pole to apply his humanistic prudence to public service.

On the one hand, Starkey seems deeply influenced by humanist theories of gathered prudence and the accumulation of knowledge as a credential for leadership. He repeatedly describes his own dialogue as "geddrid . . . by long obseruatyon," produced as a result of his desire to "geddur and confyrme" by "experyence of the manerys of other pepull in strange natyon . . . such thinges wych I had in bokys red."[75] Lupset urges Pole to serve his country because he has had so much opportunity to "geddur prudence and wyse[dom]." On the other hand, however, the worst crime in his "commonweal" proceeds from those who "loketh chefely to theyr owne profyte" instead of to "the welth of the commynalty." Pole thus rightly worries that to seek preferment would be to "spot my lyfe wyth . . . ambycyon" (85, 214).

Starkey resolves this dilemma by stressing that humanist prudence constitutes wealth that can be profitably shared by all, in contrast to aristocratic conspicuous consumption which only benefits the wealthy consumer. An educated man who is "prudent and polytyke" ought first to "make himselfe perfayte, wyth al vertues garnyschyng hys mynd; and then to commyn the same perfectyon to other," since "lytyl avaylyth tresore closyd in coffurys," and "vertue and lernyng, not communyd to other, ys lyke vnto ryches hepyd in cornerys, neuer applyd to the vse of other" (5–6). Here, the image of learning as a stored commodity, so popular in educational treatises, is dangerous unless the commodity is made "common." Starkey's concern here reflects, among other things, the rhetoricians' ambivalence about common and uncommon language, a dilemma that he resolves by imagining the use of a garnished mind in service to the state as helping, rather than manipulating, the common people.

Strongly opposed to the shared wealth of humanist learning are the signs of aristocratic superiority. Starkey repeatedly criticizes those who "besy themselfe in makyng and procuryng thyngys for the vayne pastyme and plesure of other," exporting staple commodities to "bryng in agayn vayn tryfullys and conceytys" for the rich (80). He similarly criticizes the "educatyon of the nobylyte . . . in huntyng and haukyng, dysyng and cardyng, etyng and drynkyng, and, in conclusyon, in al vayn plesure, pastyme and vanyte," arguing that they should instead be brought up in "learnyng and letturys" as well as "featys of chyualry" (129, 186). Starkey seems nervous about the advancement of middle-class men to power on the basis of their education, and yet he seems ultimately to imagine an ideal commonwealth where humanist credentials would be the primary indicator of status. His concept of "common wealth" enables him to smooth over the conflicts between the feudal tradition and the capitalist and democratic implications of humanist counsel.

Sir Thomas Elyot was essentially a failure at persuading the king that his counsel was indispensable to the commonwealth. Alistair Fox has argued that Elyot "lived" the "humanist dilemma" imagined by More in *Utopia*, first gaining power "by disguising his true beliefs for the sake of political expediency," then speaking out and losing that power.[76] Elyot was first advanced by Wolsey to the clerkship of the Privy Council but lost that position when Wolsey fell. Then, according to Fox, he sided with "the ascendant faction," even though he secretly opposed the divorce, and procured the position of ambassador to the court of Charles V. Once there, however, he was unable (or unwilling) to advance the king's cause; instead he acted secretly on Catherine's behalf and was recalled in 1532. Despite his continued efforts, he was never able to secure another government position, and Fox attributes his failure to the unrealistic idealism of his gathered Erasmian wisdom.[77]

Elyot's later political treatises (*Pasquil the Plain*, *The Image of Governance*, and *Of the Knowledge Which Maketh a Wise Man*), however, reveal the usefulness of humanist commonplace in constituting a defensive posture against failure. Elyot is able to exploit familiar concerns about profit and supplementation in order to justify withdrawal from public life. In so doing, he defines several postures that will come to be of use in Tudor poetic self-presentation.[78]

The aspect of profit and the exploitation of symbolic capital for self-promotion that bothered both More and Starkey reappears, in a different form, in Elyot's political writings. Elyot is most concerned to defend himself against the charge that his lack of material wealth and success reveals his ineptitude as a counselor. Pace's drunken nobleman, after all, saw Erasmus's poverty as discrediting humanism: "Scholars are a bunch of beggars. Even Erasmus is a pauper, and I hear he's the smartest of them all."[79] In the preface to *The Image of Governance*, Elyot acknowledges that some readers will be "dispraysinge my studies as vayne and unprofitable, sayinge in derision, that I have nothing wonne therby, but the name onely of a maker of bokes, and that I sette the trees, but the printer eateth the fruites."[80] He assures his readers that "yf I wold have employed my study about the increace of my private commodity, which I have spent in wrytynge of bokes for others necessary, few men doubt (I suppose) that do knowe me, but that I shuld have attayned or this tyme to have ben muche more welthy, and in respect of the worlde in a more estimation" (206). Instead, having in mind the parable of the talents has caused him "to take more regarde to my last rekning, than to any riches or worldly promotion" (207). Elyot here uses several strategies to defend his lack of success. First, he echoes Starkey's "commonwealth" theory in emphasizing his concern for the common good rather than private wealth or advancement. This theory enables him to interpret lack of material success as a sign of fitness to counsel. Second, he appeals to Scripture to redefine his lack of earthly wealth as a sign, again, of moral fitness for counsel and of future heavenly reward.

Elyot also echoes More's concerns about the efficacy of advice as a cure for courtly disease. In his dialogue *Pasquil the Plain*, Pasquil attempts to convince the silent Harpocrates and flatterer Gnatho that bad advice and flattery are as dangerous to the prince as poison: "is there any poison can make him to be so abhorred of man as avarice, tyranny, or bestly lyvinge?" Echoing humanist educational theory, Pasquil identifies flattery as the source of poison:

> whan Gnatho with his flateri, and ye with your silence have ones rootid in your maisters hart false opinions, and vicious affectis, which is the poyson, that we so moche spake of, though ye after repent you, and perceyue the daunger, yet shall it perchance be impossible with speche to remoue those opinions, and cure those affectis.[81]

He also seems to accord with the optimism of the educational treatises when he argues that good advice "is not onely profitable but also of necessite muste be vsed in healing the diseases, both of the soule and also the bodie."[82]

In the "proheme" to *Of the Knowledge Which Maketh a Wise Man*, however, Elyot perceives the potential of even good advice to act as poison rather than cure: "such is of some menne the nature serpentine, that lappyng swete mylke they conuerte hit forthe with in to poyson, to distroy hym of whose liberalitie they late had receyued it."[83] Under such circumstances, he imagines his advice not as "swete mylke" or a curative drug, but as the harsh goad of disciplinary education. Those who dislike his books are compared to "a galde horse abidynge no playsters" who is "always gnappynge and kyckynge at suche examples and sentences as they do feele sharpe or do byte them."[84] Imagining his "sentences" as "playsters" or a sharp, biting goad rather than defenses or cures signals Elyot's movement from adviser and teacher to disillusioned satirist and critic.

In fact, Elyot seems undecided about what role in life he wants to claim. In *Of the Knowledge*, he presents three alternative definitions of wisdom: that it consists "in moche lernynge and knowledge," that "they whiche do conducte the affayres of greatte princis or countrayes, be onely wyse men," or that "he is wysest that leste dothe meddle, and can sytte quietly at home and tourne a crabbe, and looke onely vnto his owne busynesse."[85] In contrast to the engaged adviser, "suche [as] were Solon, Aristodes, and Phocion in Athenes, Publicola, Fabritius, Curius, and Cato Uticensis at Rome" (*Image*, 210), Elyot presents an alternative stance for a learned man, as a stoic sage happy in his rustication, or as the satirist "Pasquil" who criticizes the court from a distance.

In *The Image of Governance*, what Fox has called Elyot's "humanist wish-fulfillment fantasy" of the ideal ruler, his ambivalence about the role of the counselor is in evidence. Elyot does imagine Alexander Severus as an ideal ruler who "sent often tymes for those excellente personages [learned men] communicatynge with theym thynges whiche were done as well privily as also openly. . . . sufferynge also them to reprove hym when they seemed convenyent" (218). Alexander does not value material signs of success and seems to acknowledge humanist credentials as the only criteria for advancement. He "wolde not suffer any of his courte to weare any garment myxte with golde, or other wyse preciouse or costely; nor he hymselfe delyted in ryche apparayle, saying, That governaunce was in vertue and not in beautie or costly apparayle" (231). On the other hand, however, he "ordeyned greatte salaryes" to be given to learned men (233).[86] Similarly, Elyot imagines one Gordiane who, during the reign of the wicked Heliogabalus "withdrewe hym into suche places, as he had of his owne, ferre from the citie" (235), in a pose of stoic detachment. Yet Alexander is so impressed by a letter of advice sent to him by Gordiane that he has him made consul, "affyrmynge that his youthe required for the utilitie of the publyke weale to be ioyned with suche a companyon as Gordiane was, whose wysedome, experience, and gravitie, was of all men sufficiently knowen" (245). Here again ambition is disguised as care for the public weal, and the ideal ruler is described as one who acknowledges his need for supplementary advice.

For Elyot, the commonplaces of humanist advice offered a range of self-presentational gestures that allowed ambition to appear as patriotism and failure to be masked by Christian and stoic values. The possibility that his using these commonplaces to assume a series of self-serving roles might constitute duplicity seems not to have bothered Elyot. Indeed, his own investment in the tradition of gathering and framing seems to have reassured him of his own integrity; when "lerninge is none other thinge, but an aggregation of many mens sentences and actes to the augmenta-tion of knowledge," and when it is "knowledge that maketh the wise man" (209), the very fact that one has stored up the commonplaces of tradition guarantees authenticity. Perhaps this is why Elyot can have Pasquil casually adopt the theatrical metaphor with no sense of incongruity: "if they that be called [to counsel], wolde alwaye playe the partis of good Counsaylours . . . I wolde speake never a worde."[87]

In the political arena, then, in the turbulent years of Henry's reign, the already-qualified assertions of the humanist educators become even more tentative. Certainly these humanists succeeded in making their own brand of education and discourse into a credential for promotion, but this success was achieved only at a cost. Where rhetorical and educational theorists tried to imagine sayings as guarantors of stability of thought and language, politicians more fully realized their potential for exploitation and duplicity. Where educators could be guardedly optimistic about the moral efficacy of counsel, those in power quickly learned to use that counsel for their own purposes. And while rhetoricians and educators were able to use sayings to balance the expansive and empowering force of language with safeguards and limitations, the experience of courtly reality tended to rupture the compromise and force an awareness of the dangers (to both the upwardly mobile humanist and the hierarchal social system) of that empowerment. Nevertheless, both the substance and the rhetoric of the humanist project remained powerful forces in the discursive practices of the period, and those who wanted a share of power had to learn to negotiate them.

Chapter VI

FRAMING THE STATE:

WILLIAM CECIL AND THE HUMANIST SYSTEM,

1558–1598

T HE BRIEF, politically and religiously charged reigns of Edward
and Mary disrupted, or at least temporarily displaced, the competition between humanist and aristocratic credentials for courtly
advancement.[1] After Elizabeth's accession, however, factions at court
continued to represent themselves with slightly different versions of the
courtly and humanist codes that were outlined in the previous chapter.

In recent years, such critics as Arthur Marotti, Louis Adrian Montrose,
and Stephen Greenblatt have explored the complex Petrarchan and pastoral paradigms through which Elizabeth and her courtiers both asserted
power and mystified its origins.[2] Similarly, Daniel Javitch and Frank
Whigham have stressed the rhetorical tools and tropes provided for
power struggles at court by courtesy books such as Castiglione's *The
Courtier*. These critics (with the exception of Greenblatt) confine their
attention to the 1590s and privilege the devious, role-playing Italianate
courtier and the imaginative, rhetorically adept lyrics that he used to display his courtly skills. However, Whigham and Javitch both acknowledge, as Lawrence Stone notes, that "this ideal [the Italianate courtier] did
not pass unchallenged in sixteenth-century England, for running parallel
to it was a modified, anglicized version in which prime stress was laid on
service to the Prince in either the court or the country, and in which piety
and virtue played a larger part."[3] Nevertheless, most critics (Richard
Helgerson is an exception) dismiss the alternative tradition as naive and
ill-equipped to negotiate the realities of power politics in the English
court.

We have seen, however, that under Henry the humanist practices of
gathering and framing proved quite effective as courtly strategies. The
aphoristic adviser remained an equally influential figure at Elizabeth's
court and had a shaping influence on political and literary systems
throughout the sixteenth century. The role of adviser can be most easily
explored through the semiotic strategies and educational theories of
William Cecil, Lord Burghley, who transformed the humanist practices
of gathering and framing into subtle and effective instruments of politi-

cal power. Sayings were also of central importance in constituting the social and literary devices (such as imprese) that the younger generation of courtiers developed in order to oppose and subvert Burghley's authority.

Helgerson has most clearly and convincingly demonstrated the importance of the paternal adviser in Elizabethan literature and culture.[4] He focuses on William Cecil, Lord Burghley as the representative, through the 1580s and 1590s, of what he calls "mid-century English humanism," although figures like Sir Nicholas Bacon and even, occasionally, the queen herself shared many of Burghley's values and strategies.[5] Helgerson has been most interested in charting the reaction of younger writers to the moralistic and antipoetic values promulgated by Burghley and other members of his generation. He has usefully traced some writers' use of the prodigal son story to work out their relationship to paternal authority, and also the efforts of others to define an acceptable social role for the professional poet against Burghley's condemnation of poetry as a "trifling" amateur pastime. Helgerson's account can be supplemented, however, by a more sustained look at Burghley's place in the social and literary system of his time and his relationship to the humanist project that we have been describing so far. Such an examination reveals that Burghley both continues and significantly changes the self-presentational gestures of the humanist adviser.

Because Burghley was so powerful (serving on the Privy Council, as Elizabeth's principal secretary, and finally as lord treasurer), his version of humanist discursive practice had far-reaching influence on political faction, patronage, forms of publication, and on the conception of authority and how it should be displayed. He was notorious for his sententious style (Polonius has been identified as a parody of Burghley) and used sayings to display his authority as adviser but also to efface himself and his ambition.[6] His aphoristic language often served to intertwine self-interest and public service so inextricably that they could scarcely be separated; for example, when he meshed his role as educator with his profitable and morally questionable mastership of the Court of Wards. Sayings also served to delineate a flexible authority in his relationship with the queen and the other factions at court. In Burghley's hands sayings worked more powerfully than ever before to hide the Machiavellian implications of his behavior. Finally, at the end of his life, Burghley forced aspirants for political advancement to desperate, contradictory strategies of publication and self-promotion because he refused to recognize as adequate grounds for their advancement the humanist credentials that he himself used so well. These younger men in turn redeployed sayings in new ways in order to explore and define their developing sense of subjectivity, authority, social status, and ambition.

William Cecil's family belonged (before he was made Baron Burghley in 1571) to "the lower fringe of the untitled aristocracy, the lesser gentry."[7] His father and grandfather had held minor positions at court, and Henry rewarded his father with a grant of monastic land for his service as page of the chamber and groom of the wardrobe.[8] Although the family made its way quite successfully under the old feudal system of courtly service, they seem to have realized that new credentials were necessary and arranged to send William to St. John's College, Cambridge (1535), and then to the Inns of Court so that he could accumulate them.

This he seems to have done with remarkable success. He associated himself with the prominent humanists attached to Catherine Parr's circle at court (Cheke, Ascham, Grindal); he married Cheke's sister and then, after her death, Sir Anthony Cooke's learned daughter Mildred. A near-contemporary biography, written by a member of Burghley's household shortly after his death, openly reveals the political context of his second marriage: "after he had spent some tyme at the inns of court (where though he much proffitted yet his quick spirit, [being] apter to reach at a furder fortune) [he] framed another course in the world; betaking himself to marriage."[9] Even Cecil's romantic attachments are not trifles but purposefully "framed," although whether in the sense of "shaped by accumulated wisdom" or "counterfeited on the basis of expediency" remains ambiguous.

Throughout his life, as Helgerson has shown, Cecil consciously displayed his gathered wisdom and prudence, and his assimilation of humanist values. He became, in the words of his biographer, "famous for a scholler, in Cambridg; as he was afterwards all over Europe for a grave and greate counsellor," and was known to carry a copy of that preeminent humanist text, Cicero's *De officiis*, in his pocket.[10] He gathered collections of aphorisms for both of his sons and addressed such advice to a number of other correspondents.[11] His biographer in turn "gathered" the "apophthegms and wise speeches of the Lord Burghley," which include typical expressions of humanist political theory: "that nation was happie w[h]eare the king wold take counsell and follow it"; "a good prince must heare all, but strive to follow the best, counsell"; "noe wise prince can be a tyraunt."[12] His speech was described by a contemporary as sententious, combining the paradoxical qualities of brevity and copia, commonness and eloquence, gravity and wit that humanist rhetoricians thought sayings could provide:

> His speech ... was familiar; more plaine and compendious, then often or muche. . . . His eloquence was his playne[ne]sse in familiar common wordes, without affectation. Wherein it was observed in him [as] a thinge straunge, that, in so playne terms as comonly he used, his eloquence was so excellent, as

that [what] he spake was impossible to be delivered more rhetorically, clerely, and significantlie. . . . His ordinary speeches weare comonly cherefull, merry and familiar; but witty, sharpe, and pithy . . . he colde talke aptlie and delight-fully, and, withall, so merrely, as was much pleasing to all hearers: and yet not without gravytie, nor unfitt for a grave counsellor.[13]

Throughout his life he seems to have shared the humanist opposition to trifles and to aristocratic leisure and conspicuous consumption. He was famous for his plain dress and would have made a clear visual contrast to the leaders of the opposing factions of courtiers (Leicester, Hatton, Essex).[14] His biographer repeatedly emphasizes his open avowal of hu-manist values and his opposition to aristocratic ones: "his recreation was, chiefly, in his booke, where[with], if he had tyme, he was more delighted, then others with plaie at cards"; "he hated idleness and loved no idle persons"; "he liked best and [most] desired meane and private thinges, hating all pompe and glorious showes."[15] This biography perhaps best sums up (in familiar language) Burghley's "official" persona:

his longe experience, great age, and [*grey hairs*], his painefull service so longe in such a [high] place, his incessant studie and labor, and the great delight he took in reading, meditation, practice, and agitation of mynd, joined with his greate witt, lerning, and memorie, as it weare with one consent and true har-mony, all made theire rendevouz or receptacle of all the perfections of wisdome and virtue in him! frameing in him all the partes of a wise, godlie, worthie, and perfect counsellor.[16]

Burghley presented himself, and was perceived by at least some of his contemporaries as representing, the ideal embodiment of the successful humanist project, framed by sententious wisdom and applying that wis-dom in service to the state.

Queen Elizabeth realized the importance of having such a figure publi-cally acknowledged as her adviser. By filling her Privy Council with men like Burghley (and Sir Nicholas Bacon) rather than Ralegh and Essex, she established herself as a good monarch who accepted wise coun-sel.[17] Her statement appointing Burghley to serve on her council stresses his moral authority and her own willingness to keep silent and accept advice:

I give you this charge that you shall be of my Privy Council and content to take pains for me and my realm. This judgment I have of you that you will not be corrupted by any manner of gift . . . and that without respect of my private will you will give me that counsel which you think best and if you shall know anything necessary to be declared to me of secrecy you shall show it to myself only. And assure yourself I will not fail to keep taciturnity therein and therefore herewith I charge you.[18]

In practice, of course, Elizabeth did not always take Burghley's advice. He often complains to others that she will not follow his counsel, voicing private exasperation that "I have had such a torment herein *with the Queen's Majesty* as an ague hath not in five fits so abated."[19] His collected "wise sayings" offer a significantly ambiguous assessment of the queen's relationship to advice, noting that she "had [also] so rare gyfts, as when her counsell[or]s had saied all they cold saie, she wold [then frame] [margin, MS faine] out a wise counsell beyond all theirs."[20] Does the queen "frame" counsel based on what she gathers from her advisers, her experience, and her reading, or does she "faine" the ability to give such advice? The variant reading perhaps only emphasizes the possibilities of meaning inherent in the word "frame," and in the pose of humanist counselor that Burghley assumed so well.

Elizabeth was, in fact, capable of assuming this pose herself, in addition to that of the Petrarchan mistress or Faerie Queene. She was able to maneuver with more freedom because she could play these two systems and the factions that adopted them against each other. In the early years of her reign, when Cecil was struggling with Leicester and his aristocratic faction for the queen's favor, her participation in the courtly pastime of hunting signaled a leaning toward the courtiers. Leicester wrote to Sussex in 1559 that "the Queen, thanks be to God, is in very good health and is now become a great huntress and doth follow it daily from morning till night."[21] Around the same time, Cecil noted with displeasure that "the Court is as I left it and therefore do I mind to leave it. . . . [rather than] to continue with a perpetual displeasure to myself and my foolish conscience."[22] After the suspicious death of Leicester's wife destroyed his credibility and influence, he in turn signaled Cecil's renewed ascendancy by asking his advice: "I pray you let me hear from you what you think best for me to do."[23] The queen was able to move back and forth between the two factions and their two codes as it suited her advantage.

Her use of the courtly, Petrarchan paradigms has been much noted, but her participation in the humanist system is less documented. She advertised the fact that she had received the full humanist education from Grindal, Cheke, and Ascham by speaking Latin publically and by continuing to read Greek authors with Ascham until his death.[24] She gives aphoristic advice most notably in her correspondence with James VI of Scotland, and in speeches to Parliament where she attempts to defend her right to make her own decisions on matters of prerogative. She echoes humanist commonplace when she warns James against the "Siren's songs" of bad advice: "may enough of God's reason befall you to resist so destroying advice"; and she bombards him with aphoristic counsel ranging from Isocrates to homely proverbs: "weed out the weeds lest the best corne fester."[25] In her parliamentary speeches she uses aphoristic language to establish her ability to advise herself on matters of prerogative (such as marriage and the fate of Mary Queen of Scots).[26] Nevertheless, she was more concerned to stress that she received and accepted such advice from Burghley, and contemporary accounts of her reign reflect the success of this strategy. Camden, for example, provides a good example of the relief and approval with which male subjects approached Burghley's role: "the Queen was most happy in so great a Councillor and to his wholesome counsels the state of England for ever shall be beholden."[27]

Not everyone, however, approved of Burghley, his pose, or his influence over the queen. As Richard Helgerson has shown, a younger generation of courtiers, including such men as Francis and Anthony Bacon, the earl of Essex, and Sir Philip Sidney, rebelled against him and all that he stood for. To those who belonged to the Essex faction, Burghley was known as "old Leviathan," hated for his failure to prefer younger men (other than his son, Robert) to positions at court, and for what appeared to those young men to be the Machiavellian duplicity of his pose as the wise and virtuous adviser.[28] A closer look at Burghley's career, and especially at his involvement in the education of that younger generation, reveals the ways in which he uses humanist aphorism and commonplace to mask the ruptures and contradictions in his political posture—from others, and even, I suspect, from himself.

Burghley's biographer relates an anecdote about his days at the Inns of Court, which, like Justice Shallow, Burghley evidently relished telling about himself. The story reveals the characteristic mixture of piety and self-interest, humanist and courtly values, that Burghley would manipulate so skillfully throughout his career. As Burghley evidently told it, "a mad companion [of his, whilst he was thus at Greys Inne] inticed him to plaie. Where[upon] in [a] short tyme, he lost all his monye, beddinge, and bookes to his companion; having never used plaie before." The young Cecil, however, decided that "he wold presently have a device to be evne" with his friend: "[He] made a hole in the wall, nere his plaiefellows bedshead, and, in a fearefull voice, spake thus, through the tronke. 'O mortall man, repent! repent of thy horrible time [consumed in] plaie, cousenage, and such lewednes [as thou hast committed;] or els thou art damned, and canst not be saved!' " The next day, "in presence of the yewthes," the friend called Cecil in, "asked him forgivnes on his knees; and restored all his mony, beddinge and bookes. So two gamesters were both reclaimed with this merrie device, and never plaied more."[29]

We might notice, first of all, the ambivalent engagement in aristocratic "plaie," typical of a man who "hunted, but not so often as to incur the strictures of bookish moralists that he was wasting his time on idle sport."[30] Here, Burghley engages in gambling but can offer, as a ready excuse for losing, the fact that he is not experienced in such trifling and immoral pastimes. As with Sir Thomas Elyot, lack of success is taken as a guarantee of moral superiority. Typical, too, is his ready use of religious and ethical sanction in his own self-interest: he does not hesitate to assume the voice of God and uses the threat of damnation to get back his money and personal goods. Self-interest is, however, subsumed under an overall moral purpose, since "two gamesters were both reclaimed with this merrie device, and never plaied more." Burghley seems to see no incongruity in using play (a "merrie device") to defeat play, or in using religion as the ground of a self-interested "device." For Burghley, humanist and pious ends justify, mask, and even obliterate questionable means.

The implications of such strategies for the younger generation of courtiers and writers become clearer when we examine Burghley's attitudes toward education and his involvement in the Court of Wards. Helgerson notes that he "took a leading part in the educational affairs of the nation" through his role with the wards, his chancellorship of Cambridge University, his patronage of educators such as Ascham, and his letters of advice to young men.[31] Helgerson also notes that Burghley's educational advice seems concerned with "appearance rather than reality, form rather than substance," and this is partly true.[32] But Burghley's attitudes toward education and counsel are complex, offering a contradictory mix of aristocratic and humanist values, benevolent authority and blatant self-interest, moral discipline and display of manners. In his system, as in all of the versions of the humanist system that we have examined so far, sayings serve a central purpose in, if not reconciling, then at least smoothing over the gaps between these mixed motives and goals.

Burghley's attitude toward the education of his own sons indicates some of this complexity. The "precepts" addressed to Robert are, in the first place, intended as a supplement to the instruction of his tutor who "will furnish thy life both with divine and moral documents." Burghley intends his own collection to provide "such advertisements and rules for the squaring of thy life as are gained rather by much experience than by long reading, to the end that thou, entering into this exorbitant age, mayest be better prepared to shun those cautelous courses whereinto this world and thy lack of experience may easily draw thee."[33] Burghley does not so much ignore the moral as assume that it is "furnished" by books.[34] He intends to offer precepts that he has gathered from his own experience, but not, however, because he believes that experience is a better teacher. Burghley hopes that by gathering lessons from his own experience and transmitting them to his son as textual fragments, he will enable his son to be "squared" to "shun" such experience. Burghley's goal is to turn his son's life into a text that he has framed. "Square" here serves as a significant revision of the concept of framing. It is both more aggressive and far-reaching (because a certain, rigorously determined shape is its result) and also more concerned with appearance (because the frame is to be judged by its visible shape).[35] Burghley's version of the way in which precepts are supposed to affect the student also differs from that of most previous humanist educators. He tells his son that if he will "imprint" these aphorisms "in thy mind, then shalt [thou] reap the benefit and I the contentment." Disciplinary imprinting, agricultural nurture, and capitalist accumulation are here conflated: if precepts are imprinted, then "benefits"—not a changed self, not imperviousness to evil—will be reaped. The *process* of growth, the formation of a "self," is bypassed altogether, replaced by static, impersonal, and profitable texts.

A similar mixture of concern for disciplinary rigor and for appearance appears in a less guarded moment, when an increasingly exasperated Burghley corresponds with the tutor of his rebellious older son, Thomas. Burghley had sent Thomas abroad, armed with a similar letter of advice and a humanist tutor, in order to "square" him to a virtuous and profitable life. Thomas, however, resisted these efforts, seeming to prefer precisely those aristocratic practices of consumption and leisure which Burghley hated. The irritated father wrote to the tutor describing his son as guilty of "slothfulness in keeping his bed, negligent and rash in expenses, careless in his apparel, an immoderate lover of dice and cards; in study soon weary, in game never."[36] To Thomas himself Burghley chided, "I wish you grace to spare yourself and by some virtue to recover your name of towardness, being here commonly reputed by common fame fleeing from thence . . . specially noted no lover of learning or knowledge."[37] His concern here is with "grace" and "virtue," but specifically as they yield the benefit of "name" and "repute." Burghley does not seem to be appealing to what is rather pejoratively described as "common fame"; rather, he exhorts his son to rise above it, as Burghley himself did, through (the appearance of) learning and virtue.

In April of 1562, Thomas's recalcitrance moved Burghley to harsher, and more revealing, language: "The shame that I shall receive to have so unruled a son grieveth me more than if I had lost him by honest death. . . . I could be best content that [Throgmorton] would commit him secretly to some sharp prison. . . . If you shall come home with him, to cover the shame let it appear to be by reason of the troubles there."[38] Burghley emphasizes "shame," which he seems to feel because of his inability to "rule" his own son. He goes so far as to wish, openly, that his son were dead rather than "unruly," a direct indication of Burghley's deep fear of the Oedipal struggle of young men. For Burghley, the struggle between generations for mastery is literally a fight to the death. Once humanist discipline has failed to achieve control, Burghley advocates "some sharp prison," combining the disciplinary goad ("sharp") with segregation from society ("secretly"). If his son cannot be framed by internal discipline, external coercion must be applied in order to provide a material, confining, and obscuring frame or rule.

Burghley's position and power depended both on his ability to control (especially) younger men, and on maintaining the appearance that he could do so. Nowhere is this clearer than in his involvement with the Court of Wards, of which he was made master in 1561. As Lawrence Stone describes it, the mastership of the Court of Wards was one of the most lucrative positions granted by the queen. The court itself arose from the king's right under feudal law to "the lands and disposal in marriage of any of his tenants in chief who inherited his estates while still a minor."[39] According to Stone, "The Tudors revived this authority as a fiscal device, the Court of Wards being set up to sell to individuals the Crown's rights over the minor's person and one-third of his lands. The child could be bought from the Court, either to be married to one of the purchaser's own children or to be auctioned to the mother or another."[40] Both William Cecil and his son Robert served as masters of the court, controlling what Stone calls the "sordid traffic" in wardships, granting possession of minors "often for a fat gratuity, to courtiers, noblemen, and officials, regardless of the interest of the child and its relatives, or even of the Crown."[41] Stone notes that "the notorious abuses of the system were coming under increasing criticism at the end of the sixteenth and the beginning of the seventeenth centuries," precisely during the Cecils' tenure, and Burghley's biographer felt it necessary to include a section defending the profit he obtained from this position.[42]

Burghley's role as "pater patriae," the humanist educator of the younger generation in his own household, was thus inextricably bound up with the exploitation of wards for his own (and his friends') financial and dynastic benefit. In addition to the power he held over the futures of all the wards through his control over their goods and marriages, he evidently held (unofficial and probably gratis) rights to the most noble wards who came on the market during his mastership.[43] These were the young men who were educated in his household. Oddly enough, although Stone strongly criticizes Burghley's "sordid traffic" in wards, he later refers to his role as educator with near approval: "As Master of the Court of Wards, he made himself guardian and educational director of many young fatherless noblemen, while his reputation and influence led other parents to entrust their children to his care. Upon one and all he poured out his passion for learning as the pathway to virtue, godliness, and capacity for high office, and if his efforts were not crowned with the success he felt them to deserve, at least he created a fashion for a bookish education."[44] Was Burghley an evil purveyor of a human commodity, or a benevolent educator to whom parents "entrusted" their children? It is a tribute to his astute use of the humanist system that the answer is not readily apparent.

Despite his early roots in the humanist circles of St. John's and Catherine Parr, and despite his continued use of humanist gestures to define an anticourtly faction, Burghley's involvement in the Court of Wards reveals that his educational theories are aristocratic as well as humanist. Even as early as 1559, a draft of "Considerations Delivered to Parliament," usually ascribed to Burghley, suggests his interest in education as a means of enforcing class distinction. These proposals include the injunction that "none under the degree of baron . . . keep any schoolmaster in his house to teach children," ostensibly because this would cause "the decay of universities and common schools," but also presumably to limit the educational authority of upwardly mobile gentry.[45] This kind of educational sumptuary law functions, like similar rules for dress (of which Burghley approved) to regulate signs of social status.[46]

Another proposed statute spells out the reason for educational regulation: it would enforce noble families to provide their children with a university education because "the wanton bringing up and ignorance of the nobility forces the prince to advance new men that can serve, which for the most part neither affecting true honour, because the glory thereof descended not to them, nor yet the common wealth (through coveting to be hastily in wealth and honour), forget their duty and old estate and subvert the noble houses to have their rooms themselves."[47] Another proposal enjoins that "none study the laws, temporal or civil, except he be immediately descended from nobleman or gentleman, for they are the entries to rule and government, and generation is the chiefest foundation of inclination."[48]

The perennial humanist nervousness about social mobility resurfaces with particular intensity here. Burghley preserves the old, aristocratic notion of "honour" as the central credential for preferment but acknowledges that education is also necessary. He explicitly voices the fear that education of the lower classes in fact subverts the commonwealth because they "forget their duty and old estate and subvert the noble houses to have their rooms themselves."[49] Although his aristocratic enemies regarded William Cecil himself as a "new man," his fascination with a rather farfetched Cecil genealogy indicates that he did not wish to see himself as such.[50] In any event, he was raised to a baronetcy in 1571, ironically, however, as the letters patent spell out, for the preeminently humanist and middle-class virtues of "circumspectionem, strenuitatem, prudentiam, desteritatem, vitae integritatem, providentiam, curam et fidelitatem."[51]

The academy that he set up in his own house represents a similar conflation of humanist theory and aristocratic conservatism.[52] The very idea of training young men in a noble house follows the aristocratic, rather than humanist, pattern. The curriculum, however, tends to emphasize humanist discipline, as we can see in these "Orders for the Earl of Oxford's Exercises" drawn up by his tutor Lawrence Nowell while he lived in Burghley's house:

7:00–7:30 Dancing
7:30–8:00 Breakfast
8:00–9:00 French
9:00–10:00 Latin
10:00–10:30 Writing and Drawing
The Common Prayers and so to dinner
1:00–2:00 Cosmography
2:00–3:00 Latin
3:00–4:00 French
4:00–4:30 Exercises with his pen

Before dinner the earl was to read the Epistle and Gospel in English, after dinner in their original language. He was to spend the rest of the day (!) in riding, shooting, dancing and/or walking.[53] Aristocratic pastimes (dancing, shooting, riding) are included, but marginalized, and humanist language instruction constitutes the center of the curriculum. More significant, however, is the way in which the curriculum is presented. The old humanist preoccupation with lists of books and techniques of gathering and framing is missing.[54] Instead, the emphasis is on what Foucault calls "disciplinary time," the use of a timetable to "establish rhythms, impose particular occupations, regulate the cycle of repetition."[55] "Disciplinary time" cannot easily include "pastime"; indeed, the traditional aristocratic pastimes are for the most part assigned to time left over from the daily schedule (dancing from 7:00 to 7:30 is an exception). Burghley recognizes the importance of pastime as a sign of aristocratic privilege, and his attempt to schedule and control it (even obliquely, on the margins of the curriculum) evidences his general attempt to exercise bureaucratic control through the Court of Wards over aristocratic marriage and inheritance. He also realizes, however, that such pastimes cannot constitute as effective a discipline as the humanist curriculum. Thus, the main focus of Burghley's academy is on the kinds of study that inculcate moderation, control, and submission to authority, rather than on the freer, more aggressive and self-expressive pastimes.[56]

Burghley seems to have been torn by a curious mix of old and new ideas. On the one hand, he seems to have realized that the central role of humanist education in an increasingly bureaucratic state was to train young men to take their place in the system. This training involved the mixture of empowerment and regulation that we recognize as the formation of the bourgeois "individual," able to accept his own place in an ordered hierarchy, able to exercise tactful authority over those below him, and able to find fulfillment not in extravagant outward displays of power and honor, not in personal loyalty to a feudal lord, but in private awareness of his own worth in service to the state. On the other hand, however, Burghley was more bound than his humanist predecessors by England's particular social hierarchy. He seems to have imagined the educational project as enabling, not the upward mobility of an educated middle class, but the submission of the aristocracy to middle-class values. Thus, rather than raising others like himself to office, Burghley managed, through the Court of Wards, to exercise remarkable control over those who were techically his social superiors.[57] By maintaining bureaucratic control over aristocratic education, marriage, and inheritance, Burghley was able, to some extent and temporarily, to preserve the Tudor social system into the seventeenth century.

Burghley's participation in both aristocratic and humanist codes led him sometimes to embrace aristocratic individualism, and sometimes to follow humanist practice in seeking to efface it. He seems to have justified his power and position partly by stressing his own family's place in the aristocracy, through rather fanciful genealogy, through elaborate building projects, and through skillful marriage of his children and grandchildren.[58] But he also seems to have sought, as much as possible, to hide his individual self behind its bureaucratic role. B. W. Beckingsale astutely notes that Burghley "did not personalize his own power" but was "adept at letting the vizor of officialdom fall over his features and at speaking in the anonymous voice of the State," thus relieving "himself of personal responsibilities," and fostering the impression that he was "working in accordance with the dictates of an external impersonal authority."[59] One of his mottoes, *nolo minor me timeat, despiceatve major* (I do not want inferiors to fear me, or superiors to look down on me), sums up this strategy. Although he seems acutely conscious of the social hierarchy and his own place in it, upon closer examination that place vanishes: it cannot be felt by those below or seen by those above. Veiled in this invisibility, Burghley was free to manipulate those above and below him.

Aphoristic language was, of course, a key means of effacing personality and personal ambition. Again and again Burghley phrases his own opinion as general truth. In persuading Elizabeth to reform the coinage debased by her father, Burghley spoke with aphoristic authority: "That realm cannot be rich whose coigne is poore or base": "*oportet patrem familias nagis esse vindacem quam emacem* [that a prince ought rather to be a seller than a buyer]."[60] His secretary Michael Hickes prepared a list of "sentences or adages" for use in responding to suitors whom they intended to turn down: a reply such as "let nothing be so esteemed of you that it make thee do against honesty or right" brilliantly uses a general ethical imperative to screen political maneuvering.[61] He always denied involvement in factionalism although he was clearly involved in it.[62] It is easy to see how the Burghley who accepted gratuities in order to bestow wards in ways that furthered his own interests could be on record as saying that "he can never be a good statesman, who respecteth not the publique, more then his owne private [advantage]"; and "private gain is the pervertinge of justice, and [the] pestilence of a commonwealth."[63] Burghley spoke with the voice of the commonwealth, and his private advantage was identical with the "publique" good.

We can also easily imagine the frustration that Burghley's immense power and self-effacing strategies might ignite in the young men over whom he had so much control.[64] He would indeed have appeared to be "Leviathan," the state itself, impersonal, immovable, inhuman, seeking to assimilate them into its machinery. Young aristocrats like Essex and Oxford resisted his attempts to educate them into submission, while members of the upwardly mobile gentry and middle class (Sir Philip Sidney, Edmund Spenser) were frustrated by Burghley's attempts to arrogate to aristocrats the traditional humanist credentials for upward mobility.[65] How, under Burghley, was fitness for preferment to be displayed? One had to be an aristocrat, but could not use the traditional signs of aristocratic leisure and affluence to establish that fact; one had to be educated, but without high birth such education did no good. Above all, it would have seemed impossible (and, indeed, undesirable) to emulate Burghley himself, an invisible man who claimed to be the moral voice of the commonwealth, but who bought and sold their friends for profit.

The appeal to younger men of the glamorous, aristocratic, openly Machiavellian courtier, exemplified by men like Leicester, Hatton, Ralegh, and especially Essex, is easily understood. Where Burghley seemed to represent a repressive and morally bankrupt dead end, the Italianate courtier, openly ambitious, openly concerned with "trifles" such as poetry, hunting, and the conspicuous consumption of luxury goods, provided an appealing alternative, one that the queen herself often seemed to encourage.[66] Francis and Anthony Bacon, Burghley's nephews, provide examples of young men who first pinned their hopes on Burghley but later joined the Essex faction when Burghley did nothing for them. Their father, Sir Nicholas Bacon, shared with Burghley many of the self-presentational gestures of the humanist adviser: somber clothing, fondness for self-effacing sententiae, opposition to the courtly factions.[67] Unfortunately, he did not live long enough to make the kinds of efforts on his sons' behalf that Burghley expended in securing an influential job for his son Robert. After their father's death the two Bacons looked to Burghley for help but were badly disappointed.

As late as 1592 Francis Bacon wrote a pamphlet defending Burghley against Catholic criticism. To the charge that Burghley was behind "vain and fond pamphlets and ballads," Bacon echoes Burghley's official language when he answers that "neither can his great and weighty business permit him to intend such trifles."[68] His correspondence with Burghley reveals that Burghley not only failed to offer him preferment, he seems to have lectured him about the evils of ambition and favoritism. Bacon most constantly protests that he does not seek "any extraordinary and singular note of favour," that "arrogancy and overweening is so far from my nature," and that he only seeks "some middle place that I could discharge to serve her Majesty."[69]

It is not surprising, then, that by the mid 1590s both Bacon brothers were gravitating toward the earl of Essex in hopes of the advancement they could not get through Burghley. Anthony Bacon wrote to Essex that he had received "no offer or hopeful assurance of real kindness which I thought I might justly expect at the Lord Treasurer's hands who had inned my ten years' harvest into his own barn, without any half-penny charge."[70] An exchange between Essex and Robert Cecil regarding Francis Bacon's career illustrates the different strategies used by the two sides. Cecil challenged Essex's intention to procure the attorney generalship for Francis Bacon, arguing that it would be unwise to prefer "so raw a youth to that place of such moment." Essex retorts that Cecil himself, principal secretary to the Privy Council, was "of less learning and no greater experience." Cecil uses a favorite strategy of his father's when he admits that "both his years and experience were small, yet weighing the school which he had studied in, and the great wisdom and learning of his schoolmaster, and the pains and observations he daily passed in that school, he thought his forces and wisdom to be sufficient." Cecil asserts his power through modest self-effacement, and by emphasizing the educational credential provided by contact with his father's "wisdom and learning." He further stresses the disciplinary force of his education, applied through "pains and observations." Essex's reply, on the other hand, pointedly reveals the openly ambitious, Machiavellian stance of the courtly faction: "the attorneyship for Francis is that I must have, and in that will I spend all my power, weight, authority, and amity."[71] Essex uses factional struggle to assert himself and his personal power, while Cecil uses ethical generality (young men do not deserve high place unless they have been strictly disciplined and educated in the uses of power) to conceal both factionalism and personal power.

Essex's brand of direct opposition to the older generation and its monopoly of place, its perceived hypocrisy, and its didacticism has been charted by Anthony Esler, and the similar reactions of young writers at the end of the sixteenth century have been explored by G. K. Hunter and

Richard Helgerson.[72] Nevertheless, many younger men in this period sought to develop self-presentational codes that appropriated and transformed humanist values and forms. I want to look first at their direct use of sayings in courtly imprese, and then, in the remainder of the book, at the ways in which the factors I have been tracing influenced their authorship and publication of short poems.

Imprese, or chivalric devices consisting of an allegorical picture and brief motto, enjoyed quite a vogue in the 1580s and 1590s, especially in the annual Accession Day tilts where they appeared on pasteboard shields carried by the combatants before the actual fights began. This popularity is reflected in Sir Philip Sidney's *Arcadia*, where such devices are described in elaborate detail.[73] For Sidney and other younger Elizabethans, imprese seem to have constituted a compromise between the values of the midcentury humanist and the Italianate courtier, the bureaucratic and the chivalric, aphorism and heraldry, books and experience, wisdom and wit. Most emphasis has been placed on the chivalric aspects of the tilts, but, as Frances Yates has noted, the aphoristic citations on the imprese made the tilts themselves both "military exercises" and "spectacles full of learned allusion."[74]

In fact, the tiltyard (and Whitehall, where the shields were later hung) would have resembled commonplace books as well as scenes from knightly romance.[75] The use of courtly entertainment as commonplace book is confirmed by John Bodenham's *Belvedere or The Garden of the Muses*, a published collection of poetic sententiae gathered from literary sources and also "out of many excellent speeches spoken to her Maiestie, at Tiltings, Triumphes, Maskes, Shewes, and diuises peerfourmed in prograce."[76] Such courtly commonplace books were based on different assumptions and put to different uses than were their humanist counterparts, and these differences reveal the complex and difficult situation of a younger generation struggling to accommodate rival systems of value and alternative semiotic codes.

Two important accounts of the social and linguistic uses of imprese survive from this period. Samuel Daniel's original preface to his translation of Paulus Jovius's treatise on the subject was produced in the context of the Sidney circle's interest in these devices and is essentially prescriptive.[77] William Camden's *Remains Concerning Britain*, a kind of historical commonplace book, is retrospective and descriptive.[78] Both works, however, provide remarkably clear and consistent accounts of the elaborate social semiotics associated with the impresa.

As signs of social status, it seems clear that imprese functioned as a compromise between aristocratic coats of arms and the upwardly mobile middle class's use of sayings as an educational credential. Camden's account of the orgins of "impreses" relates them to, but finally differentiates them from, "Arms . . . which were devised to distinguish Families, and were most usual among the nobility in wars, tilts and tornaments." He suggests that imprese were first adopted by French and Italian soldiers under Charles VIII, who "began to leave Arms—haply, for that many of them had none" (367–68). Daniel similarly notes that "*Impreses* are not Hereditairie, as are Armes," and says that they are used by both "Gentle-men, and noble personages."[79] Although imprese are more democratic than hereditary coats of arms, Daniel strongly emphasizes their social exclusivity: "for the valiant and hautie gentlemen, disdayning to conioine with the vile and base *Plebians* in any rustique inuention, have procured to themselues this one [device] most singulare" (24). Imprese, then, were a means for courtiers who did not (yet) merit arms to "procure to them-selues" an outward and visible sign of their courtly status.

Because they employ mottoes as well as quasi-heraldic devices, imprese also participate in the humanist code of learned display. Indeed, as Camden notes, they were "born by Noble and Learned Parsonages" (366). Daniel describes the rules for choosing the motto or "*Gnome*, a shorte sentence or Posie" in some detail (22). Ideally, the motto should consist of three or four words but should certainly not "exceed . . . a uerse in any tongue" (23).[80] Like humanist sayings, "better are they esteemed being taken out of some famous author," and they must be moral as well: "aboue all, if it be possible, let them leaue some scruple whereon to med-itate."[81] These sayings are to be chosen according to the paradoxical cri-teria that humanist rhetoricians used to define matter for gathering: they should be "not altogether manifest nor too obscure, neither yet triviall or common" (25). Camden adds that they should be "in some different lan-guage" and concurs that they ought to be "witty, short, and answerable thereunto; neither too obscure, nor too plain" (367). According to Daniel, their subject might be "either amorous or graue" (23). Like the humanist collection and use of aphorisms, then, the courtly mottoes ad-vertised knowledge of a foreign language, familiarity with canonical liter-ary texts, and a proper attitude toward "grave" moral "scruples"; unlike many humanist educational precepts, however, they sought to display wit and ambition and could deal with "trifling" amatory as well as serious moral subjects.

A more significant difference between the impresa and the aphoristic saying, especially as used by someone like Burghley, involves the relation-ship connecting a verbal formulation with, first, the subject who uses it, and, second, the ongoing experience about which it generalizes or com-ments. As we saw, Burghley and other humanist gatherers relied on say-ings as a means of achieving stability and control in and over both lan-guage and life. Humanist educators like Burghley use sayings to apply prescriptive formulas from books to life, to sum up in advance what might or ought to be done in any situation. They also imagined sayings as controlling, obscuring, and even effacing the self, both by supplying it with an already-formulated means of expression, and by hiding it behind a screen of generality and learning. Late sixteenth-century humanists grew to favor conservative, stoic *sententiae*, whose message of moderation, disdain for fortune, and warnings against ambition are reinforced by their rhetorical closure. Such sayings are static, impersonal, and rigidly hierarchical.

Imprese, however, are more active and personal. Daniel's etymology of the word "impresa" reveals the close association of these devices with the display of personal ambition:

> *Impresa* is used of the *Italians* for an enterprise, taken in hand with a firme and constant intent to bring the same to effect. As if a Prince or Captaine taking in hand some enterprise of war, or any other perticulare affaire, desirous by some figure and mot to manifest to the world his intent, this figure and mot together is called an Impresa, made to signifie an enterprise, wherat a noble mind leuelling with the aime of a deepe desire, striues with a stedy intent to gaine the prise of his purpose. (24)

According to Daniel, the impresa serves to "manifest to the world" an ambitious man's "enterprise" or "intent" to gain a particular goal. Activity is emphasized here ("enterprise," "intent," "striues," "gaine") but is balanced by a sense of disciplined control ("firme and constant," "leuelling," "stedy") just as the impresa itself ideally displayed ambition tempered by loyalty, wit moderated by learning.

Imprese also differ from humanist sayings in that they were not just gathered, but actively and creatively framed to express personal ability and intention. Camden, for example, describes how "a studious lover of good letters framed to himself only the figure of I, with this philosophical principle, 'Omnia ex uno' " (376). The point here is not only to display familiarity with a philosophical precept, but also to show an ability to choose a witty "figure" to accompany it, and to deploy it in commenting on some personal situation. "Frame" seems to have returned to something like its original sense of giving material form to some idea or conceit, but with more emphasis on the cleverness of the framer in constructing the form, and on the personal significance of the resulting device. Context, both textual and social, has become an important constituent of the process of gathering and framing.

Interpretation of the impresa was also a more active affair, involving not just familiarity with the same canonical texts but also wit and an insider's knowledge of a specific social situation; again, context has become more important. First of all, neither picture nor mot was supposed to be comprehensible without the other; instead, an onlooker would have to look at both and actively put the two together.[82] Interpretation was also dependent on relating the device to a personal situation, often ongoing, known only to insiders. Daniel, for example, relates an anecdote about a disappointed lover who appeared clad in three levels of black, "which mourning habite was no sooner seene of such as knewe the historie of his love, but they perceived what it signified, as well as if he himselfe had declared it" (20). Similarly, Sir Philip Sidney relied on onlookers' knowledge of a changing personal situation when, after the birth of Lord Denbigh ended his hopes of inheriting Leicester's title, he appeared at court with a device consisting of the word " 'speravi' dashed through." At the same occasion, Camden adds that he "signified himself to be revived with gracious favour which made the Sun shining upon a withered tree, but new blooming, with this, 'His radiis rediviva viresco' " (384).[83] Presumably, the outcome of the tilt itself would further modify the social significance of the device.[84] Rather than summing up experience and precluding change, imprese and their mottoes were intended to express ambition and desire for change, and even to procure the favor that might bring such change about.

Most of the imprese that have been recorded display a similar mix of learning, wit, topicality, and ambition stabilized by statements of loyalty or ethical generality. Sidney was a master of the form, and his several imprese illustrate its possibilities clearly. One of his "favorite" mottoes reveals the uses of imprese in expressing and controlling social aspiration as well as their relationship to literary texts. This motto, *vix ea nostra voco* (I scarcely consider these things to be our own) is unintelligible unless the reader recognizes it and recalls its context in Ovid's *Metamorphoses*: "Nam genus et proavos, et quae non fecimus ipsi / Vix ea nostra voco" (for family and ancestors, and those things which we have not performed ourselves, I can scarcely consider to be our own).[85] Sidney neatly displays (and elicits from the reader) knowledge of a saying gathered from a canonical text, but he also calls attention to his own witty ability to gather from that text an apt and riddling half-line. The saying itself comments on the difference between coats of arms (which, as signs of "genus et proavos," would be disdained as "quae non fecimus ipsi") and imprese, which specifically treat things that the bearer does intend to perform himself. Sidney seems, then, to use this motto to provide general, ethical justification for the upward mobility of self-made men and for the use of imprese as signs of their ambitious intent. However, the *vix* maintains a delicate ambiguity; it could mean "I hardly consider these things to be our own," or, less definitely, "these things are almost not our own," leaving room for the possibility (should Sidney inherit Leicester's title) that they might be. Readers who were familiar with Sidney's own uncertain social position (as well as the Ovidian intertext) would be able to read this motto in its full complexity.[86]

Another Sidney impresa expresses a more conservative position. Camden describes it as depicting the "Caspian Sea surrounded with his shores, which neither ebbeth nor floweth, and over it 'sine refluxu' " (374). In this case Sidney alludes to an arcane "fact" of natural history (of the kind popularized by Lyly's *Euphues*): that the Caspian Sea "neither ebbeth nor floweth." The motto *sine refluxu* may express stoic constancy and disregard for the vagaries of fortune, rather like the queen's *semper eadem* (always the same) or Nicholas Bacon's *mediocria firma*. In this sense it seems more closely allied to the conservative attitude of humanist *sententiae*, and it seems to express not ambition but cautious regard for social norms: I will not exceed my bounds. On the other hand, however, the motto could imply determination once an enterprise has been undertaken: I will not flow backward, or retreat. Once again, knowledge of Sidney's personal situation at the time would provide a key to interpreting the device.

Sidney's devices, and those of other courtiers as well, are balanced between personal expression and impersonal generalization. These men may have wanted to find ways to express a subjectivity more genuine than Burghley's "framed" persona yet were not willing to give up the stability and protective covering that the distanced impersonality of sayings could provide. It is often difficult to tell whether the force of an impresa is to provide an outward manifestation of an inner feeling or desire, or to prove that the bearer is able to reflect wittily and learnedly on his own situation and experience. Often, imprese function, much like Sir Thomas Elyot's use of stoic commonplace, to excuse or explain failure. Camden, for example, describes "a Gentleman Scholar, drawn from the University, where he was well liked, to the Court, for which in respect of his bashful modesty he was not fit, painted a red Coral branch, which while it grew in the Sea was green, with this, 'Nunc Rubeo, ante virebam' " (382–83). This device expresses his feeling of modesty but also provides an ethical justification for his lack of success at court, reminding the viewer that he was more successful in another milieu. The device thus labels both the bearer and his experience, and is simultaneously personal and impersonal. Similarly, Camden suggests that "it may be thought that he noted deserts to be everywhere excluded, and meer hap to raise most men, who inscribed within a Laurel Garland, 'Fato non merito' " (377).[87] Again, the subject both expresses his personal sense of disappointment and comments on the ethical status of a general situation.

Imprese, then, were one means of appropriating and reconstituting the practices of gathering and framing to suit the needs of a changing social situation. Whereas older humanists like Burghley, the elder Bacon, and the queen used gathered sayings to frame and defend a conservative, static, impersonal, and unassailable authority, younger men used them to display carefully qualified ambition and to explore a new and tentative individualism and self-awareness. While Burghley sought to transform life into a text that he could control, Sidney examines the ways in which gathered texts can represent, interpret, and even transform experience. The younger generation of courtiers and writers did not reject the discursive practices of their elders and predecessors but rather transformed them into sometimes barely recognizable shapes. In this sense, then, the literary flowering of the 1590s was informed by the drab sententiousness of the midcentury miscellanies in ways that have not been explored. I intend now to follow out the traces of the forms and codes that I have been charting, examining their manifestation in short poems—sonnets and epigrams—written during this period. In order to do so, however, I must first return to the early sixteenth century and to the close links between sententiae and short poems, commonplace books and poetic miscellanies.

Chapter VII

"IN A NET TO HOLD THE WIND": GATHERING, FRAMING, AND LYRIC SUBJECTIVITY, 1520–1540

THE *Norton Anthology of English Literature* provides as good a guide as any to our present canon of sixteenth-century poetry. This canon privileges the love lyric, focusing on the works (largely sonnets) of Wyatt, Surrey, Sidney, Spenser, and Shakespeare, and including a few selected poems by other writers.[1] These poems are for the most part aristocratic (or with aristocratic pretensions) and private, and they represent themselves as the deeply felt utterances of a self-expressive speaking voice. Joel Fineman, in his study of Shakespeare's place in this lyric tradition, articulates a common view of sixteenth-century English love poems and identifies the basis of their canonicity: such poems are valued at least in part because they are characterized by a "strikingly powerful and resonant subjective voice." According to Fineman, "the sonnet vogue itself" provides "evidence of an increasingly personal or personalizing literature, an incipiently psychological literature of subjective interiority whose self-conscious conventions evince the contours and preoccupations of a recognizably modern 'self.' "[2]

Curiously, this canon has remained virtually unchanged despite the fact that contemporary critical theory has called the "self" upon which it is based into question in a number of ways.[3] The Derridean deconstruction of presence, the Freudian theory of the "partitioned subject," the Marxist critique of bourgeois individualism, and the New Historicist focus on the cultural determinants of selfhood have not shaken our conviction that the most interesting and valuable poems of the sixteenth century are engaged in expressing a "fully present" self.[4] In general, critics who apply these theoretical perspectives to the reading of sixteenth-century poems either assume that those texts operate under a (deluded) belief in such a self which the critic can deconstruct or critique, or, perhaps more usually, argue that a given author has achieved the internal distantiation necessary to perform a limited version of the deconstruction himself.[5] Another possibility, which I intend to pursue here, is to see in the works of this early modern period a conception of the self that precedes our own and differs from it in ways that can be helpfully elucidated by the insights of theory.[6]

Theory has not generally helped to emphasize a fact that I intend to explore here, namely, that our present canon excludes many of the poems written and published in England in the course of the sixteenth century, and that the majority of the poems which our canon ignores operate on entirely different assumptions about the nature of the poem and the poetic self. This alternative poetic tradition—it has been called "drab," and "plain," but neither term is particularly useful—centered on poems that were public (not private), written (not spoken), middle-class (not aristocratic), epigrammatic (not lyric), and which, instead of purporting to express a present self, were intended to reveal the processes of gathering and framing through which a subject was consciously produced.[7] This subject was not, however, an individuated speaking voice, but something closer to the Foucauldian "author-function," openly produced by social, political, and linguistic phenomena, and gaining its authority from the public avowal of that production and from an attempt to make it accessible to the reader.[8] Such poems were not presented as the products of the human imagination or divine inspiration, but of an educational process that they were intended to manifest.[9] While the love lyric seeks to mystify its connection to political power, these poems are in general more explicitly connected to the social and political aims of their authors.[10]

The tradition of aphoristic poetry is, of course, intimately related to the humanist practices of gathering and framing that I have been tracing thus far. Although humanists are usually associated with opposition to poetry, the aphoristic tradition constituted, for most of the century, a valid and sanctioned poetic medium for even the most committed humanists.[11] In the early to middle years of the century, published and public aphoristic poetry, first in Latin and then in the vernacular, functioned as a tool of middle-class mobility and humanist (later, Protestant) political alliance.[12]

These published poems necessarily involved different attitudes toward the ownership and materiality of poems than did private, unpublished aristocratic verse. Echoing the logic and rhetoric of gathering, such poems participated in common ownership by all educated people and were presented not as spiritual and transcendent expressions of individualism but as a material commodity produced by a transferable educational technology. They were intended as signs of the possession of that *techne*, as well as a means of transferring it. Nevertheless, there was from the beginning a good deal of uncertainty about the relationship of these poems to the tradition of aristocratic love poetry, which, along with other aristocratic pastimes like hunting and dancing, was revitalized in the early sixteenth century partly in opposition to the humanist educational project. The writing of love poems served to demonstrate graceful proficiency at a courtly skill, to display a natural copia occasioned by emotional experience rather than gathered matter, and to delineate and express a private sphere of activity where feudal values might still flourish in an increasingly capitalist society. Much of the poetry of the sixteenth century in England (both canonical and noncanonical, English and Latin) was deeply concerned with working out the nature of poetic texts and authorship with reference to *both* traditions. Without an awareness of the practices of gathering and framing, without a full sense of the seriousness and viability of the aphoristic tradition, we will continue to have a partial view of sixteenth-century literary history, and even of our present canon.

In this chapter, I want to trace the English tradition of humanist poetry from its beginnings, around 1520, with the publication of three collections of Latin epigrams, Thomas More's (1518), John Constable's (1520) and William Lily's (1521). These collections were directly related to the humanist educational project and were intended to futher the political and educational aims of their authors. Many of the gestures and techniques of humanist poetry were appropriated later in the century by the Protestant poets Robert Crowley and John Parkhurst, and the ideological implications of this form of epigram can be traced in its frivolous "other," the jesting epigrams on proverbs written by the Catholic poet John Heywood. In the 1530s, this tradition came together with its courtly and aristocratic opposite in the vernacular poems of Sir Thomas Wyatt, poems that are constituted by (and torn between) the two systems.

In the next chapter, I will move to the 1550s and the first of a series of published miscellanies that bear Wyatt's double legacy, but in altered form: they reflect increased emphasis on gathering as an authorial activity, and they are published for a middle-class audience.[13] Through the seventies, eighties, and nineties, such writers as George Turberville, Barnabe Googe, Thomas Watson, George Gascoigne, Edmund Spenser, and John Bodenham experiment with combinations of the two poetic modes, presenting themselves as both authors and gatherers/editors, their poems as both aristocratic and middle-class, trifling and serious, self-expressive and aphoristic, private and published. The canonical lyricists of the nineties—Sir Philip Sidney in particular—are, as critics have long noted, self-conscious about the lyric subjectivity that they create, and that self-consciousness is based in part on their awareness of gathering and framing as alternative means of constituting the subject.

Historians of the Englsh epigram usually associate the collections by More, Lily, Constable—and, later, Parkhurst—with school exercises of the time involving the composition of epigrams on set (aphoristic) themes, or the translation of Greek epigrams into Latin and vice versa.[14] More and Lily do demonstrate just such an exercise in their joint progymnasmata, and Constable admits (as does Parkhurst) that some of his poems were written while he was still in school. The connection of these poems to humanist educational practice, is, however, politically significant in ways that have not been generally recognized. The publication of several volumes of Latin epigrams in and around the year 1520 was a conscious political gesture intimately related to the humanist social and educational project.

In 1515 Wolsey became lord chancellor of England and, as we have seen in earlier chapters, enlisted the support of humanists like More and Lily in the ongoing bureaucratization and centralization of the government.[15] Such men were particularly useful to Wolsey, first of all, because they were not members of the aristocratic class of feudal magnates that the central government was trying to control.[16] More's appointment as adviser to the king in 1518 represented the elevation of a salaried bureaucrat over the aristocracy and an abrogation of the aristocratic feudal "right" to provide counsel to the king.[17] Additionally, the humanist educational project and its goals of establishing a standardized curriculum throughout England and securing exposure to that curriculum (rather than social rank) as the primary credential for political preferment served to further the aims of the Crown. Between 1515 and 1520, several intellectual quarrels provide evidence of and resistance to the complicity of humanism with Wolsey's program: both the conflict between "Greeks" and "Trojans" at Oxford (1516) over the inclusion of Greek in the curriculum, and the "quarrel of the *Vulgaria*" (1519–1521) over the adoption of a standard grammar text were resolved in the humanists' favor.[18]

The collections of Latin epigrams that concern us here are directly related to the Grammarians' War in several ways. This conflict, as noted in chapter 4 above, arose when (in 1519) St. Paul's School abandoned Stanbridge's *Vulgaria* in favor of a humanist work by William Horman. Soon, Robert Whittinton became the champion of Stanbridge and the old method of teaching "vulgars," opposed to Horman and to William Lily, who prepared an *Accidence* to go along with Horman's text. In this context, the progymnasmata of More and Lily, as well as Lily's series of linked epigrams "qui mihi discipulos" (published with his grammar), can be seen as further attempts to explain and exemplify proper humanist methods of instruction in Latin and Greek. Constable's collection actually contains an epigram, "In Bossum Liliomastigem," that was a part of the "war."[19]

These collections can be seen as blows in a poetic war as well. The poet John Skelton also became involved in the grammar wars, on the side, however, of Whittinton. In this period Skelton was probably a partisan of the aristocratic Howard family, allied with them against Wolsey, Lily, and the New Learning.[20] Whittinton himself published a collection of epigrams in 1519, including poems praising Skelton, Henry VIII, and Wolsey, in an attempt to gain favor for himself and his texts. His poems are entirely epideictic, however, and are written in a flowery, aureate style quite different from the humanists' classical moralizing. His long poem in praise of Skelton ends by describing that poet (whom he has compared to Homer and other great poets) as "cultus," or cultivated. Perhaps the most famous document surviving from the exchange of prefaces and epigrams that made up this "war" is Lily's poem against Skelton which concludes: "Et doctus fieri studes poeta, / Doctrinam nec habes, nec es poeta" (although you want to be a learned poet, you do not have any learning, nor are you a poet).[21] Whittinton's "cultus" implies cultivation, elegance, and refinement as well as learning, all aristocratic social values. Lily's "doctus," however, had by 1520 become a technical term to describe the products of humanist education.[22] Skelton's witty, profane, satirical works are not, in humanist eyes, to be considered poems; humanists published their own volumes in order to demonstrate what did constitute both "learning" and "poetry."

As opposed to Skelton's "medieval" verses, the humanist epigrammatists demonstrated their possession of "doctrina" by writing in classical languages and by gathering their poetic matter from classical or Neo-Latin sources.[23] Their poems provided proof that they had gathered copiously from and been framed by the most important texts of the new humanist canon. Their use of such sources has been obscured, however, by the fact that their classical canon was often different from ours, and also by their use of gathering and translation rather than imitation in our sense.[24] Instead of imitating the wit and form of Martial's epigrams, More and Lily translate a selection of largely aphoristic poems from the Greek Anthology, and all three poets imitate and gather material from the anthology, the *Distichs of Cato*, the Neo-Latin pasquil tradition, and the classical tradition of epideictic verse.[25]

More, for example, bases most of his epigrams on the Greek Anthology but chooses to translate or imitate a much higher proportion of moralizing poems than are contained in the anthology itself or its Continental imitators.[26] His admonitory poems generally take the form of abstract statements on such favorite humanist themes as fortune, wealth, friendship, and death, and they counsel caution and moderation in all areas of life. This translation from the progymnasmata is typical: "Multas aedificare domos et pascere multos / Est ad pauperiem semita recta quidem."[27] The inclusion of such a poem demonstrates More's (and Lily's) ability to translate from Greek into copious Latin and to gather for translation only those poems which accord with humanist principles, in this case, their antiaristocratic opposition to conspicuous consumption.[28]

More, Lily, and Constable, were concerned to demonstrate proper doctrine or religious and moral principle as much as "doctrina" or learning. As a result, their aphoristic poems, whether based on the anthology or the *Distichs*, tend to harp on central tenets of humanist ideology. Constable, for example, seems to imitate the third-person form of the anthology in the following overtly humanist "De lingua latina": "Quot steriles viguere priori [in] tempore linguae / Tempore tot nostro docta palata virent."[29] Here he uses the garden metaphor familiar from humanist educational theory to express a rather self-congratulatory distinction between medieval and Renaissance Latin. The *Distichs of Cato*, characterized by their use of hexameters (instead of elegiac couplets) and the imperative (especially the relatively rare future imperative) could be put to similar use.[30] Lily's "qui mihi discipulos," published both separately and with his grammar text, provided a list of rules for the humanist schoolboy including instructions on gathering sayings in a notebook. Erasmus's epigram, placed over the portrait of the boy Jesus in St. Paul's School, similarly combines imitation of the *Distichs* with expression of humanist (and reformist) doctrine: "Discite me primum pueri, atque effingite puris / Moribus, inde pias addite literulas."[31] Constable turns the *Distichs* to more overtly religious doctrine, offering explicitly Christian advice in this poem: "Christicola O sacram Christi quum tendis ad aedem / Ling[u]am, oculos, pectus, dirigito ad dominum."[32]

The (pre-Reformation) religious doctrine of humanist reformers (and later of Protestants) was also expressed through another form of epigram included in the collections of More and the Protestant epigrammatist John Parkhurst.[33] The pasquil traditionally originated in Rome, where at some point in the late fifteenth or early sixteenth century a statue became a place where people posted anonymous writings—often epigrams imitating Martial—attacking prominent people, especially high officials in the church.[34] Soon annual collections of these poems were published, the most influential being a Protestant volume, *Pasquillorum tomi duo*, published in Basel in 1544. Two of More's epigrams are included in this book; however, his "pasquils" differ from the Continental analogues in several ways. In keeping with the humanist poetic tradition, they are less witty and more serious, avoiding the use of real names and stressing intellectual, rather than sexual, vices. The following poem by More, one of the two included in the Swiss volume, criticizes the ignorance of the clergy as well as their tendency to cite scriptural tags out of context in support of any position:

> Magne pater, clamas: occidit littera. In ore
>   Hoc unum, occidit littera, semper habes.
> Cavisti bene tu ne te ulla occidere possit
>   Littera, non ulla est littera nota tibi.
> Nec frustra metuis ne occidat littera. Scis non
>   Vivificet qui te spiritus esse tibi.[35]

This poem typifies the humanist poetic tradition in several ways. First, it is based on gathered matter, in this case on the scriptural aphorism "littera enim occidit, spiritus autem vivificat" (2 Cor. 3:6: "for the letter killeth, but the spirit giveth life"). On one level, the poem gives this tag a witty twist by putting it into the mouth of an antihumanist, ignorant priest who uses it to justify his own lack of learning. More demonstrates his copious and skillful command of Latin by repeating the opening words of the tag "occidit littera" in various grammatical forms and in various metrical positions. The "point" of the epigram depends upon More's knowledge (which the priest seems to lack) of the rest of the aphorism (spiritus vivificat). On a deeper level, the poem comments on the difference between the common medieval understanding of the phrase, which used it to justify allegorical interpretation of Scripture, and the humanist interpretation, which uses it to contrast the true living faith of the new covenant (and a reformed church) with the sterile rule mongering of the old covenant (and of medieval Scholasticism).[36] Indeed, the poem is itself a comment on true and false gathering. The priest gathers part of the saying and uses it to justify a discredited attitude toward texts. More gathers the whole saying and reframes it in a witty, rhetorically complex poem that explores its possible meanings and uses. In so doing, More demonstrates that he possesses the "doctrina"—humanist learning and reformed faith—that the priest lacks.[37]

These volumes also contain humanist appropriations of epideictic epigrams, poems that, as the opposite of satirical epigrams, define humanist ideology through praise rather than blame. Here again, humanist authors use a classical form in order to articulate and promulgate their own ideas, in this case by praising their friends for embodying the intellectual and moral qualities upon which their project was based.[38] These poems also reveal an attitude toward authorship which differentiates this humanist (later Protestant) tradition from that of the love sonnet. Through their prefaces, introductory poems, tables of names, and epideictic poems, the humanists attempt to define themselves not as individual and original authors but as members of a group engaged in a common project, informed by common texts. These claims of affiliation were, of course, overtly political gestures but also, I would argue, grow out of the discursive practices of gathering and framing and the concomitant concern with gaining (and providing) access to a common storehouse of authoritative matter. In addition, the awareness of ambiguous social position and nervousness about excessive singularity and upward mobility (which we traced in a previous chapter) would have encouraged these authors to emphasize the common and collective nature of their undertaking.

Thomas More, for example, opens his *Epigrammata* with five poems praising King Henry VIII on the occasion of his coronation. As Ann Coiro has pointed out, these poems provide advice as well as praise, establishing the epigrammatist as "educator of princes," a role that, as we have seen, humanists were particularly eager to fill.[39] More praises Henry for specifically humanist virtues, especially the fact that his "natural gifts have been enhanced [lit. "cultivated," also implying "supplemented"] by liberal education," and that he has been "steeped in philosophy's own precepts."[40] Constable's epigrams on his friends read like a humanist pantheon: Thomas More, John Blount, Latimer, Lily, and others are praised for exemplary learning, piety, and moral virtue. Since Constable was a lesser figure than those he praises, his volume might even have been intended to gain recognition by associating him with an ascendant party, demonstrating that he approved of the right people and the right ideas.

Parkhurst, who wrote and was published much later in the century, takes this technique even further. His volume seems in part to have been designed to identify political and religious allegiances during the difficult Marian years. Parkhurst was himself a Protestant exile, and several of his epigrams simply list the names of good and bad politicians, good and bad bishops. A poem on good politicians, "De quibusdam viris admodum praeclaris," for example, is little more than a catalog of names: "Baconus, Darcaeus, Morysinus, vosque Knolaei, / Caecilius, Cokus, Wrothus."[41] Bad bishops, on the other hand, include "Gardnerus, Sampson, Tonstallus, et illud / Monstrum Bonerus sordidum."[42] He also extends this kind of listing back in time, praising Henry VIII, Princess Elizabeth, and Catherine Parr. The volume itself emphasizes this aspect, by displaying prominently near the beginning a "Catalogus illustrium virorum et mulierum" (index of famous men and women) who are mentioned in the book. From this book readers are no doubt intended to gather human exempla as well as textual precepts. They are also from the beginning induced to define Parkhurst in terms of his political and social affiliations and antipathies, rather than on the basis of poetic originality.

Other aspects of these volumes contribute to creating a version of authorship that is based on common skills and matter rather than original or individual achievement. More, for example, opens his collection with a "*Progymnasmata* Thomae Mori et Guilielmi Lilii sodalium" jointly authored by himself and William Lily.[43] The Greek version of each epigram in this section is followed by translations by both More and Lily. Although the translations differ in details of diction and syntax, they are generally so similar that it would be virtually impossible to identify Lily's or More's contributions if they were not signed. The translators seem more interested in demonstrating the copia of terms and rhetorical forms available to all educated men than in displaying an original or personal voice.

Indeed, the poetic forms favored in these collections are conspicuously public and anonymous. The aphoristic poems of the Greek Anthology seem to represent voiceless inscriptions: couched in the third person they deliver detached pronouncements on the nature of human life.[44] The future imperative form that characterizes the *Distichs* and imitations of them is usually confined in classical Latin to laws and treaties—documents which also represent either voiceless inscription or the collective voice of the cultural code.[45] Thus, the Catonian "voice" of such epigrams derives part of its authority from its anonymity. The pasquils, too, were, in their original form, anonymous inscriptions.

Because of their origins in inscription, these poems would have seemed particularly suited for public dissemination in print. Unlike lyric, with its fiction of human presence, inscriptive forms are designed to convey themselves to the reader in the author's absence.[46] It should be clear by now that these humanist epigrammatists did not share what J. W. Saunders has called "the stigma of print," an attitude which valued the unpublished lyrics of courtly amateurs and disdained publication as both socially and intellectually "low." According to Saunders, a courtly lyric was, in its original milieu, "a statement of personal experience communicated in a manuscript between members of a group who regarded it as a necessary part of social converse and self-expression," a statement that could not survive the distancing dissemination of print.[47] True poetry "found its first audience in the circle of friends" and was "communicated orally, or through mutual exchange of scripts, or by correspondence."[48] Saunders's phonocentrism is obvious: a poem is a "statement," "a necessary part of social converse," and the author's voice is conveyed in manuscript by the authenticating presence of his own hand or that of a friend. As these poems are reproduced in print, the authenticating hand/voice of the poet is, if not lost, then at least diluted and distanced.

In Saunders's formulation, the connection between lyric voice and social class is openly drawn. According to his theory, published books appealed to "middle-class curiosity about the doings and sayings of the great and fashionable." For Saunders, the movement of a lyric poem from manuscript to print is "a tale of decline and fall" as it moves from its small, courtly circle to a wider, more heterogeneous audience.[49] Because true literature involves distinguishing between, in Saunders's words, "books which call for taste and imagination and books which are merely useful, between literature which serves the spirit of man and literature which serves his material needs," and because in Renaissance England "the printed word was circumscribed with so many non-literary considerations of religious, political, and economic kinds, . . . literature in our sense remained, in all essential respects, confined to the Court and its environs."[50]

Saunders's ideas about the stigma of print and the importance of lyric presence were, of course, espoused by some writers and readers in sixteenth-century England, but they were not universal. As we shall see, such ideas were promulgated by the aristocratic courtly poets themselves in conscious opposition to humanist, utilitarian, and public poetry, and to the increasingly powerful monarchy that it served. These aristocratic writers were engaged in reconstituting the signs of class distinction in a postfeudal society; they began to experiment with the love lyric as a way of creating and expressing a privatized, individual self which was fully present and authoritative without humanist education, and which sought to preserve, in a private sphere, aspects of feudal ideology that were disappearing in society at large. Saunders takes their ideas for general truth because he is himself still constituted by a version of that class system. What his theory obscures, however, is that such poetry does not represent an original, prior, and thus more authentic form of poetry but is rather an already-belated reaction to humanist poetry that was written, public, published, openly political, and openly the tool of a middle class in the process of fashioning its place in society.

The epigrammatists themselves articulate conceptions of purpose and audience that are mixed and complex, a reflection of their own ambivalent and supplemental position in society as advisers and teachers. Their collections seem to be addressed to a double audience of social superiors and inferiors—to be designed simultaneously to set forth a particular kind of education as a credential for preferment and to introduce to a literate public (composed largely of students) humanist ideas and practices.[51] Constable begins the preface to his collection with this statement of purpose: "I see, worthy reader, that it is a common practice among all the learned to bring forth before the public something from the storehouse of memory, by which distinguished studies might be furthered and pure studies might be rewarded."[52] First of all, Constable's volume is openly designed to demonstrate that he is one of the "learned" whose published works display the wealth of copia collected in a mental "storehouse." He also hopes that such a display will further the humanist educational project, revealing publically the fruits of "pure" studies and encouraging others to follow his example. His implied audience must certainly include higher-ups like Wolsey, More, and Lily, to whom the volume will function as a credential for preferment, but also a public who may be won over to humanist practices by reading it. Lily's "qui mihi" was actually published in two forms to appeal separately to these two audiences: once for students in his grammar, and again in a small pamphlet of (largely epideictic) epigrams, no doubt intended for court consumption. Such books seek attention for the author as a participant in a carefully controlled movement, however, and not as an ambitious individual. These volumes thus recognize, and use the printed book to exploit, the pivotal position of the humanist teacher/adviser, who hopes to employ the techniques of gathering and framing to expedite his own upward mobility and also to enable the mobility of others, without disrupting the social order.

Nevertheless, these volumes also reveal considerable uncertainty about the appropriateness of using poems, especially epigrams, to advance a serious educational and political project. Epigrams were, of course, according to classical tradition, a low and fundamentally unserious, "trifling" genre. Martial, for example, calls his epigrams *nugae* ("trifles," 8.3), and his collection a *liber iocorum* ("book of jokes," 5.15), and the Greek Anthology is largely concerned with wine, women (or boys), and song.[53] More seems to recognize this aspect of the genre by including a few scurrilous jokes in his largely serious collection.[54] Constable, however, is bothered by this side of the tradition, worrying that readers will think that a man of his profession (*artium professor*) should not be occupied "in such a frivolous and trifling thing . . . that is, in writing little epigrams."[55] Parkhurst also worries repeatedly about the propriety of publishing his youthful "ludicra," noting that his collection has been given that title because "ludricra will yield almost nothing except trifles."[56] He characterizes his almost entirely serious and religious collection as including a few "seria mixta iocis" (serious poems mixed in with the jokes).

In their attempt to create a serious version of the epigram as a vehicle for humanist political and social aims, these writers were influenced by an idea, based in poetic tradition but also current in courtly circles, that poetry was a frivolous pastime, a conspicuous expenditure of time on trifling toys.[57] They attempt consciously to counter this idea by presenting their poems as a frugal and fruitful "use," rather than waste, of time. Constable, for example, defends his own composition of epigrams as salutary because "it freed me from the vain and unfruitful leisure in which some people grow stupid."[58] More and Lily openly describe their poems as a "progymnasmata" or exercise, designed to demonstrate the use of time in a disciplinary activity. Parkhurst, writing some thirty years later, is unable to claim that writing poetry represents a fruitful use of time. Instead, he defends his poems' composition during the sad years of exile "so that I might distract from worry my mind, which was debilitated by cares and sickness, by writing." Such volumes thus work, in contrast to the courtly pastimes studied by Frank Whigham, to display rather than to efface "the traces of production on the subject."[59] Indeed, the poems themselves are explicitly the site of that production.

This preoccupation of the serious epigram with constructive use of time is given point by a tradition of trifling and joking poems and stories that seems to have developed in opposition to it. Skelton, who, as we saw before, wrote in support of aristocratic and antihumanist factions, at times presented himself and his poems in the joking tradition of the wise fool. After his death, a semifictional figure named "Skelton" was the central character in a series of anecdotes or jests that enjoyed popular circulation.[60] More, too, was ambivalent enough about the humanist and reformist cause to include jesting poems in his collection, and a fictional "More" also became the center of an anecdotal tradition.

The jesting epigram became an explicit vehicle of Catholic and aristocratic opposition to Protestant humanism when John Heywood began to publish his collections in the 1550s, perhaps as a direct response to the strongly Protestant and moralistic "One and Thyrtye Epigrammes" published in 1550 by Robert Crowley. Crowley's poems are based on material gathered from the pasquil tradition, the *Distichs of Cato*, and the Bible, especially the aphoristic wisdom books, and they are organized alphabetically in a form resembling the earliest vernacular textbooks, the hornbooks or ABCs.[61] Crowley differs from the earlier humanists, of course, in that he writes in English, favors biblical over classical matter, and emphasizes Protestant, rather than humanist, doctrine. Nevertheless, a poem like the following "Of Dicears" shares with humanist epigrams acknowledgment of its basis in gathering ("I find") as well as a disapproval of trifling pasttime: "Emonge wyttye Saiynges, this precept I finde, / To auoid and fle dice (mi son) have ever in mynde."[62]

John Heywood, author of the pro-Catholic allegory "The Spider and the Fly," on the other hand, explicitly acknowledges that his poems are "trifles" and seems, as Burton Milligan has noted, consciously to have "fostered the concept of himself as a wit and jester."[63] His "Three Hundred Epigrammes upon three hundred prouerbes," published five years after Crowley's volume, offers an example of frivolous gathering; most of the poems consist of popular proverbs followed by a flippant or ironic comment. Heywood frequently twists humanist and Protestant imagery, acknowledging that his first hundred of epigrams offers the reader little "frute," and, in his "Fifth Hundred," drawing an analogy between writing books and playing cards.[64] Puttenham's *Arte of English Poesie* provides evidence that later in the century Heywood's jesting was considered as a politically efficacious, antihumanist stance. There, Heywood is described as "the Epigrammatist who for the myrth and quicknesse of his conceits more then for any good learning [that] was in him came to be well benefited by the king."[65] The usefulness of this jesting tradition in opposition politics is further reflected in an anecdote related about Heywood by John Harington: "what think you by Haywood, that scaped hanging with his mirth, the king being graciously and (as I thinke) truely perswaded, that a man that wrate so pleasant and harmlesse verses, could not have any harmfull conceit against his procedings."[66] Thus, when Parkhurst published his volume of serious "ludicra" in 1573, his claim to be publishing because of the example "Hewodi Crowliique" reveals the sense that a collection of epigrams could help to delineate a poetic, and doctrinal, via media.

There are, however, other ways to waste time besides telling jokes, and the jestbook was not the most important poetic tradition that developed in opposition to the aphoristic epigram. Love lyric, the main focus of our canon, developed in a conscious and complex relationship to serious, middle-class poetry based on the practices of gathering and framing. The composition of love lyric was, of course, a traditional courtly pastime. A poem attributed to Henry VIII reveals the close association between courtly lyric and other pastimes as expressions of aristocratic privilege: "For my pastance, / Hunt, song, and dance, / My heart is set! / Who shall me let?"[67] As Lawrence Stone has noted, the opportunity to engage in "romantic love and sexual intrigue" was restricted to those who spent their youth experiencing the traditional feudal educational program "in the households of the prince and the great nobles."[68] Recent studies emphasizing the covert political implications of the love lyric tend to underestimate their obvious political function, like participation in hunting and the wearing of elaborate clothes, as signs of aristocratic status.[69] Only the aristocrat has the means to consume time, as well as money, in the pursuit of conspicuously frivolous romantic games, and only the aristocrat *needs* to display his natural, effortless and untaught ability to master such pastimes. In the early years of the century, love poetry was written in conscious rejection of humanist values, and it embodied different conceptions of the nature of the poem, the poet's authority, his sources, the process of composition, and the proper use of time. This began as an attempt to reestablish an aristocratic alternative to middle-class humanism, but class as well as generic lines were soon mixed and blurred.

An account of the social, political, and antihumanist contexts for love lyric might well begin with the Howard family. The Howards appeared earlier in this chapter as patrons of Skelton in his anti-Wolsey, antihumanist phase. They held the dukedom of Norfolk (restored after Flodden) and were one of only a few powerful magnate families to survive the Wars of the Roses with much of their power (not to mention bodies) intact. As representatives of the feudal aristocracy, they maintained their loyalty to the monarch (whoever that might be) but unfailingly opposed any attempt to encroach on their own feudal prerogatives. They were particularly opposed to upstart "favorites" like Wolsey, Cromwell, and More, and, as a result, to humanism in general.[70] Monarchs tended to keep a sharp eye on them, since their inherited claims to the throne were quite strong and they were always ready to strengthen their position through marriage. The poet Henry Howard, earl of Surrey was a member of this family, but I want to focus not on his poetry as such but on the Devonshire manuscript, an unpublished volume of early Tudor love lyric associated with several members of the Howard family, which reveals more directly the aristocratic agenda behind such poems.

The exact history of the Devonshire manuscript is a matter of some dispute, but its rough outlines are clear enough.[71] A blank commonplace book was probably acquired around 1533 by Henry Fitzroy, the illegitimate son of Henry VIII whose education was, to his humanist tutors' dismay, conducted according to old-fashioned aristocratic principles. Fitzroy, true to his education, used his commonplace book to collect courtly lyrics rather than humanist aphorisms.[72] Soon after this, he was married to Mary Howard who, since she was only fourteen, went to live in the household of Anne Boleyn. Two other young women, Mary Shelton and Margaret Douglas, were also members of that household, and the three women seem to have taken over the book. It circulated within a courtly circle centered on these women, Henry Fitzroy, Thomas Howard, and Thomas Clere, whose members copied into it a variety of love lyrics, some by Wyatt and Surrey, some by themselves.[73]

All this seems harmless enough, and yet the love affairs of this coterie had direct political import. The Howard family was particularly noted for regarding "marriage merely as a means of empire-building," and even nonmarital liaisons could be perceived as politically dangerous.[74] As Southall notes, "May, June, and July, 1536, were months of tragedy for the little group associated with the Devonshire Ms," and their difficulties are all related to their love lives.[75] In May, Anne Boleyn was executed for alleged adulterous love affairs that were considered treasonous. The poet Wyatt, whose poems have a central place in the volume, was also imprisoned in the Tower, probably because of accusations that he was either involved with Anne himself, or complicitous in her other affairs.[76] Margaret Douglas had been secretly married to Thomas Howard, also a treasonous act since she (as Henry's niece) was a potential heir to the throne and could not be married without his permission. Their marriage was discovered in June, and Thomas Howard was imprisoned in the Tower, where he died in 1537. Margaret Douglas survived him and was in trouble again in 1539 for an affair with Sir Charles Howard. Mary Shelton and Mary Fitzroy were members of Catherine Howard's household but survived her fall unscathed.

One set of poems in particular—those exchanged by Margaret Douglas and Thomas Howard when he was in the Tower—seems to have a direct, but carefully mystified, political function. Although their marriage was considered by the king to be a political and public act, for which they were punished, their poems attempt to privatize it, and to justify it as the expression of sincere feelings that transcend political considerations. Their poems repeatedly celebrate their relationship as a private sphere of loyalty and faith, preserving feudal values that have been abrogated in society at large. Thomas, for example, writes:

> Alas that ever pryson stronge
>   sholde such too lovers seperate!
> Yet thowgh ower bodys sufferth wronge
>   Ower hartes shalbe off one estate
>
> I wyll not swerve I you insure
>   For gold nor yet for worldly fere
> But lyke as yerne I wyll indure
>   Suche faythful love to yow I bere

(Muir, no. 7)

This poem contrasts the hostile and corrupt outside world ("pryson stronge," bribes of "gold," threats of "worldly fere") with the "hartes" of the lovers that are "off one estate" joined by "faythful love."[77] In another poem, Thomas praises Margaret's "faythfulnes" and "gentylnes" since she is true to him despite the fact that in marrying him "ye desende from your degre" (Muir, no. 13). In their world of love, true "gentylnes" or aristocratic position is determined not by official determinations of "degre," but by depth and sincerity of feeling. The love poem and its expression of a privatized, individual, feeling self is being rediscovered here as a means of countering the centralized and increasingly impersonal power of the Tudor monarchy.

A number of poems in this volume reveal the ways in which this poetry of "subjective interiority" directly counters the humanist practices of gathering and framing. Where humanists asserted gathering as the only means of securing and expressing a copious presence, the Devonshire poets locate the sources of copia in naturally occurring "passions." The engraving and goads of education are thus replaced by the wounds of love, and metaphors of watery sources, which in humanist education theory represented the powerful copia derived from texts, in these poems reappear as tears and sighs, which, transformed into words, represent the presence defined and expressed by pure feeling. Thomas Howard, for example, writes that

> With sorowful syghes and wondes smart
>   My hart ys persed sodaynly
> To morne off ryght yt ys my part,
>   To wepe, to wayle full grevously.
>
> The bytter tears doth me constrayne,
>   All tho that I wold yt eschew
> To wryte off them that dothe dysdayne
>   Faythfull lovers that be so trew.

(Muir, no. 8)

Howard has no need to undergo a program of methodical and disciplined gathering in order to write. His heart is "persed sodaynly," that is, spontaneously and immediately, not by corrective sayings, but by feelings ("sorowful syghes and wondes smart"), which automatically and naturally vent themselves in tears.[78] These "tears" of course, take the form of poems, just as the copious floods of humanist discourse took the form of eloquent Latin. Thus, he is "constrayne[d]" to write (in implicit criticism of those outside who disapprove of his love), to "wepe, to wayle full grevously" in verse.

This complex of wounds, spontaneous tears, and poems reappears throughout the manuscript. One poet's love "makes myn eys expresse /The teyres that do redresse / My lyffe in wretchednes" (Muir-Thomson, CXIV).[79] Similarly, he complains that "in my hert also / Is graven with lettres diepe / A thousand sighes and mo, / A flod of teres to wepe" (Muir-Thomson, LII, 5–8). The engraving here takes place on the heart, instead of the rational faculty, and his feeling expresses itself not only as watery "teres," but also as "sighes," a representation of voiced presence as living breath that English humanists scrupulously avoided.[80] Another poet notes that "Hartte aprest with dessperott thoughte / Ys fforsyd evere to laymentte" (Muir, no. 25). Repeatedly, these poets emphasize the naturally occurring copia directly induced in a suitably "gentle" subject by the experience of love.[81]

The other poems of the volume take up and intensify Thomas Howard's claim that private feelings of love can lead to reciprocal relationships of faithful service which replace the broken feudal system.[82] One poet asserts that

The hart and servys to yow profferd
With ryght good wyll full honestly,
Refuce yt not syns yt is offerd
But take yt to yow jentylly

(Muir-Thomson, CLXXXII)

Here, "servys," honesty, and gentleness (aristocratic status) are defined as expressions of reciprocated love. Of course, there was always the chance that love would not be requited, and some poems do complain that the beloved has broken the feudal relationship: "I serued the not to be forsaken / But that I should be rewarded again / I was content thy seruaunt to remayn, / But not to be payed vnder this fasshion" (Muir-Thomson, XIV, 3–5). In this case, the poem draws a tacit analogy between the broken love relationship and the broken feudal relationships at Henry's court; thus, as many critics have noticed, the love poem could work as an indirect means of expressing courtly frustration.[83]

As this last poem makes clear, even the Devonshire manuscript poems sometimes acknowledge that love relationships could be as corrupt,

dishonest, and dangerous—as false and "framed" in the negative sense—
as other social dealings. In fact, even so courtly a collection as this is
contaminated by humanist values and expresses some nervousness about
the lack of good framing or control inherent in its emphasis on natural
feeling and spontaneous expression. In celebrating love, and eschewing educative gathering, these poets are aware that they are elevating
"fancy" or imagination over reason. According to faculty psychology, the
fancy or imaginative faculty induced love, and the stirrings of that emotion then descended to the heart and stirred the passions that were based
there.[84] Humanist educators were, as we have seen, deeply distrustful of
the imaginative faculty and the passions, and intended the practices of
gathering and framing to strengthen the rational faculty, and to control
the more dangerous and unpredictable parts of the mind. The poems of
the Devonshire manuscript reveal an awareness of humanist attitudes
toward fancy and express some ambivalence about this aspect of their
project.

"Fancy," in these poems, is the cause of instability and betrayal in love,
even as it enables the expression of the naturally occurring copia of feelings. As one poet comments, "fansy is so fraill / And flitting still so
fast, / That faith may not prevaill / To helpe me furst nor last" (Muir-
Thomson, XLIII, 13–16). "Fancy" is also described as "vain"(a word associated with trifling pastimes) and is the enemy of reason: "Suche vayn
thought as wonted to myslede me / In desert hope by well assured mone,
/ Maketh me from compayne to live alone, / In folowing her whome reason bid me fle" (Muir-Thomson, LVI). In these poems, framing is carried
out by fancy or its alliterative companion folly ("fanecy framed my hart
ffurst" [Muir, no. 34], "foly framd my thought amys" [Muir-Thomson,
CXCVIII, 27]), and inevitably leads to deceit: "As I my self may saye / By
tryall of the same / No wyght can well bewraye / The falshed [falsehood]
loue can frame" (Muir-Thomson, CXCVII, 15–18).

Readers familiar with the Wyatt canon may have realized that many
of the Devonshire poems that express doubt about love are attributed
to him. The Wyatt corpus as a whole is even better suited than the Devonshire collection to demonstrate the conflicts I have been tracing, since
those poems are acutely torn between the humanist and aristocratic
systems.[85] Of course, just which poems from these early miscellanies are
really by Wyatt has been a subject of much discussion.[86] While some
poems exist in holograph or are reliably attributed, others (like many in
D) are unattributed, and virtually indistinguishable in style from other
poems in the miscellany. Both Saunders and Marotti acknowledge, but
fail to pursue, the tendency of manuscript collections to present poems as
the product of an anonymous author-function, the creations of a social
milieu rather than clearly defined individual poets.[87] Because they are es-

pecially concerned with asserting the link between the elite coterie and the direct transmission of poetic presence, the essential anonymity—in both style and attribution—of many of these poems must remain an unresolved paradox and an inconvenient barrier to the establishment of a definite Wyatt canon. In fact, as we have seen, the "resonant subjective voice" is a theme of these poems, rather than a necessary condition of their production.

"Wyatt" perhaps most convincingly creates that voice, partly, I would argue, because he is a product of two conflicting and incompatible systems.[88] His poems express both the allure and the dangers of a subjective self; his "self" seems particularly modern because it is informed by an awareness that it is fictional, problematic, dangerous—but desirable, perhaps even inescapable. Greenblatt has argued that Wyatt achieves a degree of "internal distantiation" from the dominant ideologies of his culture, writing poems in which "courtly self-fashioning seizes upon inwardness to heighten its histrionic power, inwardness turns upon self-fashioning and exposes its underlying motives, its origins in aggression, bad faith, self-interest, and frustrated longing."[89] The histrionic model for the self was not, I would argue, as all-encompassing for Wyatt as Greenblatt argues. Instead, humanist gathering and framing offered him a model for a stable and honest subjectivity that, unfortunately, was revealed by courtly experience to be problematic—both potentially false or framed and less vital than the lyric self produced by involvement in courtly life. On the other hand, the sayings gathered by the humanist subject warn against the pain and instability of that courtly self. To the humanist, the courtly self is frivolous, insubstantial, and inevitably hurt and frustrated. To the courtier, the humanist subject is safe, but imprisoning and even, ultimately, deadening. Wyatt's "internal distantiation," his peculiarly modern view of the self, is thus a result of his implication in both the humanist and courtly systems.[90]

Despite his role as preeminent courtly maker and most successful fashioner of an aristocratic lyric voice, Wyatt came from a nonaristocratic family and received a humanist education, matriculating at St. John's College, Cambridge, in 1516.[91] If the only surviving documents from Wyatt's pen were the two letters of advice addressed to his son in 1537, we would place him almost squarely within the tradition of humanist educator and adviser.[92] In these letters, he echoes the language of gathering and framing as used by educators, rather than courtiers, and seems to subscribe to the humanist vision of a carefully constituted subjectivity. Wyatt begins by advising his son to "gather within yourself some frame of honesty" and concludes with the hope that his "letters might work to frame you honest."[93] He warns him against "vain imaginations" and counsels a carefully controlled approach to love: "frame well yourself to love, and rule well and honestly your wife as your fellow" (1067–68).[94] Wyatt reiterates the basics of disciplinary time and advocates the practice of gathering in a passage that might have come from Vives or Elyot:

> When there is a custom gotten of avoiding to do evil, then cannot a gentle courage be contented to be idle and to rest without doing anything. Then too had ye need to gather an heap of good opinions and to get them perfectly as it were on your fingers ends: Reason not greatly upon the approving of them, take them as already approved because they were of honest men's leavings, of them of God there is no question. And it is no small help to them the good opinion of moral philosophers, among whom I would Seneca were your study and Epictetus, because it is little to be ever in your bosom. (1069)

In this classic account of gathering, Wyatt details the collection of "good opinions," the mystified criteria of selection ("reason not greatly upon the approving of them"), the importance of exercise in absorbing them ("get them perfectly . . ."), and the choice of a sanctioned moralizing canon (Seneca and Epictetus). The language here provides striking evidence that Wyatt was schooled in humanist ideology and that he thought sufficiently highly of it to recommend humanist practices to his son.

At the same time, however, these letters contain hints that the practices of gathering and framing are not always successful. Wyatt acknowledges, for example, the possibility that an honest self can be falsely assumed or framed in the duplicitous, courtly sense. More important, however, he also admits that he himself has not been able to live in accordance with the advice that he gives, and he offers himself as a negative exemplum: "I may be a near example unto you of my folly and unthriftiness that hath as I well deserved brought me into a thousand dangers and hazards, enmities, hatreds, imprisonments, despites and indignations" (1067–68). He has been aware of good advice but has not been able to follow it himself. His poems evince a similar preoccupation with aphoristic advice and a similar inability to accord with it.

Critics have noticed Wyatt's use of aphoristic language in the poems and, characteristically, have underestimated its importance. Thomas Greene sees Wyatt's use of proverbs as supplying a "certain stiffening" against the frightening ungroundedness of language and relationships, but concludes that "it scarcely suffices."[95] Stephen Greenblatt also describes Wyatt's aphoristic language as a "stiffening"; he believes that it "seems to preclude the possibility of full emotional life."[96] In the lyrics, Greenblatt believes that Wyatt's speaker has "self-consciously cultivated . . . a taste for homely proverbs, cultivated, that is, a manner that denies its own cunning."[97] Greenblatt sets Wyatt's use of "stale paradoxes" and "appropriate proverbs" against the convincing "reality of his pain and disillusionment," arguing that his proverbial persona is just another "mask" assumed, paradoxically, to deny his participation in a world of instability and double language.[98]

In fact, Wyatt's poems repeatedly problematize the role of moral sayings in constituting an authoritative self, upholding the stability of the sayings themselves at the same time that they question their role in forming the human subject. Even the verse satires, his most consistently aphoristic poems, seem uneasy about the assumption of a framed humanist stance. All three of the satires are full of sayings—"each kind of life hath with him his disease," "take a mouse as the cat can," "And on the stone that still doeth tourne abowte / There groweth no mosse"—and yet these sayings are not expressed easily or without qualification as in the humanist's aphoristic epigrams. In the first of his three epistles, Wyatt purposefully misidentifies the source of his exemplum. The tale of the city mouse and country mouse is probably taken from Horace, *Sermones* 2.6, and yet Wyatt begins by attributing it to his "mothers maydes when they did sowe and spynne." Thus, the fable of the mouse (and the saying, "Eche kynd of lyff hath with him his disease," which sums it up) is authorized by both classical literature and folk wisdom, but in failing to acknowledge a classical source that most readers would recognize, Wyatt signals the unreliability of his rustic persona.

Greenblatt has seen a similar undermining of Wyatt's pose of moral authority in "A Spending Hand," where honest proverbs are countered by cynical ones but where the notoriously corrupt Sir Francis Bryan is made to assume the honest stance.[99] In "Myne Owne John Poynz," Wyatt imitates a satire of Alamanni to express a personal experience and undercuts his stoic position when he admits, near the end of the poem, that his retirement is enforced.[100] Wyatt is honest, then, in showing how a stoic persona, "framed" by sayings, could be borrowed, forced upon him, and, perhaps, finally false.[101]

Does he then, as Greenblatt argues, present sayings framing (in the dishonest sense) just one more pose useful for courtly advancement? Although he presents this as a possibility, it is not the only possibility. Wyatt goes to some lengths to show that the truth of sayings is not dependent upon the authority of a particular self. Although sayings themselves are steadfast and true, human beings may not be able easily to participate in that "trouth." This is the point of the double authorization in "My mothers Maydes," where the exemplum and its sayings are "steadfast" because they are true for Wyatt, for Horace, and for his mother's maids. As he says of the sayings quoted at the beginning of "A Spending Hand":

A spending hand that alway powreth owte,
   Had nede to have a bringer in as fast,
   And on the stone that still doeth tourne abowte,
There groweth no mosse: these proverbes yet do last.
   Reason hath set theim in so sure a place
   That lenght of yeres their force can never wast.

(Muir-Thomson, CVII)

The steadfastness denied to the spending hand and the rolling stone is not to be found in Wyatt, or Bryan, or any persona they might assume, but in the sayings themselves. Reason, not Wyatt, has set them in a sure place, and that place does not constitute Wyatt's self.

Several critics have seen the following lines from "My mothers Maydes" as referring to the stable core of Wyatt's honest persona:

Then seke no more owte of thy self to fynde
The thing that thou haist sought so long before,
For thou shalt fele it [stickinge] in thy mynde[102]

(Muir-Thomson, CVI, 97–99)

Wyatt does not depict this "thing" as something that comprises or even is a part of an essential self. Instead, it remains a foreign object that he feels almost physically sticking in his mind. Another poem specifically identifies the "thing" as a saying:

The bell towre showed me suche a syght
That in my hed stekys day and nyght;
Ther dyd I lerne out of a grate,
Ffor all vauore, glory or myght,
That yet *circa Regna tonat*.[103]

(Muir-Thomson, CLXXVI)

The saying *circa Regna tonat*, gathered from Seneca, has been stuck in Wyatt's mind by his suffering, by his personal experience of its "trouth." He does not imagine it as a palliative wall or engraving that changes his behavior, however, but as a foreign object that is felt as an alien presence.

"Felt," here, is an operative word, since the courtly lyric was, as we have seen, largely concerned to assert a feeling presence, a genuine speaking voice engendered by desire and pain. Sayings, intended as they are to forestall painful experience, are incompatible with this feeling self and can only be incorporated into it by "experience" of their prescient validity. Wyatt's lyrics are thus repeatedly concerned with testing the efficacy of sayings in the world of the courtly love lyric. Sometimes a saying is introduced with the idea that experience in the world has proven it: "But now the proufe doth verifie / That who so trusteth ere he know / Doth hurt him self and please his foe"; "That yet *circa Regna tonat* / By proffe,

I say, ther dyd I lerne" (Muir-Thomson, CLXXVI). Sometimes, as in "My mothers Maydes," Wyatt will double the sources of authority, attributing it to his own experience and to antiquity: "Ryght true it is, and said full yore agoo: / Take hede of him that by the back the claweth" (Muir-Thomson, XLIX).[104] Often the saying is drawn out of the experience recounted in the poem: "Good is the life endyng faithfully"; "Me lusteth no lenger rotten boughes to clyme"; "But well to say and so to meane / That swete accord is seldom sene"; "For he that doth believe, berying in hand /Ploweth in water and soweth in sand." All of these sayings are presented as the hard-won conclusions of painful experience; all of them reiterate the idea that fortune is fickle, friends deceitful, and steadfastness sorely lacking.

These sayings are affirmed and reaffirmed in Wyatt's lyrics, however, by someone who does not, indeed cannot, follow their advice. This is so in part, of course, because to follow their advice would be to eschew the painful experiences that delineate the feeling presence of the self and the poems to which it gives voice. But Wyatt's dilemma goes still deeper than that. He seems to have been unable even to formulate the possibility of a choice between the two systems that constituted him. His version of two humanist "gathering" metaphors is revealing. Where humanists were able to transform the poison/cure of sayings into a legitimation of their agenda, the dilemma of the supplement seems to have rendered Wyatt powerless:

> Venemus thornes that ar so sharp and kene
> Sometyme ber flowers fayre and fresh of hue;
> Poyson off tymes is put in medecene
> And to his helthe dothe make the man renue;
> Ffyre that all thing consumith so clene
> May hele, and hurt: and if these bene true,
> I trust somtyme my harme may be my helth,
> Syns every wo is joynid with some welth.
>
> (Muir-Thomson, LXXVI, with D variants)

Humanists, of course, used the admixture of thorn and flower, poison and cure, as the justification for their practices of gathering and framing. Under such dangerous circumstances, human selves could only be framed with the help of professional technology. Wyatt sees the supplemental relationship of good and bad as a condition of the universe in the face of which man can only react as a passive sufferer. Such suffering, however, is not entirely bad, since it is what makes the self present to itself (as feeling) and to others (as the poems engendered by those feelings). Under such circumstances, a self cannot be gathered or framed; it is elusive, unpredictable, and inextricably connected to suffering.

The two systems that constitute Wyatt are as inseparable, as supplemental to each other, as good and evil in the world. The mixing of constitutive ideologies and the indecision and passivity that this causes are clearly expressed in a poem, "Ffarewell Love," which tries to make a choice:

> Ffarewell, Love, and all thy lawes for ever;
>   Thy bayted hookes shall tangill me no more;
>   Senec and Plato call me from thy lore;
>   To perfaict welth my wit for to endever.
> In blynde errour when I did perseuer,
>   Thy sherpe repulce that pricketh ay so sore
>   Hath taught me to sett in tryfels no store
>   And scape fourth syns libertie is lever.
> Therefore, farewell; goo trouble yonger hertes
>   And in me clayme no more authoritie;
>   With idill yeuth goo vse thy propertie
> And theron spend thy many britill dertes:
>   For hetherto though I have lost all my tyme,
>   Me lusteth no lenger rotten boughes to clyme.

(Muir-Thomson, XIII)

As Anne Ferry has noted, the speaker in this sonnet is "caught in the painful paradox of desiring to stop desiring what he still desires, even while he sees its rottenness." She points out his repetitious denials, and the ambiguity of the last line, which could mean "I no longer desire to climb rotten boughs" and/or "I desire to climb rotten boughs no longer."[105] The poem seems to set up a conventional choice between love and learning: an older man comes to realize the truth and utility of the humanist project, attempts to relinquish his involvement in love to apply himself to learning, but is unable, finally, to do so.

The poem undermines the very possibility of making such a choice in a number of ways. Most important, love itself is presented as a source of learning: it has "lawes" and is a "lore." It can also act as an educational goad "that pricketh ay so sore," and indeed, the deceptive "bayted hookes," as well as the "britill dartes" that cause love, like the cure and poison of the previously discussed poem, are simply alternative manifestations of that goad. Thus, it is the painful experience of love itself that has "taught" the speaker "to sett in tryfels no store," and not any lessons gathered from "Senec and Plato," who, it seems, merely call to him from a distance. The disease is its own cure; but, as a necessary corollary, the cure is itself the disease. Hence the state of affairs that Ferry has noted, wherein the speaker realizes the dangers of love but cannot give it up. The outside perspective of "Senec and Plato" does not provide a choice but merely enables him to perceive his dilemma.

This poem recapitulates and reverses Wyatt's letters of advice to his son in significant ways. There, Wyatt urged his son to eschew involvement in love. Here, the speaker encourages love to exercise its authority over "yonger hertes." In that letter, too, the lessons of Seneca were associated with coercive "framing," whereas in this poem, love is depicted as a controlling and imprisoning force from which the speaker longs to "scape fourth syns libertie is lever." Other poems will reveal, however, that this fantasy of freedom through humanist framing is not realizable. Indeed, even in this poem it is presented as a desired, rather than achieved, condition. Caught between two systems of thought, Wyatt cannot even imagine "freedom," except in another form of imprisonment.

"Who so list to hounte" (Muir-Thomson, VII), like several other Wyatt poems, uses the metaphor of hunting to figure engagement in a courtly milieu and his attempt to find and express a suitable self within it.[106] In this poem, "hunting" represents the painful process of proving the truth of a saying, in this case, that it is useless "in a nett . . . to hold the wynde." The adage "reti ventos venaris—you are hunting the winds with a net" appears in Erasmus's *Adagia* and is as important a source for Wyatt's poem as the Petrarchan sonnet that also provided its matter ("Una Candida Cerva").[107] The original version of the saying, of course, uses a metaphor drawn from the Roman practice of hunting deer with nets.[108] Erasmus's explanation that it is "used of people who toil in vain, or who chase foolishly after things they have no hope of catching, or who snatch in a futile way after futility" exactly parallels Wyatt's sense of his endeavor as a "vayne travaill," in which he "farthest cometh behinde" with no chance of catching something that is "wylde for to hold." It thus provided him with a warning about the consequences of engaging in an impossible hunt.

Hunting, of course, was the quintessential aristocratic trifling pastime, and proficiency in it was a natural demonstration of aristocratic status.[109] Because of convenient puns on heart/hart and deer/dear, hunting could also easily represent engagement in the equally aristocratic pastime of courtly love. In this case, the puns reveal the true nature of the hunt as the search for an object of desire ("dear") against which to actualize a feeling self ("heart").[110] The adage corroborates the possibility that the hunt is in some sense a search for a fully present self by introducing the idea that its object is the wind, a common representation of lyric presence as animating breath.[111]

We realize immediately that this poem is not a conventional expression of aristocratic savoir faire, since it admittedly presents the experiences of someone who is a failure at hunting: "the vayne travaill hath weried me so sore, / I ame of theim that farthest cometh behinde." Only half-engaged in the values of the court, this speaker describes hunting as "a vayne travaill"—it is work (and not a frivolous pastime), and yet it is vain or trifling. The only thing that he gets from it is a feeling of weariness. Like the speaker in "Ffarewell, Love," he desires to stop but cannot: "may I by no meanes my weried mynde / Drawe from the Diere."

The hind represents a woman, to be sure, but, as noted above, her insubstantiality as well as her alternative identity as a "hart" suggest that she also figures the lyric self engendered by the poet/lover's feelings of love and frustration. Here, then, is his problem. If he catches her, his suffering will end and the self that it engenders will vanish. If he gives up the chase (as the saying urges him to do), it will never exist at all. The poet's self and his poem depend upon his suspension in this dreary dream-world, between the knowledge that his pursuit is trivial and the realization that it is necessary. He only exists as long as he tries to hold his insubstantial self in the net of the poem.

This particular poem is (at least temporarily) resolved by a voice—or rather, inscription—from outside. The saying "noli me tangere" is identified as an expression of power by its legalistic Latin and by the fact that it is "graven with Diamonds," a sign of the jeweled displays of aristocratic conspicuous consumption. Like many of Wyatt's quotations, it has several obvious sources: the Bible (where Christ says it as a warning about the insubstantiality of his risen body), ancient history (where it appears on the collars of Caesar's deer), and, most immediately, Petrarch's sonnet.[112] It is said to be engraved on the collar of the deer yet, through the device prosopopoeia, presents itself as the voice of the deer speaking Caesar's command. The sources of authority here are not just doubled but almost exponentially multiplied: the Bible, classical tradition, Petrarch, Henry VIII, the speaker's mysterious beloved, his own heart. Despite its authority, however, this command does not have the power to create steadfastness; it cannot keep the elusive deer from being "wylde for to hold" and, like all of Wyatt's gathered sayings, can only remind the speaker of the hopelessness of his situation.

In some cases, Wyatt presents the commands of power as identical with the precepts of reason and able to enforce the speaker to make the choice that he cannot otherwise imagine. Wyatt was forcibly withdrawn from involvement in courtly life on several occasions by imprisonment and rustication. In these situations, the sayings of both power and authority became not a fortification to keep bad influences from Wyatt's mind, but a prison to keep his fancy, and ambition, at bay. However, even here the choice becomes a nonchoice between two different kinds of imprisonment. On the one hand, humanist precept reveals involvement in courtly life as a kind of prison: "who so ioyes such kinde of life to holde / In prison ioyes, fettred with cheines of gold" (Muir-Thomson, CCLIX). Love can also be depicted, from that point of view, as "the foule yoke of sensuall bondage" (Muir-Thomson, CCLXI). On the other hand, Wyatt can only find freedom from the court when "a clog doeth hang yet at my hele," and he can only learn Senecan sayings through a prison "grate." It is not surprising, then, that it comes down to a choice between "by losse of life libertye or liefe by preson" (Muir-Thomson, CCXLVI).[113]

Love and ambition and the self they constitute are, from the humanist point of view, paradoxically both insubstantial and imprisoning. But sayings are also a "grate" and a "clog" to Wyatt, and he chafes against them, knowing that to give up the courtly self is to fall silent, and, perhaps, to cease to exist. It is this chafing as much as the suffering resulting from worldly experience that leaves the "scar that shall still remain" sticking in Wyatt's mind.[114] Sayings remain for Wyatt a sign of steadfast moral authority that he cannot achieve, and of the insubstantiality of his poetic self; thus, they engrave themselves in his mind only as a scar, a painful trace of the clash between two incompatible systems and the ambivalent subjectivity that they engender.

Chapter VIII

BEND OR FRAME:

LYRIC COLLECTIONS AND THE DANGERS

OF NARRATIVE, 1550–1590

I F WE TURN again to *The Norton Anthology of English Literature* for the history of the phonocentric canon after Wyatt (and his contemporary, Henry Howard, earl of Surrey), we find that they are followed immediately by Sir Philip Sidney, even though both Wyatt and Surrey were dead when Sidney was born in 1554, and even though a stretch of more than forty years separates the periods when they were actively writing.[1] According to the values upon which this canon is based, however, the juxtaposition makes perfect sense. For it was only with Sidney's *Astrophil and Stella* sonnet sequence that the self-expressive, private lyric subjectivity explored by Wyatt was again taken up and given its definitive articulation. Of course, poetry was written in the years between 1540 and 1580, and the history of this "drab" age of verse has been charted by more than one scholar.[2] But because most attempts to define this poetic tradition have focused on style rather than on its social and ideological contexts, its crucial role in the transition from Wyatt to Sidney has not been fully understood. One of the elements missing from this story is narrative itself; that is, the realization that through the miscellanies and single-author lyric collections of the 1550s through the 1570s, the relationships between narrative and lyric, experience and aphorism, story and self, were being worked through in ways that prepared for Sidney's introduction of the lyric sequence and the distinctively "modern" self that it generates.[3]

Modern critics tend, as Marshall Grossman has recently pointed out, to "presuppose a specifically narrative disposition of history" and to assume a narrative structure behind events and texts that is, itself, a literary construction. This narrative construct was, in the sixteenth century, still under formulation.[4] Narrative was, in many ways, antithetical to the humanist practices of gathering and framing, and, not surprisingly, humanist writers in the earlier sixteenth century tend to avoid it. In the first half of the sixteenth century, English humanists imagine a subject formed not by a narrative history of personal experience but by an assimilated store of texts that seek to forestall and replace such experience. Their pedagogical focus on the extraction of fragments undermines attention to narrative sequence. Thus, for humanist educators, the most important thing about a text, whether *The Aeneid* or Plautus's *Menaechmi*, was not its narrative line but the various sayings that could be extracted from it; we remember Rainolde's injunction that "the fable was invented for the moralles sake."[5] Their extremely slow pace of reading (twelve lines of Ovid's *Metamorphoses* a week) would also tend to obscure narrative continuity. Indeed, the very concept of framing, with its emphasis on closure and control, suggests that their tendency to collapse narrative anecdotes and myths into a shortened maxim or exemplum suitable for gathering reflects ideological as well as rhetorical motives. Narrative was too dangerously errant, too free from constraints, to be valued or even enjoyed for anything other than the moral fragments it might contain.

In Roger Ascham's *Schoolmaster*, a famous passage expresses this humanist hostility to narrative.[6] Significantly, Ascham's criticism of chivalric narrative appears in the middle of his invective against Italian travel. The literal point of conjunction is the corruption of learning under papist religion, in Italy and in medieval England, but the juxtaposition also surely hinges on a deeper connection among the physical movement of travel, the linear progress of narrative, and the etymological analogy with wandering that relates "errant" and "error."[7] Both travel and narrative, for Ascham, are dangerously seductive, and perilously unframed. Italy is repeatedly likened to Circe's court, which can "entice" (he uses the word three times in three pages, 65–67) and allure young men away from learning to wickedness. Similarly, the Italian books to which he compares romance narrative are able to "carry young wills to vanity, and young witts to mischief" (69).

Chivalric narratives are also, not surprisingly, associated with the value system of aristocratic ideology. "Books of chivalry," themselves the product, as Michael McKeon has shown, of an aristocratic system, are associated by Ascham with "pastime and pleasure," "idle monks," and "toys" or trifles.[8] Such books celebrate the aristocratic codes of violence and erotic conquest, or, as Ascham describes them, "open manslaughter and bold bawdry" (68–69). Italian travel causes a similar involvement in pastime and individualistic arrogance. Those who have been to Italy are "the greatest makers of love, the daily dalliers" and also strive to be "marvellous singular in all their matters" (74).[9]

Throughout this passage, the basis of the threat posed by both travel and narrative to humanist framing is repeatedly made clear. Such experiences make a person unwilling "to live orderly" and unable to be "a quiet subject to his prince, or willing to serve God under the obedience of true doctrine or within the order of honest living" (67, 75). Mental or physical movement outside the ordered humanist frame (delineated by gathered sayings) threatens to break down all social and moral boundaries. Such an experience can corrupt even the act of gathering and can limit its framing power; Italy, notes Ascham, is "not so fit a place as some do count it for young men to fetch either wisdom or honesty from thence" (61). Indeed, the very act of considering these possibilities leads Ascham astray, and he apologizes at the end of the passage for having "wandered from my first purpose of teaching a child, yet not altogether out of the way" (75).

It is not surprising, then, that early humanists avoid writing narratives, even refusing to attempt the composition (rather than translation) of an English epic.[10] In More's *Utopia*, for example, narrative is largely replaced by dialogue and description. Thus, despite the fact that the humanist system was designed to facilitate upward mobility, the ideal humanist life was almost never described in narrative form. We have no humanist Jack of Newbury or Thomas of Reading, no popular narrative accounts of the rise of successful bureaucrats; even Elyot, who was obsessed with his own failure to achieve the expected success, does not depict the ideal humanist life story in narrative form.[11] Of course, one means by which they kept their mobility from threatening the existing social hierarchy was their refusal to depict it as a narrative. In humanist accounts, the accumulated wisdom automatically makes its possessor an adviser; any outward recognition of this by the monarch, any attendant preferment or upward mobility, is a secondary and, by implication, unimportant factor. Indeed, the humanist form of primitive accumulation was less threatening than the mercantile version partly because its fantasy of success repressed the dislocation or deterritorialization that accompanied movement across class lines. Humanists inhabited a common place of shared wisdom and did not translate their upward mobility into more dangerous spatial—that is, narrative—terms.

Without narrative, however, as Wyatt found out, there is literally no place to go. Wyatt's lyrics were, as we have seen, engendered within the clash of the courtly and humanist systems and almost obsessively trace their irresistible, and incompatible, attractions. Each poem enacts this central insoluble dilemma, torn between the gathered epigram designed to demonstrate a stable, framed humanist subjectivity, and an expressive lyric intended to display the naturally occurring copia of feelings that involvement in romantic pastime occasioned in the aristocratic subject. Each poem recognizes both forms as manifesting valid and, indeed, necessary kinds of authority; the divergent authorities negate each other, but neither can be wholly rejected or wholly embraced. Because there is no narrative movement, either within individual poems or among them, through which the subject's search for self and love might develop or be resolved, Wyatt's lyric subjectivity remains trapped in its painful state of irresolution. This impasse, of course, informs Wyatt's poems and makes them what they are, but leaves little room for subsequent poets to maneuver.

This poetic dilemma was paralleled, in the second half of the century, by a strikingly similar social and political situation. William Cecil, Lord Burghley, was, like Wyatt, produced by both systems, the aristocratic and the courtly, and in the course of his powerful career generated intensely contradictory social signals, the effect of which was what seemed at the time like an impenetrable barrier to upward mobility. As we saw in chapter 6, Burghley kept the signs and values of the humanist system alive at court until his death in 1598. Full of aphoristic advice and opposed to aristocratic pastime and display, Burghley provided a living example of a nonaristocratic humanist who used the authority generated by gathering and framing to move upward to great political power and social prestige.

Nevertheless, especially after he was elevated to the nobility in 1571, Burghley tended not to recognize humanist education alone as adequate for preferment, demanding that aspirants for courtly office combine aristocratic status with humanist education. At the same time, however, he sought to control aristocratic display and alliance through sumptuary laws and the Court of Wards, effectively bringing aristocratic status under bureaucratic control. He seems finally to have disapproved of social mobility in anyone except himself; indeed he attempted, through emphasis on a largely fictional genealogy, to efface even his own upward movement. In the course of his career he preferred relatively few people and spent most of his energy preserving his own power, helping his son's career, and securing influential marriages for his children. Younger men who hoped to emulate Burghley's own rise to power were angered and confused by the mixed signals he gave, constantly counseling adherence to humanist values, yet refusing to reward them; championing the aristocracy, yet denying its traditional forms of self-assertion.

It is not surprising, then, that those young men in the last quarter of the century who hoped to get ahead felt social, as well as intellectual, pressure to fulfill the impossible goal of presenting themselves as both aristocrats and humanists. The familiar commonplaces of humanist theory recur in their written works in new ways, and the tensions between common and uncommon, public and private, trifle and serious matter, poison and cure, gathering and self-expression, are reworked in an attempt to discover the nature and uses of poetry in these difficult social and political circumstances.

Richard Helgerson has persuasively traced the crucial role of a conventional narrative pattern of admonition, rebellion (in the form of prodigality), and repentance in the works of several of these young men.[12] Helgerson argues that these men variously used the prodigality narrative to reconcile humanist expectations and "their own unruly desires." The movement of this narrative—from humanist admonition to rebellion and immersion in experience, and finally to repentant affirmation of moral precepts—allowed them to apply a chronological solution to Wyatt's dilemma: "They could rebel, suffer guilt, and repent, and thus acquire an identity supported by the governing ethos of their age."[13]

I differ from Helgerson, as I hope I have shown in previous chapters, in arguing that there was more than one "governing ethos," and that these writers' rebellious impulses spring less from personal desire than from aristocratic expectations that worth is displayed through prodigal expenditure and through experience in love, pastime, and courtly intrigue.[14] The prodigality narratives, which, as Helgerson shows, tend to begin and end with humanist precept, are attempts to locate the authorial subject within both rival systems, and to work out the place of literary discourse between them. The very concept of narrativity is implicated, and explored, in this process. The uneasy experiments of Turberville, Gascoigne, Whetstone, Watson, and even Sidney, along the boundaries of fiction and truth, lyric and precept, originality and gathering, narrative errancy and moral frame, take place on the margins of the aristocratic and humanist systems. It is not surprising, then, that these works recapitulate and revise the familiar commonplaces that we have been following throughout the century, and that new weight and complexity adhere to the terms "fantasy" and "invention."

Despite the strong countertradition of narrative that began to lure writers away from humanist models in the 1570s, the practices and values of gathering and framing were preserved through the late sixteenth and into the seventeenth century through popular poetic collections that diverge sharply from the private, narrativized lyric sequence. Before turning to the experimental texts of the 1570s and 1580s, however, I want to trace the continued influence of humanist gathering and framing practices as a model for published collections of prose and verse. The published poetic miscellany has its roots in courtly collections like the Devonshire manuscript, but also in the student's commonplace book and its published counterparts.[15] And the history of the sixteenth-century lyric is incomplete without an account of these models.

Unpublished, courtly miscellanies like the Devonshire manuscript have obvious affinities with the commonplace book tradition. Indeed, the humanist notebook based on the collection of aphoristic material cannot always be differentiated from such poetic miscellanies; humanist commonplace books often contain some poems, while a courtly collection like the Arundel Harington manuscript includes aphoristic material.[16] However, a volume such as the Devonshire manuscript composed entirely of courtly lyrics does differ from a strictly aphoristic notebook in several ways. First, as we saw in the previous chapter, a courtly poetic miscellany is designed to express a privatized self rather than to demonstrate a subjectivity gathered and framed by a common body of aphoristic wisdom. Ownership of such a book, access to the poems that it includes, is also intended as a sign of membership in a courtly elite, a small, private coterie, rather than as a sign of participation in a broader-based educational and political project.[17] Thus, while aphoristic commonplace books lent themselves easily to publication and dissemination at large, Saunders and others have noted the incongruity of presenting the exclusive courtly collection to a wider audience.[18]

Tottel's Miscellany, published in 1557, inaugurated a series of poetic anthologies gathered and published by printers rather than authors, which established a model of editorial gathering alongside that of expressive authorship.[19] These collections spanned the second half of the century; among them were the moralizing *Court of Vertue* and the very popular *Paradise of Dainty Devices*, as well as the not-so-successful *Gorgeous Gallery of Gallant Inventions*.[20] Saunders denigrates the "dual pretense to gentility and morality" that, in his opinion, led them to "conform to a uniform, insipid pattern."[21] Although it is unsympathetic, his description does accurately pinpoint the confluence in these volumes of the humanist and aristocratic systems. The published miscellanies actually share elements of the unpublished courtly poetic anthology, the humanist epigram collection, and the published prose commonplace book.[22] And by combining elements of the versions of textuality and authorship constituted by such different systems, they establish for the latter half of the century a complex and ambivalent attitude toward the nature of poetic texts and authorship, and toward the social role of poetry.

The middle years of the century saw the publication of a number of aphoristic collections in prose and verse aimed at an audience composed of urban merchants and ambitious lesser gentry. Such works included broadside ballads of counsel, H. C.'s *The Forrest of Fancy* (1579), William Fister's *The Welspring of Wittie Conceits* (1584), Robert Greene's *The Royall Exchange* (1590), and *Polituephuia, Wit's Commonwealth* (1597).[23] The success of a book like William Baldwin's *A Treatise of Morall Philosophie* (1547) attests to the ready market for aphoristic material in the vernacular.[24] The poetic miscellany *The Court of Vertue*, intended as a moralizing response to the earlier *Court of Venus*, makes explicit the connection between published poetic miscellanies and the humanist epigram and prose commonplace traditions. Many of its poems are, like humanist and Protestant epigrams, based on passages gathered "out of many places of Scripture," particularly from Psalms and the Wisdom books. And a whole section of "Sentences of the Wyse" consists of versified sayings gathered from Baldwin's *Treatise*. Although the more secular miscellanies do not announce their affinities with these traditions quite so openly, they are nevertheless influenced by them in important ways.

The miscellanies certainly, as Saunders notes, take pains to advertise their courtly origins. And yet they also reveal traces of humanist attitudes toward the common ownership of texts—attitudes that were, as we saw, prevalent in the humanist epigram collections of the period and are also reflected in collections of prose commonplaces.[25] Tottel, for example, stresses that his collection contains poems packaged (like ideas in Lever's commodified logic) in "small parcelles"; these constitute a "treasure" which "the vngentle horders vp . . . haue heretofore enuied thee."[26] Although the title page stresses the prestige and social rank of the poets whose "treasure" Tottel has gathered for public consumption, his preface describes them as "ungentle"—an explicit denigration of their social status—in hoarding these poems as a private, courtly luxury.

Tottel thus presents his volume as a gathering designed to share among common people a textual commodity that is rightfully theirs. He twice notes that the volume will "profit" the common reader but also worries that its "statlinesse of stile" is "remoued from the rude skill of common eares." The unlearned reader can use the book, paradoxically, as both a source of cultural capital and a purgative cure: "to purge that swinelike grossnesse, that maketh the swete maierome [marjoram] not to smell to their delight" (2). His book thus shares the mixed attitude of humanist logic and rhetoric, promising to make available to the public a form of discourse that is both common and uncommon, public and private, enabling and controlling. And in a reversal of humanist theory, Tottel shifts the responsibility for proper gathering onto the reader, reserving, however, the possibility that the very process of reading the volume will effect a preemptive cure.

Later miscellanies pick up this complex and self-contradictory sense of social status in different ways. The 1578 edition of the *Paradise of Dainty Devices* seems at first to advertise itself as a gathering of aphoristic material intended for an audience of all social classes, proclaiming on the title page that it contains "sundry pithy precepts, learned Counsels, and excellent inventions, right pleasant and profitable for all estates."[27] The Horatian forumula "pleasant and profitable" takes on, in this context, ideological as well as literary significance; "pleasure" calls on the idea of poetry as aristocratic pastime, while "profit" gestures toward the humanist sense that texts ought to function as a useful commodity. The preface goes on to stress the social status of its authors, claiming that many of the poems were written by "M. Edwardes, sometimes of her Maiesties Chapel," but then shifts the social register of the volume to an emphasis on learning along with rank as a criterion of authority when it notes that

it was "penned by divers learned Gentlemen." The tension between private and public ownership of texts reenters when the preface asserts that
the volume was "collected together, through the travell of one, for his
private use," and printed because "the wryters . . . were both of honour
and worship" as well as notable for their "learnyng and gravitie" (3–4).
The printer is at pains to call on the humanist idea that a gathering of
precepts and learned counsels is profitable both to the gatherer and to a
wider audience, as well as the courtly valuation of the "private" collection of works by "Gentlemen" of "honour and worship."[28]

The common ownership of gathered matter has significant implications for the rights and status of an author. Published miscellanies also
intensify the tendency, already present in the humanist epigram books, to
devalue the individual achievement of the author. In those collections,
authorship was represented as an exercise in gathering, as the collection
and framing of already existing matter that could in turn be gathered
by the reader. Miscellanies, however, are collections of poems gathered
by an editor who is not (necessarily) himself an author and who has
great power over the texts that he gathers.[29] Saunders speaks slightingly
of the "catchpenny contempt for authors and their rights" exhibited in
such volumes, but his indignation is an anachronism.[30] In fact, authors'
"rights"—ownership of their own poems—had not yet been established
either legally or ethically.[31] If authors themselves had created their poems
out of gathered matter, then editors and readers who gathered the poems
had an equal right to "own" them. Indeed, the string of popular miscellanies published in the middle of the century seems to have gone some way
toward establishing editorship—the judicious selection and rearrangement of poems—as equal, if not in some ways superior, to original authorship.[32] Thus, it is not surprising that later poets experiment with self-
presentation in editorial as well as authorial roles.

What, exactly, were the middle-class readers of such volumes getting
for their money?[33] If we go through Tottel's Miscellany and the *Paradise
of Dainty Devices* with a notebook in hand, gathering "matter," we find
that many of the poems are moralizing, and that they carry a uniform
moral message, one which denigrates upward mobility, ambition, and
imagination: "riches hates to be content / Rule is enmy to quietnesse /
Power is most part impacient" (Tottel, no. 170); "I saw, how fansy would
retayne no lenger than her lust: / And as the winde how she doth change:
and is not for to trust" (Tottel, no. 180); "who wayteth on this wauering
world, and veweth each estate, / By tryall taught shall learne it best, to live
in simple rate" (*Paradise*, no. 100). These poems continue to promulgate
favorite ethical themes of the humanists, deploring the instability of fortune and fancy, and the dangers of false friends, ambition, and love. The
speakers in these poems stress that their own experience ("by tryall

taught") has confirmed the precepts that moderation and the mean and sure estate are the best remedies against fickle fortune.

It is, however, one thing for Wyatt or another courtier to praise the mean and sure estate, and another thing altogether for a grocer to read about it. To a readership including members of the urban merchant class, the social credentials of the authors of such poems were important not just because those readers were interested in the life-styles of the rich and famous, but because the effect of the poems is to judge the rich and famous by middle-class standards and to find them wanting.[34] Over and over these courtly poets use their own experience to "prove" the truth of sayings that reject their way of life in favor of a life of quiet and anonymous moderation. The lists of socially prominent authors are, in effect, lists of exempla to be gathered from the volume, much in the same way that the lives of the classical authors in Baldwin's *Treatise* are to be gathered along with their sayings. In these published volumes, the life stories of their famous authors are implicitly behind the poems not as narratives to be enjoyed but as sources which validate or "prove" the truth of the sayings that are gathered there. A poem such as Tottel's no. 200, an acrostic on Edward Somerset that begins "Experience now doth shew what God vs taught before, / Desired pompe is vaine, and seldome dothe it last," provides a clear example of this aspect of the volumes.[35] A narrative account of Somerset's "experience" is important only insofar as it yields the maxim "desired pompe is vaine."

Common readers, then, would purchase in such volumes on the one hand stylistic matter in the form of fashionable schemes, tropes, and other devices that would enable them to imitate their social betters, and, on the other hand, aphoristic matter that tended to confirm the superiority of their own unambitious way of life and frugal values. In so doing, the collections continue the humanists' double promise that they will teach uncommon speech grounded in the common codes of society, enabling upward mobility without disturbing the existing social hierarchy. Robert Greene's prose commonplace volume *The Royall Exchange* provides a clear parallel to this aspect of the miscellany's social project. Greene's collection of aphorisms, translated from an Italian source, advertises itself on the title page as suited for "the grauest cittizens, or youngest Courtiers," but is primarily directed at London merchants. In a dedicatory preface to the lord mayor of London, Greene repeats humanist economic theory: London citizens "attaine not to that excesse of riches" yet "grudge not to disburse any sum . . . helpfull to the common profit of theyr Countrey."[36]

Greene goes on to promise that his volume will enable them to "gather" a "principle of worth" for their own "profits," and to collect precepts with which they will be "generally furnished" (224, 227). His

volume is an "exchange" that eschews "wealthy traffique of curious mer-
chandize"; instead, citizens "may buy obedience to God . . . reuerence to
Magistrates, fayth to freendes, love to our neyghbours, and charities to
the poore . . . the duety of a Christian, the offyce of a Ruler, the calling of
a Cittizen" (227). Echoing the humanist economic theory that we traced
in chapter 5, Greene criticizes excess wealth and conspicuous consumption. His textual matter constitutes a form of wealth that can be accumulated without danger, largely because it teaches "obedience," "fayth,"
and "duety." Like the printers of the poetic miscellanies, Greene offers his
readers a form of symbolic capital that serves to reinforce their place in
the system even as it promises to aid their success within it.

Through the middle years of the century, the publication of poetic miscellanies and prose commonplace books established a market for a particular kind of volume, aimed at a nonaristocratic readership and perform-
ing a complex social function. Such volumes were themselves gatherings
of textual fragments; they were intended to serve as repositories from
which their owners could gather the fruits of humanist education and
courtly experience at second hand.[37] The gatherers of such volumes were
not authors but editors who judged, selected, and framed the authors and
poems that were included in the book. These miscellanies established a
powerful model of the published book as a material commodity, containing fragments of texts that could be bought and used by the public for its
own social and material advancement. At the same time, however, these
volumes framed whatever advancement they promised within the hierarchical system of the early modern state. The middle-class reader learned,
in effect, that his own place in society, "the mean and sure estate," was
best.

By the early 1570s, then, someone who set out to write and publish
short poems had a mixed tradition to work with. On the one hand,
courtly makers like Wyatt and Surrey offered a model of Petrarchan lyric
written as a private, courtly pastime. On the other hand, these lyrics were
circulated, alongside more blatantly aphoristic poems, in published miscellanies. Setting out to write and publish their poems in this context, men
like Turberville, Gascoigne, and Whetstone were torn between authorship and editorship, self-expression and gathering, private and public,
frivolous and useful. The confusing mixed signals given by their volumes
is testament to their genuine attraction to both systems and to their creative attempts to make these mutually exclusive systems compatible. As
Helgerson has noted, the prodigal son narrative offered a means of reconciling aphoristic precept and frivolous pastime in a single life story. But
the nature of this narrative, its relationship to the precepts that would
forestall it, and its basis in fact or fiction was extremely problematic. The
volumes of Turberville, Gascoigne, and Whetstone use different tech-

niques of gathering and different combinations of narrative and fiction in order to work through some of the problems.

The task of these poets was complicated by their own social position and project, and their mixed self-presentational gestures—as both amateur and professional, lover and moralist—attest to their own ambivalence and confusion.[38] All of them were from the merchant or lesser gentry classes, and all hoped to attract patronage and preferment at court. In essence, all were men who lacked the independent means of support deemed necessary for gentleman status but who considered themselves gentlemen and desperately sought a socially acceptable form of work. They had before them the examples of Wyatt, Surrey, and the courtly poets of an earlier generation who had established the expressive love poem as a form of courtly display. Just as potent, however, was the example of the humanist epigrammatists and the published miscellany, a tradition that sought to demonstrate (and share) the fruits of humanist education in order to prove fitness for promotion. Saunders's theory that such poets aspired to be courtly amateurs but needed the revenue generated by publication is too simple to explain the complexities of these volumes. These poets seem genuinely unsure about the nature and function of poetry, and seem equally influenced by both traditions. While Turberville seems to be able to combine them rather easily, Gascoigne and Whetstone show traces of strain.

In 1567 George Turberville published his *Epitaphes, Epigrams, Songs and Sonets, with a Discourse of the Friendly affections of Tymetes to Pyndara his Ladie*, one of the first single-author volumes to combine three models of authorship: humanist gathering, courtly self-expression, and a new, as yet un-theorized third possibility, that of fictional narrative.[39] Turberville's early career seems (if we imagine it, anachronistically, as a narrative) to exemplify an ideal humanist *cursus honorum*. Born to the lesser gentry (a "right ancient and genteel family"), he attended Winchester School, New College, Oxford, and the Inns of Court, and was sent as ambassador to Russia in 1568.[40] Later publications, however, such as *The Booke of Falconrie, or Hawking* ("collected out of the best authors," 1575) and *The Noble Art of Venerie, or Hunting*, seem to claim participation in aristocratic pastime, reflecting, perhaps, the changing criteria after William Cecil became Baron Burghley in 1571.

His *Epitaphes*, however, are torn between the two systems. The title already reveals the mixture of traditions within which Turberville is working. His volume will contain "epitaphes and epigrams" like the humanist collections, as well as "songs and sonets" in a direct echo of Tottel. The subtitle reveals a further alliance with the popular tradition of narrative romance, and the key word "affections" tells us that the narrative is included to provide a context for the feelings upon which the poems are based. Fictional narrative, here, functions at least in part as a way to authorize expressive poetry based on feelings, and at the same time to distance the author and editor from those dangerous passions by projecting them onto fictional characters.[41]

Turberville's book, like the humanist collections examined in the previous chapter, is explicitly directed at a double audience. It is dedicated to a patroness, Anne, countess of Warwick, and addressed to "the Reader," and the poems and their purpose are described quite differently in each case. When addressing the countess in his second edition, Turberville stresses that his poems are in the tradition of courtly pastime: his book is a "fond and slender treatise of sonets"; his poems are "slender trifles" and "rashe compiled toyes." His enlarging of the volume has increased his "follie," and the countess is urged to provide a concomitant increase in her "bounteous curtesie" (A2r–A4v).

The ordinary "reader," however, is addressed in quite different terms. In this preface, Turberville never calls his poems "trifles." Instead, he picks up the humanist agricultural metaphor and describes them as "the vnripe seedes of my barraine braine," perhaps not yet full-fledged fruit, but bearing that potential (A5r). He first states the purpose of the volume as "to pleasure and recreate thy wearye mind and troubled hed withall" (A5r), a description which stresses not only the "pleasure" afforded by a pastime but also a more stringent "recreation" that seems to move toward humanist exercise. Gathering first comes in as a way of defending the volume against a critical reader: "if there be any thing herein that maye offend thee, refuse it, reade and pervse the reast with pacience" (A5v). As the preface proceeds, however, this gathering becomes more explicitly moral: the reader is urged to "reade the good, and reiect the euill" (A5v), a direct application of the gathering skills taught in schools wielded here as a defense against accusations that the volume itself was immoral.

Perhaps the most original section of the preface presents one of the earliest attempts to theorize some sort of accommodation between fiction and the humanist system. Turberville explains that he has not written these poems so that young people "shoulde folow or pursue such fraile affections, or taste of amorous bait: but by meere fiction of these Fantasies, I woulde warne (if I mighte) all tender age to flee that fonde and filthie affection of poysoned and vnlawfull loue" (A6r–v). His language here reveals the pull of two systems, and the introduction of a new concept, that of "fiction," in order to mediate them. His poems are not directly expressive of dangerous affections because they are "fictions" and "fantasies," words used here for the first time in this study in a positive sense.

Like humanist educators, Turberville realizes that texts are not just harmless trifles: they carry potential for harm and for good. Their harm is, significantly, depicted as involving the seduction to movement that we associate with narrative: young readers may be led to "follow or pursue" dangerous affections. But unlike the humanists, Turberville argues that their fictionality, and not their didacticism, makes them moral. His version of the supplemental relationship of poison and cure is extremely interesting and complex, and turns in part on the shifting meaning of the word "fantasy." Realizing that love poetry might serve as a "bait" which, when swallowed, would lead to the "filthie affection of poysoned and vnlawfull loue," Turberville claims that his poems are "fiction" designed to warn against that poison. The ambiguity of the word "fantasy" is central; it could be simply a synonym for "fiction," differentiated from "fancy" or love and functioning to warn against it. On the other hand, "fiction of these Fantasies" could mean "fictional loves," in which case love warns against itself. By arguing, that is, that the poison is its own cure, Turberville justifies the writing of potentially dangerous poems. He does not, however, claim that the poems are an antidote as such, but that they simply warn readers to "flee" from poisonous love. His reasoning here seems circular: the potentially dangerous love poems themselves warn readers to flee from them and gather other more moral poems from the volume.

The volume itself reflects a similarly unproblematic reliance on both systems. He includes some moralizing poems, but they are by no means consistent. In an answer to "Maister Googe his Sonet of the paines of Loue," Turberville seems to argue that reason is the agent, rather than the enemy of love:

> Two lynes shall teach you how
> To purchase love anewe:
> Let Reason rule where Love did raigne
> And ydle thoughts eschewe. (8v)

Another poem, however, argues against the motto *Let Reason Rule*: "Shall Reason rule where Reason hath not right Nor never had? / . . . To *Cupid* I my homage earst have donne / Let *Reason* rule the hearts that she hath wonne" (79v). And while some of his poems argue against courtly pastimes like "courting, trauailing, dysing, and tenys" (79v), others represent the courtly loves of Tymetes and Pyndara in a favorable light. Turberville experiments with the narrative of Tymetes and Pyndara as a way of distancing himself from dangerous experiences but also writes some love poems in the first person. The general effect is of experimentation with different kinds of verse, with little concern for whether or not they represent incompatible attitudes and ideologies.

The clash of ideologies is also apparent in the collections of George Gascoigne and George Whetstone, who seem more consciously disturbed by the contradictions and inconsistencies into which they are drawn by their dual purposes. Both Gascoigne and Whetstone sought preferment, and both were ultimately successful in securing it, at Burghley's hands, after the publication of unambiguously didactic works.[42] Their published volumes (Gascoigne's *Hundreth Sundrie Flowers* and *Posies*; Whetstone's *Rocke of Regard*) present themselves as both gathered and expressive, public and private, and their prefaces and poems attempt to work out the nature and role of the short poem. The relationships between experience and fiction, narrative and precept, become crucial factors.

All three volumes go beyond Turberville in representing themselves as, in different ways, the products of gathering, and all three use versions of gathering to attempt to mediate between the courtly and humanist traditions. They all, for example, make extensive use of gathering metaphors that should be familiar from educational theory: Gascoigne's titles themselves describe his poems as gathered flowers, either a *Hundreth Sundrie Flowers* or *Posies*, and his division of *Posies* into "flowers," "hearbes," and "weeds" is imitated by Whetstone's division into a "Garden of unthriftinesse," "Arbour of Vertues," and "Orchard of Repentance." The gathering to which these metaphors allude is, however, variously treated in the three volumes. The author can represent himself as an editorial gatherer, or he can use the readers' role as gatherer to justify the inclusion of frivolous poems. The word "invention," previously used to mean something found or gathered, now shifts toward its modern meaning to bring in the possibility of imaginative creation, still, however, controlled and framed by its roots in gathering. And the relationship among narrative, fiction, and gathering varies, even within a single volume.

Gascoigne's *Hundreth Sundrie Flowers*, for example, claims on its title page that it is a miscellany "gathered partely (by translation) in the fyne outlandish Gardins of Euripides, O[v]id, Petrarke, Ariosto, and others: and partly by invention, out of our owne frutefull Orchardes in Englande."[43] Saunders and others have argued that Gascoigne uses this fiction to conceal his own authorship of poems of questionable moral value. However, his claim that the volume represents a gathering can also be read as literally true. The volume does include two plays, *Jocasta* and *Supposes*, gathered by translation from classical works. And the claim that the other poems are "gathered by invention" from English works may mean that some of the poems are based on conceits or "inventions," in the terms' new sense, derived from other English works. Like "fantasy" in Turberville's preface, Gascoigne's use here of "invention" is pivotal, calling on both older and newer meanings to mediate between different theories of authorship. By stressing gathering in this way and by effacing his own role as author, Gascoigne does align his volume with the miscellany tradition and the editorial model of authorship. By so doing, he is able to represent himself both as self-expressive lyric poet and as editorial gatherer and framer who has taken the works of others and "with some labour gather[ed] them into some order."

In this volume as well as in the *Posies* Turberville's defensive presentation of gathering as the reader's act reappears, exploiting supplementation in a way that both resembles and differs from humanist theory. "The Printer to the Reader" argues that the miscellany-like *Hundreth Sundrie Flowers* is "a greater commoditie than common poesies" precisely because the reader need not read the whole book page after page but "may take any one flowre by itself, and if that smell not so pleasantly as you wold wish, I doubt not yet but you may find some other which may supplie the defects thereof" (47). As in Turberville, responsibility for proper gathering is placed on the reader: "The well minded man may reape some commoditie out of the most frivolous works that are written. And as the venemous spider will sucke poison out of the most holesome herbe, and the industrious Bee can gather hony out of the most stinking weede: Even so the discrete reader may take a happie example by the most lascivious histories" (47). Here, Gascoigne's volume is simultaneously "frivolous" trifle and useful commodity, a source of poison or honey, depending on the reader's ability to gather. The supplemental relationship of matter and ornament, cure and poison, remains an instrument of justification, as it had been for humanist educators. Here, however, the responsibility for proper choice is entirely the reader's.

Throughout the volume, Gascoigne variously represents himself as an editor who gathers and comments upon the poems of others, and as a poet who bases his poems on both original and gathered matter. The "Discourse of Master F. J.," for example, is a narrative frame providing the affective context for the love poems of F. J. Here, perhaps for the first time, the narrative becomes important in itself, significant for its story line as well as for the fragments and poems that it frames.[44] Gascoigne often comments upon these poems as if he were simply their gatherer and editor, and his comments frequently call attention to the mixed emotional and literary sources for the poems. We learn, for example, that one poem is "but a rough meeter, and reason, for it was devised in great disquiet of mynd, and written in rage" (65). He comments of another poem that "I have heard F. J. saye, that he borrowed th'invention of an Italian: but were it a translation or invention (if I be Judge) it is both prety and pithy" (60). "Invention" here seems to mean both original creation and gathered matter. Yet another poem is both gathered and expressive: "this is a translation of Ariosto his xxxi song. . . . It will please none but learned eares, hee was tyed to the invention, troubled in mynd etc." (85).[45]

One of his poems, "*Gascoignes councell* to Douglass Dive," presents a new and disturbing version of gathering. This poem also has a brief narrative frame, although the narrative in this case is based on gathering. The poem, we learn, was "written upon this occasion. She had a booke wherein she had collected sundry good ditties of divers mens doings, in which booke she would needes entreate him to write some verses" (165). The poem is bitter and pessimistic, and in effect reverses the humanist metaphor that associates gathering with culling flowers from among weeds or thorns. For Gascoigne, the writing of aphoristic verse is analogous to binding "a bushe of thornes amongst swete smelling floures." As an aphoristic gatherer, he describes himself as a kite or scavenger bird among falcons, whose function is to "weede the worme, from corne and costly seedes," and to "clense the filth, / As men can clense the worthlesse weedes, from frutefull fallowed tilth" (lines 17–19). The advice that follows is standard, based on the *Distichs of Cato* and other such sources, but Gascoigne's assessment of the gatherer's role in society is new and probably more accurately reflects the way moralistic advice was received in courtly circles.

Yet another novel version of gathering is central to this volume and pulls against the idea that experience yields moral lessons. The full title, *A Hundreth sundrie flowers bound up in one small posy*, puns in a complex way on the word "posy." "Posy" here means bouquet, or gathering, of flowers, and also alludes to "poesy" or "poetry," from which the gathering is made. But the word could also mean a motto or short saying, often engraved in a ring or, with increasing frequency, used as a kind of summation or signature to a poem.[46] Gascoigne signs every poem in this volume with a posy, and the title seems to suggest that these mottoes constitute both what Gascoigne has gathered for the reader and what the reader ought to gather from the volume.

Critics have noted that Gascoigne does not use the posy, as some poets do, to sum up the moral of a poem, or as a theme upon which to expound in the poem.[47] Instead, the posies represent or express something about the poet's attitude toward the situation described in the poem. In this sense, Gascoigne's posies are similar to the imprese discussed in chapter 6, in that they are gathered from, or expressive of, experience as well as texts.[48] Gascoigne himself articulates the close connection between the posy and worldly experience when he notes that he has "sundrie tymes chaunged mine owne worde or devise. And no mervale: For he that wandreth much in those wildernesses, shall seldome continue long in one mind" (*Posies*, 17). Here, Gascoigne repeats the humanist commonplace that courtly life resembles an errant progression ("wandreth much in those wildernesses"); however, he sees sayings not as a stable frame, but as a reflection of ungroundedness.

Gascoigne's posies express a mixture of attitudes toward lack of success in love and at court: *meritum petere grave* (to seek reward gravely) defends his quest for patronage; *si fortunatus infoelix* (if fortunate, then unhappy) alludes to the proverbial fickleness of fortune; *spraeta tamen vivunt* (spurned, nevertheless they survive") suggests hope in the face of failure; *ferenda natura* (nature must bear it) suggests that nature is to blame for his failure; *haud ictus sapio* (stricken, I learn nothing), curiously, defeats the purpose of the volume by admitting that he has not learned from his troubles. Although we might expect his posies to present conventional moral judgments on the experiences recounted in the poems, they do not do so. Instead, they tend to express continued immersion in experience and an inability to gather definite lessons from it.

This inability to gather lessons from life resurfaces in what is probably Gascoigne's most famous poem, his "Woodmanship" (*Posies*, 348–52). This poem takes up the hunting metaphor for engagement in courtly life and love. Here, however, hunting has lost all trace of the pleasant "pastime" and has become a grim test of skill. The only "pastime" involved here is Lord Grey's series of jokes about Gascoigne's continued ineptitude. Like Wyatt's "Who so list to hunt," Gascoigne's hunting poem is inconclusive, but it is inconclusive in quite a different way. Where Wyatt's poem, as we saw, explores the dilemma generated by his knowledge of humanist precepts that predict his failure in love and at court, Gascoigne's poem is about his inability to find a convincing reason for that failure.

Unlike Wyatt's poem, which was characteristically suspended in time and space, Gascoigne's recounts a narrative of prodigality and failure. But his narrative neither advances him socially nor provides a clear moral exemplum. Gascoigne's speaker here owns both humanist learning (he has read "Aristotle" and "Tully") and "experience" gleaned from contact with "crafte courtiers." But he still cannot shoot straight for success. He considers various possible reasons for his failure (excessive honesty, bad luck, Providence) but ultimately finds that none provides an adequate solution, a lesson to be gleaned from his life narrative. The posy *haud ictus sapio* offers the only possible lesson that can be gathered from this story: that it is not possible to gather a lesson. Gascoigne's narrative of failure is thus ongoing and bursts its aphoristic frame.

In his *Posies*, a revised edition of the collection published a year later to counter criticism that the *Flowers* were immoral, Gascoigne shifts his account of gathering. He now admits that he has written all of the poems, and he asserts that he has rearranged them so as to aid proper gathering. His conflation of the gathering and cure/poison metaphors here is striking and reflects his problematic situation:

> in all this discourse I see not proved, that either that Gardener is too blame which planteth his Garden full of fragrant floures: neyther that planter to be dispraysed, which soweth all his beddes with seedes of wholesome herbes:

neyther is that Orchard unfruitfull, which (under shew of sundrie weedes) hath medicinable playsters for all infirmities. But if the Chirurgian which should seeke Sorrell to rypen an Ulcer, will take Rewe which may inflame the Impostume, then is hee more to blame that mistooke his gathering, than the Gardener, which planted aright, and presented store and choyse to be taken. (12)

He here explicitly attempts to place all responsibility for gathering on the reader, arguing that it is not the fault of the writer if his volume includes flowers, herbs, and even poisonous weeds, since it is the reader's job to choose and apply the proper cure. Unlike humanist educators who believed that proper gathering could separate poison and cure, Gascoigne argues that the poisonous weeds themselves, although they seem "meete to be cast away," are nevertheless "right medicinable" and have "some vertue if it be rightly handled."

When he describes these various sections separately, it becomes clear that Gascoigne is not at all certain about the criterion for gatherability, which varies from uncommon style to moral matter. Nor is he certain about the nature or purpose of the poems themselves. The "floures" were "invented upon a verie light occasion" but "have yet in them . . . some rare invention and Methode before not commonly used" (13). "Invention" seems again poised between its older sense of gathered matter and the newer idea of original composition (here based on some trifling occasion). Although the poems are trifles, they may be valuable for the uncommon matter that, in an echo of the two parts of humanist logic, they "invent" and arrange or frame (he uses the new Ramist term "method"). The "hearbes" are "morall discourses, and reformed inventions," which are "therefore more profitable than pleasant" (13), as if the old formulaic pair "pleasure and profit" can no longer work together. The "weedes," as we noted above, are offered as potential medicines, but with an intensified warning that "if you delight to put Hemlocke in your fellowes pottage, you may chaunce both to poyson him, and bring yourselfe in peril." The reader is thus urged to "look advisedly on all the Perceley that you gather, least amongst the same one braunch of Hemlock might anoy you" (13). Having said earlier that all weeds are medicinal if properly used, Gascoigne now admits that some, like hemlock, are always poisonous and ought to be discarded. In order to discern the poison, the reader must "look advisedly."

George Whetstone was influenced by Gascoigne and shows signs of a similar confusion of purpose.[49] In a prefatory epistle addressed "To all the young Gentlemen of England," he describes his poems as "worthlesse" and then in the next sentence claims that his book "importeth necessarie matter of direction, for unstayed youth." Reflecting the unsettled state of the word "invention," his title page claims that the "documents and admonitions" contained in the volume are "all the invention, collection and translation of George Whetstone, gent.," while the epistle notes that his poems are "invented for the most, of experience." The reader cannot be sure whether "invention" in the first instance suggests original composition in contrast to collection and translation, or is a synonym for them. The second formulation, introducing the idea of "invention" from experience, extends gathering (as some humanists acknowledged that it could be extended) from books to daily life.

Like Gascoigne, Whetstone variously justifies the different sections of his book, using metaphors and commonplaces gathered from both the humanist and courtly traditions. The "Garden of unthriftinesse" contains "vaine, wanton, and worthlesse sonets," which, nevertheless, are intended to urge others "to reforme their wanton lives." The "Orchard of Repentance" has been "planted with experience, the fruits therein growing . . . hoalsome, although to curious appetites, not greatly toothsome." The lack of pleasure attendant upon these moral poems gives them greater efficacy as a cure, since "the smarting wound is cured with fretting plaisters." The pain of the cure is not the reader's alone, however. Whetstone also says that "mine was the paine in framing the plots, wherin these fruits and flowers grow, yours is the pleasure and profite of both." The word "frame" has circled back to a more positive meaning. It still implies constriction and control, but also carries connotations of shaping by experience, and even of fiction or feigning—now, seen, however, in a more favorable light.

Like Gascoigne, Whetstone, in a "generall advertisement vnto the Reader," puts part of the burden of gathering onto the reader: "there is nothing written so clearkely (Diuine causes excepted) but there may bee some follie wrested out of the same: and nothing againe so fonde, but it conteyneth matter of moralitie." Whetstone makes more explicit than Gascoigne a narrative sequence in his book as a whole that serves as a key to distinguishing how the varied matter of the book should be gathered. He claims that the sequence of Delight, Unthriftinesse, Vertue, and Repentaunce "is no other than a figure of the lustie yonkers adventures," that is, the life story of a prodigal. And unlike Gascoigne's collections, Whetstone's divisions actually do follow this scheme, proceeding from stories of successful love, through descriptions of virtuous ladies, to a poem entitled "apples of admonition," derived largely from the *Distichs of Cato*. The narrative frame provides further rationale for the inclusion of youthful, frivolous, and immoral poems in the same volume as aphoristic works.

After the experiments of these midcentury poets, collections of short poems again split into two separate traditions. Thomas Watson and John

Bodenham variously develop the published, aphoristic miscellany tradition, in volumes that would influence such seventeenth-century writers as
Jonson, Herbert, and Herrick. On the other hand, Sir Philip Sidney revised and reestablished the tradition of private courtly verse in a new
form, the sonnet sequence, that built on the midcentury experiments with
fictional narrative. Yet his *Defence of Poetry* and *Astrophil and Stella* are
more informed by the other tradition—its assumptions and commonplaces—than has been generally recognized.

Thomas Watson's *Hekatompathia* (1581), like the volumes by Gascoigne and Whetstone, seeks to bridge the two traditions. Watson uses
the prodigality narrative frame of transgression followed by repentance
in order to present himself as both author and editor of his poems, and to
represent the poems as both self-expressive and gathered. In this case,
however, the editorial frame overshadows the expressive content and tips
the balance toward the humanist and miscellany traditions. In this case,
narrative acts as a literal "frame" in that Watson's subsequent repentance
and renunciation of love circumscribe his former experiences within the
confines of aphoristic advice.

Watson's title page and dedication align the volume most clearly with
the aristocratic and expressive traditions, stressing that they are trifles
which express emotions generated by the author's experiences of love.
The subtitle, for example, emphasizes that the poems "express" emotions
generated by love, and that they were "composed" (not gathered) by a
gentleman: *Hekatompathia, or Passionate Centurie of Loue, Diuided
into two parts: whereof, the first expresseth the Authors sufferance in
Loue: the latter, his long farewell to Loue and all his tyrannie. Composed
by Thomas Watson Gentleman; and published at the request of Certaine
Gentlemen his very frendes.*[50] The preface addressed to the "frendly
Reader" seeks to excuse the poems as "idle toys proceedinge from a
youngling frenzie," and an introductory poem describes the "byrth from
out my wounded hart" of this "*Toye*," since "this trifling world *A Toye*
beseemeth best" (5, 14).

Nevertheless, there are also prefatory gestures toward the humanist
tradition, hints that the volume itself develops much more forcefully.
Even in the title, Watson uses the prodigal narrative to distance his present self from the youthful Watson who was immersed in amatory experience; the book contains a second part that corresponds to the "repentance" stage of the prodigal story, in which the author renounces love.[51]
Similarly, the emphasis on the fact that the poems proceed from "a youngling frenzie" establishes an editorial persona who is able to judge, and
frame through judgment, his own earlier literary efforts.

In fact, Watson seems unclear from the beginning whether the poems
are directly expressive of love experience, or artifacts gathered from and

based upon that experience at a distance. The preface offers several preemptive excuses for aesthetic flaws in the verse, each based on a different theory of authorship. The reader is asked to tolerate faults "as ouersightes of a blinde Louer" and, at the same time, as "imperfections" placed there on purpose to express the effects of love (5).

Watson's uncertainty as to whether he is the author or editor of his volume is mirrored in the poems themselves, which are surrounded by an elaborate editorial apparatus. These editorial comments are couched in the first person; they consist, paradoxically, of claims that the poems express personal experience and pedantic references to the sources from which they are gathered. The prose preface to the first poem, for example, describes it as an introduction to his passion "the miserable accidentes whereof are sufficiently described hereafter in the copious variety of his deuises" (15). On the one hand, the poems are based on the experiences, or "accidentes," of love and the feelings that they engender; on the other hand, they are "deuises" designed to demonstrate a "copious variety" or matter.

A majority of these prefaces, however, emphasize the sources of gathered matter and the ways in which it has been organized, or framed, by the poet. They provide valuable testimony to the continuing method of imitation by gathering and reframing. The third poem, for example, is "all framed in manner of a dialogue wherein the Author talketh with his owne heart" (17). We learn that "the chief grounde and matter" of the fourth is "the rehearsall of such thinges as by reporte of the Poets, are dedicated unto *Venus*," and the author/editor helpfully cites two Latin epigrams containing such "reports."[52] The fifth is "(two verses only excepted) wholly translated out of *Petrarch*." Watson cites the original sonnet in its entirety, and he also provides a brief analysis of the "matter" upon which it is grounded, and which forms the basis of his own imitation: "herein certaine contrarieties, whiche are incident to him that loueth extreemlye, are liuely expressed by a Metaphore." He imitates Petrarch, as he learned in school, by picking out the logical (contrarieties) and rhetorical (metaphor) places from which Petrarch gathered his own device. The two "original" verses actually constitute a gathered fragment and are clearly identified as such in the margin with a Latin note ("adduntur Tuscano hij duo versus," "these two verses are added to the Tuscan"), and in the text itself as well: "and touching him, whome will hath made a slaue / the Prouerbe saith of olde, *Selfe doe, selfe haue*" (19).[53]

Watson's inclusion of Latin epigrams in his collection of largely vernacular love poems also reveals the continuing influence of the humanist tradition. His translation into English of a Petrarchan sonnet is immediately followed (poem no. 6) by a translation of the same sonnet into

Latin. Watson's attitude toward these poems is revealing. When he presents a Latin epigram as no. 45 of his volume, he apologizes for its inclusion since "he thought not to haue placed it amongst these his English toyes" (59). The Latin epigram is, as it was earlier in the century, distinguished from the trifling tradition of vernacular love poetry.

The second half of the volume, where the author describes the process of his repentance and his "long farewell to Loue," is even more sententious than the first. An introductory passage (the preface to no. 79) tells us that the rest of the poems "are all made vpon this Posie, *My Love is past*" (93). Here, the posy itself expresses the author's situation, but the poems are at one remove from it, written not directly out of the feelings and experiences of the poet but, like a school exercise, "upon" the posy. Individual poems are often based on or composed of *sententiae* expressing some moral judgment on love. The preface to poem no. 93, for example, tells us that "in the first and sixt line of this Passion the Authour alludeth to two sentencious verses in *Sophocles*" (107), and no. 88 is "nothing els but a briefe and pithy morall" (102). In no. 89, "the two first staffes . . . are altogether sententiall, and euerie one verse of them is grownded vpon a diuerse reason and authorite from the rest." Marginal notes to this poem cite author and sentence in Latin, so that, for example, as a gloss to the first line ("*Love* hath delight in sweete delicious fare") we get "1. Hieronimus: In deliciis difficile est seruare castitatem" (103).

Watson tries to demonstrate both expression and gathering, trifling wit and serious judgment, by presenting the poems as written by a frivolous youthful self, and prepared for publication by an older, wiser man. Once again, the narrative passage from one to the other is collapsed into its sententious results. But the implicit narrative frame allows him to imagine his "copious varietie" as proceeding both from the wit and passion of a courtly lover and from the gathered matter of the humanist scholar. The narrative scheme, however, breaks down when the editor describes in detail the gathered sources for the most expressive love poems. In effect, the editorial gatherer overshadows the feeling lover. This bizarre bifurcation of the self, like the conflict between poem and commentary, introduces both a self-consciousness about the process of composition and a sense of internal struggle between gathered reason and passion that will be developed within (rather than on the margins of) Sidney's sonnets.

Before turning to Sidney, however, I want to look at two aspects of Watson's poems that are taken even further by a later writer, John Bodenham, and through his work passed on to the seventeenth century. Watson's editorial interest in gathered fragments is mirrored, and amplified, in a very strange volume that appeared in 1600. Bodenham's *Belvedere* is more than just a poetic curiosity, however, since it provides evidence of the strong influence of gathering as late as 1600, and also reveals links between the miscellany tradition and such seventeenth-century poets as Herrick and Herbert. Bodenham was associated with prose miscellanies as well as other poetic anthologies, and *Belvedere* reflects aspects of both. It is a compendium of lines of poetry gathered from other writers and rearranged, under commonplace headings, as continuous verse. In several ways, it brings to a logical conclusion the humanist practices of gathering and framing.

The title of the book and its prefatory matter rehash the usual gathering commonplaces and metaphors. This *Belvedere or The Garden of the Muses* contains flowers that are "most learned, graue, and wittie sentences; each line," as in the imprese tradition, "being a seuerall sentence, and none exceeding two lines at the vttermost."[54] Bodenham realizes that unlike original poets, he does not need to "make any Apologie for the defence of this labour, because the same being collected from so many singular mens workes; and the worth of them all hauing been so especially approoued" (A3r). Far from being a product of courtly pastime, this volume urges its readers to "make vse of thy time as so rich a treasure requireth" (A3v). Because the volume is entirely gathered and framed ("subiected vnder apt and proper heads"), its curative properties are unambiguous: "if thy conscience be wounded, here are store of hearbs to heale it: If thy doubts be fearefull, here are flowres of comfort. . . . In briefe, what infirmitie canst thou haue, but here it may bee cured" (A3v).

As in the poetic miscellanies, the social rank of these gatherings' authors is prominently displayed, in such a way, however, as to present them as further matter to be gathered and not as originators or owners of their poems. These authors are listed at the beginning of the volume, but the citations are completely unattributed when they appear in the body of the book. Thus, we learn that these poetic fragments have been gathered, in descending order of social rank, "out of many excellent speeches spoken to her Maiestie" and "some especially, proceeding from her owne most sacred selfe," then "of sundry things extant, and many in priuat" written by various nobles (4r–v).[55] Then, from the works of lesser nobility and gentry, then from "other Honourable personages."[56]

Even while listing these authors by rank, however, he subverts the hierarchy by emphasizing that the poems will be arranged differently in the volume itself. Even the queen's valuable words have been "digested into their meete places," while extracts from the poems of King James of Scotland have been "reduced into their right roome and place" (A4v). The proper places for these quotations are not in the context of whole works directly attributed to their authors, no matter who the author is. Instead, the extracts are rearranged according to standard commonplace headings such as "Of God," "Of Learning," "Of Kings and Princes," "Of Counsell and Advice." We are recalled to the stress in dialectic on organization in proper "places" or "rooms," a form of framing that represents a "subiection" which is different from, but ultimately reinforces, that of the social hierarchy. The common reader is, on the one hand, empowered by access to the works of great writers rearranged for greatest practical use, but, on the other hand, controlled by the gatherer's subjection of these powerful works to their "proper" places. The editor, here, has complete power to judge, assimilate, and subject the authors' works; and yet he is completely bound to the standard "apt and proper" headings.[57]

The volume itself proceeds according to this scheme. Each section consists first of a string of sententious (unrhymed iambic pentameter) lines commenting on the subject heading, interspersed with rhymed couplets. Then, a section of "Similes on the same subiect" offers appropriate similitudes, followed by a selection of "Examples likewise on the same" (3–4). An index presents a further cross section of topical headings, so, for example, a reader could find and gather lines on "Affliction" from the sections on "Religion," "Vertue," and "Counsell and Advice." The attitude toward poetry here is very close to the humanist gatherer's tendency to regard poems as so much matter to be cut up and consumed in fragments without regard to a sense of the integrity or wholeness of the lyric source. It would seem that Bodenham's volume is about as far from the values reflected in our poetic canon as poetry can get.

Nevertheless, the influence of this odd volume shows up in unexpected places. The rhymed couplets interspersed among the quoted lines closely resemble Herrick's sententious epigrams. Bodenham, for example, writes that "God is beyond fraile sense to comprehend, / He first began all, and of all is end"; Herrick's "God is above the sphere of our esteem / And is the best known, not defining him" is very similar.[58] And the indexical cross headings resemble and prefigure Herbert's curious use of titles. In Bodenham's index, the entry "Affliction 12, 20, 74" tells us that aphoristic lines on this topic can be found on those pages. An index to *The Temple* might similarly delineate the location of Herbert's "Affliction" or "Love" poems.[59] The attitudes fostered by the discursive practices of gathering and framing were transmitted, in altered forms, to the seventeenth-century lyric.

Our canon, however, obscures the line between Bodenham and Herrick through its emphasis on the sonnet tradition, which seems to interrupt and overrule the practices of gathering and framing. Sidney's *Astrophil and Stella* sequence established a powerful and influential model that appears to ignore the gathering tradition in favor of the courtly lyric model. Sidney is (and was) the model of a courtier who wrote, as a private, courtly pastime, to express his naturally occurring wit and passions.

He uses ideas gathered from Continental sources in order, at least in the-ory, to revise the English view of education, subjectivity, and poetry, es-tablishing the dominance of what we might call the "essentialist" self and the lyric voice. Despite these innovations, however, we can still see traces of gathering and framing in the interstices of Sidney's theory and practice, and these traces contribute to the complexity, ambivalence, and ironic wit that we value in his works.

Because he did not publish his own poems, Sidney's *Astrophil and Stella* is not accompanied by prefatory material of the kind that precedes the miscellanies and collections examined in this chapter. Sidney's *Apolo-gie* or *Defence*, however, despite its more elaborate rhetorical structure and more general subject matter, has affinities with those essentially apol-ogetic prefaces.[60] Bodenham, we might recall, claimed in his preface that he did not need "to make any Apologie for the defense" of his vol-ume because his poems were selectively gathered from approved sources. The prefaces of Gascoigne, Whetstone, and Watson were largely con-cerned to defend their poems against accusations of immorality, frivolity, or falseness, and they rely, as we have seen, on various versions of gather-ing and framing as well as on narrative strategies in order to make their defense.

Sidney defends against the same sorts of accusations but shifts both the means and the matter of his defense. His *Apologie* is marked by the same kinds of conflicts between the humanist and aristocratic systems that were evident in the prefaces of Gascoigne and Whetstone. But Sidney's treatment of these varied and contradictory ideas is more complex and multilayered than that of his predecessors. He relies on imported Neopla-tonic ideas in order to justify the act of imaginative creation as in itself capable of moral efficacy, thus making gathering unnecessary.[61] Never-theless, his text itself bears traces of gathering that have frustrated critics seeking coherence and consistency in the matter of the treatise.[62] Beyond this, however, he achieves an overall tone that unifies and strengthens his case even as it undermines it.[63]

Like virtually all of the texts written in England in this period, Sidney's *Apologie* is marked by the techniques of gathering and framing with which it was written. It differs from its humanist predecessors partly in the powerful and ironic voice that it generates. This voice works to unify the gathered fragments, and to smooth over the gaps between them. Nevertheless, Sidney's *Apologie* is fundamentally a gathering of com-monplaces of literary theory arranged on the organizational frame of the classical oration. An editor has called it "a selective summary of current theories" of literature derived largely from Aristotle, Scaliger, Horace, Plato, Mantuan, Henri Estienne, and others.[64] Thus, as Ronald Levao noted, Sidney can repeat two contradictory theories of the nature of the poet (inspired "vates," or craftsmanlike "maker") without bothering to reconcile them.[65] We can find, scattered over his text, the range of Latin quotations and commonplaces that we have come to expect in the discourse of this period. The *Apologie* begins with an anecdotal exemplum, and includes standard quotations from Virgil, Cicero, and other classical authors.[66] And despite his defense of vernacular literature, he includes no quotations or tags from that body of texts.

Sidney also repeats many of the commonplaces familiar from our readings of humanist logic, rhetoric, educational theory, and poetry, but they are irrevocably altered by an infusion of new ideas from the Continent, ideas that would, in theory, destroy the practice of gathering.[67] His description of the means and purpose of education is a typical example, combining old and new into a synthesis that looks more "modern" (that is, pre-postmodern) than anything we have seen so far.[68] Sidney's revision of supplementation is particularly significant because, unlike the humanists, he elevates the natural over the artificial. While humanist educators openly admitted that their project involved artificial supplementation, or the construction of a subject out of foreign bits of text, Sidney claims that education simply guides what is already present.

He first describes education, conventionally enough, as both enabling and controlling separate faculties of mind: "this purifying of wit—this enriching of memory, enabling of judgement, and enlarging of conceit—which commonly we call learning." But he goes on to describe its purpose in (what was in England) a new way: "the final end is to lead and draw us to as high a perfection as our degenerate souls, made worse by their clayey lodgings, can be capable of" (82). The idea, here unqualified by images of imprisonment and coercion, that the purpose of learning is to "lead and draw" the self to "as high a perfection" as possible is different from humanist theories depicting learning as the necessary supplementation of an imperfect and incomplete subject with fragments of canonical texts. For Sidney, the soul is degenerate, but complete, and needs only to be led. In using a metaphor of "leading" rather than "framing," Sidney also signals an antihumanist willingness to embrace process, experience, and narrative.

His account of the nature of poetry is based on a similar version of the supplemental relation between nature and art. Sidney uses his Neoplatonic theories to redeem the imagination, redefining it as a source of natural copia already controlled by judgment. The organic metaphors that humanists used to depict the interaction of self and text here represent the workings of the fertile imagination, and "invention" shifts to its modern sense. The poet, lifted up with the vigour of his own invention, doth grow in effect another nature, in making things either better than nature bringeth forth, or, quite anew. . . . Nature never set forth the earth in so rich tapestry as divers poets have done; neither with so pleasant rivers, fruitful trees, sweet-smelling flowers, nor whatsoever else may make the too much loved earth more lovely. (78)

Here, "invention" is the poet's "own" possession, and he is able to generate within himself all the authorizing faculties of logic and rhetoric: within his own mind he produces the woven tapestry of schemes and tropes, the rivers of originary authority, the fruitful trees of education, and the sweet smelling flowers of rhetoric. The effect of this self-generative power is the formation of both the organic work of art and the transcendent artistic self, as the poet is "lifted up" by his own powers.

Because the poet is able to create his own copia, his own authority, and his own self, from within himself, gathering is, at least in theory, not necessary. Indeed, it is denigrated as the unnecessary supplement to discourse, which is now described as visual or vocal, and not as a material entity. The "poet only bringeth his own stuff, and doth not learn a conceit out of a matter, but maketh matter for a conceit" (99).[69] Imitation can now be described, in Continental terms, as the ingestion and assimilation of whole works: "by attentive translation (as it were) devour them whole, and make them wholly theirs" (117). Gathered matter is denigrated as "far-fet maxims" (93), "far-fet words" (117), or "figures and flowers, extremely winter-starved" (117), while proper poetry embodies "a speaking picture" (86). Dramatically reversing the humanist account of the action of sayings, Sidney says that the precepts of philosophy offer a "wordish description, which doth neither strike, pierce, nor possess the sight of the soul so much as" poetry (85). Thus, Aesop's fables, previously described as "invented for the moralles sake," are now said to let the reader "hear the sound of virtue from these dumb speakers" (87).

Sidney's theory of naturally occurring copia is controlled, or framed, by the rational faculty and its knowledge of decorum. The poet is superior to the historian, for example, because he can "frame his example to that which is most reasonable" (87). Similarly, the "imaginative and judging" powers of the mind can be paired, where previously they were at odds. Sidney describes at great length the superior educative power of poetry that can "guide," "lead," "illuminate," and give "insight" into virtue, but he does not discuss how the rational power of the poet is to be developed in the first place.

At this point, the social implications of Sidney's theories become obvious. True eloquence, properly controlled by reason and decorum, occurs naturally and cannot be gathered or learned. Thus, Sidney has inevitably "found in divers smally learned courtiers a more sound style than in some professors of learning" because they "by practice" find a style that is "fittest to nature" (118–19). Sidney has hit what Derek Attridge has termed "Puttenham's perplexity"—the problem of defining a socially constituted decorum as natural.[70] He may be less able than his humanist predecessors to accept cultural difference because he is more implicated in defining an "essential" human self, and, as a result, conflates failure to maintain discursive decorum with cultural otherness.

In Sidney's text, the ear becomes a dangerously contested site of colonization. He describes users of commonplace books as being "like those Indians, not content to wear earrings at the fit and natural place of the ears, but they will thrust jewels through their nose and lips" (117). And once a certain kind of culturally determined speech is defined as "natural," any "art" that diverges from it becomes an unnecessary supplement, so that overuse of similitudes is a "surfeit to the ears" (118). Similarly, the power of uncommon speech over common people, in a striking reversal of humanist rhetorical theory, is denied: in order to "win credit of popular ears," a writer must use "these knacks [of art] sparingly" (118). While humanists had made the dangerous claim that their art enabled control over the populace, Sidney denigrates the power of artifice and also, perhaps, the ability of the common people to appreciate it.

Of course, the treatise itself makes effective use of similitudes and other such gathered rhetorical knacks. And in his conclusion, Sidney denigrates his own work as a worthless trifle or "ink-wasting toy" (121). The *Apologie* seems to have layer upon layer of argument. First, he makes use of humanist techniques and, at times, acknowledges their theoretical and moral force. In other places, however, he adduces Continental theories about the natural creative power of the imagination that seem to explode English humanist practice and provide the first serious theoretical basis in England for aristocratic modes of behavior and discourse. Beyond this, however, is the ironic voice of this oration's speaker, who, as various critics have noted, undermines his own argument as a courtly jeu d'esprit.[71] Thus, although Sidney seems to have "solved" the dilemma of his generation, the solution turns out to be, at least in part, a rhetorical illusion. What remains, however, is the captivating, ironic voice, which locates itself—quite consciously—in between the two systems that constitute it.

Sidney's *Astrophil and Stella* sequence also seeks to establish a naturally occurring aristocratic copia, based in imagination and aware of, if not entirely framed by, the force of reason. Sidney resolves the uneasy experiments of Gascoigne and others with fictionality and narrative by creating a clearly established and consistent persona, who both is, and is not, Sidney.[72] Through Astrophil, Sidney is able to treat the problematic nature of poetic composition, the moral status and purpose of poetry, and its social status, without directly implicating himself. His ironic distance protects him from his dangerous experiments with poetry and the poetic self, and that irony is again a product of the clash of the humanist and courtly systems. He treats some of the same problems as does Wyatt in the form of conflicts between reason and passion, virtue and desire, but uses narrative to effect a complex double movement. Each individual sonnet tends to narrate the victory of courtly over humanist values; the sequence as a whole, on the other hand, depicts the failure of courtly desire, even as it maintains the witty self fashioned in its shadow.

As various critics have argued, *Astrophil and Stella* is a text with strong social and political implications. Most of these critics understand the sequence to use love as a kind of substitute for frustrated social and political ambition.[73] But I believe that we can be more precise about the social context of these poems, that we can place their political project in the context of Lord Burghley and the conflicting humanist and aristocratic systems which he used to forestall upward mobility.[74] In *Astrophil and Stella*, Sidney uses a quasi-fictional love affair in order both to rebel against Burghley and to forge a version of the aristocratic self that contains, but is not contained by, the humanist ethical frame.

Despite his reputation (now, and soon after his death) as the archetypal Elizabethan courtier, Sir Philip Sidney was, after all, just a knight.[75] As the heir of Leicester and Warwick, he had aristocratic hopes, but they were never realized.[76] In fact, Sidney, more than any other writer of the period, was located at the juncture of humanist and aristocratic systems. He had a humanist education but also participated in courtly pastimes.[77] He was the recipient of a typically humanist letter of advice from his father, Henry Sidney, and wrote a similar letter to Edward Denny.[78] His most notorious failure at court, however, stemmed from his attempt to assume the role of adviser to the queen, writing a "Letter" that argued against her proposed marriage with Alençon and earned her disfavor. Thus, although he ought to have been uniquely suited to achieve success even within the contradictory system instituted by the queen and Burghley, he unfortunately achieved it only after his death.

In this context, it seems quite plausible that Sidney, like the earlier poets of the Devonshire manuscript, used love poetry to assert his proficiency in romantic pastime and to create a privatized sphere in which he could rehearse, and rewrite, courtly failure as amorous success. But throughout his life, Sidney's involvement in love relationships was more bureaucratic than courtly, and was itself implicated in the conflict between humanist and aristocratic values. For, unlike Sir Thomas Howard and Margaret Douglas, Sidney was in no position to assert his status or aristocratic prerogative through an independent marriage. That he was not was testimony to his ambiguous social situation and also to the power of Lord Burghley, through the Court of Wards, over marriage arrangements in this period. Until his marriage in 1583 to Frances Walsingham, Sidney, his father, and Burghley were constantly engaged in complex negotiations regarding the possibility of his marriage to various women.[79]

Because of Philip's liminal place in society, these negotiations were particularly delicate. In 1569, Burghley seriously considered a match between Philip and his daughter Anne but withdrew in 1571 when he discovered how little Henry Sidney's property was worth, and was himself made a peer.[80] In 1576, Penelope Devereux's father (Walter, first earl of Essex) realized that he was dying and tried to forestall Burghley's control over his minor children by making arrangements for them before his death.[81] He attempted to set up a marriage between Philip and Penelope, but the Sidneys turned it down, probably because she did not have enough money or status to be considered a suitable match for Leicester's heir.

When Penelope Devereaux's marriage to Lord Rich was arranged by Burghley in 1581, however, Sidney was at the nadir of his fortunes and was evidently not even considered as a prospective husband for her.[82] For in 1579, Leicester, who had married Lettice Knowles, widow of the earl of Essex, had a son, Lord Denbigh, who lived until 1584. While this child lived, Sidney was, of course, no longer his uncle's heir.[83] Around the same time, Sidney wrote his ill-fated letter of advice to the queen and failed as a humanist adviser as well. At this low point of his fortunes, Sidney married Frances Walsingham, of a respectable family but no great catch. She would surely not have been considered even a few years earlier.[84] By the early 1580s, then, Sidney seemed to have failed as both aristocratic courtier and humanist bureaucrat. The complex and ongoing negotiations with Burghley about his marriage possibilities suggest, however, that the erotic sphere was as fully implicated in Sidney's difficult situation as were the social and political. Under such circumstances, love poetry would hardly serve as a way to escape from or evade his problems.

A sequence written at this time, fantasizing about an illicit affair with a woman who was once not good enough but is now too good for him, is at once a protest against Burghley's control of the marriage market and against Sidney's own devaluation within both the aristocratic and humanist systems. The sequence asserts the naturally occurring copia of imagination and style, and demonstrates that the author is aware of humanist precepts and at least toys with their willful rejection. He need not be given humanist advice; he has internalized it and tests it against various courtly values. It is also a muted assertion of the dangerous power of the imagination and the will to persuade others to act against the precepts of reason and the stifling social hierarchy. The poems are, as various critics have noticed, largely about their own composition and almost obsessively interested in exploring their own sources in the conflicting systems of value. Sidney has a vocabulary with which to do this because he is engaged in creating, from two contradictory systems, a new, enabling, discourse.

The opening poem of the sequence establishes its terms; it might serve as a summation of many of the ideas and practices discussed in this study. It is essentially a narrative account of its own composition and incorporates within itself a number of the contradictions that had been played out on the margins of previous collections of poems. It begins with a bold programmatic assertion of antihumanist principles:

> Loving in truth, and faine in verse my love to show,
> That the deare She might take some pleasure of my paine;
> Pleasure might cause her reade, reading might make her know,
> Knowledge might pitie winne, and pitie grace obtaine.[85]

The poet asserts that he writes out of his present experience of love, and the participle "loving" emphasizes that this experience is present and on-going (not a rejected experience of the past). He already possesses the naturally occurring copia of feelings and is now concerned to translate them into words. He is "faine," or desirous of doing this, with a pun on the alternative sense of "fictionalize." The pun suggests, perhaps, that the expression of feeling in verse necessarily involves imagination, and, perhaps, even deceit.[86] Whetstone's assertion to the reader that "mine was the paine in framing the plots, wherin these fruits and flowers grow, yours is the pleasure and profite of both" provides a context for the next lines. Sidney's felt pain (not the pains he has taken in writing) will lead to a particular reader's "pleasure" and, he hopes, to his own eventual profit. The *concatenatio* disguises his new and questionable purpose (seduction) as a conventional account of the process of reading.[87] Humanists had argued that pleasure led to reading which led to knowledge; but rather than seeing poetry as leading to right action, Sidney stresses its affective power: it will cause pity, which will lead to "grace." Use of the religious term again masks the sexual purpose. The poem, despite its use of humanist terminology, advertises itself as a maneuver in the courtly pastime of love.

Sidney then turns to an account of composition by gathering, which is nevertheless altered by some of the new ideas expressed in his *Apologie*:

> I sought fit words to paint the blackest face of woe,
> Studying inventions fine, her wits to entertaine:
> Oft turning others' leaves, to see if thence would flow
> Some fresh and fruitfull showers upon my sunne-burn'd braine.

The poet approaches composition, as taught in school, by searching for matter to gather. He seeks "fit words," which, to a humanist, would be words that were properly framed, but to the Sidney of the *Defence* would mean decorous and socially apt. He wants to use these words to create a "speaking picture," however, and not a moral argument. And, as Anne Ferry has noted, he intends to use this gathered matter in order to "paint" a sad face, implying that his feelings are artificial, and even false.[88] Sidney here in fact questions the natural copia of feeling, since he must "faine" or "paint" his woe using inventions gathered from elsewhere.

Nevertheless, he proceeds as he has been taught, "oft turning others' leaves," in search of matter. These gathered "leaves" are to be contrasted, perhaps, with the natural growth of the poet's imagination described in the *Apologie*. Sidney uses the pivotal word "invention" for the first (of three) times in the poem, here in a sense that is closest to its older meaning of "gathering." Here, it could mean matter that he finds in the work of other writers, or matter that they have found, or matter that they have made up and he has found. He hopes that the "fresh and fruitfull showers" of originary authority will flow, as humanist theorists said it would, from their pages to him. But these showers are needed, ironically, because his brain has been parched by too much contact with the ancients.

The conflicts between the various theories of discourse available to Sidney become even more intense in the sestet, and the conclusion of the poem does not resolve them:

> But words came halting forth, wanting Invention's stay,
> Invention, Nature's child, fled step-dame Studie's blowes,
> And others' feete still seem'd but strangers in my way.
> Thus great with child to speake, and helplesse in my throwes,
>   Biting my trewand pen, beating my selfe for spite,
>   "Foole," said my Muse to me, "looke in they heart and write."

The gathering method does not work, paradoxically, because Astrophil lacks the frame provided by invention, its "stay." In this context "invention" seems to mean gathering, but we learn in the next line that invention is "Nature's child," and that it flees the coercive goads of education, which is a stepmother or a cruel and unnecessary supplement.[89] In a reversal of Agricola's sense of gathering as a means of following the footsteps of the ancients to reach one's own goal, Sidney finds that "others' feete" are "strangers in my way," presumably in accordance with the theories of the *Defence* in which the purpose of education is to lead the self in its own way.

For Sidney's problem is not that he lacks matter. He is already pregnant with his own child, "invention." But he is, for some reason, unable to give birth to it. The birth metaphor, studiously avoided by English humanists, here reflects Sidney's new sense that the imagination is redeemable. Sidney attempts to discipline himself, applying to himself the educative goads of "Step-dame Studie." And this self-discipline seems to resolve his problem. A mysterious muse appears, insults him, and tells him to "looke" in his own heart and copy the natural copia that he finds there.[90] The poem implies, however, that this copia cannot be tapped unless some sort of discipline is applied. The pain of love cannot be expressed unless it is coercively framed and controlled. But, unlike humanist versions of the educative and discursive process, this coercion must be internalized, and it does not ensure either the efficacy or the morality of what it produces.

The struggle between Reason and Passion, Virtue and Desire, that continues throughout the sequence, represents a similar internalization of humanist ideals. On the one hand, individual poems tend to enact a brief narrative sequence in which Reason or Virtue struggles with Passion and Desire, and is defeated. Sonnet no. 19, for example, resembles Wyatt's "Ffarewell, Love" in enacting the speaker's inability to choose between humanist precept and courtly pastime. It differs from Wyatt, however, in the addition of narrative values, in ultimately seeming to reject reason for love, and in the ironic wit that the speaker uses to distance himself from his dilemma.

This sonnet begins with a truncated hunting metaphor: the speaker's condition of immersion in love involves having his "heart-strings bent" on "*Cupid's* bow."[91] The "bend" suggests the wayward errancy of feelings that have wandered away from serious moral purpose. Like Wyatt's speaker (in both "Ffarewell, Love," and "Who so list to hunt"), Astrophil is trapped in an inconclusive situation involving attraction and repulsion, involvement and repentance: he sees his "wracke" and embraces it, runs toward his desire and repents his running.

Unlike Wyatt, however, Astrophil is self-consciously aware of the problematics of poetic composition in this situation. He watches himself trying to write out of two conflicting systems, but his inability to choose yields ironic distance rather than hopeless angst. From a humanist point of view, he sees his "best wits still their owne disgrace invent." Instead of the "grace" that he hoped to obtain from his beloved, he "invents" (in a fully ambiguous use of the term—both finds and creates) his own disgrace. His undisciplined pen eludes the framed stay of wise precepts and wanders or "turnes straight to *Stella's* name." He is, however, fully aware that this is a frivolous pastime: as he, ironically, "frame[s]" these unframed words, they themselves provide humanist "avise" that they are "vainely spent" in the conspicuous expenditure of courtly display.

The sestet seems to mark a turn away from the allure of love. Astrophil asks himself "what is all / That unto me," and cites a common saying to describe his condition as one who "Lookes to the skies, and in a ditch doth fall." Like Wyatt's wind in the net, this saying, often used as a critique of Platonism, describes the situation of someone who fails while striving for something insubstantial.[92] It also descibes the consequences of errancy; of unframed "turning" toward love, and uncontrolled expenditure of natural copia. Astrophil seems to reject this path, asking to be able to "prop" his "mind" (undoubtedly with the frame of "Invention's stay") so that it will be able to produce the humanist "fruits" for which it has been made fit. But the final line, with a movement typical of Sidney's sonnets, "turns" away from this solution: the *volta* literally re-turns to and voluntarily embraces the initial "bend" of desire: " 'Scholler,' saith *Love* 'bend hitherward your wit.' "

The complex play on "bend" and "frame" in this poem reenacts, in little, the social and intellectual conflicts of Sidney's age. But although courtly pastime seems to win out, that victory is itself contained by the ironic self-awareness of the voice that proclaims it. For that voice, unlike Wyatt's, is not engendered by pain, but by alienation. It perceives the incompatibility of the two systems in which it works, and uses that distance to create the space in which it exists and reflects on itself. When the speaker ends the poem with Love's advice to bend the wit away from the humanist frame, he establishes his own freedom to imagine and to choose such an act, without, however, committing himself to it. The narrative movement of the sequence as a whole is equally inconclusive—although the predictions of the humanist adviser seem to come true as the projected seduction of Stella fails. So it is perhaps the greatest irony of all that, despite his rebellious stance, Astrophil's narrative finally is confined within the social and intellectual conventions he would deny.

The sequence as a whole, then, depicts the failure of passion, desire, and literary persuasion to overcome reason, virtue, and advice as they exist outside the poet. The sequence thus establishes the poet's self as a private space for subversion, while, at the same time, asserting the power of the status quo in the world outside. More important, however, the sequence establishes the myth of a "whole" essential self that is sufficient even in its natural state to see its situation clearly and speak its own desires, if not persuasively, then ironically. The sequence, indeed, performs the constitution of that self and that myth before our eyes. It is a powerful myth, and the long and well-established tradition of gathering would ultimately have little strength in its face.

There is, however, a postscript to this story, one which hints that Sidney was aware of the misrecognition that is bound up with this version of the self, however self-aware it tries to be. In his description of Sidney's deathbed, Fulke Greville applies a prodigal narrative of sorts, making Sidney order that his *Arcadia* be burned because "beauty itself, in all earthly complexions, was more apt to allure men to evil than to frame any goodness in them."[93] Whether this is a reflection of Sidney's words or a

pious invention of the more conventional Greville, it nevertheless reflects deep uncertainty about Sidney's formulations. For if literature is designed to "lead" rather than "frame," it is perhaps more likely to lead to evil than to good. Sidney may have seen that the "allure" must simply camouflage the disciplinary frame, just as the fiction of an essentialist self hides its social construction.

CONCLUSION

S IDNEY, of course, did not mark the end of the humanist practices of gathering and framing. But he did formulate versions of self and text which so brilliantly accommodated humanist and courtly practice that they become more difficult to separate. Those who wrote after Sidney inherited a version of gathering and framing that was transformed, almost beyond recognition, in both theory and practice.

Shakespeare's sonnets, for instance, seem even further removed from the aphoristic epigrams of the 1520s, or the lumbering fourteeners of Tottel's Miscellany. And yet, their curiously modern subjectivity, characterized, as Fineman has argued, by a simultaneous construction and deconstruction of their present self, is generated in part by the rival versions of the self that we have been tracing here.[1] Shakespeare famously reworks the relationship between advice and love, epigram and sonnet, in a mixture of new complexity.[2] But where the disjunction between adviser and lover led Sidney to a detached and ironic pose, Shakespeare's sonnet speaker projects a self that combines, and questions, both attitudes. Similarly, his detachable and enigmatic couplets test the efficacy of aphoristic formulations to sum up and forestall experience.

Many of his sonnets replay the commonplaces that we have traced throughout this period—gathering and expending (129), copia and closure (1), engraving and planting (15, 5), poison and cure (118)—but combined and recombined with dazzling and confusing rapidity, in new contexts and situations. In 122, Shakespeare's speaker explicitly takes up the supplemental role of a commonplace book in generating and preserving the lyric subject. In this sonnet, the speaker contrasts actual notebooks or "tables" with those "within my brain / Full character'd with lasting memory."[3] The actual books are, at least on one level, derided as an unnecessary "adjunct" to memory, a cure that, as Plato argued of writing itself, will "import" (imply, but also bring in) forgetfulness. To this extent, Shakespeare seems to reject the humanists' belief in the power of supplemental gathering and framing in a notebook to preserve and shape the subject.

But the poem also acknowledges that the boundary between mental and actual "tables" cannot be so strictly drawn. In the first line of the poem, the speaker seems initially to be talking about actual notebooks that have been received as a gift: "Thy gifts, thy tables." Not until the third line are the mental tables contrasted with the "idle rank" (now connecting commonplace books with frivolous pastimes) of actual tables. And the use of "character'd" to describe the engraving of the beloved on the mind is significant in several ways. First of all, Shakespeare here, unusually, depicts his record of the young man *not* as an image, but as a written "record," engraved on the memory as sayings were in humanist educational theory. But "character'd" also implies the power of such engraving to shape the subject itself, in the very process of recording the object.

In the second quatrain, the speaker also admits that mental tables are only temporary; that is, they can only "subsist" as long as "raz'd oblivion" spares them. "Subsist" here, from the Latin root *subsistere* (to stand under and support) implies material existence supported by a stay, prop, or frame. The speaker here seems more intent on rejecting the accumulation of cultural capital ("nor need I tallies thy dear love to score") and the use of external tables to display it, than the actual writing down or recording of his love. The couplet, of course, acknowledges the danger of writing as supplement but does not explicitly reject it. Indeed, as the poem has shown, it cannot be rejected.

Nor could the practices of gathering and framing be rejected by such central seventeenth-century figures as Bacon, Jonson, Herbert, and Herrick. Sir Francis Bacon, with roots in the same problematic milieu as Sidney, with a similarly difficult relationship to powerful humanists like his father and Burghley, carried gathering into the seventeenth century in a form that was more controlled, and less powerful. Bacon's new science is based, to a greater extent than many critics have realized, on gathering "textualized" fragments from nature, and reframing them as scientific aphorisms. Jonson, Herbert, and Herrick write poems that are, in various ways, influenced by the traditions of commonplace miscellany and aphoristic epigram that I have been tracing.[4] Indeed, Herrick wrote some epigrams that might have been taken directly from Bodenham.

Nevertheless, the seventeenth century effectively ended the social efficacy of these humanist practices. The conflict of humanist and courtier was replaced by (or subsumed into) the more volatile and violent conflict of Puritan and Royalist. Pastime, for instance, takes on new political connotations in the context of the controversy over the Book of Sports. And secular sayings are replaced, in large part, by biblical citations.[5] True index of the change is probably Milton, who kept a commonplace book but did not fill it with aphorisms, who used and assimilated classical works as wholes, and who replaced gathering with something more like imitation as we understand it.[6] Yet even Milton retained a sense that the primary intellectual activity involved gathering and framing as well as choice. In "Of Education," for instance, he argues that literary composition in prose and verse should be "the finall work of a head fill'd by long reading, and observing, with elegant maxims, and copious invention."[7]

More telling is his fondness for the exemplum of Orpheus as inspired poet, an analogy that would seem to conceive of literary invention in terms very different from those implied by gathering and framing. But in our fallen world, the inspired poet exists in fragments, torn apart, to be reconstructed by his readers.[8] Thus, although

> Truth indeed came into the world with her divine Master, and was a perfect shape, most glorious to look on. . . . [there] arose a wicked race of deceivers, who . . . took the virgin Truth, hewd her lovely form into a thousand peeces, and scatter'd them to the four winds. From that time ever since, the sad friends of Truth, such as durst appear, imitating the careful search that *Isis* made for the mangl'd body of Osiris, went up and down gathering up limb by limb still as they could find them.[9]

Not until the second coming will these fragments be framed or "molded" into their prelapsarian form. That Milton, in such different circumstances, retained this much of the humanist practices suggests how powerful they were. And although they are now hard for us to piece together, we must attempt to do so if we are to begin to understand the English Renaissance in all its otherness.

NOTES

INTRODUCTION

1. R. R. Bolgar, *The Classical Heritage and Its Beneficiaries* (Cambridge: Cambridge University Press, 1954), 265–75.

2. Notable exceptions include important articles by Walter Ong, John M. Wallace, Marion Trousdale, and Daniel Kinney, as well as Anne Ferry's *The Art of Naming*, Richard Halpern's *The Poetics of Primitive Accumulation*, and, for the medieval period, Mary Carruthers's *The Book of Memory*. Ong, in several places, including *Interfaces of the Word: Studies in the Evolution of Consciousness and Culture* (Ithaca: Cornell University Press, 1977), 147–79, stresses the importance of the commonplace tradition as an element of oral culture preserved even beyond the invention of printing. Wallace, " 'Examples Are Best Precepts': Readers and Meanings in Seventeenth-Century Poetry," *Critical Inquiry* 1 (1974): 273–90, argues that Plutarch's essay on "How a yoong man ought to heare poets" influenced Renaissance readers to mine whatever they read for ethical precepts. Trousdale, "A Possible Renaissance View of Form," *ELH* 40 (1973): 179–204, recognizes that Elizabethan writers and readers took an "essentially expedient approach to literature," considering it primarily as a store of illustrative exempla. She includes a similar argument in *Shakespeare and the Rhetoricians* (Chapel Hill: University of North Carolina Press, 1982). Daniel Kinney, "Erasmus' *Adagia*: Midwife to the Rebirth of Learning," *Journal of Medieval and Renaissance Studies* 11 (1981): 169–92, argues that Erasmus believed classical wisdom could best be assimilated in fragments rather than wholes. He does not, however, discuss the commonplace book. Anne Ferry, *The Art of Naming* (Chicago: University of Chicago Press, 1988), 83–124, notes the importance of "borrowing" and the commonplaces as part of her discussion of metaphor. Richard Halpern, *The Poetics of Primitive Accumulation: English Renaissance Culture and the Genealogy of Capital* (Ithaca: Cornell University Press, 1991), 48–49, 91, discusses some of the economic implications of copia and commonplace books. Mary Carruthers, *The Book of Memory: A Study of Memory in Medieval Culture* (Cambridge: Cambridge University Press, 1990), traces the role of the commonplaces in the medieval memory tradition. Sister Joan Marie Lechner, *Renaissance Concepts of the Commonplaces* (New York: Pageant Press, 1962), also notes the importance of the "places" but does not go much beyond summarizing contemporary descriptions of them. Lawrence Manley, "Proverbs, Epigrams, and Urbanity in Renaissance London," *English Literary Renaissance* 15 (1985): 247–76, discusses the role of proverbs as a repository of community values.

3. Thomas M. Greene, *The Light in Troy: Imitation and Discovery in Renaissance Poetry* (New Haven: Yale University Press, 1982), 318. He suggests that Italian writers for seventy-five years after the death of Petrarch "failed to produce interesting discussions of imitation" partly because of "the pedagogic method of the commonplace book, which tended to foster syncretic textures of fragmentary allusions or topoi and left little room for extended reflection" (147). He speaks

more positively, however, about *"eclectic* or *exploitative"* imitation, which "treats all traditions as stockpiles to be drawn upon ostensibly at random" (39). I will argue that the commonplace book in sixteenth-century England fostered this type of imitation.

4. H. A. Mason, *Humanism and Poetry in the Early Tudor Period* (New York: Barnes and Noble, 1959), 111, and Paul Oskar Kristeller, "Humanist Moral Philosophy," in Albert Rabil, Jr., ed., *Renaissance Humanism: Foundations, Forms, and Legacy,* vol. 3 (Philadelphia: University of Pennsylvania Press, 1988), 281. Mason acknowledges the influence of the commonplace book but believes that it was almost entirely negative. Geoffrey Bennington, *Sententiousness and the Novel: Laying Down the Law in Eighteenth-Century French Fiction* (Cambridge: Cambridge University Press, 1985), suggests that "the formal incompatibility of sententious propositions and the narrative-descriptive complex . . . is something of an embarrassment to rhetoricians" and critics (50). Critics may also be bothered by the lack of originality and individualism attendant upon the use of commonplaces.

5. Bolgar, *Classical Heritage,* 268. William G. Crane, *Wit and Rhetoric in the Renaissance: The Formal Basis of Elizabethan Prose Style* (New York: Columbia University Press, 1937), chapter 3, argues that commonplace books provided material for the witty "amplification and ornamentation of compositions" (33), and gives a useful list of titles of some published volumes. Arthur Kinney, *Humanist Poetics: Thought, Rhetoric, and Fiction in Sixteenth-Century England* (Amherst: University of Massachusetts Press, 1986), 11, provides a typical account of the commonplace book as a tool of imitation.

6. "Gather" and "frame" are used, throughout the sixteenth century, with such frequency that they become virtually technical terms. Part of the purpose of this book will be to trace their usage and shifts in meaning in the course of the period. Although they at first seem to be rough English equivalents for *inventio* and *dispositio,* the two parts of logic, their connotative force shifts as these discursive practices gain currency and fail to achieve humanist goals. "Frame," for example, begins by meaning either "to give material form to an immaterial idea" or "to arrange in coherent order according to some natural system." In political and social contexts, it later comes to mean something like "feign" or "falsify," and eventually, under the influence of Ramism, becomes a synonym for methodical organization.

7. Of course, as Mary Carruthers and others have shown, the topoi of gathering and framing originated in ancient texts and were current throughout the Middle Ages. However, early English humanists took over these traditional commonplaces and reshaped them in response to their own particular needs.

8. For a recent restatement of this version of individualism and authorship in the earlier sixteenth century, see Joel Fineman, *Shakespeare's Perjured Eye: The Invention of Subjectivity in the Sonnets* (Berkeley and Los Angeles: University of California Press, 1986), 84–85, who relates the sonnet tradition of "literature of subjective interiority" to "analogous Renaissance impulses to individuation" that led to the formation of "privatized, bourgeois, psychological identity." He goes on, however, to question this "Burckhardtian Renaissance 'first person,' " especially as it applies to the later sixteenth century and to Shakespeare's sonnets. A number of critics have similarly questioned the existence of a "modern" concept

of the self in the sixteenth century. Anne Ferry, *The "Inward" Language: Sonnets of Wyatt, Sidney, Shakespeare, Donne* (Chicago: University of Chicago Press, 1983), has traced its gradual development, toward the end of the century, through the medium of the sonnet. Stephen Greenblatt, "Psychoanalysis and Renaissance Culture," in Patricia Parker and David Quint, eds., *Literary Theory / Renaissance Texts* (Baltimore: The Johns Hopkins University Press, 1986), 210–24, argues that the concept of the self upon which psychoanalysis is based was "made possible by (among other things) the legal and literary proceedings of the sixteenth and seventeenth centuries" (221). Jonathan Dollimore, *Radical Tragedy: Religion, Ideology and Power in the Drama of Shakespeare and His Contemporaries* (Chicago: University of Chicago Press, 1984), locates the dissolution of "humanism and the transcendent subject" in Jacobean tragedy.

9. As Thomas Greene, for example, traced in various texts from this period. Greene's brilliant discussion of imitation "fits" Continental texts better than sixteenth-century English ones; he notices what he calls a "the gradual, *filtered* reception of Elizabethan neoclassicism," and does not find a clear exemplar of classical *imitatio* until Ben Jonson in the early seventeenth century (*Light*, 270). In general, theorists of imitation tend to rely on Italian discussions that had, I will argue, limited influence in England before the 1580s.

10. In this regard, I accord with the recent work of Anthony Grafton and Lisa Jardine, *From Humanism to the Humanities* (Cambridge: Harvard University Press, 1986), xiii–xiv, who argue that humanist education throughout Europe "fitted the needs of the new Europe that was taking shape." In the first two chapters of his book, Halpern suggests some of the ways in which "the stylistic education offered by the Tudor schools helped produce a nascent form of bourgeois culture" (*Poetics*, 60). The application of class labels (such as "middle-class") to early modern England has been the subject of much debate. Michael McKeon, *The Origins of the English Novel 1600–1740* (Baltimore: The Johns Hopkins University Press, 1987), 159–75, provides a particularly good account of the historical controversy over the use of such terms as "gentry," "merchant class," and "middle class," arguing that those terms are so hard to pin down precisely because this was a period of profound "status indeterminacy," when concepts of status were being replaced by concepts of social class. Nevertheless, "middle-class" remains a useful term to describe the social role—as working gentlemen— that these writers were attempting to construct.

11. See Victoria Kahn, "Humanism and the Resistance to Theory," in Parker and Quint, *Literary Theory*, 373–96. Kahn argues that humanists all over Europe harbored a "pedagogically motivated resistance to theory conceived of as undecidability" (374). I use the term "theory" here to distinguish texts that offer guidelines for discourse and teaching from "practical" documents more immediately embedded in social and political interaction. The version of "theory" that I find in humanist commonplaces is precisely designed to counter what Kahn describes as the threat of "undecidabilty" or skepticism.

12. Manley ("Proverbs") has recognized a close link between proverbs and epigrams in a slightly different context toward the end of this period.

13. Alistair Fox, "Facts and Fallacies: Interpreting English Humanism," in Fox and John Guy, eds., *Reassessing the Henrician Age: Humanism, Politics and Reform 1500–1550* (Oxford: Blackwell, 1986), 9–33, provides a useful summary

204 NOTES TO INTRODUCTION

of the controversy over the constituents, scope, and influence of English humanism in the political sphere. He cites R. W. Chambers, *Thomas More* (London:
Cape, 1935), and Frederic Seebohm, *The Oxford Reformers* (London, 1869), for
the idea that humanism in England dies out with More and Fisher or was "sub-
merged" under the Reformation, a view countered by Douglas Bush, *The Renaissance and English Humanism* (Toronto: University of Toronto Press, 1939). On
the other hand, both James McConica, *English Humanists and Reformation Politics under Henry VIII and Edward VI* (Oxford: Oxford University Press, 1965),
and Arthur B. Ferguson, *The Articulate Citizen and the English Renaissance*
(Durham, N.C.: Duke University Press, 1965), argue that Erasmian humanism in
England directly fostered political and religious reform. Fritz Caspari, *Humanism
and the Social Order in Tudor England* (Chicago: University of Chicago Press,
1954), argues that English humanism both defended the hierarchical social system and encouraged the growth of republicanism. Fox himself believes that Erasmian humanism had little or no direct influence on politics or political reform.
Daniel Javitch, *Poetry and Courtliness in Renaissance England* (Princeton:
Princeton University Press, 1978), 18–19, provides a summary of definitions of
humanism and goes on to argue that in England the humanist model of orator was
insufficiently sophisticated to succeed at court. As for literary influence, Bush
traces the influence of Christian humanism on Milton, while Mason (*Humanism*)
is concerned to distinguish "false" humanism, which inhibited literature, from its
true forms, which particularly influenced Ben Jonson. Arthur Kinney (*Humanist
Poetics*) traces the influence of humanism on prose fiction in sixteenth-century
England. G. K. Hunter, *John Lyly: The Humanist as Courtier* (Cambridge: Harvard University Press, 1962), argues that the literature of the 1580s and 1590s
was produced in part by the failure of humanism to achieve its social goals.

14. For Louis Althusser's "anti-humanism" see especially *For Marx* (London:
New Left, 1977), and *Lenin and Philosophy and Other Essays* (London: New
Left, 1977). For an application of Althusser to Renaissance literature, see Dolli-
more, *Radical Tragedy*, especially 17–19, 153–82. For some of the ideological
implications of the term in modern culture, see Raymond Williams, *Keywords*
(New York: Oxford University Press, 1976), 122–23.

15. Stephen Greenblatt, *Renaissance Self-Fashioning: From More to Shakespeare* (Chicago: University of Chicago Press, 1980), 174. The "syncretic structures" of English humanism often seem conflated, in the works of Greenblatt and
other New Historicists, with the structures (such as Tillyard's "Elizabethan world
picture" or Dover Wilson's assertions of Shakespearean orthodoxy) erected by
the earlier generation of scholars against which these more recent critics react.

16. Paul Oskar Kristeller has suggested such a definition in a number of places.
See also Hanna Gray, "Renaissance Humanism: The Pursuit of Eloquence," *Journal of the History of Ideas* 24 (1963): 497–514, for the role of rhetoric in this
curriculum. Victoria Kahn, *Rhetoric, Prudence, and Skepticism in the Renaissance* (Ithaca: Cornell University Press, 1985), argues persuasively that the Renaissance rhetorical tradition involved an "active conception of reading" designed
to "educate the reader's prudential judgment" (20). She is concerned to trace the
role of argument *in utramque partem* in developing this rhetorical praxis; I will
suggest that gathering and framing provided, particularly in England, a similar
practical and prudential strategy on the level of the brief textual fragment.

17. Both Mason (*Humanism*) and Fox ("Facts") consider a fondness for commonplaces constitutive of at least a branch of English humanism (Mason's "false" humanism, Fox's ineffectual "Erasmian humanism"). I believe that this aspect was more important, more widespread, and less damaging than either Mason or Fox suggests, however. A partial list of early English humanists (according to my criteria) might include More (before the break with Rome), William Lily, Sir John Cheke, Thomas Starkey, John Palsgrave, Richard Croke, Richard Pace, Sir Thomas Elyot, and Roger Ascham.

18. Although he does not specifically discuss "humanism" as such, Perry Anderson, *Lineages of the Absolutist State* (London: Verso, 1974), 48–51, traces the bureaucratization of government and the concomitant need for the aristocracy to "learn the new avocations of a disciplined officer, a literate functionary, a polished courtier, and a more or less prudent estate-owner" (48), all of which humanist education fostered. Lawrence Stone, *The Crisis of the Aristocracy 1558–1641* (Oxford: Clarendon Press, 1965), 673–722, traces the rise of humanist education as a credential for advancement that "increased the opportunities of the gentry to compete on more equal terms with the nobility" for political position. Mervyn James, *Society, Politics, and Culture: Studies in Early Modern England* (Cambridge: Cambridge University Press, 1986), 309, notes the importance of "humanistic 'wisdom' " in achieving the "moralization of politics" necessary for the state to obtain a monopoly of the "honour" and "violence" previously wielded by the aristocracy as the basis for a power rivaling that of the monarch. Fox and Guy, of course, argue that "the idealistic, didactic intent in Erasmian humanism rendered it an ineffectual force in politics" (*Reassessing*, 44).

19. I have borrowed the term "cultural capital" from the work of Pierre Bourdieu, especially (with Jean-Claude Passeron) his *Reproduction in Education, Society, and Culture*, trans. Richard Nice (London: Sage, 1977), and *Outline of a Theory of Practice*, trans. Richard Nice (Cambridge: Cambridge University Press, 1972). I will argue, however, that his critique of education is not entirely applicable to the premodern system of the sixteenth century. I have not been able fully to take account of Richard Halpern's recent book (*Poetics*); however, he also traces the role of the Tudor grammar school in the context of primitive accumulation. Although he discusses, as I do, the relationship of those schools to upward mobility and social regulation, he does not focus specifically on the notebook method.

20. For a clear explanation of the distinction between "subject" and "individual," see Kaja Silverman, *The Subject of Semiotics* (Oxford: Oxford University Press, 1983), 126–30. Silverman defines "individual" as a concept implying "an entity that is both autonomous and stable" (126), while "subject," on the other hand, suggests that "human reality" is a "construction . . . and the product of signifying activities which are both culturally specific and generally unconscious" (130). She locates the origin of the concept of "individual" in "the Renaissance," but I will argue that in sixteenth-century England humanists conceived of something more closely resembling her "subject," with this difference: they tried to make the "signifying activities" that formed the subject both conscious and, as far as possible, controllable.

21. I do not, however, agree with Alan Macfarlane's argument, in *The Origins of English Individualism: The Family, Property, and Social Transition* (Cam-

bridge: Cambridge University Press, 1979), that English society fostered a strong sense of individualism at all levels from the early Middle Ages.

22. The quoted phrases are from Steven Mullaney, *The Place of the Stage: License, Play and Power in Renaissance England* (Chicago: University of Chicago Press, 1988), 132.

23. Erasmus, in the *Adagia*, defines an adage as "a saying in popular use [*celebre dictum*], remarkable for some shrewd and novel [*novitate*] turn," cited from *Adages Ii1 to Iv100*, trans. Margaret Mann Phillips, ed. R.A.B. Mynors, vol. 31 in *The Collected Works of Erasmus* (Toronto: University of Toronto Press, 1982), 4. He goes on to stress that "there are then two things which are peculiar to the character of a proverb, common usage and novelty" (4). Similarly, the English rhetorician Henry Peacham, *The Garden of Eloquence*, ed. W. G. Crane (Gainsville, Fla.: Scholars' Facsimiles and Reprints, 1954), 29–30, states that a proverb must have two qualities: that it be "commonly knowen. . . . and much spoken of, as a sentence in everie mans mouth. The other that it be witty, and well proportioned, whereby it may be discerned by some speciall marke and note from common speech and be commended by antiquitie and learning."

24. Kahn, "Resistance," argues that humanist pedagogy was "a practice of examples or of an exemplary practice, on the assumption that such examples will involve the reader in a practice of interpretation which is essential for the active life" (377–78).

25. In a process similar to what William Kerrigan describes in "The Articulation of the Ego in the English Renaissance," in Joseph Smith, ed., *The Literary Freud: Mechanisms of Defense and the Poetic Will* (New Haven: Yale University Press, 1980), 261–308.

26. My use of masculine pronouns here is not an oversight. Although a few women in this period did receive a version of humanist education, this humanist program for authorization and empowerment in a public forum was unavailable to them. In fact, few women seem to participate in the discursive practices of gathering and framing, and as a result their writings lack the particular hallmarks of patriarchal authority that men learned to manifest in school. Elizabeth I is perhaps the one exception; her use of these practices will be treated in chapter 6.

27. Bennington, *Sententiousness*, 3–63, discusses a number of classificatory schemes, including imagistic, rhetorical, and generic criteria, and explains why each is only partially adequate.

28. The quoted phrases are from ibid., 50 and 56. As "substantial" summation, sententious fragments often restate common beliefs, while as ornamentation, they represent uncommon devices of style.

29. There are a number of useful accounts of the place of sayings in logic and rhetoric: B. J. Whiting, "The Nature of the Proverb," *Harvard Studies in Philology and Literature* 14 (1932): 273–300; Elizabeth McCutcheon, ed., *Sir Nicholas Bacon's Great House Sententiae, English Literary Renaissance* Supplements, no. 3 (1977): 22; Rudolph Habenicht, ed., *John Heywood's "A Dialogue of Proverbs"* (Berkeley and Los Angeles: University of California Press, 1963), introduction; Thomas K. Mauch, "The Role of the Proverb in Early Tudor Literature" (Ph.D. diss., University of California at Los Angeles, 1963), 106–11.

30. Patricia Parker, *Literary Fat Ladies: Rhetoric, Gender, Property* (New York: Methuen, 1987), especially "Motivated Rhetorics: Gender, Order, Rule," 97–125; and Derek Attridge, "Puttenham's Perplexity: Nature, Art, and the Supplement in Renaissance Poetic Theory," in Parker and Quint, *Literary Theory*, 257–79.

31. On the spatialization of logic and rhetoric, see *Ramus, Rhetoric, and the Decay of Dialogue* (Cambridge: Harvard University Press, 1958); and on commonplaces, *Interfaces*, 147–79. I accept much of Ong's theory about the impact of print and the increasing importance of the textual and visual, but do not agree that commonplaces were primarily a residual feature of oral culture.

32. See, for example, Barbara Kirshenblatt-Gimblett, "Toward a Theory of Proverb Meaning," in Wolfgang Mieder and Alan Dundes, eds., *The Wisdom of Many* (New York: Garland, 1981), 111–12. See also Peter Seitel, "Proverbs: A Social Use of Metaphor," *Genre* 2 (1969): 143–61; and Paul D. Goodwin and Joseph W. Wenzel, "Proverbs and Practical Reasoning: A Study in Socio-Logic," in Mieder and Dundes, *Wisdom*, 140–60; Grigorii Permiakov, *From Proverb to Folktale: Notes on the General Theory of Cliche*, trans. Y. N. Filippov (Moscow: Yanka, 1979); and A. K. Zolkovskij, "At the Intersection of Linguistics, Paroemiology, and Poetics: on the Literary Structure of Proverbs," *Poetics* 7 (1978): 309–32.

33. Versions of this kind of reading have been applied to Renaissance texts most notably by Thomas Greene, *The Light in Troy*; Terence Cave, *The Cornucopian Text: Problems of Writing in the French Renaissance* (Oxford: Clarendon, 1979); Patricia Parker, *Literary Fat Ladies*; John Guillory, *Poetic Authority: Spenser, Milton and Literary History* (New Haven: Yale University Press, 1983); and David Quint, *Origin and Originality in Renaissance Literature* (New Haven: Yale University Press, 1983). However, these authors differ widely in their attitude toward and use of Derrida and deconstruction.

34. Again, see Kahn, "Resistance," for the argument that humanists opposed the practical qualities of prudence and rhetorical skill to theoretical formulation. I am suggesting that humanist rhetorical practice subsumed "theory" within its practice of redeploying significant commonplaces.

35. See, for example, Greenblatt's "Psychoanalysis and Renaissance Culture"; and also Timothy J. Reiss, "Montaigne and the Subject of Polity," in Parker and Quint, *Literary Theory*, 115–49, who argues that Montaigne was one of the "precursors" of the modern form of subjectivity critiqued by Marxists.

36. See, for example, the work of Joseph Loewenstein on copyright law and the development of the "modern bibliographic ego": "The Jonsonian Corpulence, or the Poet as Mouthpiece," *ELH* 53 (1986): 497–504; and "The Script in the Marketplace," in Stephen Greenblatt, ed., *Representing the English Renaissance* (Berkeley and Los Angeles: University of California Press, 1988), 231–64.

37. See Richard Helgerson, "Barbarous Tongues: The Ideology of Poetic Form in Renaissance England," in Heather Dubrow and Richard Strier, eds., *The Historical Renaissance: New Essays on Tudor and Stuart Literature and Culture* (Chicago: University of Chicago Press, 1988), 273–92, for an account of the quantitative verse movement as just such a crucial "misdirection." Helgerson argues that "we need at least to entertain the possibility of valuing the terms that

have failed, as both Spenser and Harvey apparently did, over those that have succeeded" (277).

CHAPTER I
FINDING A PLACE

1. Aristotle maintained a strict distinction between logic or *apodeixis*, which dealt with matters amenable to scientific certainty and valid proof, and dialectic (*dialektos*), which dealt with fuzzier areas of experience not subject to certainty (see *Topica* 100a 27–30). As Richard McKeon explains, "the shift from science or demonstration to dialectic is from principles grounded in the nature of things to principles based on the authority of those who hold them," "Aristotle's Conception of Language and the Arts of Language," in R. S. Crane, et al., eds., *Critics and Criticism: Ancient and Modern* (Chicago: University of Chicago Press, 1952), 205. Scholastic logicians were more aware of this distinction than humanists, and were logically much more rigorous; however, humanists still believed that dialectic was at least potentially more stable and valid than the rhetoric of stylistic ornamentation.

2. Ong, *Ramus*, 100, describes in detail how Rudolphus Agricola's *De inventione dialectica* replaced more rigorous medieval logic with what is essentially a method of rhetorical invention. See also Grafton and Jardine, *From Humanism*, xii–xiv, on humanist efforts to displace the well-established Scholastic curriculum.

3. It is actually quite difficult to distinguish absolutely between logical, rhetorical, and pedagogical treatises, so intertwined were these three disciplines in the humanist project. Erasmus's *De copia* is a case in point. Although some scholars consider it as a dialectic, I treat it with both rhetorical and educational works.

4. For "authentic discourse," see Cave, *Cornucopian Text*, 53; For the "ungrounded contingency of language," see Greene, *Light*, 5.

5. Michel Foucault thus defines the cultural code in *The Order of Things: An Archaeology of the Human Sciences* (New York: Vintage, 1973), xx. Sayings have been associated with the cultural code by a number of scholars. See especially Roland Barthes, *S/Z*, trans. Richard Miller (New York: Hill and Wang, 1974), 97–100, as well as the work of a number of folklorists: Seitel, "Proverbs," 143–61; Kirshenblatt-Gimblett, "Toward," 111–12; and Goodwin and Wenzel, "Proverbs," 140–60.

6. Cave (*Cornucopian Text*) essentially explores the concept of copia as a response to the first problem, while Greene (*Light*) traces the ways in which imitation theory attempts to take account of the uncontrollability of language.

7. Ong, *Ramus*, 92, notes the humanist "determination that linguistic expression was to be controlled by the *written* words of Cicero and his coevals"; Cave, *Cornucopian Text*, 136–41, mentions the "special difficulty of extemporization in a non-vernacular tongue."

8. Ong, "The Oral Residue of Tudor Prose Style," in *Rhetoric, Romance, and Technology: Studies in the Interaction of Expression and Culture* (Ithaca: Cornell University Press, 1971), argues that the central function of sayings in this period was to transmit just such an "oral residue."

9. Javitch, *Poetry*, 13, comments that the English court "tended to be indifferent to Latin."

10. T. W. Baldwin, *Shakspere's Small Latine and Lesse Greeke* (Urbana: University of Illinois Press, 1944), vol. 1, cites these relevant grammar school rules: "Lastly, whatever they are doing in earnest or in play they shall never use any language but Latin or Greek" (166; Canterbury, 1541); "none above the first fourme shall speake englishe in the schoole or when they are togither at playe. And for that and other faults allso lett there be two monytors who shall give vp their Roles euery ffridaye at afternoone" (311; Harrow, 1591); "Both the Master and the Usher must see diligently that all and every one of the Scholars, as their wits will serve, do exercise themselves daily in speaking Latin" (350; Winchester, 1570–1576). These passages may indicate that Latin speaking at school declined in the course of the century, since in 1541 the requirement that students speak Latin (or Greek) is simply stated, but by the end of the century either a mechanism for punishing noncompliers is provided, or the requirement is qualified by the phrase "as their wits will serve."

11. On this, see R. F. Jones, *The Triumph of the English Language* (Stanford: Stanford University Press, 1953), especially chapter 2.

12. On the vernacular as supplement in the Derridean sense, see Attridge, "Perplexity," 263.

13. Jones, *Triumph*, 68–141.

14. Cave, *Cornucopian Text*, 33–34, points to Erasmus's attempts at controlling the "centrifugal movement" of language and the "Protean current of *verba*."

15. Jones, *Triumph*, 167. See also Parker, "Motivated Rhetorics: Gender, Order, Rule," in *Literary Fat Ladies*, 101, for an account of Thomas Wilson's treatment of the figure amphibology as offering "the possibility of an unsettling lack of control over language, as if the very instrument of civil order—in Wilson's strategic formulation of Cicero—were open to radical inversion."

16. Greene, *Light*, 7, on "the historicity of the signifier."

17. For the problems that necessarily accompanied a claim to be able to teach rhetorical or behavioral skills that would enable upward mobility, see Attridge, "Perplexity," 269–70; Parker, *Literary Fat Ladies*, 97–125; and Frank Whigham, *Ambition and Privilege: The Social Tropes of Elizabethan Courtesy Theory* (Berkeley and Los Angeles: University of California Press, 1984), 1–6.

18. On this, see especially Anderson, *Lineages*, and Richard Halpern, "Skelton and the Poetics of Primitive Accumulation," in Parker and Quint, *Literary Theory*, 228, who gives a succinct description of some of these changes: "the deracination of the peasantry by enclosure, engrossment, and commutation of dues, the destruction of the petty artisan by usurer's capital and merchant oligarchies" as well as the creation of "a concentrated hoard of money that could be used to hire the newly proletarianized workers as wage labor." He discusses the role of humanist rhetoric and education in relation to these events at some length in his book.

19. The term "deterritorialization" is used by Gilles Deleuze and Felix Guattari, *Anti-Oedipus*, trans. Robert Hurley, Mark Seem, and Helen R. Lane (Minneapolis: University of Minnesota Press, 1983), 222–40. On the shift from the marketplace as "a situated phenemenon . . . assigned to precise sites—in space and

time," to an "abstract" and "multiplied" set of processes, see Jean-Christophe Agnew, *Worlds Apart: The Market and the Theater in Anglo-American Thought, 1550–1750* (Cambridge: Cambridge University Press, 1986), 1–47.

20. See Agnew, *Worlds Apart*, 43. For a slightly different account of the relevance of deterritorialization and primitive accumlation for literature in the period, see Halpern, "Skelton," 225–56.

21. Halpern, *Poetics*, 91, notes that "copia . . . had always had metaphorical associations with wealth" and links the humanist program with the definition of primitive accumulation which Marx ascribed (falsely) to Adam Smith.

22. I realize that the concept of class is problematic when applied to this period; see, especially, McKeon, *Origins*, 159–75. These humanist theorists seem to have been operating on the margins of a shift from concepts of status to economically determined concepts of social class, using economic metaphors to define their status in society.

23. Whigham discusses the way in which Thomas Wilson "uncouples the existing order from transcendent authority and refounds it on the sheerly formal, learnable, vendible skills of persuasion" (*Ambition*, 3). Attridge ("Perplexity") identifies a similar maneuver in Puttenham's *Arte of English Poesie* and explicitly links it to Derridean supplementation. Patricia Parker makes a similar point in "Motivated Rhetorics," 118, as does Victoria Kahn, "Resistance," 383–84.

24. Whigham (*Ambition*) and Parker ("Motivated Rhetorics") do note that in establishing the need for supplementation, Wilson establishes its teachability and "vendibility."

25. Nancy Struever, *The Language of History in the Renaissance: Rhetoric and Historical Consciousness in Florentine Humanism* (Princeton: Princeton University Press, 1970), 102, notes the "emphasis on the mediated experience" in humanist attempts to assert their political function. Ong, *Ramus*, traces the virtual identification of dialectic and teaching in this period, but does not discuss the social implications of this fact. Attridge, "Perplexity," 263, acknowledges the problem of supplementing classical literature: "Vernacular verse is necessarily only an addition to the already complete and fully realized body of classical verse, and if it appears to be making claims to be an improvement on, or substitute for, classical verse, which it must do in order to escape perpetual secondariness, it constitutes a threat to the classical verse's exemplary status, and therefore to its own *raison d'etre*."

26. Daniel Kinney, "Erasmus' *Adagia*," 172–73, sees a similar attitude on the part of Erasmus toward his *Adagia*: "Where Boccaccio offers his work [*Genealogia deorum*] as an epic of assimilation, thus disguising his grander more perilous scheme for a radical mythopoetic renewal, Erasmus presents his recovery quest more humbly still, as an 'epic' of simple collation."

27. Bennington, *Sententiousness*, 50.

28. Ong, *Ramus*, 100.

29. W. S. Howell, *Logic and Rhetoric in England, 1500–1700* (Princeton: Princeton University Press, 1956), describes the influence of Agricola on Thomas Wilson (15–16), John Seton (49–50), Richard Sherry's *Treatise of Schemes and Tropes* (131), and on Ramus (152).

30. Lechner, *Renaissance Concepts*, 66–69, discusses a confusion on the part of Renaissance logicians and rhetoricians between commonplace considered as "a pigeonhole in the mind" and commonplace as "a more concrete subject heading under which ideas, images, maxims, or excerpts of all sorts could be stored." Agricola acknowledges both of these concepts, but the second is an intermediate stage in the progressive textualization that I trace here. Carruthers acknowledges that "the relationship between mnemonic places or topics and what came to be known as 'topics' in logic is a vexed one" (*Book of Memory*, 308). Walter Ong, *Interfaces*, 166, notes in the course of the sixteenth century a shift from "place" conceived of as a "vague region in consciousness" to a "place" in the text, and he ties this to the influence of print as a visual medium.

31. The definition of topos is itself controversial. Both before and after Aristotle, writers have tended to think of topoi as "ready-made arguments or commonplaces," while Aristotle seems to consider the topos to be a "form or type of argument of which you need grasp only the basic structural idea to apply it forthwith to discussions about any and every subject." See Friedrich Solmsen, "The Aristotelian Tradition in Ancient Rhetoric," in Rudolph Stark, ed., *Rhetorica* (Hildesheim: Georg Olms Verlag, 1968), 317. Eleanor Stump, ed. and trans., *Boethius' De topicis differentiis* (Ithaca: Cornell University Press, 1978), 167–70, discusses this issue and argues that a topos is essentially a strategy. For slightly different accounts of the definition of topos, see Walter de Pater, "La Fonction du lieu et de l'instrument dans les *Topiques*," in E. L. Owen, ed., *Aristotle on Rhetoric* (Oxford: Oxford University Press, 1968).

32. Ong (*Ramus*, 104) gives this general list.

33. Aristotle defines dialectic as dealing with matters involving not absolute scientific certainty, but the realm of *endoxa* or common opinion. He defines endoxa as "those things that seem likely to be true to all men, or the many, or the wise" ("endoxa de ta dokounta pasin e tois pleistois e tois sophois"); *Topica et Sophistici Elenchi*, ed. W. D. Ross (Oxford: Clarendon, 1963), *Topica* 100b, 21–22. For a discussion of Aristotelian "endoxa," see J.D.G. Evans, *Aristotle's Concept of Dialectic* (Cambridge: Cambridge University Press, 1977), 77–79. Roland Barthes calls doxa the "cultural code"; see *S/Z*, 97–100. I use "doxa" and "cultural code" interchangeably.

34. Aristotle discusses *martures*, or "witnesses," including sayings, in his *Rhetorica*, ed. W. D. Ross (Oxford: Clarendon, 1959), 1375b; the *locus ab auctoritate* appears in the pseudo-Ciceronian *Ad C. Herennium Libri IV De Ratione Dicendi*, trans. Harry Caplan (Cambridge: Harvard University Press, 1954), 2:3, 48 as a part of the conclusion of an oration. Cicero includes the *locus* "testimonium" in his *Topica*, in *Rhetorica*, ed. A. S. Wilkins, vol. 2 (Oxford: Clarendon Press, 1903; rpt. 1978), 19; and he associates sayings with a *locus ab auctoritate* in the peroration of an oration in his *De inventione* 1.53.101. Quintilian, in his *Institutio oratoria*, admits the use of authoritative sayings under three headings: *testimonia* (5.7.1–2; 11.41), *iudicia* (5.11.36), and *exempla*. Boethius, *De topicis differentiis* 2:54, explicitly links this locus to Aristotle's definition of *endoxa*: "quod omnibus vel pluribus, vel sapientibus hominibus videtur, ei contradici non oportere" (what seems true to everybody, or to most people, or to the wise, ought

not to be contradicted). Peter of Spain repeats the Boethian formula virtually verbatim.

35. Kinney, "Erasmus' *Adagia*," 177.

36. I am indebted to Ong's account in *Ramus*, 92–130, of Agricola's role in the spatialization of thought.

37. "Omnisque adeo sermo, quo cogitata mentis nostrae proferimus, id agere, hocque primum et proprium habere videtur officium, ut doceat aliquid eum qui audit." Rudolph Agricola, *De inventione dialectica libri tres*, ed. Willhelm Risse (Hildesheim: Georg Olms Verlag, 1976), 1, my translation. I have expanded abbreviations and repunctuated. Throughout this section most translations of Agricola are my own, although I have occasionally relied on J. R. McNally, "Rudolph Agricola's *De Inventione Dialectica Libri Tres*: A Translation of Selected Chapters," *Speech Monographs* 34 (1967): 393–422.

38. "qui consilio rempublicam gubernant," Agricola, *De inventione*, 3.

39. Ong, *Ramus*, 101–4, comments on Agricola's virtual identification of dialectic with teaching.

40. Translation is McNally's, 375. "Iamque alii mentis acumine freti, uberius expeditiusque argumentum, id est (ut inquit Cicero) probabile inventum ad faciendam fidem excogitent: alii contra hebetiore mentis vi, ad rerum obtutum caligent, et vel nihil vel sero quid quaque de re dici possit, invenire queant," 2.

41. "utilissimum videntur fecisse, qui sedes quasdam argumentorum (quos locos dixerunt) excogitavere: quorum admonitu, velut signis quibusdam, circunferremus per ipsas res animum, et quid esset in unaquaque probabile aptumque instituto orationis nostrae, perspiceremus," 2. My translation.

42. Anne Ferry, *Art*, 90–96, discusses the "spatial terms" associated with invention in English based on the places, and notes that these spatial metaphors "reflect the deep-rooted assumption that language exists in some space external to itself and to the mind of the writer" (93). I believe that this assumption may have been fostered by the humanist desire to think and speak in an alien language which existed only in printed texts.

43. "iremus, et duceremus inde argumentum propositis rebus accommodatum," 8. My translation.

44. Cave, *Cornucopian Text*, 19, discusses the fact that *res* can mean both "subject matter," and "extra-linguistic reality," concluding that Erasmus uses it in essentially the first sense. Agricola, however, qualifies *res* with *ipsas*, "the things themselves," indicating that he means real objects in nature, which, according to his system, do not necessarily constitute ideas unless organized by the places.

45. Ferry, *Art*, 93, argues that the places rely particularly on metaphor as the means of linking mind and matter. I believe that Agricola's text presents all, or most, of the places as able to do this.

46. "Nec instruere solum os facultas ista, et tantum dicendi copiam subministrare, sed providentiam animi, et recte consulendi quoque aperire viam videtur. Quando non alia re prudentiam constare apparet, quam perspicere quid in quaque re sit positum, et consentanea repugnantiaque, et quo quicque ducat, quidve evenire possit, colligere," 3. My translation.

47. Here I might seem to differ from Victoria Kahn's account of the relation-

ship between rhetoric and prudence. She argues (in her book *Rhetoric, Prudence, and Skepticism in the Renaissance*) that Renaissance humanists were influenced by the Aristotelian rhetorical tradition to regard reading as an activity or "praxis, which educates us in the very act of reading at the same time that it moves us to the application of prudence in human affairs" (40). She admits, however, that this optimistic view of the moral efficacy of rhetoric did not survive unchanged in the northern Renaissance, and I would argue that Agricola's "gathering" of selected fragments represents a more cautious approach to the praxis of reading.

48. "Inest tamen omnibus, tametsi suis quaeque discreta sint notis, communis quaedam habitudo, et cuncta ad naturae tendunt similitudinem, ut quod est omnibus substantia quaedam sua, omnia ex aliquibus oriuntur causis, et omnia aliquid efficiunt. Ingeniosissimi itaque virorum, ex effusa illa rerum varietate, communia ista capita, ut substantiam, causam, eventum, quaeque relique mox dicemus, excerpsere, ut cum ad considerandam rem quampiam animum advertissemus, sequentes ista, statim per omnem rei naturam et partes, perque omnia consentanea et dissidentia iremus, et duceremus inde argumentum propositis rebus accommodatum," 8. My translation.

49. I would argue, therefore, that the system of resemblances which Foucault attributes in *The Order of Things* to the sixteenth century was neither easily nor automatically perceived. As Agricola notes, the supplementation of dialectical instruction was necessary in order for people to perceive the resemblances and use them as a basis of authentic discourse.

50. Agricola, *De inventione*, 98–100.

51. "homini proprium, natum esse ridere," 34.

52. "Proximum in locorum notitia est, quodque difficilius est, traditas ab autoribus argumentationibus suis locis reddere. Idque non in hoc solum est utile, quod plurimum confert in intelligendis virtutibus autorum, et in discernenda varia apud eos argumentandi ratione, ut quandoque tanquam crebris densisque ictibus, sic multis argumentationibus celeriter coagmentatis, feriant adversarios: quandoque argumentatione late copioseque fusa, multarum impetum, unius pondere exaequent: iam confodiant acumine, iam viribus prosternant, iam de re iudicent: iam sicubi parum est in re fiduciae, in adversarium conversa oratione, velut flexu eludant," 305. My translation.

53. Quintilian says that sententiae are useful because "they strike the mind and often produce a decisive effect by one single blow, while their very brevity makes them cling to the memory, and the pleasure which they produce has the force of persuasion" ("feriunt animum et uno ictu frequenter impellunt, et ipsa brevitate magis haerent et delectatione persuadent") in Quintilian, *Institutio oratoria*, ed. and trans. H. E. Butler (Cambridge: Harvard University Press, 1934), 4.12.10.48.

54. John Wallace (" 'Examples' ") links this defensive approach to reading in the Renaissance to Plutarch's essay on "How a yoong man ought to heare poets." Where Wallace stresses the importance of separating precept from example, Agricola's text seems to me to allow a wider range of material for gathering.

55. "copia quaedam et thesaurus paratur, qui semper nobis in promptu sit, ut quoties ex locis quaeremus similibus in rebus, similes nobis argumentationes occurrant," 305. My translation.

56. Daniel Kinney, "Erasmus' *Adagia*," 177, attributes a similar realization to Erasmus: "Even before Erasmus began the *Adagia*, even before Petrarch and Boccaccio first conceived of a bodily revival of classical culture, the common lore of their own culture comprised a great number of the same adages, the same elemental opinions, which helped shape the cultural stance of the classical past." Kinney does not explore the logic theory that helped establish the existence of this shared space and the means of accessing it.

57. "Unde apud Platonem, Aristotelem, Ciceronem, Quintilanum, reliquosque quorum in illustri nomen est, omnium artium omnisque humanitatis peritia elucet. Quam quidem eis qui in populo maioreque civilium negotiorum turba versantur, usus utcunque et crebra audiendi experiendique consuetudo suppeditat. Qui vero tecto et umbra gaudentes, intra studiorum secreta se condiderunt, nisi ab eis quae in literas isti miserunt deprompserint, non video unde ea consequi possint," 401. My translation.

58. "eorum quoque sequi vestigia, quos quantumlibet de longinquo posse sequi, in hac saeculi nostri desidia, vel praecipuam arbitror laudem," 402. My translation.

59. Greene, *Light*, especially chapter 2, "Historical Solitude."

60. Ibid., 98.

61. "Quae strictim breviteque dicta sunt ab alio, ipse copiose: quae ubertim alius, ipse angustius dicat," 402.

62. "expedite, copiose, subito, de omni re proposita dicere possimus, 403.

63. "Res autem numero sunt immensae, et proinde immensa quoque proprietas atque diversitas earum. Quo fit, ut omnia quae singulis conveniant aut discrepent, sigillatim nulla oratio, nulla vis mentis humanae possit complecti," 8. My translation.

64. "Tegunt enim saepe, et in ipsa dicendi copia delitescunt, vel variis dicendi figuris occuluntur," 306.

65. Jones, *Triumph*, 68, 281–84.

66. Cited in ibid., 15, from *Scholemaster* (1570) fol. 56v.

67. *Pace* Wallace, " 'Examples,' " 280, who strictly separates precept and example. In the sixteenth century, both were considered matter for gathering.

68. On the social implications of a "defense" of the vernacular in sixteenth-century France, see Margaret W. Ferguson, "Joachim du Bellay: The Exile's Defense of His Native Language," in *Trials of Desire: Renaissance Defenses of Poetry* (New Haven: Yale University Press, 1983), 18–46.

69. On the criticism of neologisms or "inkhorn terms," see Jones, *Triumph*, 94–118. On the problems of "borrowing," see Ferry, *Art*, 83–90.

70. See, for example, Howell, *Logic*, 12–13. Baldwin, *Small Latine*, 2:40, describes both of Wilson's treatises as "vernacular equivalents of conventional Latin texts." This is truer of his rhetoric than of his logic.

71. Daniel Kinney attributes to Erasmus a similar view that adages represent "the sole pristine vestiges of God's shaping presence in history" ("Erasmus' *Adagia*," 191–92).

72. Thomas Wilson, *The Rule of Reason*, ed. Richard S. Sprague (Northridge, Calif.: San Fernando Valley State College Renaissance Editions, 1972), 7. Subsequent references are provided parenthetically in the text.

73. Carruthers, *Book of Memory*, 62, notes that Quintilian employs a similar metaphor to describe the use of mnemonic techniques. However, the fact that the metaphor is commonplace does not preclude the argument that Wilson "gathered" it in response to pressing contemporary concerns. We will see in later chapters that "hunting" often represents an aristocratic pastime, the kind of frivolous behavior which humanist education was designed to replace. It may be that Wilson here intends to include aristocratic hunters in his Protestant frame. Also, Wilson's rural analogy serves to reterritorialize logic, by associating it with knowledge of the English countryside.

74. In locating this source of invention in the writer's heart, Wilson admits into dialectic an alien source of authenticity—inspiration. For an account of inspiration and imagination as sources of authority, see Guillory, *Poetic Authority*.

75. Derrida, *Dissemination*, ed. Barbara Johnson (Chicago: University of Chicago Press, 1981), 355–58, describes all writing as grafting and associates the insertion of gathered matter into a text with a graft: "Inserted into several spots, modified each time by its exportation, the scion eventually comes to be grafted onto itself. The tree is ultimately rootless. And at the same time, in this tree of numbers and square roots, everything is a root, too, since the grafted shoots themselves compose the whole of the body proper, or the tree that is called present: the subject's career or quarry" (356). Wilson, of course, uses the concept of "God" to resolve the apparent paradox of no root/all root.

76. Wilson's image of de- and reconstruction in a religious context is echoed, on the other side of the fence, by the Catholic epigrammatist John Heywood: "*Roome was not bylt on one day*: that is well knowne, / Nor in one day Rome wyll not be overthrowne. / For where Rome semd puld downe in one day brother, / There is Roome set up agayn in an other." Burton A. Milligan, ed., *John Heywood's "Works" and Miscellaneous Short Poems* (Urbana: University of Illinois Press, 1956), "Three Hundred Epigrams," 274.

77. See Howell, *Logic*, 57–59, for the conjecture that Lever wrote his logic in 1549–1551 but delayed publication until 1573 because Wilson's vernacular logic appeared in 1551.

78. Bourdieu, *Outline*, 187. Strictly speaking, Bourdieu is talking about an earlier phase of society undergoing a shift from orality to literacy. However, the invention of printing and the growing importance of education as a means of political advancement re-create similar conditions in sixteenth-century England. Halpern, *Poetics*, is, of course, concerned with situating Tudor education within the transition described by Marx as "primitive accumulation" (95); he briefly notes that "copia clearly offered an analogy to material wealth, and the collection of commonplaces an analogy to . . . primitive accumulation" (91). I am arguing that these practices insert themselves into the economic system as more than analogies.

79. For an account of the political career of Walter Devereux, first earl of Essex, see *The Dictionary of National Biography*, vol. 5 (London: Smith, Elde, 1908), 893–97. Walter Devereux's actual financial situation at this time was not good, and his attempts to remedy it and provide for his children after his death will figure in the final chapter of this book.

80. Offering a commodified logic to an impecunious aristocrat had complex social significances that will become clearer in the course of this study. We will see

that in the earl's youth, disdain for humanist education was a sign of aristocratic prerogative; however, by 1573, times had changed. Lever probably seeks to capitalize on such a shift in his choice of dedicatee.

81. Ralph Lever, *The Art of Reason* (Menston, England: Scolar Press, 1972), viii (verso). Subsequent references are provided parenthetically in the text.

82. Although the treatise is explicitly directed to Essex, it probably had a middle-class readership in mind as well. This kind of double audience (both an influential patron and the ambitious middle class) was a hallmark of humanist publication practice and will be treated at greater length in chapter 8 below.

83. Carruthers, *Book of Memory*, 34–35, traces ancient and medieval metaphors describing "*designed* memory as an inventory of all experiential knowledge" (34). Lever is not talking here about memory but about a different technology for access to knowledge, although, as Carruthers observes (*Book of Memory*, 307–8 n. 122), the system of topics is similar in many ways to techniques of artificial memory.

84. Struever, *Language*, 109, notes that humanist rhetoricians in Italy offered not "esoteric knowledge but a shared intellectual apparatus, the *topoi* of common sense." Lever differs in his emphasis on transforming these topoi into a commodity.

85. See Ferry, *Art*, 88, for the idea that those who practice certain "physical operations" (sheepherding, for instance) are the "proper owners" of metaphors and proverbs gathered from their work. In this sense, Lever's logic teaches would-be courtiers and bureaucrats how to appropriate the language properly owned by those they desire to rule.

86. Struever, *Language*, 61, attributes to humanist rhetoricians the idea that "the thought unexpressed is not worth having." Lever's appropriation of this attitude shows the rhetorical cast of his logic.

87. Of course, there are significant differences between Ramist dialectic and the conventional dialectics that we have been discussing, for which see Ong, *Ramus*, 171–292. For one thing, the Ramist emphasis on "method" stressed an overall scheme of organization that implied greater interest in a coherent shaping of the whole text. I would, however, cautiously differ from Ong's argument that Ramism represented a "deathblow to profusion of expression as something consciously cultivated" (212). Although it did so eventually, Fraunce's text reveals that in sixteenth-century England Ramism was assimilated quite comfortably into the pervasive method of gathering and framing.

88. Howell, *Logic*, 219.

89. For a description of Fraunce's career and relation to Ramist texts, see ibid., 222–28.

90. Dudley Fenner, "The Artes of Logike and Rethorike," in *Four Tudor Books on Education*, ed. Robert D. Pepper (Gainsville, Fla.: Scholars' Facsimiles and Reprints, 1966), 146. Subsequent references are provided parenthetically in the text.

91. Fenner uses only scriptural citations to demonstrate the invention of arguments and the nature of the rhetorical tropes and figures; he uses doctrinal points to demonstrate syllogistic reasoning, for example, "*No sinner is iustified by his workes: / Every man is a sinner,* Therefore / *No man is iustified by his workes*" (165).

92. Abraham Fraunce, *The Lawiers Logike, exemplifying the precepts of Logike by the practise of the common Lawe* (Menston, England: Scolar Press, 1969), 2r. Subsequent references are provided parenthetically in the text.

93. Fenner's text, according to its title page, was initially intended to include similar exercises based on Scripture, including "The Order of Householde, described methodically out of the worde of God," and "The resolution and interpretation of the Lordes Prayer, out of Mat. 6.9. and Luke 11.2." In part, Fenner employs Ramist method as a way to apply gathered scriptural fragments to framing human behavior.

CHAPTER II
COMMON PEOPLE, UNCOMMON WORDS

1. For example, Agricola (*De inventione*) lists these forms that make up the thesaurus needed to supply copious speech: "exempla, sententiae, diverbia," which he defines as "ad omnem orationis usum apta quaedam supellex" (which [provide] a certain appropriate supply suited to any speech).

2. See ibid., 305–6. Humanist logics are, of course, "rhetorical" logics in the sense that they eschew absolute scientific validity and concern themselves with the invention and disposition of plausible arguments; indeed, "invention" and "disposition" were traditionally also the first two parts of rhetoric, although in this period rhetoric focuses increasingly on the ornamentation of style through schemes and tropes. However, even the rhetoricized logics were considered to be more grounded in matter and closer to truth than rhetoric defined largely as ornamentation.

3. Milton, in *Paradise Regained* (*Complete Poems and Major Prose*, ed. Merritt Y. Hughes [Indianapolis: Odyssey Press, 1957]), has Christ describe the Greek rhetorical tradition in exactly these terms: "Remove their swelling Epithets thick laid / As varnish on a Harlot's cheek, the rest, / Thin sown with aught of profit or delight" (4.343–45) On the "quarrel of rhetoric and philosophy" dating back to antiquity, see Struever, *Language*, 5–39. Traditional accounts of humanist rhetoric often attempt to deny this aspect of rhetoric: see, for example, Gray, "Renaissance Humanism," 498, who argues that "by 'rhetoric,' the humanists did not intend an empty pomposity, a willful mendacity, a love of display for its own sake, an extravagant artificiality, a singular lack of originality." However, accounts informed by New Historicism tend to emphasize just these qualities. Javitch, *Poetry*, 1–75, and Whigham, *Ambition*, both emphasize the duplicity and display associated with rhetoric at the Elizabethan court. I am concerned with the role of the notebook in the attempts of earlier humanists to come to terms with the dangerous side of rhetoric.

4. Attridge, "Perplexity," 257–79, shows how in Puttenham's rhetorical *Arte of English Poesie*, the oppositions between nature and art, dialectic and rhetoric, dissolve into the supplementation of nature by art, and art by nature. According to Attridge, Puttenham presents the figures of speech in such a way that "that which is unnatural and deceitful is able to cure nature of its faults" (265). See also Parker, *Literary Fat Ladies*, chapter 6.

5. As Kahn notes in *Rhetoric*, 47, the "crisis of confidence in Renaissance humanist rhetoric in the later Renaissance. . . . can be explained in part by the

different political conditions that prevailed in northern Europe." The power of rhetoric to move emotions is more threatening in a quasi-absolutist monarchy. Kahn argues that rhetoric, at least for Italian humanists, provided an active model of reading as a mean of developing prudence. I believe that in the northern Renaissance, the more cautious interpretive model of gathering supplemented the practice of argument "in utramque partem" and provided a more guarded form of the optimistic concept of reading as moral education which Kahn posits.

6. "Flowers" and "jewels" represent exactly the sort of "trifling" imports that economic theorists like Thomas Starkey believed were destroying the English economy in the early 1500s. On this, see chapter 5 below.

7. Leonard Cox, *The Arte or Crafte of Rhethoryke*, ed. Frederic Ives Carpenter (Chicago: University of Chicago Press, 1899), 41–42. As Carpenter demonstrates, Cox is translating from and expanding upon a rhetorical treatise by Melanchthon, but the introduction (from which this passage is taken) and many of the commonplaces and examples are additions to Melanchthon's simple and schematic text.

8. Thomas Wilson, *Arte of Rhetorique*, ed. Thomas J. Derrick (New York: Garland, 1982), 6. Subsequent references are provided parenthetically in the text.

9. On Wilson's relationship to Dudley, see Howell, *Logic*, 99.

10. For a discussion of Wilson's machinations in this passage, see Whigham, *Ambition*, 1–3.

11. Henry Peacham, *The Garden of Eloquence*, ed. W. G. Crane (Gainsville, Fla.: Scholars' Facsimiles and Reprints, 1954), A3r. I have expanded abbreviations. Subsequent references are provided parenthetically in the text.

12. On this, see Howell, *Logic*, 65.

13. Cox's text (except for his introduction) is essentially a translation of book 1 of Melanchthon's *Institutiones rhetoricae* with material added from Cicero's *De inventione*; see Cox, *The Arte or Crafte of Rhethoryke*, 29–31. Wilson's text follows Cicero's *De oratore* and the pseudo-Ciceronian *Ad herennium*. On this, see Lee A. Sonnino, *A Handbook to Sixteenth-Century Rhetoric* (London: Routledge, 1968), 238–40.

14. Sherry's treatise is based on Mosellanus's *Tabullae de schematibus et tropis* (1529), the *Ad herennium*, and Erasmus's *De copia*; see Crane, *Wit and Rhetoric*, 99. Peacham also uses Mosellanus and Susenbrotus's similar *Epitome troporum ac schematum et grammaticorum et rhetoricorum*. Aphthonius's *Progymnasmata* (based on Hermogenes' work of the same name) dates from late antiquity and was in use throughout the Middle Ages. Renaissance schools commonly used one of the Latin translations by Rodolphus Agricola or Ioannes Maria Cataneus. Rainolde translates from Reinhard Lorich's Latin text; see Howell, *Logic*, 140–41, and Crane, *Wit and Rhetoric*, 61–63.

15. Cox, *The Arte and Crafte of Rhethoryke*, 44.

16. On "farfet," see Ferry, *Art*, 103.

17. Studies of the role of proverbs and aphorisms in the Renaissance have tended to stress their classification as one of the figures of speech but generally do not recognize their connection to all of the figures. For the place of sayings among the rhetorical figures, see McCutcheon, *Bacon*, 22; Habenicht, *Heywood*, 11; and Mauch, "Role of the Proverb," 106–11.

18. Richard Sherry, *A Treatise of Schemes and Tropes* (Gainesville, Fla.: Scholars' Facsimiles and Reprints, 1961). Subsequent references are provided parenthetically in the text.

19. Howell, *Logic*, 138.

20. Richard Rainolde, *The Foundacion of Rhetorike* (New York: Scholars' Facsimiles and Reprints, 1945), A4r. Subsequent references are provided parenthetically in the text.

21. Bennington, *Sententiousness*, 46–47, notes that in Bernard Lamy's *Rhetorique*, "these figures of the *sententia* are figures of figures, insofar as the *sententia* is itself a figure of discourse. . . . But the situation of the *sentence* as a figure cannot be so simple, insofar as it has an important privilege with respect to the general classical desire to subordinate language to 'things.' " Bennington also notes, however, that "if the *sentence* has a privilege among figures, it is also the site of a danger attendant on all figures," namely, the possibility of manipulating emotion rather than expressing truth.

22. See Javitch, *Poetry*, 76–92, for the idea that Puttenham gains from the Elizabethan court the "confidence to recommend the contrived and deceitful uses of language so cautiously treated by other Tudor rhetoricians" (90).

23. Wilson is referring to John Heywood's *Dialogue of Proverbs*.

24. Dudley Fenner's Ramist *Rethorike* uses only scriptural sayings to illustrate the figures. See Fenner, "The Artes of Logike and Rethorike," in *Four Tudor Books on Education*, 168–76.

25. Different rhetoricians make different distinctions among the terms "figure," "scheme," and "trope." In general, however, "trope" (from the Greek for "turn") is used of figures involving a metaphorical shift in meaning, while "scheme" (Greek for "figure" or "pattern") denotes a shift from the usual order of words. I use "figure" as a blanket term including both tropes and schemes. For a discussion of these terms, see Richard Lanham, *A Handlist of Rhetorical Terms* (Berkeley and Los Angeles: University of California Press, 1968), 90, 101–3.

26. Barbara Herrnstein Smith, *Poetic Closure* (Chicago: University of Chicago Press, 1968), 168, discusses "the formal reinforcement of alliteration, assonance, and syntactic parallelism that gives . . . maxims their intimidatingly oracular quality, that makes them seem so incontrovertibly *so*." The formal qualities she lists are all, of course, schemes.

27. Erasmus, *Adages*, in *Collected Works* 31:6, 21.

28. Ibid., 22.

29. On the reinforcing effects of such devices of style, see Herrnstein Smith, *Poetic Closure*.

30. George Puttenham, *The Arte of English Poesie*, ed. Gladys Willcock and Alice Walker (Cambridge: Cambridge University Press, 1936; rpt. 1970), 196–97. I have accepted their argument that George Puttenham was, in fact, the author of this treatise.

31. For a discussion of problems involved in dating this text, see the Willcock and Walker edition. On Puttenham and the link between poetic rhetoric and other forms of courtly manipulation or deception, see Javitch, *Poetry*.

32. Patrick Grant, *Literature and the Discovery of Method in Renaissance England* (Athens: University of Georgia Press, 1985), 43, sees a similar "contra-

diction" in the humanism of More and Erasmus. He argues that they want "plain-ness, openness and cooperation, based on ordinary speech and common mean-ing" and at the same time realize that "clarity and plainness are never sufficient because their abuses can only be guarded against by those who know the unrelia-bility of language."

33. Cox, *The Arte or Crafte of Rhethoryke*, 48.

34. "Gay" and "delectable," as qualities of discourse more frivolous than plain matter, may be linked to the persistent sixteenth-century tendency to con-sider some kinds of poetry as "trifles." For this, as well as for some of the social implications of the term in this period, see Jeffrey Knapp, "Error as Means of Empire in *The Faerie Queene*," *ELH* 54 (1988): 818–19; and, for an account that differs from Knapp's in several ways, chapter 5 below. "Delectable," of course, is derived from the Latin word "deligere," "to choose," suggesting, perhaps, that its pleasantness furnishes grounds for gathering.

35. Ferry, *Art*, 83–124, associates the concept of borrowing primarily with metaphorical figures.

36. On the multiple denotations of "file," meaning both "the literal act of polishing metal" and "to deceive," see Ferry, *"Inward" Language*, 89.

37. See *OED*, 9:690.

38. Javitch, *Poetry*, 90, notes briefly "the courtly elite's appreciation of idioms that depart from or even defy common usage."

39. Sherry associates with exaggeration one form of "commonplace," which he defines as "sentences whyche we exaggerate as it were wythoute the cause, but so that they serve to the cause whiche wee have in hande: as bee the amplificacions of vertues, and the exaggeracions of vices" (86–87).

40. For similar readings of this passage, see Whigham, *Ambition*, 1–3, and Parker, *Literary Fat Ladies*, 97–98.

41. Wallace, " 'Examples,' " 273–90, traces this notion of defensive reading to its source in Plutarch's essay on "How a yoong man ought to heare poetes, and how he may take profit by reading poemes." In the context of these rhetori-cal treatises, the recommendations of Plutarch and Quintilian (which Wallace contrasts) are conflated, and gathering is presented as a means of reading *and* writing.

42. The 1593 edition of Peacham's work is bolder in its claims to enable speech, claiming that the book is "Profitable and necessarie, as wel for priuate speech, / as for publicke Orations."

43. Pope's couplet, in fact, almost perfectly states the idea that sayings supple-ment nature by reformulating a bit of the cultural code in a striking way: "*True Wit* is *Nature* to Advantage drest, / What oft was *Thought*, but ne'er so well *Exprest*." From *An Essay on Criticism*, lines 297–98, in E. Andra and Aubrey Williams, eds., *Pastoral Poetry and An Essay on Criticism* (New Haven: Yale University Press, 1961).

44. The definition in the Latin reads "celebre dictum, scita quapiam novitate insigne." See Erasmus, *Adages*, 4–5.

45. Bennington, *Sententiousness*, ix, defines maxims and aphorisms as "sen-tences which *lay down the law*."

46. The *Book of Common Prayer* (1559), Order for Morning Prayer, "Gen-eral Confession," includes this phrase: "We have left undone those things which

we ought to have done, and we have done those things which we ought not to have done." See *Liturgical Services of the Reign of Queen Elizabeth*, ed. Rev. William Clay (Cambridge: Cambridge University Press, 1847), 55. In thus seeking to associate linguistic framing with religion, Peacham accords with Wilson's Protestant logic.

47. See Attridge, "Perplexity," 268–70, on nature, art, decorum, and supplementation.

48. Because sayings are simultaneously common and uncommon, they offer, at least in theory, a way out of what Attridge describes as Puttenham's "perplexity," his need to "produce a manual that is designed to fail" ("Perplexity," 270).

CHAPTER III
SEED OR GOAD

1. For an excellent source of school curricula, see Baldwin, *Small Latine*. Important elementary texts include William Horman, *Vulgaria*, ed. M. R. James (Oxford: Oxford University Press, 1931); Beatrice White, ed., *The Vulgaria of John Stanbridge and the Vulgaria of Robert Whittinton*, Early English Text Society (London: Kegan Paul, 1932); William Lily, *A Shorte Introduction of Grammar* (New York: Scholars' Facsimiles and Reprints, 1945).

2. "Frame" is more common than "fashion" in these texts, and suggests an activity at once more coercive (because inflicted on the self by another person, the teacher) and more empowering than Greenblatt's "self-fashioning." In this context, framing suggests something like what Foucault means by "discipline" in seventeenth-century education; see Michel Foucault, *Discipline and Punish: The Birth of the Prison*, trans. Alan Sheridan (New York: Vintage, 1979); Grafton and Jardine, *From Humanism*, 136–37, who link Erasmian "method" with a similar sense of discipline; and Halpern, *Poetics*, part 1.

3. William Kempe, *The Education of Children in Learning*, in *Four Tudor Books on Education*, 220, 223.

4. Grafton and Jardine, *From Humanism*, 122–60.

5. They focus, instead, on the role of the *Progymnasmata* as an orderly "method" of progressive exercises. But, as we saw in the previous chapter, the *Progymnasmata* was itself concerned with the collection and redeployment of commonplaces and sententious fragments.

6. For an early and influential formulation of Renaissance individualism, see Jacob Burckhardt, *The Civilization of the Renaissance in Italy* (rpt. London: Phaidon, 1965). For a discussion of more recent versions of this view, see Dollimore, *Radical Tragedy*, 175–81. For a good general account of the difference between the concepts of "individual" and "subject," see Silverman, *Subject*.

7. See *Outline*, 171–88, on education as a means of the "primitive accumulation of cultural capital." And see Bourdieu and Passeron, *Reproduction*, 5–13, on "pedagogic authority" as "a power to exert symbolic violence which manifests itself in the form of a right to impose legitimately" and thus "reinforces the arbitrary power which establishes it and *which it conceals*."

8. On the established practice of so "educating" aristocratic children in the households of prominent noblemen, see James, *Society*, 271–78, and chapters 4 through 6 below.

9. Usury was, in this period, widely condemned at least partly on the grounds that barren metal was not supposed to be able to reproduce itself; see, for example, *The Merchant of Venice*, act 1, sc. 3, for a discussion of this issue.

10. James, *Society*, 271–78.

11. Thomas Elyot, *The Boke Named the Governor* (1531) (Menston: Scolar Press, 1970), 13v. Subsequent references are provided parenthetically in the text.

12. On the elevation of country gentry and urban merchants to power in the early Tudor period, see Caspari, *Humanism*, 1–6; for the accompanying reduction of aristocratic power and the resistance of the aristocracy to humanist education as a means of empowerment, see Stone, *Crisis*. And see Ferguson, *Articulate Citizen*, 133, for the "new sense of citizenship" on the part of educated men in the early Tudor years.

13. Francis Clement, *The Petie Schole*, in *Four Tudor Books on Education*, 92.

14. On the impact of humanism at the court of Henry VIII, see McConica, *English Humanists*, and Maria Dowling, *Humanism in the Age of Henry VIII* (London: Croom Helm, 1986), 15–22; see also chapter 5 below.

15. For a more detailed account of these different curricula, see chapters 4 and 5 below.

16. Grafton and Jardine, *From Humanism*, ix, note the complicity of humanist education all over Europe with hierarchy and absolutism.

17. Wayne A. Rebhorn, "Thomas More's Enclosed Garden: *Utopia* and Renaissance Humanism," *English Literary Renaissance* 6 (1976): 149–52, gives a brief but suggestive account of humanist use of agricultural and fortification metaphors. He reads these metaphors as providing an essentially optimistic and unproblematic view of the ability of education to ameliorate fallen human nature. Carruthers, *Book of Memory*, 16–45, traces a number of metaphors used to describe the workings of memory in the Middle Ages.

18. Foster Watson, trans., *Vives: On Education* (1913; Totowa, N.J.: Rowman and Littlefield, 1971), 84. Subsequent references are provided parenthetically in the text. For the Latin text, see Juan Luis Vives, *De tradendis disciplinis*, in vol. 6 of *Opera omnia* (Benedicti Monfort, 1745; London: Gregg Press, 1964), 293, "in usum discipuli decerpere." Vives, like Erasmus, was born on the Continent but had a direct influence on English education, writing an earlier treatise *De ratione studii puerilis* for Princess Mary, for which see McConica, *English Humanists*, 54.

19. Elyot notes that in Aesop's fables "is included moche morall and politike wisedome" (30v), that in Homer's "bokes be contained . . . incomparable wisedomes" (31v), and that in Horace's works "is contayned moche varietie of lernynge and quicknesse of sentence" (34r).

20. Roger Ascham, *The Schoolmaster*, ed. Lawrence V. Ryan (Ithaca: Cornell University Press, 1967), 130.

21. John Foxe, *Pandectae locorum communium* (London, 1585), Aiiii (verso): "non solum in literis sacris, sed in quotidiana etiam vita se offerant." My translation.

22. "Eodem referuntur *proverbia*, et *sententiae*, omnia denique, quae ex quorundam animadversione annotata, in populo remanserunt tamquam *publicae opes in aerario communi*," *De tradendis*, 263.

23. "Et praeceptori facile erit ejusmodi flosculos ex philosophis et sacris auctoribus tamquam e pratis vernantissimis in usum discipuli decerpere" (ibid., 293).

24. This connection between the garden metaphors common in poetic anthologies and some form of rhetorical gathering has been noted by Ong, *Interfaces*, 170, and Ferry, *Art*, 92–93.

25. "Quasi horto quodam fragrantissimo ... selectae sunt, et excerptae"; Nicholas Udall, *Floures For Latine Spekynge* (1533) (Menston, England: Scolar Press, 1972), "Epistola nuncupatoria." My translation.

26. Foxe, *Pandectae*, A2v, "Sicutque flosculis aliena manu lectis libenter quidem vtimur, at cum ipsi in pratorum vireta expatiantes, atque ex radice adhuc spirantes recens, cum libero delectu eos quas cupimus, reuellimus, duplex demum accedit amoenitas." This he compares to "adolescentes ... ex autoribus ipsis." My translation.

27. "Venit iam ad lectionem gentilium, tamquam in agros venenis. . . . meminerit se per gentiles iter facere, id est, inter spinas, inter toxica, aconita, et pestes praesentissimas, ut ex eis sola sumat utilia, rejiciat cetera," *De tradendis*, 320–21.

28. "Delibabit magister, tamquam ad morbos remedia," ibid., 279.

29. Craig R. Thompson, trans., *Literary and Educational Writings 2: De Copia / De Ratione Studii*, in vol. 24 of *Collected Works of Erasmus* (Toronto: University of Toronto Press, 1978), 639. For the Latin text, see Desiderius Erasmus, *De copia verborum ac rerum*, in vol. 1 of *Opera Omnia* (Leiden, 1704; London: Gregg Press, 1962), col. 102; "Itaque studiosus ille velut apicula diligens, per omnes auctorum hortos volitabit, flosculis omnibus adsultabit, undique succi nonnihil colligens, quod in suum deferat alvearium."

30. Greene, *Light*, 147; and G. W. Pigman III, "Versions of Imitation in the Renaissance," *Renaissance Quarterly* 33 (1980): 1–32.

31. Greene, *Light*, 98, cites as an example this passage from Petrarch: "We should write as bees make sweetness, not storing up the flowers but turning them into honey, thus making one thing of various ones, but different and better." On the Lucretian version, see 74.

32. Plutarch, *Moralia*, ed. Frank Cole Babbit (Cambridge: Harvard University Press, 1949), 1:171. See Wallace, " 'Examples,' " on the importance of this essay in Renaissance England.

33. Kinney, "Erasmus' *Adagia*," 172.

34. Foxe, *Pandectae*, A3r, A4v.

35. Thompson translation of *De copia*, 638; Latin text, "Addieris locos communes sive sententias, jam quicquid usquam obvium erit, in ullis auctoribus, praecipue si sit insignius, mox suo loco annotabis sive erit fabula, sive apologus, sive exemplum, sive casus novus, sive sententia, sive lepide, aut alioque mire dictum, sive paroemia, sive metaphora, aut parabolae," 397.

36. "Preface" to Nicholas Udall, *The Apophthegmes of Erasmus* (Lincolnshire: Roberts, 1877), xii–xiii. Subsequent references are provided parenthetically in the text.

37. Foxe, *Pandectae*, A3v: "Rerum pondere, grauitate, sapentia, ingenio, doctrina, methodo, tractandique felicitate metiamur."

38. Habent antiquitatis et omnis memoriae cognitionem, exempla tot dictorum et factorum, acute, graviter, festive, sancte, quibus excolitur prudentia atque adiuvatur," *De tradendis*, 269.

39. See Cave, *Cornucopian Text*, 4–5, on the etymological relationship between "copia" and "copy."

40. Yates describes a number of these systems in *The Art of Memory* (London: Routledge and Kegan Paul, 1966). McCutcheon, *Bacon*, 20, notes the difference between verbal sayings and the images used for artificial memorization. For a detailed account of the place of memory in medieval culture, see Carruthers, *Book of Memory*. She argues that in that culture, memory went beyond mnemonic systems to embrace virtually all areas of human knowledge. Renaissance theorists, however, differentiated themselves from medieval writers in part by consciously reducing (and denigrating) the role of memory per se in their systems of thought. Gathering and framing become partial replacements for the elaborate medieval technologies of memory.

41. Greene, *Light*, 318 n. 1.

42. The passage appears in Foxe, *Pandectae*, B2r; "Etenim quum in tanta scriptorum turba nullius sufficiet memoria retinendis omnibus, profuerit certe non parum, memoriae fragilitatem scribendi atque adnotandi securitate, sublevari, adhibito locorum communium volumine, in quod velut in quandam memoriem bibliothecam, cunctas eruditionis tuae simul opes congerere licebit." On supplementation, see A4r.

43. In the introduction to his *Pandectae*, Foxe stresses his own use of print technology in preparing a ready-made commonplace book and index in order to help his readers collect and organize such material.

44. Ascham, *Schoolmaster*, 114.

45. See Carruthers, *Book of Memory*, 33–45, for medieval versions of these metaphors applied to memory systems.

46. Bennington, *Sententiousness*, 56. He also argues that the jewel metaphor conveys "the notion that the aphorism is a detachable unit of the economy of wisdom."

47. Preface to *Adages*, 13–14. Thomas Greene, "Erasmus' 'Festina Lente': Vulnerabilities of the Humanist Text," in *The Vulnerable Text in the English Renaissance* (New York: Columbia University Press, 1986), 3–6, notes that for Erasmus the jewel metaphor implies that a saying is a "hard, secret, precious, time-resistant capsule of signification." He goes on to argue that this view of a saying is accompanied by the contrasting idea that it is also "a creature of history" in need of explanation (9). Because I believe that sayings always articulate an overlapping of the cultural codes of antiquity and modernity, I disagree with Greene's conclusion that for Erasmus the "center" of a saying is not its kernel of meaning but its "etiology."

48. Erasmus, *Adages*, 17; "Proinde si scite et in loco intertexantur adagia, futurum est ut sermo totus, et antiquitatis ceu stellulis quibusdam luceat, et figurarum arrideat coloribus, et sententiarum niteat gemmulis." The Latin text is from vol. 2 of *Opera Omnia* (Leiden, 1703; London: Gregg Press, 1962), col. 8.

49. "Itaque unusquisque puerorum habebit librum chartae vacuum, in partes aliquot divisum, ad ea accipienda, quae ex ore praeceptoris cadent, utique non viliora, quam gemmae," *De tradendis*, 310.

50. Erasmus, *De copia*, 638; "Sunt enim qui plurima teneant velut in mundo reposita, cum in dicendo scribendoque mire sint inopes ac nudi," col. 101.

51. Desiderius Erasmus, *Antibarbari*, trans. M. M. Phillips, vol. 23 of *Collected Works of Erasmus* (Toronto: Toronto University Press, 1978), 90.

52. Greene, *Light*, 183; "Concoquendum est, quod varia diutinaque lectione devoraris, meditatione traiiciendum in vaenas animi, potius quam in memoriam aut indicem, ut omni pabulorum genere saginatum ingenium ex sese gignat orationem, quae non hunc aut illum florem, frondem gramenve redoleat, sed indolem affectusque pectoris tui."

53. Sir Philip Sidney, "A Defence of Poetry," in Katherine Duncan-Jones and Jan Van Dorsten, eds., *Miscellaneous Prose of Sir Philip Sidney* (Oxford: Oxford University Press, 1973), 117, associates shallow imitation of Cicero and Demosthenes with the use of "Nizolian paper-books of their figures and phrases," and suggests as an alternative that students "by attentive translation (as it were) devour them whole, and make them wholly theirs." Again, the contrast is not between imitation and the notebook, but between proper and improper treatment of texts.

54. Hugh of St. Victor, *Didascalion*, trans. Jerome Taylor (New York: Columbia University Press, 1961), 93–94. Carruthers, *Book of Memory*, 219, argues that Renaissance use of the digestive and apian metaphors represents "a restatement of the very medieval description of reading and composing we encountered . . . in Hugh of St. Victor." However, Renaissance writers in England consciously attempt to differentiate their own methods of learning from medieval memorization (even though, as Carruthers argues, there are more similarities than they would like to admit).

55. Ascham, *Schoolmaster*, 79.

56. "Condient haec jocis salis, fabellis scitis ac lepidis, exemplis atque historiolis jucundis, paroemiis, parabolis, apophthegmatis, sententiolis acutis, argutis nonnumquam et gravibus, ut sic libentius haariuntur, et magno cum fructu non linguae tantum, sed etiam prudentiae atque usus vitae," *De tradendis*, 326.

57. Letter cited in John Palsgrave, *Acolastus*, ed. P. L. Carver, Early English Text Society (London: Kegan Paul, 1937), lvi.

58. Sir Thomas Elyot, *The Bankette of Sapience* (London, 1534), introduction.

59. *Adages*, 18. "Ut illis utamur non tanquam cibis, sed, condimentis," col. 9.

60. Ascham, *Schoolmaster*, 39. He goes on to note that when young men become "englutted with vanity," their parents will "reap only in the end the fruit of grief and care."

61. Ascham may here be seeking an excuse for the failure of humanist education to cause lasting moral transformation in every single case, displacing that failure onto experiences after the child leaves school.

62. "Velut vascula angusti oris, quae superfusam humoris copiam respuant, sensim instillatam recipiant: itaque initio pauca et facilia objiciet," *De tradendis*, 309.

63. "Admiscent tamen his tam salutaribus *perniciosa* non pauca, et quasi venenum melle aut suavissimo vino temperant, ibid., 270.

64. Erasmus, *Institutio principis christiani*, vol. 4, col. 587 of the Leiden edition. Vives, *De tradendis*, 125, 320.

65. Erasmus, *Institutio*, col. 587; Vives, 89: "illinc nonnulla delibabit magis-

ter, tamquam ad morbos remedia, quantum quidem videbitur sufficere," *De tradendis*, 297.

66. *Institutio*, 589, offers as a *philtron* the saying "amet qui cupiat redamari," and on 595ff. offers law as the prince's *pharmacon*.

67. Jacques Derrida, "Plato's Pharmacy," in *Dissemination*, 61–156.

68. Erasmus, *De copia*, 295; "Ut non est admirabilius, vel magnificentius quam oratio, divite quadam sententiarum verborumque copia, aurei fluminis instar, exuberans," col. 3.

69. "Prima in homine peritia est loquendi, quae statim ex ratione ac mente, tamquam ex fonte, profluit," *De tradendis*, 298.

70. Guillory, *Poetic Authority*, 26; and Quint, *Origin*, 23–28.

71. *De ratione studii*, 669. Thus, the humanist battle cry, *Ad fontes*.

72. Christian texts are also likened to fountains. Elyot, for example, calls God "the fountayne of Sapience" (*Bankette*, 274), and Erasmus, *Institutio*, urges that princes be given the collected teachings of Christ, since "from them as from fountains, from which they may drink not only more purely, but also more effectively" ("ex ipsis statim fontibus, unde non solum purius hauriuntur, verum etiam efficacius," col. 565). My translation.

73. *De copia*, 303; "Magnopere juvabit et illud, si eum locum qui maxime videbitur scatere copia, ex auctore quopiam aemulemur," col. 7.

74. "Habebit amplam et copiosam verborum latinorum supellectilem, sed vere latinorum, ut ad eo possint pueri tamquam ex fonte incorrupto haurire," *De tradendis*, 307.

75. *Institutio*, col. 569; "si ab eo maxima Reipublicae malorum pars oriatur, ubi fontem bonorum oportebat esse."

76. Richard Mulcaster, *The First Part of the Elementary (1582)* (Menston, England: Scolar Press, 1970), 13.

77. *Institutio*, col. 564; "jam tum infantulo, fabellis amoenis, apologis festivis, lepidis parabolis, insinuet, quae post grandiori sit serio praecepturus"; cols. 587, 589, 595.

78. "Plato's Pharmacy," 152.

79. Bourdieu, *Reproduction*, 31, makes a similar point when he defines "pedagogic work" as "a process of inculcation which must last long enough to produce a durable training."

80. "Semina disciplinorum omnium in illorum libris esse sparsa," 324; "ex ambabus multa reliquaram artium semina accipiet, *De tradendis*, 300.

81. Richard Morison, trans., *Introduction to Wisedome* (London, 1546), A5r.

82. *Institutio*, col. 564; "Etenim quo melior est soli natura, hoc magis corrumpitur, et inutilibus herbis ac fruticibus occupatur, ni vigilet agricola. Itidem ingenium hominis, quo felicius, quo generosius et erectus, hoc pluribus ac tetrioribus obducitur vitiis, ne salubribus praeceptis excolatur."

83. Kempe, *Education*, pp. 237–38.

84. Ascham, *Schoolmaster*, 13, 45.

85. Plutarch, *Moralia*, 1:81.

86. Clement, *Petie Schole*, 81.

87. Accounts of faculty psychology, with minor variations in detail, can be found in many sources. For a sixteenth-century version, see Thomas Elyot, *Castel*

of Health (1541) (New York: Scholars' Facsimiles and Reprints, 1936); for a modern summary, see William Rossky, "Imagination in the English Renaissance: Psychology and Poetic," *Studies in the Renaissance* 5 (1958): 50–51. Carruthers, *Book of Memory*, 46–79, recounts the many "confusing inconsistencies" (47) that exist in medieval accounts of faculty psychology, especially in what she calls "the neuropsychology of memory."

88. Rossky, "Imagination," 51–53.

89. Ibid., 53–59.

90. Ibid., 53; both Rossky and Guillory (*Poetic Authority*) trace the process by which the poetic imagination was "rehabilitated" in the course of the sixteenth century.

91. Ong, *Ramus*, 211.

92. J. L. Halio, "The Metaphor of Conception in Elizabethan Theories of Imagination," *Neophilologus* 50 (1966): 454–61; for the Erasmus quotation, see Greene, *Light*, 183.

93. Morison, *Introduction to Wisedome*, A3v–A4r.

94. The phrases are Silverman's, *Subject*, 132.

95. Kerrigan, "Articulation of the Ego," 284–85, suggests that "the learning of a second language in the Renaissance grammar school resembles a staged re-dramatization of the birth of the ego."

96. Ascham, *Scholemaster*, 13, 46.

97. Cited in Baldwin, *Small Latine*, 1:203–4.

98. The passage also notes that the prince has learned "to be thankfull to them that telleth hym of hys fawtes."

99. Rainolde, *Foundacion of Rhetorike*, 20r.

100. From his "De liberorum educatione," in *Vittorino de Feltre and Other Humanist Educators*, trans. W. H. Woodward (1897; New York: Columbia Teachers College, 1970), 137.

101. Erasmus, *Institutio*, col. 564; "ea littora solemus diligentissime communire, quae vehementissimam fluctuum vim excipiunt. . . . Quo diligentius erit optimis decretis, laudatorum Principum exemplis, adversus haec praemuniendus."

102. Ibid., col. 563; "qua senserit illum proclivem ad vitium, ea primum muniat animum illius salubribus decretis ac praeceptis accommodis; coneturque sequax adhuc ingenium, in diversum habitum trahere."

103. On theories of habitus in the Middle Ages and the Renaissance, see Thomas Greene, "The Flexibility of the Self in Renaissance Literature," in Peter Demetz et al., eds., *The Disciplines of Criticism* (New Haven: Yale University Press, 1968), 243–44. See also Bourdieu, *Reproduction*, 31, who stresses that to be an effective cultural tool, education must "produce a durable training, i.e. a *habitus*, the product of the internalization of the principles of a cultural arbitrary." However, see Carruthers, *Book of Memory*, 65–70, for a patristic and medieval connection between trained memory, habitus, and prudence.

104. Eramus, *Institutio*, col. 563; "Neque satis est, huiusmodi decreta tradere, quae vel a turpibus avocent, vel invitent ad honesta, infigenda sunt, insulcienda sunt, inculcanda sunt, et atque alia forma renovanda memoriae, nunc sententia, nunc fabella, nunc simili, nunc exemplo, nunc apophthegmate, nunc proverbio, insculpenda annulis, appingenda tabulis, adscribenda stemmatis, et se quid aliud

228 NOTES TO CHAPTER IV

est, quo aetas ea delectatur, ut undique sint obvia, etiam aliud agenti." See also *De ratione studii*, 671, where he repeats this advice, and the introduction to *Adagia*, where he relates it to practice in antiquity.

105. Mason, *Humanism*, 111.

106. McCutcheon, *Bacon*, makes this connection.

107. Ibid., 18–20, lists several examples of similar wall decorations in the Renaissance, including Montaigne's study.

108. As Frances Yates points out, memory, and especially memory of moral exempla and sayings, has a traditional association with the virtue *prudentia* (*Art*, 20–21). Bacon's chamber thus served as public manifestation of his prudence, the virtue most needed by the humanist adviser.

109. The saying *gnothi seauton*, "know yourself," engraved on the shrine of Apollo at Delphi was sometimes described in this way, as in Juvenal, *Satire* 11, line 27, "e caelo descendit gnothi seauton."

110. *Adages*, 13–14. "Proinde pro foribus templorum veluti digna diis inscribebantur: passimque columnis ac marmoribus inscalpta visebantur tanquam immortali digna memoria," col. 6.

111. Clement, *Petie Schole*, 81, 89. The saying so engraved is "If thou love learnyng wel, thou shalt be well learned."

112. "Seneca; habet *idem* sententias concinnas, argutas, breves, quas jaculatur tamquam spicula amentata," *De tradendis*, 364.

113. Clement, *Petie Schole*, 98.

114. Stanbridge, *Vulgaria*, 13.

CHAPTER IV
EDUCATIONAL PRACTICE IN EARLY SIXTEENTH-CENTURY ENGLAND

1. Kahn, "Resistance," 373–96.

2. Again, see McKeon, *Origins*, 159–60, for a good brief account of the controversy over the application of these class labels to early modern England. Particularly at issue is the extent to which the "gentry" class shared aristocratic values, or, as R. H. Tawney has argued, the values of urban merchants. See Tawney's "The Rise of the Gentry, 1558–1640," *Economic History Review* 11 (1941): 1–38; J. H. Hexter, "Storm over the Gentry," in *Reappraisals in History: New Views on History and Society in Early Modern England*, 2d ed. (Chicago: University of Chicago Press, 1979), 128–29; and Lawrence Stone, *Crisis*, with whom I accord in accepting the division between "gentleman" and "common," distinguished by the need (or lack of need) to work for a living (50). My "middle-class" humanists were trying to establish a kind of work compatible with gentleman status.

3. In the later stages of education, and particularly at the university, texts were more often considered as wholes. Erasmus himself, who was one of the central advocates of the notebook method, also recommended and demonstrated techniques for the "disciplined reading" of whole texts, especially in works like the *Methodus* (a treatise attached to his *Novum instrumentum*) that were intended not for school use but for the adult reader; see Grafton and Jardine, *From Humanism*, 146–49.

4. Greene, *Light*, 42. Here Greene is describing what he calls "heuristic imitation," one of the two forms that he privileges. He does identify a version of imitation that is closer to what I am tracing here when he describes the "eclectic or exploitative," in which "allusions, echoes, phrases, and images from a large number of authors jostle each other indifferently" (39). Greene feels that this technique "could not mediate effectively between a past and a future if the past was fragmented, jumbled, in effect dehistoricized" (40). In northern Europe, however, it was precisely this effect of fragmentation and dehistoricization that made gathering and framing such a powerful mediator. Pigman similarly identifies a kind of imitation involving the "gathering or borrowing of phrases, sentences, passages" but values what he calls "transformative" imitation more highly ("Versions," 32).

5. Greene, *Light*, 96.

6. Halpern, *Poetics*, 91, notes that "the habits of thrift, diligence, and application gained through a literary education were felt to be transferable to the economic world."

7. Grafton and Jardine, *From Humanism*, chapter 6, "Northern Methodical Humanism."

8. For these documents in translation, see Baldwin, *Small Latine*, 1:123–26 (Ipswich, based on St. Paul's), 135–43 (Eton and Winchester), 164–68 (Canterbury). Baldwin stresses differences among these schools and argues that the curriculum became increasingly uniform and "classical" in the course of the century. I am more interested in their common elements.

9. Ibid., 136.

10. From the Canterbury curriculum, 1541, in ibid., 165.

11. By "sententious" I mean a brief statement that employs some of the devices associated by Barbara Herrnstein Smith (*Poetic Closure*) with "maximal closure": rhyme, balance, antithesis, alliteration, brevity. In addition, Latin takes on qualities of sententiousness when hexameter meter is used. Sir Thomas Elyot (*Governor*, 31r) notes the mnemonic force of verse when he suggests that Aristophanes is a better school text than Lucian because "that they be in metre they be the sooner lerned by harte."

12. The "war" was waged through an interchange of polemical epigrams and prefaces. It began in 1519 when William Lily, master of St. Paul's School, chose to replace the traditional *vulgaria* written by John Stanbridge with a newer "humanist" version written by Robert Horman, master of Eton. Stanbridge's student (and successor as master of Magdalen School) Robert Whittinton published his own *Vulgaria* in 1520 as a direct response to Horman. Whittinton's text maintained the basic structure and values of Stanbridge's traditional method but also attempted to assimilate some humanist attributes. In 1521, Horman and Lily published a collection of epigrams entitled *Antibossicon* ("against Bossus," Whittinton's Latin pen name), and the poet John Skelton became involved in support of Whittinton. In the course of the quarrel, Lily accused Skelton of being "neither learned, nor a poet" ("doctrinam nec habes, nec es poeta"), and we can recognize in "doctrinam" a code word for humanist education. For an account of this quarrel and its bibliography, see Maurice Pollet, *John Skelton: Poet of Tudor England* (Lewisburg, Pa.: Bucknell University Press, 1971), 113–19, and chapter 7 below.

13. For more on what this training involved, see chapter 5 below. Young aristocrats sometimes studied some Latin and modern languages, but they spent most of their time learning music and dancing, serving at table, and practicing their skill at hunting, riding, and other aristocratic pastimes.

14. However, Greg Walker, *John Skelton and the Politics of the 1520s* (Cambridge: Cambridge University Press, 1983), chapter 1, has countered long-accepted views by arguing both that the Howards did not oppose Wolsey's policies in the 1520s, and that Skelton was not a long-term client of the Howard family.

15. Whittinton seems to be trying to combine traditional methods of teaching Latin grammar, traditional aristocratic training in manners and behavior, and a few elements of humanist innovation, perhaps in an attempt to meet the educational challenge posed by the increasing prestige of humanist teachers.

16. "Plurima cuique fere mortalium statui atque professioni accommodata." William Horman, *Vulgaria* (London, 1519; rpt. Norwood, N.J.: Walter J. Johnson, Inc., 1975). Subsequent references are provided parenthetically in the text.

17. By "unclassical" I mean that the sentences follow English, rather than Latin, word order and do not attempt to reproduce Latin idioms or confine themselves to Ciceronian vocabulary.

18. John Stanbridge, *Accidence (ca 1496)* (Menston, England: Scolar Press, 1969), A1r.

19. For example, when describing exceptions to the rules for the comparison of adjectives, the following verse outlines the use of "magis" for the comparative form of adjectives ending in *-ius, -eus, -uus,* or *-uis:* "Quod sit ius vel eus uus aut uis or caruere / Per magis et pium quod comparat instituere" (A2r). The presence of rhyme gives even these hexameters an unclassical sound.

20. Beatrice White, ed., *Vulgaria Stanbrigiana,* Early English Text Society (London: Kegan Paul, 1932), 1. Subsequent references are provided parenthetically in the text.

21. White, ed., *Vulgaria Roberti Whitintoni Lichfeldiensis,* Early English Text Society (London: Kegan Paul, 1932), 35. Subsequent references are provided parenthetically in the text.

22. Ascham, *The Schoolmaster,* 13. Subsequent references are provided parenthetically in the text. John Colet, founder of St. Paul's School, reiterates this idea that the rules of grammar are themselves simply "gathered" from the example of speech: "For in ye begynnyng, men spake not laten bycause such rulers [*sic*] were made, but contrary wyse, bycause men spake such laten. Upon yt folowed yt rules were made"; from *Rudimenta Grammatices* (1529) as cited in the introduction to Palsgrave, *Acolastus,* lxiii.

23. Lily, *Shorte Introduction* (1567 edition), 104v. In this section, many rules are exemplified by classical sententiae, for example, on the same page, "Amantium irae, amoris redintigratio est" (the falling out of friends is the renewing of love).

24. Ibid., E2v. "A personal verb agrees with its nominative in number and person: as in 'The way to good morals is never too late.' 'Fortune is never perpetually good' . . . Ovid: 'You will be my master, my husband, my brother.' " My translation.

25. Note, too, that the sententiae reinforce humanist values: the importance of moral behavior, and the untrustworthiness of fortune.

26. Erasmus, of course, includes a treatment of manners in his *De civilitate morum puerilium* (1520); however, this book, dedicated to the prince of Burgundy, was not intended as a school text, nor did Erasmus assume that table service should constitute a major part of the educational program. See Barbara Correll, "Malleable Material, Models of Power: Women in Erasmus' 'Marriage Group' and *Civility in Boys*" *ELH* 57 (1990): 252, who sees in the *De civilitate* "concern with the instabilities of social mobility." She argues that although Erasmus here attempts "to balance the aristocratic model with a reconciliation and unification of noble and bourgeois standards," the result is, in the end "bourgeois" (254). Whittinton translated Erasmus's *De civilitate* into English in 1532.

27. "Sunt enim electa / pura / casta / vereque latina / et e latinorum hominum optimis ac celeberrimis longo certoque iudicio deprompta," "Epistle from Robert Aldrich."

28. "plurimi triviales / nugivendi et credulae iuventutis impostores," from the introductory epistle from Horman to Robert Aldrich. "Triviales," and "nugivendi" (trivial and trifling) are, as we will see in the next chapter, terms associated with aristocratic pastime as opposed to humanist discipline.

29. "On Piety," "On Impiety," "Medicine," "Cooking," "On Civil Administration," "Marriage." Ascham, however, lumps Horman with Whittinton as the author of a text that provides faulty examples for "making Latins" (*Schoolmaster*, 13).

30. Each of these sentences is accompanied by a Latin equivalent, which I have not always transcribed.

31. The partial exclusion of the vulgar and scatological language so common in Whittinton's *Vulgaria* may represent what Peter Stallybrass and Allon White, *The Politics and Poetics of Transgression* (Ithaca: Cornell University Press, 1986), describe as the common bourgeois practice of defining itself by excluding the "low." Humanist teachers, however, recognize the schoolroom as a place, like the fair or marketplace, where different strata of society come together and boundaries are blurred; they also seem to have realized that too-rigid repression of such elements guarantees their return as forms of desire.

32. Lily, "To the Reader," A3r.

33. Baldwin, *Small Latine*, 1:144.

34. Cited in ibid., 124.

35. See Lily, *Shorte Introduction*, D5r: "Si quid dictabo scribes, at singula recte, / Nec macula aut scriptis menda sit ulla tuis. / Sed tua nec laceris dictata aut carmina chartis / Mandes, quae libris inseruisse decet. (Whenever you write down what I dictate, let your writings not be blotted or corrected, but single and correct. But do not commit your dictations or poems to torn sheets, which you ought to ingraft in a book.)

36. The connection between framing and handwriting is made more explicitly by Clement, *Petie Schole*, 105, who urges the student who practices his handwriting to "give diligent heede to frame eche letter in every part according to your copy." See also Jonathan Goldberg, "Hamlet's Hand," *Shakespeare Quarterly* 39 (1988): 307–27, who discusses sixteenth- and seventeenth-century penmanship

texts to conclude that "it is precisely because there is no notion of human character save as a locus of inscription that the literal act of copying can be an ideological practice" (316). Halpern, *Poetics*, 79, discusses the penmanship in Tudor schools as an example of "an essentially sedentarizing regime into which certain 'nomadic' elements were nevertheless absorbed."

37. Actual commonplace books of the period tend to follow these instructions. For examples of student notebooks containing sententiae neatly transcribed in roman or italic characters, see BM Additional MS 38,923, belonging to Sir Edward Hoby, which includes sayings copied on the flyleaves in an italic hand (contrasting with various notes in the body of the book in a secretary hand); Additional MS 46,398, which includes a section of sayings arranged under headings in an italic hand, and various recipes in secretary; Harley 4484, with sayings on the endpapers in both Latin and English that seem to be used to practice an italic hand; Additional MS 32,494, which consists of sayings and quotations in clear roman characters.

38. White, ed., *Vulgaria*, xxx.

39. W. Keith Peraval, "Renaissance Grammar," in Albert Rabil, Jr., ed., *Renaissance Humanism: Foundations, Forms, and Legacy*, vol. 3 (Philadelphia: University of Pennsylvania Press, 1988), 79, notes that "the reading list of the average Renaissance humanist scholar or student would strike the modern classical scholar . . . as extremely bizarre." In the United States, beginning Latin students traditionally read (selections from) Caesar's *Gallic Wars*, then move on to selected orations and letters of Cicero (usually the first oration against Catiline, or *Pro Caelio*), then to selections from Ovid (usually *Metamorphoses*), and finally Virgil's *Aeneid*. In Greek, beginners read selections from Plato, Xenophon, Homer, then tragedy (often the *Oedipus Rex* and Euripides' *Medea* or *Hippolytus*.

40. The *Distichs of Cato* are a series of aphoristic distichs in Latin that were believed in the Renaissance to have been written by the Roman moralist Cato. Most modern scholars believe that they are a later (third-century) compilation of earlier materials. On the place of the *Distichs* in Tudor education, see Mary Thomas Crane, "*Intret Cato*: Authority and the Epigram in Sixteenth-Century England," in Barbara K. Lewalski, ed., *Renaissance Genres: Essays on Theory, History, and Interpretation*, Harvard English Studies, 14 (Cambridge: Harvard University Press, 1986), 165–67.

41. Rainolde, *Foundacion of Rhetorike*, in his section on how to "make an Oracion by a Fable." He also notes that "Esope, for his godly preceptes, wise counsall and admonicion, is chiefly to bee praised."

42. Udall, *Floures*, "Epistola Nuncupatoria": "si vos aliquando ad eas in disciplina vires accrescere, et pervenire videro, ut exuperatis evictisque istis grammaticarum praeceptionum, et rudimemtum difficultatibus, ac velut salebris, ad iucundissimam, eandemque multo uberrimi fructus latinorum authorum lectionem studium transferre valeatis."

43. Elyot, *Governor*, 31r, notes that "the nexte lesson wolde be some quicke and mery dialoges, elect out of Luciane, whiche be with out ribawdry, or to moche skorning, for either of them is exactly to be eschewed, specially for a noble man, the one anoyeng the soule, the other his estimation, concernyng his gravitie

... it were better that a childe shuld never rede any part of Luciane than all Luciane." We should notice his emphasis on proper choice when gathering the "elect" dialogues, as well as his belief that the nature of the rhetoric can influence the "soule" and "gravitie" of a student.

44. Baldwin (*Small Latine*), of course, considers the influence of all these works on Shakespeare. Charles G. Smith, *Shakespeare's Proverb Lore* (Cambridge: Harvard University Press, 1963) and *Spenser's Proverb Lore* (Cambridge: Harvard University Press, 1970), finds traces of two elementary collections (Culman's *Sententiae Pueriles* and the *Sententiae* of Publilius Syrus, often printed with Cato) in those authors' works. For the importance of Cato for the Neo-Latin epigram in England, see Crane, "*Intret Cato.*"

45. Baldwin, *Small Latine*, 1:153. Grafton and Jardine note a similarly slow pace in the teaching of Guarino Guarini of Verona: "To cover texts in the gruelling detail shown here, given an hour's lecturing per day per text, can hardly have taken less than an academic year for each book. Accordingly, a student who spent several years attending Guarino's lectures on rhetoric would probably have studied only the equivalent of a few hundred modern pages of text *in all*" (*From Humanism*, 20). They cite R. R. Bolgar, "Classical Reading in Renaissance Schools," *Durham Research Review* 6 (1955): 2–10, as arguing that Renaissance grammar schools could only have covered "a fragment of the projected curriculum" (21).

46. Palsgrave, *Acolastus*, 1.

47. P. L. Carver, in the introduction to ibid., lxxix.

48. Kempe, *Education*, 232. Subsequent references are provided parenthetically in the text.

49. The quotations that follow, and the in-text parenthetical references, are based on the Rainolde version. On the use of Agricola's text in northern European grammar schools, see Grafton and Jardine, *From Humanism*, 129–35. They stress the importance of the *Progymnasmata* as a means of "structuring the transmission of the rhetorical skills required to produce active and influential members of the community," thus instilling "discipline" (131).

50. Greene, *Light*, 270, assumes that formulary rhetoric was based on imitation.

51. The phrases are Greene's with reference to Ben Jonson's imitative achievement; see *Light*, 273.

52. Baldwin, *Small Latine*, 1:251–53, reprints some of the school exercises of Edward VI, which consist of just such fragments and tags soldered together.

53. See ibid., 2:386.

CHAPTER V
PASTIME OR PROFIT

1. Halpern, *Poetics*, 91, makes a similar point.

2. As in the modern sense of "framing" someone to bear responsibility for a crime.

3. "Realism" and "fresh" are both Ferguson's terms. And see Caspari, *Humanism*, 1, for the idea that English humanists use classical philosophy to

justify an existing social hierarchy. As we have seen, however, their concern was at least in part to justify their own advancement without unduly disrupting that hierarchy.

4. Fox, "Facts," 33–39.

5. Fox, "Elyot and the Humanist Dilemma," in Fox and Guy, *Reassessing*, 68.

6. Ferguson, *Articulate Citizen*, 142, 401.

7. Richard Helgerson, *The Elizabethan Prodigals* (Berkeley and Los Angeles: University of California Press, 1976), is again an exception, although he focuses on the Elizabethan period.

8. Roger Ascham is a master of this.

9. Ferguson, *Articulate Citizen*, 17, 9.

10. Ibid., 121.

11. Ibid., 117–18. On Fortescue and the limited monarchy, see also John Guy, "The King's Council and Political Participation," in Fox and Guy, *Reassessing*, 126, 137.

12. G. R. Elton, *The Tudor Constitution* (Cambridge: Cambridge University Press, 1960), 13–14.

13. Brian P. Levack, "Law and Ideology: The Civil Law and Theories of Absolutism in Elizabethan and Jacobean England," in Dubrow and Strier, *Historical Renaissance*, 226–27, notes that during the sixteenth century, "the actual relationship between the king and the two houses of parliament was never made clear," and argues that the phrase "constitutional monarchy . . . does not say much more than that sovereignty in England was shared in some unspecified way."

14. Elton, *Tudor Constitution*, 17–18; Levack, "Law," 226.

15. Greenblatt, *Self-Fashioning*, 116; Whigham, *Ambition*, 186.

16. Cited in Guy, "Council," 137.

17. Also cited in ibid., 121.

18. Thomas Starkey, *A Dialogue between Pole and Lupset*, in Sidney J. Herrtage, ed., *England in the Reign of King Henry the Eighth*, Early English Text Society (London: Trübner, 1878), 104. Subsequent references to the *Dialogue* are provided parenthetically in the text. On the duty of subjects to depose a tyrant, see 169, where Starkey recommends that if Henry's heir succeeds him, Parliament should approve him as king only if "to hym must be joynyd a counsele by commyn authoryte; not such as he wyl, but such as by the most parte of the parlyament schal be jugyd to be wyse and mete therevnto."

19. James, *Society*, 193, 259–60, argues that works like Lydgate's *Fall of Princes* suggest that God inevitably punishes a bad monarch through popular rebellion. Discussions of bad counsel thus provided a way for influential subjects to imply that the king was a tyrant and at risk for rebellion without expressing open disobedience to him. The idea that rebellion might be justified when the monarch follows bad advice is clearly related, but not identical, to the "resistance theory" formulated by Protestants against Catholic monarchs. The view of resistance that I am tracing here is based in secular, rather than religious, ideology, and is much less radical in its implications, since its goal is not "liberty of conscience" but a share of power. On Protestant resistance theory, see Donald R. Kelley,

"Ideas of Resistance before Elizabeth," in Dubrow and Strier, *Historical Renaissance*, 48–76.

20. Guy, "Council," 126.

21. Ibid., 121. And see J. D. Mackie, *The Earlier Tudors* (Oxford: Clarendon, 1952), 385–91, for a traditional account of this northern uprising. Mackie summarizes their demands: "that the king should suppress no more abbeys, should impose no more taxation, should surrender Cromwell to the people, and get rid of heretical bishops" (387). Mervyn James has argued against the idea, found in Mackie as well as A. G. Dickens, *Thomas Cromwell and the English Reformation* (94–95), and G. R. Elton, *England under the Tudors* (147–48), that the Pilgrimage of Grace and Lincolnshire rebels were "neo-feudal instigators of civil conflict, conniving at the renewal of the Wars of the Roses and seeking to plunge the country into prolonged anarchy and bloodshed" (*Society*, 191). Instead, James feels that the leaders of the Lincolnshire rebellion were attempting to "transform 'rebellion' into a 'loyal' demonstration against unworthy councillors and precipitate a change of regime at the centre" (241).

22. The quotation is from the Eltham Ordinances, 1526, naming the members of the council (including Wolsey and Sir Thomas More), in C. H. Williams, ed., *English Historical Documents 1485–1558* (London: Eyre and Spottiswoode, 1967), 517.

23. William Baldwin, *A Treatise of Morall Philosophie*, ed. Robert Bowers (Gainesville, Fla.: Scholars' Facsimiles and Reprints, 1967), 127.

24. Ibid., 129–30.

25. On the range of jobs held by humanists, see Arthur J. Slavin, "Profitable Studies: Humanists and Government in Early Tudor England," *Viator* 1 (1970): 307–25.

26. Frank Whigham, "The Rhetoric of Elizabethan Suitors' Letters," *PMLA* 96 (1981): 864–82, discusses the rhetoric of letters from Christopher Hatton's *Letter Book*. Whigham emphasizes the use of "peripheral and formulaic assertions of courtesy" (868) to signal status and relationship.

27. McConica, *English Humanists*, 212.

28. J. A. Giles, ed., *The Whole Works of Roger Ascham*, vol. 1, pt. 1 (London: John Russell Smith, 1865), 68: "Ad hanc rem PLATONEM et ARISTOTELEM, ex quorum fontibus inter Graecos loquens illa prudentia optime hauriri potest, adhibemus."

29. To Cecil, ibid., 2:48; To Gardiner, 1 (pt. 2):405.

30. Herrtage, *England*, xliii.

31. Pole refers to a "commun saying," on 3, to "Arystotyl" and a common proverb that make the same point (32–33); and he refers to a number of unattributed commonplaces and sententiae.

32. McConica, *English Humanists*, 127–33, lists in addition to Starkey Richard Morison, Richard Taverner, Leonard Cox, Thomas Paynell, John Rastell, Stephen Vaughan, Robert Wakefield, William Marshall, Thomas Swinnerton, Richard Sampson, Edward Fox, and David Clapham. McConica describes a commonplace book kept by Paynell, containing classical and scriptural sayings, that places him within our tradition.

33. Ferguson, *Articulate Citizen*, 221.

34. Herrtage, *England,* xxvix.

35. James, *Society,* 259, describes how Pole "attempts to posit a theory of limited obedience by reminding the English that in the past they had deposed tyrannical kings and by pointing to Henry VIII's trust in evil councillors." Pole's *Pro ecclesiasticae unitatis defensione,* received by Henry in June of 1536, argued for papal supremacy.

36. For these sayings, see the near-contemporary (anonymous) biography of Burghley reprinted in Francis Peck, *Desiderata curiosa,* 2d ed. (London, 1779), 46.

37. James, *Society,* 48–90.

38. Stone, *Crisis,* 672–722.

39. Ibid., 722, 673.

40. As Stone describes it, "over-consumption led to sale of land, which generated social mobility and psychological insecurity among the purchasers; in its turn insecurity caused a struggle for status, exacerbated by the inflation of honours, which found expression in competitive consumption" (185). For an account of some religious and imperialist implications of "trifles" in this period, see Knapp, "Error," 801–34. Patricia Fumerton, *Cultural Aesthetics: Renaissance Literature and the Practice of Social Ornament* (Chicago: University of Chicago Press, 1991), focuses at length on what she calls the "trivial selfhood of the aristocracy in the English Renaissance" (1). I have not had time to take full account of her argument here.

41. On this, see James, *Society,* 271–78.

42. Richard Pace, *De fructu qui ex doctrina percipitur,* ed. Frank Manly and Richard Sylvester (New York: Ungar, 1967), 123. "Decet enim generosum filios, apte inflare cornu, perite venari, accipitrem pulchre gestare et educare" (122).

43. Whigham, *Ambition,* 88. James discusses aristocratic and feudal education, centered on music, service in hall, and hunting; and he investigates its role in furthering a "concept of honour" that "could both legitimize and provide moral reinforcement for a politics of violence" (271–78, 309).

44. James, *Society,* 309.

45. Dowling, *Humanism,* 209–11, discusses the education of Fitzroy and cites Croke's letters to Wolsey and More.

46. The Pilgrimage of Grace, like several other rebellions encouraged by the aristocracy, was centered in the North.

47. Elizabeth Rogers, ed., *The Correspondence of Sir Thomas More* (Princeton: Princeton University Press, 1947), 404.

48. Richard Croke to Wolsey, Wolsey correspondence iii. 93, cited in Henry Ellis, *Original Letters Illustrative of English History,* ser. 3, vol. 1 (London: Richard Bently, 1846), 335–36.

49. Ibid., 343. Humanist "good letters" are here combined with the instruction in manners advocated by Whittinton and, beyond even that, explicit emphasis on aristocratic "pastime."

50. Ibid., 344.

51. Ibid., ser. 1, 2:136. "Ex literis autem tuis multum fructus accepi, quod in illis me hortaris, atque veluti stimulum mihi addis ad perdiscendas bonas literas, quae mihi usui futurae sint cum ad virilem perveniam aetatem."

52. Sir Thomas Elyot, *The Image of Governance* (1541), in Lillian Gottesman, ed., *Four Political Treatises* (Gainesville, Fla.: Scholars' Facsimiles and Reprints, 1967), 233.

53. The phrase "pet humanist" is G. R. Elton's, cited by Greenblatt, *Self-Fashioning*, 21.

54. J. H. Hexter, *More's Utopia: The Biography of an Idea* (Princeton: Princeton University Press, 1952), 113–14. Hexter argues that Erasmus's failure to acknowledge this dilemma is "evidence of the superficiality of the humanist social criticism of which he was the leading protagonist" (114).

55. Ibid., 103.

56. The marginal glosses were evidently written by Giles and Erasmus in consultation with More, and should be considered an integral part of the volume (along with the prefatory material). On the importance of these glosses, see Dana G. McKinnon, "The Marginal Glosses in More's *Utopia*," *Renaissance Papers* (1970): 11–27.

57. Thomas More, *Utopia*, ed. Edward Surtz, S.J., and J. H. Hexter, vol. 4 of *Complete Works of Sir Thomas More* (New Haven: Yale University Press, 1965), 121, 123. Subsequent references are provided parenthetically in the text. Utopian disdain for jewelry is illustrated by the anecdote of the Anemolian ambassadors, designated in the margin as "Elegantissima fabula," and a number of other basic principles of their society ("likeness begets harmony," "What is Common to All is Borne Lightly") are articulated as sayings (152, 113). McKinnon notes that these "maxims . . . spell out the sententiae which easily fit into the humanist's creed" ("Marginal Glosses," 18).

58. Greenblatt, *Self-Fashioning*, 35.

59. Fox, "English Humanism and the Body Politic," in Fox and Guy, *Reassessing*, 38, who notes Hythlodaeus's love of travel and preference for the Greek language.

60. See, for example, "Astrophil and Stella," 1.7–8, "Oft turning others' leaves, to see if thence would flow / Some fresh and fruitful showers upon my sunne-burn'd braine," in William A. Ringler, ed., *The Poems of Sir Philip Sidney* (Oxford: Clarendon, 1962).

61. "Si apud aliquem regum decreta sana proponerem, et perniciosa malorum semina, conarer ille evellere." Rebhorn, "Enclosed Garden," 140–55, notes the similarities between this passage and comparable metaphors in humanist educational theory. He does not, however, discuss the contradictions and problems that accompany the analogy of disease and cure.

62. Louis Adrian Montrose, "Of Gentlemen and Shepherds: The Politics of Elizabethan Pastoral Form," *ELH* 50 (1983): 426.

63. On More's use of litotes, see Greenblatt, *Self-Fashioning*, 23; and Elizabeth McCutcheon, "Denying the Contrary: More's Use of Litotes in the *Utopia*," in Richard Sylvester and G. P. Marc'hadour, eds., *Essential Articles for the Study of Thomas More* (Hamden, Conn.: Archon Books, 1977), 263, 271–72.

64. Arthur Kinney, *Humanist Poetics*, 62, puts the decision in the hands of the Syphogrants: "Only the secret voting of the syphogrants allows some men to abjure manual labor for scholarly pursuits."

65. Who, nevertheless, do not have tenure, since those who "falsify" expectations of scholarly diligence can be "reduced to the rank of workingman" (131–33).

66. Kinney, *Humanist Poetics*, 88, describes Utopia as a "state of self-examination."

67. Richard Marius, *Thomas More* (New York: Knopf, 1985), 167, comments that "if the Utopians let down their guard for an instant, sin will rush in." He attributes More's pessimistic view of human nature to the fact that he was "a medieval Christian, saturated with pessimism about a frail humankind weakened by original sin" (167). From this viewpoint, humanist optimism might well seem foolish.

68. As Rebhorn notes, "Enclosed Gardens," 147–48.

69. "Terrae sic medentur industria." My translation.

70. Rebhorn cites the same passages to draw the very different conclusion that More's "language reveals the basic connections he accepted between sound agriculture, health, cleanliness, connections which demonstrate the profound imaginative unity of his work" ("Enclosed Gardens," 147–48). I believe that the disturbing facets of Utopian society force us to see the ruptures in this vision, ruptures which at least in part More was conscious of.

71. Herrtage, *England*, xxxix–xxxxi.

72. Ibid., liii–liv.

73. Ferguson, *Articulate Citizen*, 244–314.

74. This was behind More's complaint in *Utopia* that "in a society where we make money the standard of everything, it is necessary to practice many crafts which are quite vain and superfluous, ministering only to luxury and licentiousness," 131.

75. Herrtage, *England*, lxxiv. He also says that he has "geddryd a certayne commentary" from his observations and "compylid as hit were a lytill boke of the same" (lxxiv).

76. Fox, "Elyot," 53.

77. Ibid., 52–73.

78. Montrose, "Gentlemen and Shepherds," argues that in contrast to earlier pastorals, Elizabethan versions of the form allowed "gentlemen who may be alienated or excluded from the courtly society that nevertheless continues to define their existence [to] create an imaginative space within which virtue and privilege coincide" (427). I would argue that Elyot begins to develop this and several related strategies.

79. Pace, *De fructu*, 23.

80. Elyot, *The Image of Governance*, in *Four Political Treatises*, 206. Subsequent references are provided parenthetically in the text.

81. *Pasquil the Plain*, in *Four Political Treatises*, 91–92.

82. Ibid., 95.

83. Thomas Elyot, *Of the Knowledge Which Maketh a Wise Man*, ed. Edwin Howard (Oxford, Ohio: Anchor Press, 1946), 5.

84. Ibid., 4.

85. Ibid., 10.

86. Elyot lists "rhetorycians, teachers of grammar, phisitions, astronomers, geometricians, musiciens, devisers of building and ingines" as the recipients of these funds.

87. *Pasquil the Plain*, 97–98.

CHAPTER VI
FRAMING THE STATE

1. Although versions of their strategies remained useful as survival tactics, in particular the generality of aphorism and commonplace allowed humanists like Burghley and Ascham to use the same ideologically vague but self-consciously moralistic language in order to maintain and defend their alignment with opposed factions. See, for example, Ascham's use of the same aphorism from Sophocles in asking preferment from Gardiner and from Cecil, in the previous chapter.

2. Arthur F. Marotti, " 'Love is not Love': Elizabethan Sonnet Sequences and the Social Order," *ELH* 49 (1982): 398–400; Louis Adrian Montrose, " 'Eliza Queene of Shepheardes,' and the Pastoral of Power," *English Litary Renaissance* 10 (1980): 153–82, "Gentlemen and Shepherds," and " 'Shaping Fantasies': Figurations of Gender and Power in Elizabethan Culture," *Representations* 1 (1983): 61–94; Stephen Greenblatt, *Sir Walter Ralegh: The Renaissance Man and His Roles* (New Haven: Yale University Press, 1973), 52–59, and *Self-Fashioning*, 165–69.

3. Stone, *Crisis*, 400. Javitch (*Poetry*) calls this alternative ideal the "orator" and argues that it was ineffective under an absolutist government. Whigham attributes this attitude to the "old order" of Ascham and Burghley (*Ambition*, 176). Richard Helgerson, *Prodigals*, 16–43, most clearly acknowledges the importance of this attitude as reflected in the "prodigal son" paradigm that rebels against it.

4. In *Prodigals*, especially chapter 1, and in *Self-Crowned Laureates: Spenser, Jonson, Milton and the Literary System* (Berkeley and Los Angeles: University of California Press, 1983), 25–49.

5. *Prodigals*, 41. Anthony Essler, *The Aspiring Mind of the Elizabethan Younger Generation* (Durham, N.C.: Duke University Press, 1966), discusses the reaction of that younger generation against an older generation, born in the 1520s and 1530s, which included Burghley, Bacon, and the queen.

6. On Burghley's use of adages, see B. W. Beckingsale, *Burghley: Tudor Statesman* (New York: St. Martin's, 1967), 199.

7. Ibid., 270.

8. Ibid., 7–9.

9. "The Compleat Statesman Exemplified in the life and actions of Sir William Cecil, Lord Burghley," written by a contemporary and published in Peck, *Desiderata*, 5.

10. Beckingsale, *Burghley*, 249.

11. Helgerson, *Prodigals*, 28–29.

12. Peck, *Desiderata*, 45–46. The biographer lists thirty-nine "wise speeches," which do not include the precepts addressed to his sons.

13. Ibid., 37.

14. A famous portrait, for example, depicts him seated on a mule, in clear contrast to heroic equestrian portraits of men like Essex. For a copy of this portrait, see Beckingsale, *Burghley*, facing 151.

15. Peck, *Desiderata*, 36–38.

16. Ibid., 39.

17. As we saw in the previous chapter, it was important even for a king to appear to receive such advice. It was even more important for a young woman to appear to do so. On this, see Mary Thomas Crane, " 'Video et Taceo': Elizabeth I and the Rhetoric of Counsel," *Studies in English Literature* 28 (1988): 5–7.

18. As quoted in Conyers Read, *Mr. Secretary Cecil and Queen Elizabeth* (London: Cape, 1955), 119, from PRO., SP xii-1-7.

19. See ibid., 171, for a letter to Throgmorton of 7 May 1560, in which Cecil complains about the queen's refusal to follow his advice.

20. Peck, *Desiderata*, 46.

21. Quoted in Read, *Cecil*, 199.

22. Ibid.

23. Ibid., 201.

24. On her education, see J. E. Neale, *Queen Elizabeth* (New York: Harcourt, 1934), 13–16. And see also Crane, " 'Video et Taceo.' "

25. G. B. Harrison, ed., *The Letters of Queen Elizabeth I*, 2d ed. (New York: Funk and Wagnalls, 1968), 228. John Bruce, ed., *Letters of Queen Elizabeth and King James VI of Scotland* (London: Camden Society, 1849), 45, 165.

26. Crane, " 'Video et Taceo,' " 7–10.

27. William Camden, *Annals*, as cited in Read, *Lord Burghley and Queen Elizabeth* (New York: Knopf, 1960), 546.

28. See Esler, *Aspiring Mind*, for an extended account of the generational tension at the Elizabethan court. He particularly focuses on an "older generation" born in the 1520s and 1530s, and a younger group born in the 1560s and including Ralegh, the younger Bacons, and the earl of Essex.

29. Peck, *Desiderata*, 5.

30. Beckingsale, *Burghley*, 276.

31. Helgerson, *Prodigals*, 29.

32. Ibid., 20.

33. "Certain Precepts for the Well-Ordering of a Man's Life," in Louis B. Wright, ed., *Advice to a Son* (Ithaca: Cornell University Press, 1962), 9.

34. "Furnish" here alludes to the Latin word *supellex*, "furniture," commonly used for the "matter" constituting copia, for example, in the epigraph to Ben Jonson's commonplace book *Timber*: "Tecum habita, ut noris quam sit tibi curta supellex."

35. The word "square" also has stoic overtones, based on Erasmus's account of the "quadratus homo" ("square man," *Adagia* 1131), derived from Aristotle's concept of the man whose happiness is not dependent on fortune or material goods. On this, see McCutcheon, *Bacon*, 58.

36. Read, *Cecil*, 215.

37. Ibid., 216.

38. Ibid.

39. Stone, *Crisis*, 600. And see Lisa Jardine, *Still Harping on Daughters:*

Women and Drama in the Age of Shakespeare (1983; New York: Columbia University Press, 1989), 80–93, for an excellent account of the implications of the Court of Wards and inheritance practice for the status of women in this period.

40. Stone, *Crisis*, 600.

41. Ibid., 601. As an example, Stone cites the case of Walter Astor, a ward who was bought in 1597 by Burghley's friend Sir Edward Coke. Coke paid the standard fee of three hundred pounds to the Crown, and an additional thousand to Burghley for control of Astor.

42. Stone, (ibid., 603) cites passages from plays containing such criticism. For the defense, see Peck, *Desiderata*, 21–22.

43. These included the earl of Oxford, Philip Howard earl of Surrey, the third and fifth earls of Rutland, the earl of Essex, and the earl of Southampton. On this, see J. Hurstfield, "Lord Burghley as Master of the Court of Wards, 1561–98," *Transactions of the Royal Historical Society*, 4th ser., 31 (1949): 95–115. Hurstfield speculates that Burghley obtained these noble wards "from the Queen by word of mouth" since no records of the transactions exist (104).

44. Stone, *Crisis*, 679.

45. "Considerations delivered to Parliament, 1559," in R. H. Tawney and Eileen Power, eds., *Tudor Economic Documents*, vol. 1 (London, 1824), 326.

46. On sumptuary laws in this period, see Jardine, *Still Harping*, 141–68.

47. "Considerations," 326.

48. Ibid. This document goes on to condemn conspicuous consumption in terms almost identical to those of the Henrician and Edwardian commonwealth pamphlets, prohibiting importation of "caps, pins, points, dice, gilt stirrups, etc., . . . for they are not only false and deceitful wares, rather serving for the gaze than any good use, but for such trifles they filch from us the chief and substantial staple wares of the realm" (327).

49. The image of "rooms" reserved for aristocratic occupants directly counters Ralph Lever's use of similar imagery to suggest that "place" logic can provide "rooms" for an upwardly mobile merchant class.

50. Beckingsale, *Burghley*, 273, comments on the general acceptance of this genealogy: "When most family trees grew in glass-houses of pretence there were few who cared to throw stones."

51. Read, *Burghley*, 33; "circumspection, stoutness, wisdom, dexterity, integrity of life, providence, care, and faithfulness."

52. William Cecil became master of the Court of Wards in 1561 and did not become Baron Burghley until 1571. It is not clear, however, whether he educated wards in his home before achieving that rank.

53. Read, *Burghley*, 125.

54. Lawrence Nowell was presumably familiar with them, since he kept a commonplace book of French sayings and idioms. See BM Additional ms 43,708.

55. Foucault, *Discipline and Punish*, 149–50.

56. In a letter to the earl of Rutland during a vacation, Burghley seeks to reimpose a disciplinary schedule: "you will, when you are wearying of hunting, recontinue some exercise of hunting in your book"; see Beckingsale, *Burghley*, 248.

57. Burghley's power over the aristocracy, exercised through the Court of Wards, can hardly be exaggerated. It would have been extremely difficult for an

aristocratic marriage to take place without Burghley's approval. In fact, evidence about marriages during this period survives largely in Burghley's correspondence.

58. He married his daughter Anne to his ward, the earl of Oxford, and arranged for her daughter Elizabeth to marry the earl of Derby. His will specified that her two remaining daughters should inherit four thousand pounds if they married earls, three thousand for barons, and two thousand for any other rank. Both married earls. On this, see Beckingsale, *Burghley*, 290–91.

59. Ibid., 193.

60. Peck, *Desiderata*, 11.

61. See Hurstfield, "Lord Burghley," 110, who cites this adage from Lansdowne MS 98, 215r–217r. Hurstfield describes these "sentences or adages" as "masterpieces of sanctimoniousness and ambiguity," and associates their use with the Court of Wards.

62. A letter to Henry Sidney (1565) tries to take a stance above the factional struggle between Leicester and Sussex (even though Cecil actually opposed Leicester): "surely this court here is not free from many troubles, amongst others none worse than emulations, disdains, backbitings, and such like. . . . I wish that God would direct the hearts of those two earls to behold the harm that ensueth of small sparks of dissention betwixt noble houses. . . . I, as a mean man, can but wish it, for neither is my power nor my credit of value to do so good a deed"; quoted in Read, *Cecil*, 332–33. Note his uses of moralistic and religious language to express distance from and disapproval of factionalism, as well as his reference to his own "mean" position.

63. Peck, *Desiderata*, 45–46.

64. Esler makes this point at some length but overstates the intrinsic tendency of younger men to dislike what he calls the "platitudinous nonsense" and "rank hypocrisy" of humanist aphoristic language (*Aspiring Mind*, 66).

65. Hurstfield, "Lord Burghley," 106, quotes Oxford's response to Burghley's attempts to control him: "I mean not to be youre ward nor youre chyld. I serve her majestie and I am that I am" (Lansdowne 42, 97r). We should note that Oxford feels Burghley's power as a threat to his subjectivity and is compelled to assert "I am that I am."

66. She knew better than Burghley that young men must have something to do, some hope for advancement, and succeeded in keeping many of them safely lodged in her court spending their energy and funds on "trifles" that posed no threat to her power.

67. See McCutcheon, *Bacon*, for an account of this fondness for sententiae.

68. Francis Bacon, "Observations on a Libel," in James Spedding, ed., *The Letters and Life of Francis Bacon*, vol. 1, in *The Works of Francis Bacon*, vol. 8 (London: Longman, 1861), 200.

69. Spedding, *Letters*, 1:59, 108. Bacon's famous statement that he has "taken all knowledge to be my province" occurs in the second of the letters cited above, and is followed by remarks which place this claim clearly in the context I have been exploring: "I have taken all knowledge to be my province; if I could purge it of two sorts of rovers, whereof the one with *frivolous* disputations, confutations, and verbosities, the other with blind experiments and auricular traditions and impostures, hath committed so many spoils, I hope I should bring in *industrious*

observations, *grounded* conclusions, and *profitable* inventions and discoveries" (109, emphasis mine).

70. Cited by Read, *Burghley*, 479.

71. Conversation cited in ibid., 496–97.

72. Helgerson, in *Prodigals*, emphasizes their use of the prodigal son plot to test the didactic teaching of their fathers and further explores their attempts to define themselves as poets in *Laureates*. G. K. Hunter, *John Lyly: The Humanist as Courtier* (Cambridge: Harvard University Press, 1962), 1–36, stresses the importance of the inability to find preferment at court in shaping the career and prose style of John Lyly.

73. Sir Philip Sidney, *The Countess of Pembroke's Arcadia*, ed. Albert Feuillerat (Cambridge: Cambridge University Press, 1922), book 2, chapter 21, where the Iberian games are described.

74. See Yates, "Elizabethan Chivalry: The Romance of the Accession Day Tilts," in *Astraea* (London: Routledge and Kegan Paul, 1975), 88.

75. On the display of shields in Whitehall, see ibid., 91.

76. John Bodenham, *Belvedere or The Garden of the Muses* (1600), Spenser Society Reprint, vol. 8 (1875), A4r.

77. On imprese and the Sidney circle, see John Buxton, *Sir Philip Sidney and the English Renaissance*, 2d ed. (New York: St. Martins, 1964), 148. Two of its members, Daniel and Abraham Fraunce, wrote treatises on imprese, and Sidney's *Arcadia* attests to his interest in them.

78. See William Camden, *Remains Concerning Britain* (London, 1870), 366–86. Subsequent references are provided parenthetically in the text.

79. Alexander Grosart, ed., *The Worthy Tract of Paulus Jovius*, in *The Complete Works in Verse and Prose of Samuel Daniel*, vol. 4 (London, 1885), 24, 17. Subsequent references are provided parenthetically in the text.

80. Camden (*Remains Concerning Britain*, 367) notes that an impresa is "most commended when it is an Hemistich, or parcel of a verse."

81. Daniel provides a suggested list of "famous authors," including Ovid, Horace, Catullus, Homer, Hesiod, Callimachus, Petrarch, Ariosto, Dante, and Bembo.

82. In this respect, imprese resemble the religious and moral emblem collections that were so popular in the period, but differ in their social and political function. On such emblems, see Barbara K. Lewalski, *Protestant Poetics and the Seventeenth-Century Religious Lyric* (Princeton: Princeton University Press, 1979), 179–88.

83. Yates notes that the astronomical (particularly solar and lunar) imagery which was so popular in Accession Day imprese derives at least in part from Ramon Lull's *Book of the Ordre of Chyvalry* ("Elizabethan Chivalry," 106–8). Sidney uses the sun here in a typical way, to reinforce the Tudor hierarchy and to suggest that by advancing him it will only enhance its own stature.

84. Naomi Miller called this possibility to my attention.

85. Buxton, *Sidney*, 149, cites this motto and identifies its source.

86. On Sidney's uncertain social position, see especially Maureen Quilligan, "Sidney and His Queen," in Dubrow and Strier, *Historical Renaissance*, 171–96.

87. George Gascoigne used this motto; for more on his ambivalent position in society, see chapter 8 below.

CHAPTER VII
"IN A NET TO HOLD THE WIND"

1. M. H. Abrams et al., eds., *The Norton Anthology of English Literature*, 5th ed., vol. 1 (New York: Norton, 1986).

2. Fineman, *Perjured Eye*, 9, 84. He goes on to argue that Shakespeare's sonnets differ from this tradition, offering a "genuinely new effect of subjectivity" by recording "the difference between their vision and their speech" (25).

3. For a discussion of the role of New Criticism and its assumptions about the lyric self in the formation of our canon, see the introduction to Chaviva Hosek and Patricia Parker, eds., *Lyric Poetry: Beyond New Criticism* (Ithaca: Cornell University Press, 1985), especially 18–21, where some changes prompted by theory in the Romantic canon are noted.

4. Fineman, *Perjured Eye*, 9, notes that "the poetic self of the Renaissance sonnet characteristically presents itself as a *full* self, present to itself, or potentially so, by virtue of the complementarity it discovers or hopes to discover, between objective and subjective pointing." I borrow the term "partitioned subject" from Silverman, *Subject*, 132. Her chapter on "The Subject" provides a useful summary of the impact of some of these systems on the individualist self.

5. For the first approach see, for example, Derek Attridge, "Perplexity," 257–79, who sees in the inconsistencies and self-contradictions of Puttenham's text "a cheerful pragmatism in the face of the perplexing field of discourse" (275). Richard Halpern, "Skelton," 225–56, reads Skelton from a Marxist perspective and discovers in his poems "a politics that does not entirely coincide with his explicitly stated beliefs" (231). For the second, see Greenblatt, *Self-Fashioning*, on Wyatt, or Fineman, *Perjured Eye*, on Shakespeare's sonnets. Greenblatt uses the term "internal distantiation" to describe Wyatt's position (153).

6. Greenblatt, "Psychoanalysis," 210–24, argues that the self upon which psychoanalysis is based was not yet fully formed in the Renaissance. Timothy J. Reiss, "Montaigne and the Subject of Polity," in Parker and Quint, *Literary Theory*, 115–49, similarly argues that Montaigne's conception of the public and private subjects differs significantly from our own. Anne Ferry, *"Inward" Language*, discusses the linguistic manifestations of the differences between a sixteenth-century view of the self and our own, pointing out, for example, that the word "individual" was not in use until 1645 (34).

7. See C. S. Lewis, *English Literature in the Sixteenth Century Excluding Drama* (Oxford: Clarendon, 1954), 239, for "drab" aphoristic poetry. Douglas L. Peterson, *The English Lyric from Wyatt to Donne* (Princeton: Princeton University Press, 1967), traces "plain" and "eloquent" poetic traditions. Yvor Winters, "The Sixteenth Century Lyric in England: A Critical and Historical Reinterpretation," in Paul J. Alpers, ed., *Elizabethan Poetry: Modern Essays in Criticism* (Oxford: Oxford University Press, 1967), 93–125, distinguishes a plainer expository mode of poetry and defends it against the more popular Petrarchan tradition. Although Winters is clearly more sympathetic to this kind of poetry, he, like

Lewis and Peterson, defines it solely by style. This is misleading in part because many aphoristic poems are as rhetorically elaborate as their Petrarchan rivals. I would argue that this tradition is more accurately delineated by its participation in the discursive practices of gathering and framing, and by the writers' attitudes toward publication, the nature of the poetic text, and the role of the author.

8. On the "author-function," see Michel Foucault, "What Is an Author?" in Josue V. Harari, ed., *Textual Strategies: Perspectives in Post-Structural Criticism* (Ithaca: Cornell University Press, 1979), 141–60.

9. On imagination and inspiration as authorizing principles for poetry in sixteenth-century England, see Guillory, *Poetic Authority*.

10. Frederic Jameson, *The Political Unconscious* (Ithaca: Cornell University Press, 1981), 20, links our tendency to distinguish political and nonpolitical texts with "that structural, experiential, and conceptual gap between the public and the private, between the social and the psychological, or the political and the poetic, between history or society and the 'individual' "—a gap which the two poetic traditions that I am tracing here were instrumental in constituting.

11. Helgerson, *Laureates*, argues that "amateur" poets at the end of the century could only make "a place for poetry . . . by systematically inverting the values of midcentury humanism" (28), which taught that "poetry was wasteful folly" (17). He focuses on the efforts of men like Spenser, Jonson, and Milton, who attempted to fashion roles and voices suitable for a serious, professional poet. He does not, however, explore the tradition of serious humanist poetry that was a precursor to and model for these later "laureate" poets.

12. A few Protestant writers in the sixteenth century wrote poems in this tradition. Later, English Protestants found acceptable models for personal, private lyric, as Lewalski (*Protestant Poetics*) has shown.

13. I use "middle-class" here to differentiate this audience from the small, court-centered groups in which aristocratic lyric circulated in manuscript. The wider audience no doubt included some members of the nobility and gentry, but the poetry seems largely intended for an urban merchant class.

14. See, for example, Hoyt Hopewell Hudson, *The Epigram in the English Renaissance* (1947; rpt. New York: Octagon, 1966), 145–55. For a more unsympathetic view of these poets' failure to imitate Martiallian wit and point, see T. K. Whipple, *Martial and the English Epigram from Sir Thomas Wyatt to Ben Jonson*, University of California Publications in Modern Philology, 10, no. 4 (Berkeley and Los Angeles: University of California Press, 1925), 302. I am including some references to Parkhurst in my discussion of the humanist epigrammatists of the 1520s because his poems are closely modeled on theirs and represent a later version of many of the same techniques and practices.

15. For an account of this process from a Marxist perspective, see Anderson, *Lineages*, 48–49. On Wolsey's role, his use of humanists, and the opposition of aristocratic families like the Howards, see Stanley Fish, *John Skelton's Poetry* (New Haven: Yale University Press, 1965), 126–27.

16. On the replacement of aristocratic magnates by educated bureaucrats, see chapter 5 above, and also Stone, *Crisis*, 199–201.

17. On the struggle, in this period, over who should provide advice to the king, see chapter 5 above.

18. On these two controversies and Wolsey's involvement on the humanist side, see Pollet, *John Skelton*, 113–19. On the grammar controversy, see chapter 4 above.

19. "Bossus" was the pen name that Whittinton assumed. Constable's poem asserts that "Bossus" has fallen silent, ashamed of his inept epigrams against Lily (D2r).

20. See Pollet, *John Skelton*, 115–19; and Fish, *Skelton's Poetry*, 126, who notes that "at some point between 1515 and 1520 the Cardinal became for the aging poet [Skelton] the symbol of all that was dangerous in the contemporary scene. Not only to Skelton, but to the great families whose unofficial propagandist he was in the 1520s, Wolsey seemed to be the architect of the centralizing process that was steadily undermining their feudal position." Skelton was praised by Erasmus and Lily as a humanist ally around the turn of the century but by 1520 is clearly against them. The Howard family did not actively participate in the Grammarians' War but probably encouraged Skelton to write against Wolsey (see Pollet, 135–37). (However, see Walker, *John Skelton*, for the idea that the Howards did not oppose Wolsey in the 1520s.)

21. On this poem and its place in the "war," see Pollet, *John Skelton*, 115.

22. "Humanist," was not, of course, a term generally used by these writers. They designate their project as the study of "bonae litterae" (*not* generally *litterae humaniores*), their teaching as "bona doctrina," themselves as "doctus," taught.

23. Gordon Kipling, "Henry VII and the Origins of Tudor Patronage," in Guy Fitch Lytle and Stephen Orgel, eds., *Patronage in the Renaissance* (Princeton: Princeton University Press, 1981), 117–64, argues that Skelton writes very much in the "Franco-Burgundian" tradition favored at the court of Henry VII. A library inventory of the period reveals that this tradition was "without humanist direction," consisting largely of "histories, romances, and poetry—heavily chivalric in emphasis and composed in copious aureate prose" (124).

24. In stressing these models, I hope to supplement Ann Baynes Coiro's account of the "epigram book tradition" in the early sixteenth century, in *Robert Herrick's "Hesperides" and the Epigram Book Tradition* (Baltimore: The Johns Hopkins University Press, 1988), 45–77.

25. For a more extended account of their use of these source materials, see Crane, "*Intret Cato*," 158–86.

26. Of More's 253 poems, about 25 percent are aphoristic, about 30 percent are satiric, and the rest are divided among a number of kinds including the epideictic (some of which are also moralizing), amatory, and anecdotal. On More's sources, see Leicester Bradner and Charles Arthur Lynch, eds., *The Latin Epigrams of Thomas More* (Chicago: University of Chicago Press, 1953), introduction. They note that he differs from Continental epigrammatists in imitating a higher proportion of satiric poems, but they tend to overlook his high proportion of aphoristic poems. Ann Coiro, "*Hesperides*," 61–67, also discusses More's sources, noting that his poems "prune away mythological decorations and aim instead for the Anthology's aphoristic style" (62).

27. Bradner and Lynch, *Latin Epigrams*, 7. "To build many residences and to feed many people is surely the direct road to poverty" (130).

28. In 1516 Wolsey and Henry VIII had passed sumptuary laws attempting to curtail aristocratic display. Thomas Howard, Skelton's patron, resigned from the king's council in protest (Pollet, *John Skelton*, 81). Ann Coiro, "*Hesperides*," 65–71, provides an excellent discussion of More's epigrams on kingship, which express ideas about tyranny similar to those found in the humanist political treatises of the period.

29. "Ioannis Constablii Londinensis et artium professoris epigrammata" (London, 1520), A2v. "As many sterile tongues as flourished in an earlier age, so many learned palates thrive in our own time." My translation.

30. Although today most scholars believe that the *Distichs* represent a late (third-century) compilation of earlier materials and consider them to be a minor, uninteresting work, English humanists believed that they were written by the great Roman moralist Cato the Elder. As I noted in chapter 4, they were highly valued for their aphoristic moralizing and their pure style, and were a required school text in the first and second forms of almost every humanist school, usually in Erasmus's edition; this contained variously the *Distichs* themselves, Erasmus's commentary on them, Greek translations by Maximus Planudes (who compiled the Greek Anthology), the Apophthegmata of Ausonious, the "Mimi" of Publilius Syrus, and versions of the creed and other religious texts translated into Latin elegiacs by Erasmus himself. For a modern scholarly edition, see Marcus Boas, ed., *Disticha Catonis* (Amsterdam: North Holland Publishing Co., 1952). For an account of Erasmus's text and its importance in English education, see Baldwin, *Small Latine*, 1:595–96, 603; and chapter 4 above. For further evidence that these poems were considered to be epigrams, see Crane, "*Intret Cato*," 166–68.

31. Cornelis Reedijk, ed., *The Poems of Desiderius Erasmus* (Leiden: Brill, 1956), no. 86. "Learn from me first, boys, and frame pure moral habits, then add pious letters." It is clear that Erasmus has the *Distichs* in mind because of his use of the distinctive future imperative "discite," and also because of the resemblance of his poem to this selection from the *Distichs*: "Disce sed a Doctis, indoctos ipse doceto, / Propaganda etenim rerum doctrina bonarum" (from Erasmus's 1523 edition: "Learn only from the learned, and teach the unlearned, for the teaching of 'good doctrine' must be propagated").

32. "Ioannis Constablii," A2v. "O Christian, when you move toward the sacred hall of Christ, direct your eyes, your tongue, and your heart to the Lord." Again, we know he consciously imitates the *Distichs* because of his future imperative "dirigito," and because of the resemblance between this poem and sections of Cato and Lily that direct students to pay attention in school.

33. In this period, of course, religious affiliations shifted rather quickly, so that while More was initially sympathetic to some aspects of religious reform (and to proto-Protestants like Colet), he later defended Catholic orthodoxy.

34. John W. Spaeth, "Martial and the Pasquinade," *Transactions of the American Philological Association* 70 (1939): 242–46.

35. Bradner and Lynch, *Latin Epigrams*, 85. "You, mighty father, exclaim 'The letter kills.' This single phrase 'The letter kills' you have always in your mouth. You have taken good care so that no letter may kill you; you do not know any letter. And not idle is your fear that the letter may kill; you know that you do not have the spirit which will give you life" (206).

36. On 2 Cor. 3:6 as the basis for allegorical interpretation, see *The Cambridge History of the Bible*, ed. G.W.H. Lampe (Cambridge: Cambridge University Press, 1969), 2:89–90.

37. The poem by Lily against Skelton with which this section began has obvious affinities with the pasquil tradition. John Parkhurst, in his *Ludicra sive epigrammata juvenilia* (London, 1573), writes a number of doctrinal pasquils, condemning the sale of indulgences (47), the doctrine of justification by works (40), and the lack of learning among priests (32); and supporting the marriage of priests (68–69). Hudson, *Epigram*, 98, mentions that some of Parkhurst's poems resemble pasquils, but he does not indicate which collection he used or the extent of his reliance on it. Parkhurst used the *Pasquillorum tomi duo* of Caelius Secundus Curio (Basel, 1544), and several of his poems are based on poems in that volume: Parkhurst's "De Innocento Octavo Pontifice Romano," from "De Innocentio VIII" (*Pasquillorum*, 78); "De Ioanne eius nominis octavo" (82), from "De Pararum creandorum ritu immutato" (*Pasquillorum*, 70); "In Episcopos Romanenses" (83), from "In Alex. VI. Pont. Max." (*Pasquillorum*, 78); "In eandem Lucretiam" (Parkhurst, *Ludicra*, 83), from "Lucretiae Alexandri VI filiae tumulus" (*Pasquillorum*, 79).

38. Compare, for example, the epideictic poems of Whittinton, which do not seem concerned to advocate any particular moral or intellectual program.

39. Coiro, "*Hesperides*," 65–67.

40. Bradner and Lynch, *Latin Epigrams*, 19. "Cui cultum ingenuis artibus ingenium est," and "Imbuit et monitis Philosophia suis." We should note More's use of "cultum" in the first passage, implying, perhaps, that Henry did not receive the full humanist "indoctrination" under his tutor, Skelton. His use of "imbuit" hints at the highly problematic liquid metaphor for instruction; it also echoes the passage in *Utopia* where he reveals the secret of Utopian obedience as the fact that all citizens are "imbued" with good letters. Steeping in philosophical precepts would be carried out partly through gathering and the notebook method, but More's use of "imbuit" may, even here, reveal a trace of his uncertainties about this project, especially as applied to rulers.

41. Parkhurst, *Ludicra*, 55. He seems to refer here to, among others, Sir Nicholas Bacon, Richard Morison, the two Nowell brothers, William Cecil, and Sir Anthony Cooke.

42. Ibid., 55–56. He means Stephen Gardiner, Richard Sampson, Cuthbert Tunstall, and Edmund Bonner.

43. "Sodalis" literally means "comrade" or "companion." The Bradner and Lynch edition introduces an anachronistic idea of individual competition into the exercise when it translates the word as "friendly rivals."

44. George B. Walsh, "The Voices of Epitaph and Alexandrian Poetics," *Abstracts of the One Hundred and Twentieth Annual Meeting of the American Philological Association* (Athens, Ga.: Scholars' Press, 1989), 118, notes of the Greek inscriptive epitaphs that "it is hard to imagine a medium that needs a voice more or owns one less."

45. See David Daube, *Forms of Roman Legislation* (Oxford: Oxford University Press, 1979), 93–96. This form appears in Cato's *De agricultura* and may have first appeared in edicts written by Cato.

46. Harry Berger, Jr., "Bodies and Texts," *Representations* 17 (1987): 149, notes that "mechanical inscription . . . progressively abstracts the means of production from the control of the body and thus alienates the production of meaning."

47. J. W. Saunders, "From Manuscript to Print," *Proceedings of the Leeds Philosophical and Literary Society* 6 (1951): 527.

48. J. W. Saunders, "The Stigma of Print: A Note on the Social Bases of Tudor Poetry," *Essays in Criticism* 1 (1951): 153.

49. Saunders, "Manuscript to Print," 527–28.

50. J. W. Saunders, *The Profession of English Letters* (London: Routledge and Kegan Paul, 1964), 4, 67.

51. The fact that such poetry was in Latin prevented it from being addressed to a wider audience; however, we should be careful not to attribute the later status of Latin as a sign of an upper-class education to this period. In the early sixteenth century, Latin was a middle-class language, and humanist educators used it to extend the authority of the educated middle class and its values.

52. "Commune esse video studiosis o[mn]ibus optime lector e memoriae thesauro aliquid in medium proferre / unde honesta possint adiuuari & candida promoueri studia," "Ioannis Constablii," A1v.

53. See Martial, *Epigrammata*, ed. W. M. Lindsay, 2d ed. (1903; rpt. Oxford: Clarendon, 1969). Peter Jay, ed., *The Greek Anthology* (London: Lane, 1973), 16–17, comments on the "presence of so much occasional and light verse" in the anthology.

54. It is typical of More simply to include, without comment, two traditions— serious aphoristic poetry and trifling jokes—that others found disturbing and incompatible.

55. "In re frivola et nugaci . . . scilicet in pauculis condendis epigrammatis" (A1v).

56. "Nil praeter nugas ludicra pene dabunt" (*Ludicra*, 1).

57. Frank Whigham, "Interpretation at Court: Courtesy and the Performer-Audience Dialectic," *New Literary History* 14 (1983): 623–40, discusses the importance to aristocrats of "effortlessness . . . designed to imply the natural or given character of one's social identity, and to deny any earnedness, any labor or arrival from a social elsewhere" (626).

58. "Qui an inani atque infrugifero (quo alii torpent) ocio nos liberaverit" (A1v).

59. Whigham, "Interpretation," 626, citing Frederic Jameson, "Marxism and Historicism," *New Literary History* 11 (1979): 57.

60. The first "Skelton" anecdote appears in John Rastell's *Hundred Merry Tales* (1526), which, according to Pollet, "entitles us to think that the Skelton legend originated in English humanistic circles" (*John Skelton*, 150). It is tempting to draw a connection among Catholicism, antihumanism, and jestbook fools; however, the fool "Skelton" was actually later appropriated by Protestants because of stories about his "wife" and illegitimate child (166). It does seem safe to say that Catholic writers (like Skelton, More, and Heywood) tend to adopt a more frivolous stance, and Protestant writers tend to be more serious—at least early in the century.

61. John King, *English Reformation Literature* (Princeton: Princeton University Press, 1982), 344, connects Crowley's organizational scheme with "moralized Renaissance hornbooks." For more on Crowley's sources and relation to the Latin epigram tradition, see Crane, "*Intret Cato*," 173–76.

62. Robert Crowley, *Select Works*, ed. J. M. Cowper, Early English Text Society (London: Trübner, 1872), "Of Dicears," 25.

63. First Hundred, published 1550, in Milligan, *John Heywood's "Works,"* 104. Milligan, 4, cites the final poem of the fifth hundred ("Art thou Skelton with the mad mery wit?") as evidence for his self-presentation as a jester. Knapp, "Error," 813, argues that Spenser repeatedly connects papistry with "trifles."

64. Milligan, *John Heywood's "Works,"* 107, 200.

65. Puttenham, *Arte of English Poesie*, 60. Note Puttenham's use of the near-technical term for humanist teaching, "good learning" (*bona doctrina*). Like Skelton, Heywood is said to lack humanist doctrine.

66. Elizabeth Story Donno, ed., *Sir John Harington's A New Discourse of a Stale Subject, Called the Metamorphosis of Ajax* (New York: Columbia University Press, 1962), 99–103. Harington, interestingly, precedes the Heywood anecdote with two stories about Sir Thomas More's wit on the scaffold. Like More, Heywood was indicted for treason stemming from pro-Catholic beliefs, but unlike More, he used his jest persona to procure the king's pardon.

67. Cited in Elizabeth Longford, ed., *The Oxford Book of Royal Anecdotes* (Oxford: Oxford University Press, 1989), 208.

68. Lawrence Stone, *The Family, Sex, and Marriage in England 1500–1800* (New York: Harper and Row, 1977), 103. Only there did young men and women have virtually unrestricted and only loosely chaperoned contact with each other.

69. Thus, Marotti, " 'Love is not Love,' " 396–428, argues that the Sidneyan sonnet sequence functions as "a form of mediation between socioeconomic and sociopolitical desires and the constraints of the established order" (399), but does not discuss the importance of the courtly lyric, earlier in the century, in constituting that desire. Similarly, Javitch (*Poetry*) focuses on the close relationship in the Elizabethan period between the duplicities of courtly intrigue and the ambiguities of poetic language, but does not examine the somewhat different relationship between them at Henry's court.

70. They were recusant all through the Reformation, and, indeed, remain Roman Catholic today.

71. For accounts of this manuscript, see Raymond Southall, *The Courtly Makers* (Oxford: Blackwell, 1969), 15–23; Kenneth Muir, "Unpublished Poems in the Devonshire Manuscript," *Proceedings of the Leeds Philosophical and Literary Society* 6 (1947): 253–82 (cited hereafter in the text as Muir); Kenneth Muir and Patricia Thomson, eds., *The Collected Poems of Sir Thomas Wyatt* (Liverpool: Liverpool University Press, 1969) (cited hereafter in the text as Muir-Thomson); and Richard Harrier, *The Canon of Sir Thomas Wyatt's Poetry* (Cambridge: Harvard University Press, 1975), 23–54. My account is largely based on Southall, 16–25, as corroborated by Harrier, 23.

72. The practice of collecting poems in a notebook is related to, but in some ways different from, the collection of sayings. Notebooks exist that contain sayings and abstracts alone (BM Additional MS 32, 494, kept by Gabriel Harvey;

Harley 783; Harley 1327). There are others that contain a mixture of sayings and poems (Lansdowne 679, which was kept by Samuel Fox and ranges from moral maxims to jestbook anecdotes and obscene poems; or the Arundel Harington MS, ed. Ruth Hughey, 2 vols. [Columbus: Ohio State University Press, 1960], which contains a section of "dyvers sentences," 98–103, included in a collection that largely consists of courtly verse). The Devonshire is actually unusual in its sole focus on love lyric. Courtly miscellanies seem at least partly designed to display the owner's participation in the courtly pastime of writing, exchanging, and collecting love lyrics; however, in the case of the Arundel Harington MS, this is mixed in with the gathering of aphoristic matter as well. See the next chapter for a more detailed discussion of these various kinds of collection.

73. Harrier, *Canon*, 23. On Thomas Clere's feudal relation to the Howard family, see Sheldon Zitner, "Surrey's 'Epitaph on Thomas Clere': Lyric and History," in Hosek and Parker, *Lyric Poetry*, 106–15. Zitner sees in this poem (and in Surrey's poem on Fitzroy) evidence that he "had made the early sixteenth-century struggles among kinship factions the substance of his emotional life" (111). I am arguing that poetry provided, in the Howard circle particularly, a central means of mystifying such political relations as emotional and private.

74. Patricia Thomson, *Sir Thomas Wyatt and His Background* (Stanford: Stanford University Press, 1964), 16, notes the marriage of Mary Howard to Henry Fitzroy, as well as the marriages of the Howard nieces Anne Boleyn and Catherine Howard to the king himself, in support of this allegation. This idea is supported by Stone, who notes that "the larger the property and status . . . the greater the participation of the kin in the formation and daily life of the conjugal family," *Family, Sex, and Marriage*, 85.

75. Southall, *Courtly Makers*, 19.

76. Thomson, *Sir Thomas Wyatt*, 37–39, on Wyatt's imprisonment.

77. Ferry, *"Inward" Language*, has argued that writers in this period seem unable to distinguish between inward and outward experience. In Thomas Howard's poem, I believe that we can see a clumsy attempt to assert such a difference, even here contaminated by the attribution of a condition of "outward" experience (social "estates") to the sphere of the inward. However, Howard exploits this contamination in order to construct a version of inward experience that recapitulates and revises the social relations of courtly life.

78. Here again the conflation of "syghes" and "wondes" supports Ferry's contention that inward and outward levels of experience were imperfectly differentiated. Here again, however, Howard seems specifically concerned to present the expression of inward feeling as spontaneous and natural, and to link the outward causes of his pain directly with his criticism of it in verse.

79. In this section, I have printed the D variants of the Wyatt poems that are found in the Devonshire manuscript.

80. Probably because it was so insubstantial. Humanist educators preferred to imagine speech as framed into substantial materiality.

81. As Ferry notes, *"Inward" Language*, 67–70, there is not yet a gap between what is felt and what can be expressed. The lack of such a gap is essential to the idea that love copia is natural, and not in need of supplemental gathering. For the commonplace that members of the aristocratic class were subject to stronger emo-

tions, see Geoffrey Chaucer, "The Knight's Tale," in Larry Benson, ed., *The Riverside Chaucer*: For pitee renneth soone in gentil herte" (line 1761).

82. Southall, *Courtly Makers*, 23, notes that, considering the circumstances of its owners, "it is not difficult to understand why . . . love, loyalty, and secrecy, the three ideal regulations of courtly love, should dominate the attentions of the poets represented in the [Devonshire] manuscript." He does not, however, pursue the cultural and political implications of these ideals.

83. Several critics have discussed the use of love lyrics to vent frustration resulting from the instabilities and duplicities their authors experienced while seeking courtly advancement; see, for example, Marotti, " 'Love is not Love,' " 398, for treatment of a slightly later period. See also Jonathan Kamhholtz, "Thomas Wyatt's Poetry: The Politics of Love," *Criticism* 20 (1979): 359, who argues that "love and the state both try to subject the courtier to authority," and that while "Wyatt sees both love and politics as a constant process of slipping and falling" (357), he seeks stability through his involvement in love and courtly life.

84. For a contemporary account of this process, see Thomas Wright, *The Passions of the mind in general (1601)*, ed. Thomas O. Sloan (Urbana: University of Illinois Press, 1971). Anne Ferry, *"Inward" Language*, 72, discusses the link between love and imagination.

85. Several critics have commented on Wyatt's ties to both systems. Mason, *Humanism*, 167–99, sharply divides the Wyatt canon into worthless "courtly" lyrics (largely found in the Devonshire MS) and worthwhile humanist translations. Thomas A. Hannen, "The Humanism of Sir Thomas Wyatt," in Thomas Sloan and Raymond Waddington, eds., *The Rhetoric of Renaissance Poetry* (Berkeley and Los Angeles: University of California Press, 1974), 37–57, argues (against Mason) that Wyatt's "humanism" consists in his attempt (in both original lyrics and translations) "to find an eloquence that would reconcile thought and action" (57), and to "bring to public life the wisdom and stability usually found only in philosophy" (39). Similarly, Thomson sees "courtly wisdom" and "courtly love" integrated into "a total complex" in Wyatt's poems without serious contradiction. I am primarily interested in the incompatibility of the two systems, and the traces, in Wyatt's poems, of that rupture.

86. See, for example, Harrier, *Canon*.

87. See, for example, Marotti, *John Donne, Coterie Poet* (Madison: University of Wisconsin Press, 1986), 13–14, who notes that although the content of poetic miscellanies "approaches the condition of such [Foucauldian] authorless discourse," it is also personal and "self-advertising."

88. By "Wyatt" I mean the reputed author of the set of texts I now intend to discuss, a figure who was, I argue, a particularly concentrated and articulate focal point for the conflicting social and intellectual systems that I have been tracing. I include in this discussion poems that are of doubtful attribution. However, if, in fact, some of these poems are not by Wyatt, they are nevertheless the products of a similar conflation of forces in some other contemporary subject. It might therefore be more accurate to enclose the name in quotation marks throughout this section.

89. Greenblatt, *Self-Fashioning*, 154–56.

90. Anne Ferry, *"Inward" Language*, 71–118, explores Wyatt's use of the sonnet form to experiment with a "new sense of distance between what is within the lover's heart and his outward modes of expression, including the poem itself" (118). Where she is interested in the modes of expressing that distance, I am concerned to follow the textual traces of its causes.

91. See Thomson, *Wyatt*, 7–8, for Wyatt's education. Wyatt's father was a privy councillor to both Henry VII and Henry VIII and served as a soldier against the French and Scots, thus acting as both adviser and feudal liege. He seems to have brought up his son in both traditions; in 1516, for example, the younger Wyatt both matriculated at the preeminent humanist college and served as a ewer at the christening of Princess Mary (5–7).

92. The very act of writing such letters was a self-presentational gesture intended to define the author as a humanist patriarch: they were written by Sir Henry Sidney, Lord Burghley, and King James. See the introduction to Louis B. Wright's collection of such letters (*Advice to a Son*) and Habenicht's introduction, in *Heywood*, to Heywood's "Dialogue."

93. Thomas Wyatt's advice to his son, in *English Historical Documents*, ed. C. H. Williams (London: Eyre and Spottiswoode, 1967), 1066, 1070. Subsequent references are provided parenthetically in the text.

94. Wyatt admits that he himself is not to be taken as an example in such matters.

95. Greene, *Light*, 258.

96. Greenblatt, *Self-Fashioning*, 132.

97. Ibid., 143.

98. Ibid., 143 and 137.

99. Ibid., 134–35. As Jerry Mermel, "Wyatt's Satires and the Humanist Debate over Court Service," *Studies in the Literary Imagination* 11, no. 1 (1978): 69–70, points out, Bryan's "A Dispraise of the Life of the Courtier" (1548) "managed the feat of denouncing in print most of the courtly vices which he was notorious for commiting in practice." Bryan, then, had actually tried to assume the "honest" persona, a fact that may have occasioned some of Wyatt's doubts about it.

100. Greenblatt, *Self-Fashioning*, 132, makes this point.

101. Mermel, "Wyatt's Satires," 79, has argued that Wyatt's satires "speak to the conflicting attitudes that the problem of court service generated among the humanistically trained readers and writers of Tudor England," and that he uses different "voices" to explore different positions on the issue. I am arguing that the satires are as much about the assumption of any kind of "voice" as about the opinions such voices might express.

102. Muir-Thomson prints "sitting in thy mind," but "stickinge" is a variant reading found in A2 and T. See Donald Friedman, "The 'Thing' in Wyatt's Mind," *Essays in Criticism* 16 (1966): 380, on the "thing" as a stoic "inviolable core of personal identity."

103. Southall, *Courtly Makers*, 69, identifies the "thing" in the previous poem with the lesson of the bell tower "concerning the insecurity and instability of court favor." Friedman ("'Thing'") argues against Southall that the "thing" is Wyatt's stable personal identity.

104. Similarly, CCXIII quotes several sayings on love from "Therence in his commedis poeticall" and then notes that "we see by experience" that such observations are true.

105. Ferry, *"Inward" Language*, 84.

106. Two other notable hunting poems are, of course, "They Flee from Me," and "The Long Love."

107. Erasmus, *Adages*, 363.

108. Virgil describes this in several passages, for example, *Georgics* 1.307, "retia ponere cervis."

109. We might recall Gregory Cromwell's tutor and his assurances about his charge's natural ability to hunt: "for his recreation he useth to hawke and hunte, and shote in his long bowe, which frameth and succedeth so well with hime that he semeth to be thereunto given by nature"; see chapter 4 above.

110. Cf. Fineman, *Perjured Eye*, 9; see n. 4 to this chapter.

111. We might recall the copious "sighs" of the Devonshire MS, or, at the risk of anachronism, Shelley's "Ode to the West Wind" and Wordsworth's "gentle breeze."

112. On these sources, see Greenblatt, *Self-Fashioning*, 148–49, who is, however, largely interested in "the wrenching transformation of the sacred to the profane which is the essence of Wyatt's treatment of Petrarch."

113. Similarly, CCXXXII describes the "dedelie stroke" or suicide that will release his "harborid syghes" and will "loose the bonde of my restore / Wherein is bounde my liberte."

114. Hannen makes a similar point when he says, of the inscription following "who lyst his wealth," that "the enemies who surround him are innocence, truth and faith as well as those people at court who have had him imprisoned. It is the desire of his mind for stability as much as his courtly companions which prevents him from living comfortably in the real world of eternal change" ("Humanism," 56). I argue that this "desire," is, for Wyatt, bound up with the practices of gathering and framing.

CHAPTER VIII
BEND OR FRAME

1. Wyatt died in 1542, Surrey in 1547. Abrams, *Norton Anthology*: Wyatt, 461–71; Surrey, 473–80; Sidney, 481–528.

2. C. S. Lewis, *English Literature in the Sixteenth Century*, 227, introduced the term "drab," which, he insisted, was not a pejorative term. More recently, Douglas L. Peterson, *English Lyric*, has argued that these poems represent a "plain" (as opposed to "eloquent") stylistic tradition that reflected "the idiom of the common man" and provided an antecedent for Donne. Peterson's argument resembles mine in his sense that the "plain" and "eloquent" traditions "represent . . . the values of distinct cultural groups" (349). But he differs in his purely stylistic definition of the two kinds of poem (a definition that, I believe, does not hold up, since aphoristic poems are often as stylistically elaborate as love poems), and in his belief that the "plain" style directly reflects "common" people instead of upwardly mobile humanists. He also differs in linking the plain style more closely

to a "Christian Contemplative Ideal" that earthly life is vain, and in reading it as "dedicated only to content—to truth and reality" (352).

3. Arthur Kinney traces the formative influence of humanism on English prose fiction in the sixteenth century. The fact that he focuses on "fiction" rather than "narrative" gives his account a different shape from mine. I concur, however, in his sense that Gascoigne marks a phase of distrust of humanist optimism and in his acknowledgment that it might be "self-serving in the employment of sophistry" (*Humanist Poetics*, 36).

4. Marshall Grossman, "Literary Forms and Historical Consciousness in Renaissance Poetry," *Exemplaria* 1 (1989): 248. Grossman argues that in the Renaissance we see "a body of poetry that self-consciously engages a formal tension between lyric and narrative" (253), and he traces its presence in Marvell's "The Garden."

5. Richard Rainolde, *Foundacion of Rhetorike*, Bir.

6. Roger Ascham, *The Schoolmaster*, ed. Lawrence V. Ryan (Ithaca: Cornell University Press, 1967), 68–70. Subsequent references are provided parenthetically in the text.

7. On both travel and narrative as dilatory wandering, see Patricia Parker, *Inescapable Romance: Studies in the Poetics of a Mode* (Princeton: Princeton University Press, 1979).

8. McKeon, *Origins*, 131–50, on the class origins of chivalric narrative.

9. Such singularity is, of course, at odds with the humanist emphasis on nonthreatening corporate success. Ascham notes that this desire for singularity is pitted against humanist bureaucrats when he describes the Italianate Englishmen as considering themselves "so singular in wisdom (in their own opinion) as scarce they count the best counselor the prince hath comparable with them" (74).

10. A possible exception to this rule is the *Mirror for Magistrates*, begun in 1559 by a group of men who were generally sympathetic to humanist ideas. However, as the full title and prefatory material make clear, these complaints are narratives of failure rather than success and are intended as sources of exempla illustrating humanist ethical and political values. The title of the 1559 edition, for example, is *A Myrroure for Magistrates. Wherein may be seen by example of other, with howe grevous plages vices are punished and howe frayle and unstable worldly prosperite is founde, even of those whom Fortune seemeth most highly to favoure*, in Lily B. Campbell, ed., *The Mirror for Magistrates* (Cambridge: Cambridge University Press, 1938). William Baldwin's introduction begins with this gathered saying: "Plato Among many other of his notable sentences concerning the government of a common weale, hath this: Well is that realme governed, in which the ambicious desyer not to beare office" (63). As Mervyn James has noted (*Society*), the *Mirror* was closely implicated in the absolutist monarch's ongoing effort to replace aristocratic with humanist values.

11. Of course, as McKeon has pointed out, Deloney's narratives of "upwardly mobile apprentices" also qualify the social threat: "Deloney both proclaims, and effaces the evidence of, the elevation of the humble" (*Origins*, 223–24).

12. In *Prodigals*, Helgerson treats Gascoigne, Lyly, Greene, Lodge, and Sidney.

13. Ibid., 155.

14. Helgerson does note that the prodigality narrative allowed these men to embrace both "civic humanism" and "courtly romance" in "a dialectic of opposites" (ibid., 41); however, he is largely concerned with the relationship between fact and fiction, biographical self-expression and conformity to convention, in their works.

15. Of course, there was a long tradition of collecting short poems, preserved in classical sources such as the Greek Anthology and in Continental imitations of it. Coiro "*Hesperides*," traces the influence of one aspect of it in England. But in the middle years of the sixteenth century, English collections seem more strongly influenced by the model of the commonplace book than by that of the epigram book.

16. See Hughey, *The Arundel Harington Manuscript of Tudor Poetry*, especially 1:98–104 for aphoristic material under the heading "dyvers sentences." For manuscript commonplace books containing both sayings and poems, see the notebooks of Samuel Fox (BM Lansdowne 679), Sir E. Hoby (BM Additional MS 38,823), and William Norden (BM Sloane 1606).

17. On the importance of the coterie, see Arthur Marotti, *Donne*, especially 7–14.

18. Marotti, (ibid., 12) argues that the emphasis in published miscellanies on the authors' social prestige constitutes an attempt to preserve the "social environment" of the courtly coterie. See also Saunders, "Manuscript to Print," 528.

19. Richard C. Newton, "Making Books from Leaves," in Gerald P. Tyson and Sylvia S. Wagonheim, eds., *Print and Culture in the Renaissance* (Newark: University of Delaware Press, 1986), 246–64, argues that print technology enabled poets to become editors as well as authors and "to discover a new authority over their texts, an editorial majesty that had not generally been available to them since classical antiquity" (246). According to Newton, Ben Jonson first achieves this new authority. He sees the miscellanies as collections based on pastoral values, "an absence of narrative and, in a sense, of personality" (250) in favor of a dialogue of voices.

20. For a more complete description of these volumes, see the editions of Hyder Rollins (cited below, nn. 26–28) and also Elizabeth Pomeroy, *The Elizabethan Miscellanies* (Berkeley and Los Angeles: University of California Press, 1973).

21. Saunders, "Manuscript to Print," 528.

22. Marotti, *Donne*, 7, sees them as a "compromise" between manuscript circulation and the "printing of individual authors' works" but does not discuss the nature of these printed works in detail.

23. For an account of such collections and their audience, see Louis B. Wright, *Middle-Class Culture in Elizabethan England* (Chapel Hill: University of North Carolina Press, 1935). On ballads of counsel such as "A Table of Good Nurture" based in part on the *Distichs of Cato*, see 130–32. On the prose commonplace collections, see 150–54.

24. See Baldwin, *Treatise*. Bowers's introduction describes this book as "an Elizabethan best seller" that went through twenty-three editions.

25. On the commonwealth writers and their attitudes toward textual gathering, see chapter 5. H. C., in the preface to his *Forrest of Fancy*, notes that he has collected matter that "the common sorte" will be able to use.

26. Hyder Rollins, ed., *Tottel's Miscellany (1557–1587)* (Cambridge: Harvard University Press, 1926; rev. ed. 1966), 1:2. Subsequent references are provided parenthetically in the text. As noted in chapter 1, Ralph Lever's *Art of Reason* describes the predicaments as functioning as "notes sette on packets" so that "as the good and ready marchaunt provideth store of sundry wares, and sorteth every kinde by it selfe . . . so the quicke and sharpe reasoner, must gather general rules together, and place them in order."

27. Hyder Edward Rollins, ed., *The Paradise of Dainty Devices* (Cambridge: Harvard University Press, 1927), facing page xviii. Subsequent references are provided parenthetically in the text.

28. The *Gorgeous Gallery* (1578), ed. Hyder Rollins (Cambridge: Harvard University Press, 1926), seems to have experimented with two versions of self-presentation. The Stationer's Register records, in 1577, "a handefull of hidden Secretes conteigninge therein certaine Sonetes and other pleasaunte Devises pickt out of the Closet of sundrie worthie writers" (xiv). The title page of 1578 tries another tactic, however, offering "A gorgeous Gallery of gallant Inventions, Garnished and decked with *diuers dayntie deuises*, . . . First framed and fashioned in sundrie formes, by divers worthy workemen of late dayes: and now, ioyned together and builded up" (1). The first version stresses an aristocratic version of gathering as "secretes . . . pickt out of the closet of sundrie worthie writers," and expressive of their inner feelings. The second moves toward the humanist model, stressing that the poems have been "framed" by "workmen."

29. For example, Tottel took notorious liberties with Wyatt's poems, refashioning their meter to accord with the smoother and more regular verse that had become standard by 1557.

30. Saunders, "Manuscript to Print," 525.

31. On this, see Joseph Loewenstein, "The Script in the Marketplace," in Greenblatt, *Representing*, 265–78.

32. Newton, "Books from Leaves," acknowledges the importance of editorship in this period.

33. Wright, *Middle-Class Culture*, 151, notes that "provided with such books, one did not need to labor through pagan writers in search of apt phrases." This explanation is certainly true, but it leaves out the complex social function of such volumes.

34. Saunders, "Manuscript to Print," 527, argues that these volumes were published in order to exploit "middle class curiosity about the doings and sayings of the great and fashionable."

35. In this respect, such volumes participated in the ongoing efforts of the Tudor monarchs to achieve a "monopoly" of power (at the expense of once-powerful nobles) by encouraging all subjects to "internalize" what Mervyn James has called "a system of social controls and moral sanctions" that devalued aristocratic codes of honor (*Society*, 309).

36. In Robert Greene, *Works*, ed. Alexander Grosart, vol. 7, (London, 1881–1883), 216, 223. Subsequent references are provided parenthetically in the text.

37. We might recall Ralph Lever's *Art of Reason*, a logic text published in this period (1573) that promised an easy way to gather the basics of logic.

38. Helgerson, *Laureates*, introduces the terms "self-presentational gesture" and "amateur."

39. I have used the 1570 edition of Turberville's collection, the *Epitaphes, Epigrams, Songs, and Sonets, with a Discourse of the Friendly affections of Tymetes to Pyndara his Ladie* (London, 1570). Subsequent references are provided parenthetically in the text.

40. *Dictionary of National Biography*, 19:1248.

41. On the popularity of romance in this period with a middle-class audience, see Wright, *Middle-Class Culture*, 375–81. Berger, "Bodies and Texts," 149, provides another reason why a fictional narrative might be a necessary supplement to love poems in a printed book. He argues that "mechanical inscription . . . progressively abstracts the means of production from the control of the body and thus alienates the production of meaning." This would be particularly acute in poems that purport to express directly the voice produced by a suffering body, thus necessitating the addition of a narrative to supply the missing "bodily" context.

42. Gascoigne published *The Glasse of Government* in 1575, *The Steele Glas* in 1576, and he received preferment after the publication of *A Delicate Diet for Dainty-Mouthed Drunkards*. The early view of Gascoigne's shift to wholly moral works was that his repentance was "sincere," for which see C. T. Prouty, *George Gascoigne: Elizabethan Soldier and Poet* (New York: Blom, 1942), 239. Helgerson (*Prodigals*) ties this life pattern to the prodigality narrative, while Richard C. McCoy, "Gascoigne's 'Poetmata Castrata': The Wages of Courtly Success," *Studies in English Literature* 27 (1985): 24–55, takes the more cynical view that Gascoigne's "creative autonomy diminished as his proximity to power increased" (30). But this view is based on the idea that didactic poetry was a "subservient" (52) form, without any attractions of its own.

43. C. T. Prouty, ed., *George Gascoigne's "A Hundreth Sundrie Flowers,"* *University of Missouri Studies* 17 (1942): 45. Subsequent references are provided parenthetically in the text.

44. The idea of a narrative "frame" is interesting, since, as I have been arguing, the forward movement of narrative is antithetical to the stasis that humanists sought to achieve within their didactic "frames."

45. Interestingly, when Gascoigne revised the "Discourse of Master F. J." for *Posies*, he added a conclusion which claims that the narrative has been offered as a source of moral exempla: "I have recyted this Fable which may serve as ensample to warne the youthful reader from attempting the lyke worthles enterprise"; from George Gascoigne, *The Posies*, ed. J. W. Cunliffe (Cambridge: Cambridge University Press, 1907), 453. Subsequent references are provided parenthetically in the text.

46. For a description of these practices, see Puttenham's *Arte of English Poesie*, 58–59.

47. On Gascoigne's use of the posy, see Prouty's introduction to the *Hundreth Sundrie Flowers*, 28–39. Gascoigne does include a set of five poems written on aphoristic "theames," such as "Dominus iis opus habet," 159–60.

48. Camden, *Remains Concerning Britain*, mentions one of Gascoigne's posies in his section on "Impresses": "It may be thought that he noted deserts to be everywhere excluded, and meer hap to raise most men, who inscribed within a Laurel Garland, 'Fato non merito' " (377).

49. For Whetstone's career, which was similar in many respects to that of his friend Gascoigne, see Thomas C. Izard, *George Whetstone: Mid-Elizabethan Gentleman of Letters* (New York: Columbia, 1942). For the text of his poems, see George Whetstone, *The Rocke of Regard* (London, 1576).

50. Thomas Watson, *Hekatompathia or Passionate Centurie of Loue*, Spenser Society, vol. 6 (London, 1869). Subsequent references are provided parenthetically in the text.

51. Helgerson (*Prodigals*) does not explicitly discuss Watson, but his paradigm is clearly relevant.

52. One of these Latin poems is by Watson himself.

53. Watson's combination of Petrarchan and proverbial sources recalls Wyatt's practice in "Who so list to hunt"; however, Watson is less conscious of the contradictory nature of his sources.

54. John Bodenham, *Belvedere or The Garden of the Muses (1600)*, Spenser Society, vol. 8, (London, 1875), A3v. Subsequent references are provided parenthetically in the text.

55. Bodenham lists "Thomas Earle of Surrey. The Lord Marquesse of Winchester. Mary, Countesse of Pembrooke. Sir Philip Sidney."

56. The first list includes "Edward, Earle of Oxenford. Ferdinando, Earle of Derby. Sir Walter Raleigh. Sir Edward Dyer. Fulke Greuile, Esquier. Sir John Harington." The second includes Henry Constable, Samuel Daniel, Thomas Lodge, Thomas Watson, Christopher Marlow, "Beniamin Johnson," William Shakespeare, Nicholas Breton, and others.

57. By 1600, some of this emphasis on "apt" and "meet" headings may be derived from Ramist interest in "method," or methodical organization. But, as I argued in chapter 2, Ramism represents a culmination of gathering and framing, rather than a departure from it.

58. L. C. Martin, ed., *Herrick's Poetical Works* (Oxford: Clarendon Press, 1956), 340.

59. Anne Ferry pointed out this similarity to me. Whatever other organizational schemes lie behind *The Temple*, the commonplace book (or commonplace miscellany) is surely one of them.

60. Two versions of this work were published, under different titles, in 1595: William Ponsonby brought out "The Defence of Poesie," and Henry Olney "An Apologie for Poetrie." For the text, see the Duncan-Jones and Van Dorsten edition of Sidney's *Miscellaneous Prose*. Subsequent references are provided parenthetically in the text.

61. For an account of one of Sidney's Platonic sources, see S. K. Henninger, Jr., "Sidney and Serranus' *Plato*," in Arthur F. Kinney, ed., *Sidney in Retrospect* (Amherst: University of Massachusetts Press, 1988), 27–44. O. B. Hardison, "The Two Voices of Sidney's Apology for Poetry," in the same volume, associates Sidney's Platonism with "humanist poetics" (59). By humanism, however, Hardison seems to mean Italian humanism, since he lists Boccaccio, Politian, Daniello, and Tasso as major exponents. Indeed, what Hardison terms "neoclassicism" and opposes to humanism seems closer to the versions of English humanism that I have been tracing.

62. Ronald Levao, for instance, in "Sidney's Feigned Apology," *PMLA* 94

(1979): 223–44, describes Sidney's "discussion of poetic inspiration" as "deliberately tangled and ambivalent" (224), and he suggests that "by treating his arguments as conjectures, he can arrange a variety of them without strict regard for consistency" so that "running counter to . . . the central theory" is "the testing of more conservative possibilities" (230). Margaret Ferguson, *Trials of Desire*, 138, notes the "intellectual condescension" of modern critics who find Sidney's "eclecticism" disappointing. For the older argument that Sidney achieves coherence despite his eclecticism, see John Hunt, "Allusive Coherence in Sidney's 'Apology for Poetry,' " *Studies in English Literature* 27 (1987): 1–16.

63. Both Ferguson and Levao argue, in different ways, that the "Apology" undermines its own argument. According to Ferguson, Sidney's text "establishes and undermines rhetorical authority, its own and others' " (*Trials of Desire*, 162), while Levao argues that Sidney's text "act[s] out the tensions characteristic of the best Renaissance thought" ("Feigned Apology," 232). I hope to clarify the intellectual antecedents of Sidney's ideas and his rhetorical practice.

64. Duncan-Jones and Van Dorsten, *Miscellaneous Prose*, 63–64. Source hunting in the *Apologie* has occasioned a number of articles; see, for example, the one by Hunt cited above (n. 62) as well as Anthony Miller, "Sidney's 'Apology for Poetry' and Plutarch's *Moralia*," *English Literary Renaissance* 17 (1987): 259–76.

65. Levao, "Feigned Apology," 224. Hunt, "Allusive Coherence," 1, similarly notes that "Sidney confounds logical tidiness by maintaining both sides of the argument" on many issues.

66. From Virgil, for example, "Arma amens capio nec sat rationis in armis" (76); from Cicero, his famous definition of history (84).

67. The edition of Duncan-Jones and Van Dorsten, *Miscellaneous Prose*, 63–64, suggests that among Continental humanists Sidney was most influenced by Henri Estienne. See also J. A. Van Dorsten, *Poets, Patrons and Professors: Sir Philip Sidney, Daniel Rogers, and the Leiden Humanists* (London: Oxford University Press, 1962).

68. Hunt, "Allusive Coherence," 3–13, notes a number of different sources for Sidney's account of the ends of learning, but argues that he "has his own vision to enact" and uses many sources because he "will not rely on any one man's ideas to do it for him" (12). I believe, however, that this argument is based on an anachronistic view of gathering.

69. Sidney does, however, occasionally fall back on more traditional language, as when he notes that "Plutarch teacheth the use to be gathered" from poems (109).

70. Attridge, "Perplexity," 257–79.

71. Both Ferguson (*Trials of Desire*) and Levao ("Feigned Apology") make similar points.

72. Helgerson, *Prodigals*, 130, argues that "the poems invite us to see Sidney as Astrophil, and they suggest that his purpose in writing was the simple, if ignoble, desire to seduce Lady Rich." A closer look at Sidney's situation in the early 1580s, however, serves to separate Sidney and Astrophil.

73. See, for example, Marotti, " 'Love is not Love,' " 396–428, who argues that Sidney was "a politically, economically, and socially disappointed young

man" who used love poetry to replay and rewrite his failure at court, failing, ultimately, because his sequence is "a painful repetition of the experience [of courtly failure] in another mode" (405); similarly, Ann Rosalind Jones and Peter Stallybrass, "The Politics of *Astrophil and Stella*," *Studies in English Literature* 24 (1984): 53–68, suggest that in Sidney's sequence, "love, modeled upon an idealization of court hierarchies, could refashion in mystified form those very relations of power and submission that had structured it in the first place" (53).

74. Maureen Quilligan, "Sidney and His Queen," 171–96, places the sequence in the context of Sidney's conflict with the earl of Oxford in 1579, arguing that "Sidney's use of a self-abasing emphasis on his socially inferior position paradoxically redounds to his greater honor in the challenge to the earl of Oxford; in *Astrophil and Stella*, Sidney gains mastery by a similar strategy of self-abasement, taking control not merely of his text, but of his inferior social situation" (171). I want to place the sequence in a slightly different context.

75. As Marotti, " 'Love is not Love,' " and Quilligan, "Sidney and His Queen," point out.

76. Marotti points out that when Sidney wrote his sonnets, "he was and *he was known as* a politically, economically, and socially disappointed young man" (" 'Love is not Love,' " 400).

77. F. J. Levy, "Philip Sidney Reconsidered," in Kinney, *Sidney in Retrospect*, notes that the curriculum at Shrewsbury was designed "to produce statesmen," and that Sidney chose to become a statesman rather than a "courtier" (4–7). I believe that he chose to attempt to combine the two.

78. For the text of this letter, dated 22 May 1580, see James M. Osborn, *Young Philip Sidney* (New Haven: Yale University Press, 1972), 537–40. In it, Sidney notes the lack of opportunities under Burghley and applauds Denny's response to it: "let me reioyse with you, that since the vnnoble constitution of our tyme, doth keepe us from fitte imployments, you doe yet keepe your selfe awake, with the delight of knowledge" (537). Sidney provides standard humanist advice: not "to loose your tyme" (537), to study the "toungs of Latine and Greek (which be as it were the treasure howses of learninge" (538); to "let Tully be for that mater your foundation" next to the "foundation of foundations . . . the holy scripture" (539). Denny is also urged "to exercise your hand in setting downe what you reed," and to "forget not to note what you conceave of that you reed" (539–40).

79. On these negotiations, see D. E. Baughan, "Sir Philip Sidney and the Matchmakers," *Modern Language Review* 33 (1938): 506–19. Baughan's purpose in the article is to prove that Sidney was never in love with anyone; it is, nevertheless, a useful source of information.

80. Baughan notes that "Cecil's elevation to power as Lord Burghley . . . coincided with Sir Henry's waning patrimony and his disfavor at court" (ibid., 510). Anne married the earl of Oxford.

81. Ringler's edition of Sidney's poetry (*Poems of Sir Philip Sidney*) notes that Essex sought to marry Penelope to Sidney, to have his heir, Robert, made a ward of Burghley himself, and to have his other children given to the earl of Huntington. These requests (except for the Sidney marriage) were carried out; Penelope also went to the Huntingtons.

262 NOTES TO CONCLUSION

82. Ringler (ibid., 438) cites this letter from Huntington to Burghley of 27 February 1581: Lord Rich "hath lefte to hys heyre a propper gentleman and one in yeares very fytte for my ladye penelope devereux." Rich's son was almost twenty-one when he died; he was evidently spared wardship and allowed to inherit his lands and titles. Nevertheless, perhaps because Penelope was a ward, Burghley's approval was needed for the match to be made. They were married on 1 November 1581; Leicester's heir had been born in July.

83. Camden, *Remains Concerning Britain*, tells how at this time Sidney appeared with the impresa "Speravi"; see chapter 6 above.

84. Ironically, after Sidney's heroic death, she was considered worthy to marry the archetypal courtier of the day, Robert Devereux, second earl of Essex.

85. Ringler, *Poems of Sir Philip Sidney*, 165.

86. Ferry, *"Inward" Language*, 128–31, stresses this pun on "faine."

87. Richard A. Lanham, "*Astrophil and Stella*: Pure and Impure Persuasion," in Kinney, *Sidney in Retrospect*, 100–15, argues that a central purpose of the sequence is the seduction of Stella.

88. *"Inward" Language*, 128–29.

89. Patricia Fumerton, " 'Secret' Arts: Elizabethan Miniatures and Sonnets," in Greenblatt, *Representing*, suggests that "only by considering commonly used 'fine' 'inventions' can the poet make the turn inward in the last line of the sonnet toward the kind of plain speech and sincere emotion that belong 'in' his own 'heart' " (121). I believe that there may be more tension between the two alternatives than her reading acknowledges.

90. Ringler, *Poems of Sir Philip Sidney*, 459 n. 14, argues that " 'heart' refers to the mind in general, the seat of all the faculties. What the poet will see when he looks in his heart is the image of Stella." I believe that "brain" and "heart" are contrasted here, in accordance with faculty psychology. His natural copia, however, may very well be engendered by Stella's image.

91. Ibid., 174.

92. It appears in the *Apologie*, where it qualifies the optimistic idea that learning serves "to lead and draw us to as high a perfection" as we are capable of: "But when by the ballance of experience it was found, that the astronomer, looking to the stars might fall in a ditch, that the inquiring philosopher might be blind in himself" man realized that "all these are but serving sciences" to "the ethic and politic consideration, with the end of well-doing, and not of well-knowing only" (Duncan-Jones and Van Dorsten, *Miscellaneous Prose*, 82–83). Here Sidney seems to contrast Neoplatonic idealism and English humanist pragmatism. However, for a different reading of the passage, see Hunt, "Allusive Coherence," 4.

93. Cited in Helgerson, *Prodigals*, 127.

CONCLUSION

1. Fineman, *Perjured Eye*, 25, comments on the sonnets' "genuinely new effect of subjectivity. . . . poised between a visionary and a verbal self." Fineman argues that the sonnets "record the difference between their vision and their speech."

2. On this, see Marotti, " 'Love is not Love,' " 412–13, who discusses the social implications of Shakespeare's use of sonnet (a socially inferior stance) and epigram (which is more authoritative). Rosalie Colie, *The Resources of Kind: Genre-Theory in the Renaissance* (Berkeley and Los Angeles: University of California Press, 1973), 69–75, also explores Shakespeare's mixing of these genres.

3. G. Blakemore Evans, *The Riverside Shakespeare* (Boston: Houghton Mifflin, 1974), 1771.

4. For the influence of this tradition on Ben Jonson's "Epigrammes," see my article "*Intret Cato*"; and " 'His Owne Style': Voice and Writing in Jonson's Poems," *Criticism* (1990). In chapter 8, I cited Anne Ferry's suggestion that Herbert's titling practice owes something to commonplace book headings.

5. Unpublished commonplace books in this period tend to consist of biblical passages arranged under headings to facilitate sermon or tract writing; see, for example, BM Harley 4050, which includes some classical sayings, and Harley 6565, "A Commonplace Book on Theological Subjects."

6. For Milton's imitation and transformation of various classical kinds, see Barbara K. Lewalski, "*Paradise Lost*" and the Rhetoric of Literary Forms (Princeton: Princeton University Press, 1985).

7. *Complete Prose Works of John Milton*, ed. Ernest Sirluck (New Haven: Yale University Press, 1959), 2:372.

8. See "Lycidas," in Hughes, ed., *Complete Poems*, lines 58–63.

9. From "Areopagitica," in *Complete Prose Works of John Milton*, 2:549.

INDEX

Caspari, Fritz, 204n.13
Castiglione, Baldassare, 116
Cataneus, Ioannes Maria, 218n.14
Catherine of Aragon, 112
Cato, Marcus Porcius (the Elder), 248n.45.
　See also *Distichs of Cato*
Catullus, Gaius Valerius, 243n.81
Cave, Terrence, 12, 14, 209n.14, 212n.44
Cecil, Anne, 191, 242n.58, 261n.80
Cecil, Mildred [Cooke]. *See* Cooke, Mildred
Cecil, Robert, 121, 122–23, 124, 128
Cecil, Thomas, 123
Cecil, William: "Considerations Delivered
　to Parliament," 125; epigrams on, 143,
　248n.41; and Henrician politics, 95, 98,
　100; personal life of, 118, 121–22, 125,
　127, 241n.50, 242n.58, 253n.92
—and Elizabethan politics: as adviser, 116–
　17, 118–21, 127, 240n.19; in aristocratic
　education, 78, 125–26, 127, 241nn. 48,
　49, and 56; compared to younger courti-
　ers, 131, 134, 135; in factionalism, 117,
　120, 121, 128–29, 240n.28, 242nn. 62,
　64, 65, and 66, 242–43n.69; in humanist
　education, 7, 78, 121, 122–23, 124, 126–
　27, 240n.34; influence of on lyric poets,
　5, 165, 172, 175, 190, 191, 198, 261nn.
　78, 80, and 81, 262n.82; as master of the
　Court of Wards, 117, 122, 124–25, 126,
　127, 165, 191, 241 nn.41, 43, and 52,
　241–42n.57, 242n.61; mentioned,
　239nn. 1 and 3
Chambers, R. W., 204n.13
Charles, duke of Burgundy, 104
Charles I (king of Spain), 112
Charles VIII (king of France), 131
Cheke, Sir John, 7, 56, 103, 118, 120,
　205n.17
Chrysoloras, Manuel, 3
Cicero, Marcus Tullius: *De Amicitia*, 37;
　De inventione, 211n.34, 218n.13; *De of-
　ficiis*, 88, 118; *De oratore*, 218n.13; in
　education, 58, 90, 91, 230n.17, 232n.39;
　influence of in Agricola, 18, 211n.34; in-
　fluence of in logic, 18, 19, 22, 37,
　209n.15; influence of in politics, 98, 118;
　influence of in Wilson's rhetoric text,
　218n.13; influence of on Sidney's lyric
　poetry, 187, 260n.66; letters of, 87; and
　rhetoric, 41, 218n.13; *Topica*, 211n.34
Ciceronianus (Erasmus), 63, 71
Clapham, David, 235n.32

"Classical Reading in Renaissance Schools"
　(Bolgar), 233n.45
Clement, Francis, 69–70, 75, 231n.36
Clere, Thomas, 149
Coiro, Ann, 142–43, 246n.26, 247n.28,
　256n.15
Coke, Sir Edward, 241n.41
Colet, John, 56, 230n.22
Collectanea satis copiosa, 99
Colloquies (Erasmus), 87
commonplace books: physical form of, 86,
　232n.37; poems in, 149, 166, 250–
　51n.72; summary of history and criticism
　of, 3, 201n.2, 201–2n.3, 202nn. 4 and 5
common vs. uncommon sayings: in educa-
　tional practice, 77; in general, 8, 206nn.
　23 and 28; in imprese, 131; in rhetoric,
　40, 46, 49–51, 219–20n.32, 220n.43,
　221n.48
conception metaphor. *See* birth metaphor
"Considerations Delivered to Parliament"
　(Cecil), 125
Constable, John: collection of epigrams by,
　138, 139, 140–41, 143, 145, 146,
　246n.19, 247n.32; and educational prac-
　tice, 78
constitutional monarchy, 96, 234n.13
control of language: anxiety over, 13–14,
　209nn. 14 and 15; for control of others,
　16, 48; through rhetoric, 48–49
control of others: through education in gen-
　eral, 56–57, 61, 69–70, 72–74, 76,
　233n.49; through education under Eliza-
　beth I, 126–27; through education under
　Henry VIII, 108; through logic, 16;
　through rhetoric, 16, 48–49, 52, 189
control of self through education, 54–55,
　76, 108
Cooke, Sir Anthony, 118, 143, 248n.41
Cooke, Mildred, 118
Cornucopian Text, The (Cave), 209n.14,
　212n.44
Correll, Barbara, 231n.26
counsel. *See* advisers
Courtier, The (Castiglione), 116
Court of Venus, 167
Court of Vertue, 167
Court of Wards, 117, 122, 124–25, 126,
　127, 165, 191, 241nn. 41, 43, and 52,
　241–42n.57, 242n.61
Cox, Leonard: and politics, 235n.32; on
　rhetoric, 40, 41, 46, 218nn. 7 and 13